Routledge Questions & Answers

G000135034

Equity & Trusts
2013–2014

Routledge Q&A series

Each Routledge Q&A contains approximately 50 questions on topics commonly found on exam papers, with comprehensive suggested answers. The titles are written by lecturers who are also examiners, so the student gains an important insight into exactly what examiners are looking for in an answer. This makes them excellent revision and practice guides. With over 500,000 copies of the Routledge Q&As sold to date, accept no other substitute.

New editions publishing in 2013:

Civil Liberties & Human Rights
Company Law
Commercial Law
Constitutional & Administrative Law
Contract Law
Criminal Law
Employment Law
English Legal System
Equity & Trusts
European Union Law

Evidence
Family Law
Jurisprudence
Land Law
Medical Law
Torts

Published in 2012:
Business Law 2012–2013
Intellectual Property Law 2012–2013

For a full listing, visit http://cw.routledge.com/textbooks/revision

Routledge Questions & Answers Series

Equity & Trusts

2013–2014

Mohamed Ramjohn

LLB, LLM, CIOT, JP, Barrister at law
Principal Lecturer in Law, University of West London

Routledge
Taylor & Francis Group

LONDON AND NEW YORK

Eighth edition published 2013
by Routledge
2 Park Square, Milton Park, Abingdon, Oxon OX14 4RN

Simultaneously published in the USA and Canada
by Routledge
711 Third Avenue, New York, NY 10017

Routledge is an imprint of the Taylor & Francis Group, an informa business

First edition published by Cavendish Publishing 1995
Seventh edition published by Routledge 2011

British Library Cataloguing in Publication Data

A catalogue record for this book is available from the British Library

Library of Congress Cataloging in Publication Data
Ramjohn, Mohamed.
  Equity and trusts / Mohamed Ramjohn. — 7th ed.
    p. cm.—(Routledge questions & answers series)
  Rev. ed. of: Equity and trusts, 2009–2010. 6th ed. 2009.
  Includes bibliographical references and index.
  ISBN 978–0–415–59912–2 (pbk : alk. paper)—ISBN 978–0–203–82997–4 (ebk)
  1. Equity—England—Examinations, questions, etc.   2. Trusts and trustees—England—Examinations, questions, etc.   I. Ramjohn, Mohamed. Equity and trusts, 2009–2010   II. Title.
  KD1480.r363 2011
  346.4205'9076—dc22

                                                                                        2010036347

ISBN: 978–0–415–69592–3 (pbk)
ISBN: 978–0–203–08387–1 (ebk)

Typeset in TheSans
by RefineCatch Limited, Bungay, Suffolk

Printed and bound in Great Britain by the MPG Books Group

Contents

	Table of Cases	vii
	Table of Legislation	xv
	Guide to the Companion Website	xvii
	Introduction	1
1	The Creation of Trusts	5
2	Secret Trusts	43
3	The Inherent Attributes of a Trust: The Three Certainties and the Beneficiary Principle	62
4	The Law of Charities	99
5	Resulting Trusts	139
6	Constructive Trusts 1: The Duty Not to Make a Profit from the Trust and Co-ownership Trusts	159
7	Constructive Trusts 2: The Liability of Strangers to the Trust	194
8	The Law of Tracing	216
9	Breach of Trust	237
10	The Office of Trustee and its Powers and Duties	248
	Index	259

Table of Cases

Abbey, Malvern Wells Ltd v Minister of Local Government and Housing (1951) Ch 728 118

Abbott, Re [1900] 2 Ch 326 82, 130, 142, 147

Aberdeen Town Council v Aberdeen University (1877) 2 App Cas 544 165, 175

Abou-Ramah v Abacha [2006] All ER (D); EWCA 1492 164, 195, 199, 203, 208, 213, 222, 258

Abrahams v Trustee in Bankruptcy of Abrahams [1999] BPIR 637 144

Adams and Kensington Vestry, Re (1884) LR 27 Ch D 394 69

AGIP (Africa) Ltd v Jackson [1991] Ch 547; [1990] 1 Ch 265 198, 202, 203, 204, 208, 214, 220, 222, 225, 226, 234

Air Jamaica Ltd v Charlton [1999] 1 WLR 1399 PC 146, 149, 150, 154

Allen, Re [1958] 1 All ER 401 70, 72

Ames, Re (1884) 151, 153

Andrews Trust, Re [1905] 2 Ch 48 157

Anker-Petersen v Anker-Petersen [1981] 88 LS Gaz 32 254

Armitage v Nurse [1997] 3 WLR 1046; [1998] Ch 241 203, 242, 244, 256

Artistic Upholstery Ltd v Art Forma Ltd [1999] 4 All ER 277 84, 90, 92, 146, 147

Astor, Re (1952) Ch 534 82, 118

Attorney General for Hong Kong v Reid [1994] 1 AC 324 162, 168, 176

Attorney General of the Bahamas v Royal Trust Co [1986] 3 All ER 423; [1986] 1 WLR 1001 104, 106, 121

Attorney General v Sidney College (1869) LR 4 Ch 722 128

Ayliffe v Murray (1740) 2 Atk 58 171

Bacon v Pianta (1966) 114 CLR 634 90, 93

Baden Delvaux and Lecuit v Société Générale pour Favoriser le Devéloppement du Commerce et de l'Industrie en France, SA [1983] BCLC 325 164, 197, 198, 202, 204, 209, 214, 234, 257

Baden's Trusts (No 1), Re McPhail v Doulton [1971] AC 424 see McPhail v Doulton (Re Baden's Deed Trusts (No 1)) [1971] AC 424

Baden's Trusts (No 2), Re McPhail v Doulton [1973] Ch 9 see McPhail v Doulton (Re Baden's Deed Trusts (No 2)) (1973) [1973] Ch 9

Bahin v Hughes (1886) 31 ChD 390 242, 246, 247

Baillie, Re (1886) 2 TLR 660 47, 57, 61

Ball, Re [1968] 1 WLR 899 253

Bank Tejarat v Hong Kong and Shanghai Banking Corporation (Ci) Ltd and Hong Kong and Shanghai Bank Trustee (Jersey) Ltd [1995] 1 Lloyd's Rep 239 225

Banque Belge pour L'Etranger v Hambrouck [1921] 1 KB 321 226

Banque Financière de la Cité v Parc (Battersea) Ltd [1998] 1 All ER 737 231

Barclays Bank Ltd v Quistclose Investments Ltd [1970] AC 567 84, 143, 150, 151

Barlow, Re [1979] 1 WLR 278; 1 All ER 296 70, 76

Barlow Clowes International Ltd (in liquidation) v Eurotrust International Ltd and others [2006] 1 All ER 333 164, 195, 199, 203, 208, 212, 213, 257, 258

Barlow Clowes International Ltd (in liquidation) v Vaughan [1992] 4 All ER 22 232

Barnes v Addy (1874) 9 Ch App 244 198, 202, 212

Barralet v Attorney General [1980] 1 WLR 1565 111

Bartlett v Barclays Bank Trust Co Ltd (No 2) (1980) Ch 515 245

Bartram v Lloyd (1904) 90 LT 357 176

Bateman, Re [1970] 1 WLR 1463 51, 52, 57

BCCI Ltd v Akindele [2000] Ch 437 164, 197, 198, 199, 200, 202, 204, 208, 209, 214, 257

Beatty (deceased), Re [1990] 3 All ER 844 64

Beaumont, Re [1902] 1 Ch 889 39

Belmont Finance Corporation v Williams Furniture Ltd (No 2) [1980] 1 All ER 393 198, 204, 207, 209, 214

Beswick v Beswick [1968] AC 58 15, 35

Biscoe v Jackson (1887) 35 Ch D 460 132

Biss, Re [1903] 2 Ch 40 167

Blackwell v Blackwell [1929] AC 318 46, 51, 52, 56, 60

Blair v Duncan [1902] AC 37 104, 123

Boardman v Phipps [1965] Ch 992 (CA); [1967] 2 AC 46 (HL) 163, 168, 175, 177, 178, 257

Boscawen v Bajawa [1995] 4 All ER 769, [1996] 1 WLR 328 218, 227, 231

Bowden, Re [1936] Ch 71 23

Bowman v Secular Society Ltd [1917] AC 406 118, 127

Box v Barclays Bank plc [1998] Lloyd's Reports Bank 185 84, 144, 198, 204, 207, 208, 214, 220, 226, 236

Boyes, Re (1884) 26 ChD 531 52, 78

Bray v Ford [1896] AC 44 165, 170, 174

Brinks v Abu-Saleh (No 3) [1995] 1 WLR 1478 199, 203, 212, 258

Bristol and West Building Society v Mothew [1998] Ch 1 162, 256

Brooks v Brooks [1996] AC 375 253

Brown v Bennett [1999] 1 BCLC 649 207, 211

Bucks Constabulary Widows' & Orphans' Fund Friendly Society (No 2), Re [1979] 1 WLR 937 143, 146, 147–8, 152

Burns v Burns [1984] Ch 317; [1984] 1 All ER 244 178, 181, 187, 192

Burrough v Philcox (1840) 5 My & Cr 72 104

Burton v FX Music (1999) *The Times*, 8 July 84

Caffoor v Income Tax Commissioner [1961] AC 584 128

Cain v Moon [1896] 2 QB 283 16

Cannon v Hartley [1949] Ch 213 35, 36, 37

Cape Breton Co, Re (1885) 29 Ch D 167

Carl Zeiss Stiftung v Herbert Smith (No 2) [1969] 2 CH 276 198, 204

Carreras Rothmans Ltd v Freeman Mathews Treasure Ltd [1985] Ch 207 84, 143, 150, 153

Cavendish Browne's ST, Re [1916] WN 341 34–5, 37

Central London Property Trust Ltd v High Trees House Ltd [1947] KB 130 22

Chapman v Chapman [1954] 1 All ER 798 251, 252

Chase Manhattan Bank NA v Israel-British Bank (London) Ltd [1981] Ch 105 222

Chichester Diocesan Fund and Board of Finance v Simpson [1994] AC 341 104

Chillingworth v Chambers [1896] 1 Ch 685 241, 242, 247

Chinn v Collins [1981] AC 533, 31

Choitram International SA v Pagarani [2001] 2 All ER 492; [2001] 1 WLR 1 6, 7, 10–11, 24, 39

Christian v Christian (1981) 131 NLJ 43 187

Christ's College Cambridge (1757) 128

Clayton's Case (1816) 1 Mer 572 218, 231, 232

Cochrane, Re [1955] Ch 309 158

Cocks v Manners (1871) LR 12 Eq 574 92, 96

Collins, Re (1886) 32 Ch D 229 252

Commerzbank Aktiengesellschaft v IMB Morgan [2004] EWHC 2771 232

Commissioners for Special Purposes of the Income Tax v Pemsel [1891] AC 531 80, 91, 135

Compton, Re [1945] Ch 123 96, 113, 118

Conolly, Re [1910] 1 Ch 219 55, 69

Conservative & Unionist Central Office v Burrell [1982] 1 WLR 522 91, 93, 96

Construction Industry Training Board v Attorney General [1973] 1 Ch 173 118

Cook, Re [1965] Ch 902 11, 14, 38, 40

Corelli, Re [1943] Ch 332 123

Cowan de Groot Properties Ltd v Eagle
Trust plc [1992] 4 All ER 700 198, 204,
209, 214

Cowcher v Cowcher [1972] 1 WLR 425 144

Coxen, Re [1948] Ch 747 123

Cradock v Piper (1850) 1 Mac and G 664
166, 172

Craven's Estate, Re [1937] Ch 423 41, 252

Crown Dilmun Ltd v Sutton [2004] All ER
(D) 222 159, 166, 176

Cunnack v Edwards [1896] 2 Ch 679; [1895]
1 Ch 498 98, 152

D (a child) v O [2004] 3 All ER 780 253

Danish Bacon Co Ltd Staff Pension Fund, Re
[1971] 1 WLR 248; [1971] 1 All ER 486 21

Daraydan Holdings v Solland Interiors
[2004] EWHC 622 168, 176

Davis v Hutchings [1907] 1 Ch 356 241

Davis v Richards and Wallington Industries
Ltd [1991] 2 All ER 563 148

Dawson, Re [1966] NSWR 211 245

Dean, Re (1889) 41 ChD 522 84

Denley, Re [1968] 3 All ER 65 69, 81, 82, 84,
85

Denley's Trust Deed, Re [1969] 1 Ch 373 83,
89, 90, 93, 120–1, 126, 127, 143, 147

Dimes v Scott (1828) 4 Russ 195 245

Dingle v Turner [1972] AC 601 112, 113, 116,
118

Diplock, Re [1948] Ch 465, 209, 221, 222,
226, 227, 229, 230, 231, 233, 234, 235, 236,
244, 246

Dominion Students' Hall Trust, Re [1947]
Ch 183 132

Dougan v Macpherson [1902] AC 197 167

Douglas, Re (1887) 35 Ch D 472 126

Dover Coalfield Extension, Re [1908] 1 Ch
65 168, 175

Downshire, Re [1953] Ch 218 252

Drake v Whipp [1996] 1 FLR 826 180, 192–3

Dubai Aluminium Co v Salaam [2002]
UKHL 48 197, 242

Duffield v Elwes (1827) 1 Bli (NS) 497 16

Duke of Norfolk's Settlement Trust, Re
[1982] Ch 61 166, 171

Dundee General Hospital Board v Walker
[1952] SC (HL) 78 76, 80

Dyer v Dyer (1788) 2 Cox Eq Cas 92 144, 152

Eagle Trust plc v SBC Securities Ltd [1992]
4 All ER 488 198, 202

Eaves v Hickson (1861) 30 Beav 136 200, 207

El Ajou v Dollar Land Holdings plc [1993] 3
All ER 717; [1994] 2 All ER 685 163, 198,
257

Endacott, Re [1959] 3 All ER 562 69

Endacott, Re [1960] Ch 232 (CA) 82, 83, 86,
88, 91, 120, 126, 131, 135, 142, 147, 235

English v Dedham Vale Properties [1978]
1 All ER 382 214

Eves v Eves [1975] 1 WLR 1338 180, 187

EVTR, Re [1987] BCLC 646 150, 154

Falconer v Falconer [1970] 3 All ER 449 180

Faraker, Re [1912] 2 Ch 488 131, 137, 138

Farrant v Blanchford (1863) 1 De GJ & Sm
240

Ferrotex v Banque Français de l'Orient
[2001] EWCA Civ 1387 202

Finger, Re [1972] Ch 286 137

Fleetwood, Re (1880) 15 Ch D 46

Fletcher v Collis [1905] 2 Ch 24 240, 241

Fletcher v Fletcher (1844) 4 Hare 67 7, 11, 14,
15, 38, 39, 40

Flinn, Re [1948] 1 All ER 541 88

Forrest v Attorney General [1986] VR 187
129, 134

Foskett v McKowen [2000] 2 WLR 1299 216,
217, 221, 223, 227, 230, 232, 235

Foster v Spence (1996) 2 All ER 672 171

Fowler, Re (1914) 31 TLR 102 88

Francis, Re (1905) 92 LT 77 168, 175

Freeland, Re [1952] Ch 110 42

Fry, Re [1946] 1 Ch 312 9, 41

Funnell v Stewart [1996] 1 WLR 288 121

Gardner (No 2), Re [1923] 2 Ch 230 46, 47,
51, 56

Gee, Re [1948] Ch 284 175

Gibbons, Re [1917] 1 Ir R 448 84, 87

Gillingham Bus Disaster Fund, Re [1958]
    Ch 300; [1958] 2 All ER 749 97, 142, 146,
    148–9, 152

Gilmour v Coats [1949] AC 426 122

Gissing v Gissing [1971] AC 886 178, 179,
    180, 181, 184, 187, 188, 192

Golay's WT, Re [1965] 1 WLR 969 78

Goodman v Charlton [2002] All ER (D) 284 190

Goodman v Gallant [1986] 2 WLR 236 190

Gower, Re [1934] Ch 365 252

Grainge v Wilberforce (1889) 5 TLR 436 20,
    21, 30

Grant, Re [1980] 1 WLR 360 93

Grant v Edwards [1986] 1 Ch 638 178, 180,
    181, 192

Grey v IRC [1960] AC 1 18, 19, 20, 21, 27, 30

Griffith v Owen [1907] 1 Ch 195 167, 177

Grove-Grady, Re [1929] 1 Ch 557 126

Guild v IRC [1992] 2 AC 310 102, 108, 116,
    117, 127

Guinness plc v Saunders [1990] 2 AC 663
    168, 177

Gulbenkian's Settlements, Re [1970] AC
    508; [1968] Ch 126 64, 65, 66, 74, 75, 88

Hadden, Re [1932] Ch 133 127

Hallett's Estate, Re (1880) 13 ChD 696 218,
    226, 229, 231

Hambro v Duke of Marlborough [1994] 3 All
    ER 332 251, 252

Hanchett-Stamford v AG [2008] All ER (D)
    391 98

Harrison v Randell (1852) 9 Hare 397 244

Harwood, Re [1936] Ch 285 132, 138

Hay's Settlement Trusts, Re [1981] 3 All ER
    786 64, 66

Head v Gould [1898] 2 Ch 250 247

Heseltine v Heseltine [1971] 1 All ER 952 180

Hetherington, Re [1990] Ch 1 84

Holder v Holder [1968] Ch 353 167, 177, 240

Holmden, Re [1968] AC 685 254

Holt's Settlement, Re [1969] 1 Ch 100
    21, 253, 254

Hooper, Re [1932] 1 Ch 38 84, 87

Hopkins Will Trust, Re [1964] 3 All ER 46 107

Horley Town Football Club, Re [2006] WTLR
    1817 84, 90, 92

Houbourn Aero Components Ltd, Re [1946]
    Ch 144 98, 152

Houghton v Fayers [2000] 1 BCLC 571 197

Houston v Burns [1918] AC 337 122

Hulkes, Re (1886) 33 Ch D 552 212

Huntingford v Hobbs [1993] 1 FCR 45; [1993]
    1 FLR 736 182, 191

Incorporated Council of Law Reporting for
    England and Wales v Attorney General
    [1971] 3 All ER 1029; [1972] Ch 73 111, 123

Independent Schools Council v Charity
    Commission [2011] UKUT 421 111, 123

Industrial Development Consultants v
    Cooley [1972] 1 WLR 443 163

International Sales Ltd v Marcus [1982] 3 All
    ER 551 197, 198, 204, 209, 214, 234

IRC v Baddeley [1955] AC 572 96, 108, 109,
    112, 113, 116

IRC v Broadway Cottages [1954] 3 All ER 120
    70, 74, 88

IRC v Broadway Cottages Trust [1955]
    Ch 20 66

IRC v City of Glasgow Police Athletic
    Association [1953] AC 380; [1953] 1 All ER
    747 101, 108

IRC v Educational Grants Association Ltd
    [1967] Ch 123, affirmed [1967] Ch 993
    116, 128

IRC v McMullen [1978] 1 WLR 664; [1981] AC
    1 116, 117, 123, 124, 127

Irvine v Sullivan (1869) LR 8 Eq 673 51

Isaac v Defriez (1754) Amb 595 112

Jackson v Dickinson [1903] 1 Ch 947 239

James v Williams (1999), The Times, 13 April
    197

Jeffreys v Jeffreys (1841) Cr & Ph 138 15

Jones v Jones see Trustee of the Property of
    FC Jones and Sons (a firm) v Anne Jones
    [1996] 3 WLR 703, [1996] 4 All ER 721

Jones v Kernott [2011] UKSC 53 144, 179,
    182–3, 184, 187, 188, 190, 193

Jones v Lock (1865) LR 1 Ch App 25 9, 25

Jyske Bank v Heinl [1999] Lloyd's Rep Bank
511 199, 210, 213

Karak Rubber v Burden [1972] 1 WLR 602
197, 225

Kay, Re [1939] 1 All ER 245 12, 16, 34, 35, 37

Kayford, Re [1975] 1 All ER 604 25, 69

Keech v Sandford (1726) Sel Cas Ch 61 162,
167

Keen, Re [1937] Ch 236 45, 50, 51, 52, 54, 57

Khoo Cheng Teow, Re [1932] Straits
Settlements LR 226 87

Knight v Knight (1840) 3 Beav 148 64, 68

Knocker v Youle [1986] 2 All ER 914 253

Koeppler's WT, Re [1986] Ch 423 118

Koettgen, Re [1954] Ch 252 117, 128

Lacey, Ex p (1802) 6 Ves 625 167

Lambe v Eames (1870–71) LR 6 Ch App 597
69

Lambert v Thwaites (1866) LR 2 Eq 151 123

Lassence v Tierney (1849) 1 Mac & G 551 69

Le Foe v Le Foe [2001] 2 FLR 970; [2001] All
ER (D) 325 181, 192

Leahy v Attorney General for New South
Wales [1959] AC 457 89, 91, 92

Lee v Brown (1798) 4 Ves 362 244

Lepton's Charity, Re [1972] Ch 276 134

Leslie Engineers Co Ltd, Re [1976] 1 WLR 29
236

Life Association of Scotland v Siddal (1861)
3 De G F & J 240

Lightfoot v Lightfood-Brown [2005] EWCA
Civ 201 181

Linsley, Re [1904] 2 Ch 785 242, 246

Lipinski's Will Trusts, Re [1976] 1 Ch 235;
[1977] 1 All ER 33 93, 96

Lipkin Gorman v Karpnale Ltd [1989] 1 WLR
1340; [1991] 2 AC 548; [1991] 3 WLR 10
200, 204, 220, 221, 222, 225, 226, 227,
235, 236

Lister & Co v Stubbs (1890) 45 ChD 1 162,
163, 168, 176

Lloyds Bank plc v Markandan and Uddin
[2012] EWCA 65 241

Lloyds Bank plc v Rosset [1991] 1 AC 107;
[1990] 1 All ER 1111 144, 178, 181, 182, 184,
186, 187, 188, 192, 193

LSE v Pearson (2000) LTL 4/7/2000 168, 176

Macadam, Re [1946] Ch 73 168, 175

Macaulay's Estate, Re [1943] Ch 435 122

Macduff, Re [1896] 2 Ch 451 111

Maddocks, Re [1902] 2 Ch 220 51, 52

Makin (William) & Sons Ltd, Re [1993] BCC
453 65

Manifest Shipping Co v Uni-Polaris
Shipping Co [2001] UKHL 1 209

Manisty's Settlement, Re [1974] Ch 17 66,
76, 79

Mara v Browne [1896] 1 Ch 199 197

Margulies v Margulies and others [2000]
All ER (D) 344 50, 55

Mariette, Re [1915] 2 Ch 284 117, 124

Mascall v Mascall (1984) 50 P & CR 119
10, 40

Mason v Fairbrother [1983] 2 All ER 1078 252

McCormick v Grogan (1869) LR 4 HL 82 45,
46, 50, 54

McGovern v Attorney General [1982] Ch 321
107, 116, 118, 127

McPhail v Doulton [1970] 2 All ER 228 71

McPhail v Doulton (Re Baden's Deed Trusts
(No 1)) [1971] AC 424 65, 66, 72, 73, 79,
104

McPhail v Doulton (Re Baden's Deed Trusts
(No 2)) (1973) [1973] Ch 9 70, 72, 73, 74,
75, 76, 79, 80

Mettoy Pension Trustees v Evans [1991]
2 All ER 513; [1991] Conv 364 65, 79

Meux, Re [1958] Ch 154 252

Midland Bank plc v Cooke [1995] 4 All ER
562 144, 178, 182, 187, 188, 192

Milroy v Lord (1862) 4 De GF & J 264; (1862) 31
LJ Ch 798 7, 8, 9, 14, 22, 24, 33, 38, 39, 50

Mitford v Reynolds (1848) 16 Sim 105 84

Montague's Settlement Trusts, Re [1987] Ch
264 164, 198, 202, 204, 209, 214, 251, 257

Morice v Bishop v Durham (1804) 9 Ves 399
82, 83, 104

Moss v Cooper (1861) 1 John & H 352 51, 54, 59

Mumford v Ashe [2001] BPIR 1 144

Mussett v Bingle [1876] WN 170 84, 87

National Anti-Vivisection Society v IRC [1948] AC 31 107, 111, 116, 121, 126

Nelson v Greening [2007] EWCA 1358 20, 30

Nestlé v National Westminster Bank plc [1993] 1 WLR 1260 245

Neville Estates v Madden [1962] Ch 832 90, 96, 117, 122

Neville v Wilson [1996] 3 All E R 171 CA 18, 20, 21, 28, 32

New, Re [1901] 2 Ch 534 251

News Group Newspapers Ltd v SOGAT 1982 [1986] ICR 716 92

Niru Battery Manufacturing Co v Milestone Trading Ltd (No 2) [2004] 2 WLR 1415 222

Northcote's Will Trusts, Re [1949] 1 All ER 442 166, 171–2

Northern Developments (Holdings) Ltd, Re (unreported) 6 October 1978 84, 143

Norton's Will Trusts, Re [1948] 2 All ER 842 122

Nottage, Re [1895] 2 Ch 649 108, 117, 127, 129

Oatway, Re [1903] 2 Ch 356 218, 226, 230

Oldham Borough Council v Attorney General [1993] Ch 210 132

Oppenheim v Tobacco Securities Trust Co Ltd [1951] AC 297 96, 110, 112, 113, 117, 118, 121, 128

Osoba, Re [1979] 1 WLR 247; 2 All ER 393 69, 82, 88, 142, 157

Ottaway v Norman [1972] Ch 698 47, 57

Oughtred v IRC [1960] AC 206 17, 18, 20, 28, 31

Oxford Group v IRC (1949) 2 All ER 537 121

Oxley v Hiscock [2004] EWCA 546 188, 193

Paradise Motor Co Ltd, Re [1968] 1 WLR 1125 21

Paragon Finance v Thakerar [1999] 1 All ER 400 195, 199, 202, 258

Park (No 2), Re [1972] 2 WLR 276 42

Paul v Constance [1977] 1 WKR 527, 9 25

Pauling, Re [1962] 1 WLR 86; [1964] Ch 303 240

Peel, Re [1921] 2 Ch 218 136

Peggs v Lamb [1994] Ch 172 111, 123, 134

Pennington v Waine [2002] 1 WLR 2075; (2002) All ER (D) 24 7, 10, 25, 26, 31, 40, 41

Pettinghall v Pettingall (1842) 11 LJ Ch 176 84

Pettitt v Pettitt [1970] AC 777 178, 180, 181, 184, 186, 192

Pinion, Re [1965] Ch 85 103

Plumtree's Marriage Settlement, Re [1910] 1 Ch 609 42

Polly Peck International plc v Nadir (No 2) [1992] 4 All ER 769 197, 204, 209

Popat v Schonchhatra [1997] 1 WLR 1367 167, 177

Printers and Transferrers Amalgamated Trades Protection Society, Re [1899] 2 Ch 84 98, 146, 152

Prison Charities, Re (1873) LR 16 Eq 129 131

Protheroe v Protheroe [1968] 1 WLR 519 (CA) 167, 177

Pryce, Re [1917] 1 Ch 234 12, 16, 34, 37

Pullan v Koe [1913] 1 Ch 9 11, 15, 36, 42

R v Common Professional Examination Board ex p Mealing-McCleod (2000), The Times, 2 May 151

R v District Auditor, ex parte West Yorkshire Metropolitan County Council [1986] RVR 24 66, 72, 76, 79, 80, 104

R v Ghosh [1982] EWCA Crim 2 195, 203, 208, 212, 257

Raikes v Lygon [1988] 1 All ER 884 252

Raine, Re [1956] Ch 417 122

Ralli, Re, Re [1964] Ch 288 7, 10, 26, 39, 42

Reading v Attorney General [1951] AC 507 162, 168, 176

Recher's Trust, Re [1972] Ch 526 84, 86, 90, 92, 96, 143, 146, 147, 148

Rees, Re [1950] Ch 204 45, 51, 57

Regal (Hastings) Ltd v Gulliver [1942] 2 All ER 378; [1967] 2 AC 134 163, 166, 168, 175, 176

Remnant, Re [1970] 1 Ch 560 253

Richards v Delbridge (1874) LR 18 Eq 11 9, 14,
  26, 39
Roberts, Re [1963] 1 WLR 406 131, 137
Robertson, Re [1960] 3 All ER 146 253
Robinson v Pett (1734) 3 P Wms 249 166, 170
Rochefoucauld v Boustead [1897] 1 Ch 196
  26, 45
Rose, Re [1952] Ch 499 CA; [1949] 1 Ch 78
  9–10, 25, 31, 40, 41
Royal Brunei Airlines Sdn Bhd v Tan [1995]
  2 AC 378 164, 195, 198, 199, 200, 201,
  202, 203, 207, 209, 212, 227, 258
Royce, Re [1940] Ch 514 122
Rymer, Re [1895] 1 Ch 19 131, 132, 136, 137,
  142
Sainsbury, Re [1967] 1 All ER 878 253
Salisbury v Denton (1857) 3 K&J 529 106
Sanderson, Re (1857) 3 K & J 497 82
Satterthwaite's WT, Re [1966] 1 WLR 277 138
Saunders v Vautier (1841) 4 Beav 115 31, 250,
  251, 253
Scarisbrick, Re [1951] Ch 622 112
Scottish Burial Reform & Cremation Society
  Ltd v Glasgow Corporation [1968] AC
  138 111, 116
Segelman, Re [1996] 2 WLR 173 112
Sen v Headley [1991] Ch 425; [1991] 2 WLR
  1308 16
Shalson v Russo [2003] EWHC 1637 (Ch) 218
Shaw, Re [1957] 1 WLR 729; [1957] 1 All ER
  745 103
Shaw's Will Trust, Re [1952] Ch 163 86, 102–3
Sinclair Investments v Versailles Ltd [2011]
  EWCA 347 162, 163, 168, 176
Sinclair v Brougham [1914] AC 398 222
Slevin, Re [1891] 2 Ch 236 133
Smith, Re [1896] 1 Ch 71 247
Smurthwaite, Re (1871) 52
Snowden, Re [1979] Ch 528 52, 55, 60
Somerset, Re [1894] 1 Ch 231 241
Sonley v Clock Makers Company (1780)
  1 Bro CC 81 51
South Place Ethical Society, Re [1980] 1 WLR
  1565 103

Southwood v Attorney General [2000]
  WTLR 1199 118, 127
Sprange v Barnard (1789) 2 Bro CC 585 130
Stack v Dowden [2007] UKHL 17 144, 179,
  182, 183, 186, 187, 188, 190, 191, 193
Stafford v Stafford (1857) 1 De G & J 240
Starglade Properties Ltd v Nash [2010] EWCA
  (Civ) 1314 195, 199, 203, 208, 213, 258
Statek Corp v Alford [2008] EWHC 32,
  199–200 213
Stead, Re [1900] 1 Ch 237 55–6, 60
Steed, Re [1960] 1 All ER 487 253
Strakosch, Re [1949] Ch 529, 118
Strong v Bird (1874) LR 18 Eq 315 10, 12, 13,
  17, 26, 42
Swindle v Harrison [1997] 4 All ER 705
  245
Tanner v Tanner [1975] 1 WLR 1346 186
Target Holdings Ltd v Redferns [1995] 3
  WLR 352; [1996] 1 AC 421 239, 244, 245
Taylor v Plummer (1815) 3 M & S 562 225
Thompson, Re [1934] Ch 342 177
Thynn v Thynn (1684) 1 Vern 296 50
Tilley, Re [1967] Ch 1179 221, 230, 232, 235
Timpson's Executors v Yerbury (HM
  Inspector of Taxes) [1936] 1 KB 645
  19, 20, 27, 29, 30, 31
Tinsley v Milligan [1994] 1 AC 340 179
Tito v Waddell (No 2) [1977] Ch 106; 3 All ER
  129 56, 69, 167, 234
Trustee of the Property of FC Jones and
  Sons (a firm) v Anne Jones [1996]
  3 WLR 703, [1996] 4 All ER 721 217, 220,
  221, 226, 227
T's Settlement Trusts, Re [1964] Ch 158 253
Tuck, Re [1978] 1 All ER 1047 70
Turton v Turton [1988] Ch 542 188
Twinsectra Ltd v Yardley [2002] 2 All
  ER 377 151, 164, 199, 203, 208, 212, 226,
  257, 258
Valuation Commissioner for Northern
  Ireland v Lurgan BC [1968] NI 104 127
Vandervell v IRC [1967] 2 AC 291 17, 18, 21,
  27, 28, 31, 142, 151, 153, 154

Vandervell's Trusts (No 2), Re [1974] Ch 269
    18, 21, 22, 142, 150–1, 153
Vandervell's Trusts, Re (1970) 18
Verge v Somerville [1924] AC 496 106
Vernon, Re [1972] Ch 300 137
Verrall, Re [1916] 1 Ch 100 123
Vinogradoff, Re [1935] WN 68 152
Vyse v Foster (1874) LR 7 HL318 245
Ward-Smith v Jebb (1964) 108 SJ 919 241
Wedgwood, Re [1915] 1 Ch 113 126, 136
Weekes, Re [1897] 1 Ch 289 104
West Sussex Constabulary's Widows,
    Children & Benevolent (1930) Fund
    Trusts, Re [1971] Ch 1 97, 141, 142, 143,
    146, 147, 148, 149, 152, 153
Westdeutsche Landesbank Girozentrale
    v Islington Borough Council [1996] AC
    669 53, 139, 140, 142, 144, 146, 147, 148,
    149, 150, 153, 182, 184, 188, 197, 201, 204,
    209, 218, 222, 226, 230
Weston, Re [1969] Ch 223 251, 253
William-Ashman v Price [1942] 1 Ch 219 207
Williams Trustees v IRC [1947] AC 447 111,
    113, 116, 122, 123
Williams v Barton [1927] 2 Ch 9 168, 176
Williams v Byron (1901) 18 TLR 172 234, 241
Willis v Kibble (1839) 1 Beav 559 170
Wilson, Re [1913] 1 Ch 314 132, 136
Wokingham Fire Brigade Trusts, Re [1951] 1
    Ch 373 128, 133
Wood, Re (1949) Ch 498 82
Woodard v Woodard [1991] Fam Law
    470 41
Woodhams, Re [1981] 1 WLR 493 132
Wynn, Re [1952] 1 Ch 271 76, 80
Young, Re [1951] Ch 344 46, 56, 112

Table of Legislation

STATUTES

Charities Act 1960
  s 13 131, 132
  s 14 132
Charities Act 1993
  s 13 131
  s 14 133
Charities Act 2006 99
  s 4(2) 111
Charities Act 2011 99
  s 1 106
  s 1(1)(a) 104, 106, 121
  s 2(1)(b) 110, 111, 121
  s 3 95, 106, 115, 121
  s 3(1) 126
  s 3(1)(a) to (m) 111
  s 3(1)(b) 100, 102, 116, 123, 128
  s 3(1)(c) 121
  s 3(1)(d) 135–6
  s 3(1)(g) 95–6, 100, 101, 102, 108, 117, 119, 124, 129
  s 3(1)(i) 119, 122
  s 3(1)(j) 102, 135–6
  s 3(1)(k) 126, 136
  s 3(1)(l) 129
  s 3(1)(m) 102, 111, 112, 121, 123, 126
  s 3(1)(m)(i) to (iii) 123
  s 3(1)(m)(iii) 112
  s 3(2)(a) 121
  s 3(2)(d) 101, 102, 108, 117, 124
  s 3(3) 102, 107, 121, 126
  s 4 109, 121, 126
  s 4(1) 102
  s 4(2) 102, 117
  s 4(3) 102, 109, 111, 117

  s 5 100, 102, 105, 108, 114, 115, 117, 119, 124, 127, 129
  s 5(2) 127
  s 5(3) 108, 127
  s 5(3)(a) 108
  s 5(3)(b)(i) 108
  s 5(3)(b)(ii) 108
  s 30 121
  s 37 121
  s 62 129, 131, 132, 133, 134
  s 62(1)(a)(i) 134
  s 62(1)(c) 134
  s 62(1)(d) 134
  s 62(1)(e) 134
  s 62(3) 132
  s 67 133
  ss 63–66 132
Civil Liability (Contribution) Act 1978 242, 246
Civil Partnership Act 2004 182
Companies Act 2006 40
Contracts (Rights of Third Parties) Act 1999 12, 15, 32–7, 42
  s 1 16
  s 1(1) 35
  s 1(2) 35
  s 1(3) 35
  s 1(5) 16, 35–6
Equality Act 2010 156
Inheritance (Provision for Family and Dependants) Act 1975 12
Judicial Trustee Act 1896 166
  s 1(5) 171
Law of Property Act 1925 24

s 53 22, 24, 47
s 53(1)(b) 17, 19, 26, 47, 54, 57, 61, 186, 190
s 53(1)(c) 17, 18, 19, 20, 21, 27, 28, 29, 30, 31, 32, 254
s 53(2) 20, 21, 26, 28, 31, 32, 61, 186
s 184 158
s 205(1)(ii) 21
s 205(1)(x) 19, 29
Limitation Act 1980 238
s 21(1)(a) 242
s 21(1)(b) 242
Matrimonial Causes Act 1973 253
ss 23–25 182
Matrimonial Proceedings and Property Act 1970
s 37 182
Mental Health Act 1983 253
Perpetuities and Accumulations Act 2009 83, 89, 93, 124, 129
Public Trustee Act 1906
s 4(3) 171
s 9 171
Settled Land Act 1925
s 64 250, 252, 253
Statute of Charitable Uses (Statute of Elizabeth) 1601 108
Preamble 102, 111, 117, 126
Statute of Frauds 1677
s 9 29
Stock Transfer Act 1963 40
Trustee Act 1925
s 23 246
s 30 246
s 31 249
s 32 249, 253
s 42 171
s 53 250, 252
s 57 250, 254
s 57(1) 252
s 61 238, 241, 244
s 62 238, 241

Trustee Act 1942
s 42 166
Trustee Act 2000 169, 171, 249
Part IV 246
s 1 212, 244, 246, 255
s 3 212, 213
s 4 212, 213
s 6 212
s 7 244
s 11 207, 225
s 11(2), 64
s 14 214
s 22 246
s 23 247
s 28 170
s 28(4)(a) 170
s 29 172
s 29(1) 172
s 29(2) 172, 175
s 30 172
s 61 234
ss 28–30 166
Sched 1 244, 246, 255
Sched 1(1)
para 1 207
Trusts of Land and Appointment of Trustees (TOLATA) Act 1996 69
s 6 250, 251
s 7 252
Variation of Trusts Act (VTA) 1958 21, 250
s 1(1)(a) 253
s 1(1)(b) 253
s 1(1)(c) 253
s 1(1)(d) 253
Wills Act 1837 43, 46, 47, 50, 53, 56
s 9 27, 45, 48, 60–61
s 15 54
EUROPEAN LEGISLATION
European Convention on Human Rights
Protocol 1, Art 1 98

Guide to the Companion Website

http://cw.routledge.com/textbooks/revision

Visit the Routledge Q&A website to discover even more study tips and advice on getting those top marks.

On the Routledge revision website you will find the following resources designed to enhance your revision on all areas of undergraduate law.

The Good, The Fair, & The Ugly
Good essays are the gateway to top marks. This interactive tutorial provides sample essays together with voice-over commentary and tips for successful exam essays, written by our Q&A authors themselves.

Multiple Choice Questions
Knowledge is the foundation of every good essay. Focusing on key examination themes, these MCQs have been written to test your knowledge and understanding of each subject in the book.

Bonus Q&As
Having studied our exam advice, put your revision into practice and test your essay writing skills with our additional online questions and answers.

Don't forget to check out even more revision guides and exam tools from Routledge!

Lawcards
Lawcards are your complete, pocket-sized guides to key examinable areas of the undergraduate law.

Routledge Student Statutes
Comprehensive selections; clear, easy-to-use layout; alphabetical, chronological, and thematic indexes; and a competitive price make *Routledge Student Statutes* the statute book of choice for the serious law student.

Introduction

The trust concept has been heralded as a unique development of English law over the centuries and its principles are enshrined essentially in case law that has occasionally been tempered by statutory intervention. The principles of trusts law were initially created out of necessity to achieve fairness or justice to litigants who were aggrieved by the harshness of the common law. Today, as the principles of trusts law have become settled, some of its rules are still regarded as relatively flexible and adaptable enough to meet the changing needs of modern society. Such developments are best understood by considering the exposition of judges and the precise words used in statutes.

Many students are initially filled with trepidation in reading this module at undergraduate level (or its equivalent). This may be due to the inherently complex nature of property law concepts, its overlap with many other subject heads, such as contract law, commercial law, revenue law, land law, succession law, company law, bankruptcy law, etc, or the fine distinctions that judges sometimes make in an effort to resist undesirable precedents. That aside, the study of trusts law is stimulating, challenging and dynamic.

Students sometimes confess to being unclear about how to present answers to examination questions in trusts law. The aims of writing a book on questions and answers on trusts law are to assist the student in analysing a variety of standard examination questions and demonstrating some of the techniques involved in writing examination answers. Although this book is not intended to be a substitute for the reading of textbooks, cases, statutes and articles, it is a book full of questions and answers and could be an important acquisition that you, as a student, make in preparation for your examination. Having experienced similar questions on subjects covered in the syllabus will give you a tremendous advantage and greater confidence before sitting down to write the examination. Having actually answered, say, 50 questions on the same topics as those on which you are to be examined must give you a good chance of meeting the complexities and peculiarities that arise in an examination paper on trusts law.

The book is laid out by dividing the subject into ten chapters. Each chapter commences with an introduction to the topic by summarising the salient points within the chapter. This is followed by a variety of essay and problem questions that are engineered within the confines of the issues raised in each chapter. Each question is analysed with an answer plan for quick reference and each chapter contains questions with 'aim higher' and 'common pitfalls' comments for the benefit of students.

ADVICE ON REVISION AND EXAMINATION TECHNIQUE

1. REVISION STRATEGY

There is no substitute for hard work. During this time (revision) it is of the utmost importance that you concentrate on a full and structured revision of the subject. Listed below are some guidelines to assist you in your revision.

(i)   Draft a revision plan that will give you sufficient time to revise each topic in full.

(ii) It is necessary to find the right balance in distributing your time to the various topics so that you do not concentrate on your weak topics at the expense of your strong ones.

(iii) Working from memory, devote some time (say 30 minutes) to jot down in your notebook what you consider to be the key points of any topic you have selected for your revision. Re-read the topic from the textbook and add any further points to the list in your notebook. This technique has the advantage of giving you an overview of the topic. This process will sharpen your ability to recognise topics (including relevant details) in dealing with examination questions.

(iv) Always work towards the examination. That is the object of revision. Obtain a generous selection of past examination papers and analyse examination questions on topics you have revised. Structure skeleton answers to these questions. In addition, if you have a friendly tutor, perhaps he or she may be persuaded to mark full examination answers with constructive comments. These answers should be written under simulated examination conditions. Note, however, that drafting full examination answers is fairly time-consuming. Your decision to undertake such a task would depend on the time that is available and, indeed, the enormous effort that is needed to compile full answers.

(v)   Keep up to date with new articles and important cases. Examiners tend to be impressed by candidates who demonstrate knowledge of innovations in the law. Adopt the habit of reading one or more of the recent law journals. There is a wide selection of these available, such as *New Law Journal, Modern Law Review, Journal of Business Law, Conveyancing and Property Lawyer, Law Quarterly Review* and *Trust Law International*.

2. EXAMINATION TECHNIQUE

The essence of a good answer to an examination question is one which has a sound structure with sub-headings, and which addresses the issues posed in the question. What follow are useful tips in presenting good examination answers under examination conditions.

(a) Take some time to read all the questions in the examination paper and select the ones with which you are most comfortable. If you are required to answer four questions from eight, then it is prudent to select the four questions that you wish to answer before you start writing. This process has the advantage of avoiding a late change of heart and consequent time wasting. You should bear in mind that the period spent in the examination hall is the most valuable time you may spend on the law of trusts. For these purposes your knowledge of the law is measured by the content of your examination script.

(b) Having selected the questions, it is most important that you are fully conversant with the facts of the problem or the focus of the essay. If necessary, re-read the question and underline or highlight key words or phrases.

(c) Plan your answers as quickly as possible by jotting down notes (cases, phrases and sections of statutes).

(d) Assemble the points in a logical order. This involves the structure of your answer. With a sound structure it is possible to build on it, and the structure itself ought to take top priority.

(e) Get stuck into the issues posed by the question. Avoid writing vague introductions or preambles to your answers. This is distinct from identifying the issues in the first paragraph. Identifying the issues goes some way in structuring your answer. It indicates to the examiner that you appreciate what he or she is asking you to deal with.

(f) Avoid rewriting the question. Many students believe (mistakenly) that they can, in effect, alter the emphasis of a question or even change it completely. Answer the specific question set.

(g) You should not assume that the examiner knows everything pertaining to the question. He or she probably does, but it is up to the examinee to prove to him or her that you do. If you neglect to deal with relevant issues you run the risk of losing marks.

(h) Apportion the time to be spent on each question carefully and try to stick to this plan. If, perchance, you miscalculate your time and feel that you are likely to run short, then, as a last resort, present your answer in note form. This is better than nothing. In any event, you are more likely to be rewarded with five marks for a new question than the last five marks of an earlier one.

(i) One of the skills that the examiner is looking for is your ability to analyse the issues posed by the question, and the application of the relevant principles of law. Accordingly, it is advisable that you present your arguments as clearly as possible, in neat and legible handwriting. It is good practice to use sub-headings and present your answer in short paragraphs, each of which involves a distinct point.

(j) In your concluding paragraph you should try to address the issues raised by the question. It is advisable to relate back to the instructions set out in the question, such as: 'In the light of the arguments set out above, my advice to A is as follows . . .'

Common Pitfalls

The most common mistake made when using Questions & Answers books for revision is to memorise the model answers provided and try to reproduce them in exams. This approach is a sure-fire pitfall, likely to result in a poor overall mark because your answer will not be specific enough to the particular question on your exam paper, and there is also a danger that reproducing an answer in this way would be treated as plagiarism. You must instead be sure to read the question carefully, to identify the issues and problems it is asking you to address and to answer it directly in your exam. If you take our examiners' advice and use your Q&A to focus on your question-answering skills and understanding of the law applied, you will be ready for whatever your exam paper has to offer!

The Creation of Trusts

INTRODUCTION

It might be thought prudent at the start of any book on the law of trusts to attempt to define exactly what a 'trust' is. Unfortunately, that is not as easy as we might hope. Of course, the essential ingredients of a trust are well known: there is a 'trustee', who is the holder of the legal (or 'paper') title to property, and this person holds the trust property 'on trust' for the 'beneficiary' (or *cestui que trust*). The beneficiary is the equitable owner of the property and this is the person (or persons) to whom the real or 'beneficial' advantages of ownership will accrue. The interest enjoyed by the beneficiary is proprietary, or '*in rem*'. Thus, he is able to trace his property and recover it from any intermeddler with the exception of the bona fide transferee of the legal estate for value without notice. Further, although, as just indicated, the trustee usually holds the 'legal' title and the beneficiary holds the 'equitable' title, it is perfectly possible for an equitable owner to create a trust of *that* interest. In such cases, the first equitable owner is the trustee (as well as the beneficiary under the first trust!), holding an equitable interest on trust for a beneficiary. Sometimes this is known as a 'sub-trust'. However, whatever the precise configuration of legal and equitable ownership, necessarily there is a relationship between the trustee and the beneficiary – sometimes referred to as a 'fiduciary relationship' – and it is clear that the former has certain responsibilities and duties to the latter. Furthermore, sometimes the property which is the subject matter of the trust – and this can be any property, tangible or intangible, real or personal – will have been provided by a 'settlor' or a 'testator' and it is they who have set up the trust either during his or her lifetime (settlor) or on death (testator). Indeed, in the case of a trust established by *inter vivos* gift (that is, not by will), the settlor and the trustee may be the same person and, in such cases, the settlor is said to have declared himself or herself trustee of the trust property. Finally, it should be noted that a trustee may also be a beneficiary under a trust. This quite often happens with trusts of cohabited property where the man may hold the property on trust for himself and his lover in some defined shares.

This, then, is a very simple picture of a trust and beyond this it is not easy to make general statements about the nature of a trust without also explaining the one or more exceptions that exist to nearly every rule. The law of trusts is not something that can be neatly dissected nor can its principles be safely pigeonholed. Perhaps the best way to understand it is through an analysis of the substantive law without recourse to *a priori* definitions and assumptions that may prove wholly inadequate in explaining how the unique legal concept of the trust actually works in practice. With that in mind, the first topics to consider are the requirements imposed by general statute law and general principles of common law for the creation of a valid trust.

There are two sets of formal requirements which must be met before a valid trust can exist. On the one hand, there are those rules imposed by statute – principally the Law of Property Act 1925 – which establish formality requirements for the creation of trusts of certain kinds of property. These are requirements of writing and the like which are not inherent in the concept of the trust *per se*, although failure to comply with them will render the trust unenforceable. Rather, they are 'external' requirements imposed in order to ensure the proper working of the trust concept, especially the prevention of fraud by the trustee. Second, there are those rules of common law and equity which require the declaration of trust and/or the transfer of ownership of the trust property to the trustee to be achieved in specific ways according to the particular type of trust property. Examples include the need for a deed or registered disposition for the transfer of land to the trustee and entry in the company's register for the transfer of shares. These rules are not peculiar to the law of trusts, but given that the property which is the subject matter of the trust must pass into the hands of the trustee before the trust can exist (if it is not already there), the mode of transfer appropriate to each particular kind of property must be used if the trust is to be regarded as properly constituted. Failure to constitute the trust because of a failure to transfer the trust property to the trustee by the appropriate method has serious consequences.

Thus, the issues covered in this chapter require an understanding of the following matters:

(a) the different formality requirements for the creation of trusts of land and those for the creation of trusts of other property;

(b) the distinction between the creation of a trust and the 'disposition' of a 'subsisting' equitable interest under an existing trust and the reasons why an accurate distinction must be made;

(c) the necessity of properly constituting a trust and the manner in which this may be achieved relative to specific types of trust property; and

(d) the consequences of failure to constitute the trust properly.

QUESTION 1

'Although equity will not aid a volunteer, it will not strive officiously to defeat a gift' (*per* Lord Browne-Wilkinson in *Choithram International SA v Pagarani* (2001)).

▶ Evaluate this statement by reference to decided cases.

Aim Higher

Students are urged to read the judgments in the controversial decision *Pennington v Waine*. In this case, Arden LJ's view of unconscionability was based on the discretion of the court and varies with the circumstances of each case. This approach introduces notions of justice and fairness in outcomes to transactions that involve the process of the transfer of the legal title to property. In *Pennington v Waine*, what would have been the position if registration of the shares were declined by the company? If the constructive trust theory is to be maintained, despite the refusal to register the new owner, this would result in equity treating an ineffective transfer as a valid declaration of trust. But in *Pennington v Waine* the donor had not declared a trust, nor made a gift, nor had she done everything in her power to make a gift, yet the court decided that the transfer was effective in equity.

Common Pitfalls

Students are urged to approach this question by highlighting the various occasions when the court in purporting to apply the *Milroy v Lord* principle, in effect, extended the test in a number of landmark decisions. Simply 'trotting out' the popular cases without a structure will not stand you in good stead with the examiners. Students should be clear as to the significance of the principles in the controversial decisions, *Choithram v Pagarani*, *Pennington v Waine* and *Fletcher v Fletcher*.

How to Answer this Question

- ❖ The *Milroy v Lord* test.
- ❖ Transferor completing everything required of him.
- ❖ No self-declaration following imperfect transfer.
- ❖ The principle in *Re Ralli*.
- ❖ Multiple trustees, including the settlor.
- ❖ Trust of a chose in action.
- ❖ Consequences of a trust being perfect.
- ❖ Exceptions to the rule that equity will not assist a volunteer.

Answer Structure

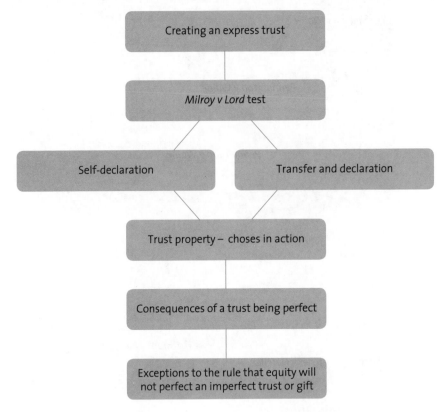

This diagram illustrates the methods and consequences of creating trusts, including gifts.

ANSWER

This statement by Lord Browne-Wilkinson highlights two fundamental principles of equity: the notion that equity will not assist a volunteer and that there is no policy in equity to defeat a perfect gift. These are self-evident propositions. However, a number of landmark cases have striven to perfect gifts which, on orthodox theory, ought to be considered as imperfect.[1]

The principle laid down by Turner LJ in *Milroy v Lord* (1862) identifies the various modes of creating an express trust. Generally, there are two modes of constituting an express trust and the onus is on the settlor to execute one (or in exceptional circumstances

1   Identify and address the issues posed by the question directly.

both) of these modes for carrying out his intention. The two modes of creating an express trust are:

(a)   a self-declaration of trust; and
(b)   a transfer of property to the trustees, subject to a direction to hold upon trust for the beneficiaries.

A settlor may declare that he presently holds specific property on trust, indicating the interest, for a beneficiary. In this respect he simply retains the property as trustee for the relevant beneficiaries. Clear evidence is needed to convert the status of the original owner of the property to that of a trustee. This form of creating an express trust is as effective as the transfer and declaration mode. In the absence of specific statutory provisions to the contrary, no special form is required as long as the intention of the settlor is sufficiently clear to constitute himself a trustee, for 'equity looks at the intent rather than the form'.[2] Thus, the declaration of trust may be in writing or may be evidenced by conduct or may take the form of a verbal statement or a combination of each of these types of evidence: see *Paul v Constance* (1977); contrast *Jones v Lock* (1865). What is required from the settlor is a firm commitment on his part to undertake the duties of trusteeship in respect of the relevant property for the benefit of the specified beneficiaries. The effect of this mode of creation is to alter the status of the settlor from a beneficial owner to that of a trustee. The test that is applicable here is the 'three certainties' test, i.e. certainty of intention, subject matter and objects.

The alternative mode of creating an express trust involves a transfer of the relevant property to another person (or persons) as trustee(s), subject to a valid declaration of trust. In this context the settlor must comply with two requirements, namely a transfer (gift or sale) of the relevant property or interest to the trustees complemented with a declaration of the terms of the trust. If the settlor intends to create a trust by this method and declares the terms of the trust, but fails to transfer the property to the intended trustees, it is clear that no express trust is created.[3] The court will not automatically imply a self-declaration of trust: see *Richards v Delbridge* (1874) and *Jones v Lock* (1865).

The formal requirements, if any, concerning the transfer of the legal title or equitable title to property vary with the nature of the property involved, in accordance with the *Milroy v Lord* (1862) principle; but if the transferor has done everything required of him to transfer the legal title to property and something has yet to be done by a third party, the transfer will be effective in equity: see *Re Rose* (1952); contrast *Re Fry* (1946) in respect of the transfer of shares in a private company. The effect of this rule (known as the rule in *Re Rose*) is that although the transfer of the legal title is not complete, the transferor will

---

2   Use the equitable maxim in the appropriate context.
3   Highlight the significance of the modes of creating an express trust.

nevertheless hold the legal title to the property as constructive trustee for the transferee. It is unclear as to the precise role played by the third party. Some third parties may have a purely ministerial role while others may have a discretion to refuse registration of the legal title. It would appear that the *Re Rose* principle is applicable irrespective of the role of the third party – dispositive or not. In *Mascall v Mascall* (1984), the rule was extended to a delivery by the transferor of a registered land certificate and duly executed transfer form to the transferee. Indeed, in *Pennington v Waine* (2002), the Court of Appeal decided that the delivery of the share transfer form to the company could be dispensed with. If it would be *unconscionable* for the transferor to have recalled what she intended to donate, the transfer would be effective in equity. This notion of unconscionability was based on analogy with the principle laid down by the Privy Council in *Choithram International SA v Pagarani* (2001). However, the Privy Council in that case had decided that the trust was perfectly created and thus it would have been unconscionable for the settlor to deny the existence of the trust, whereas in *Pennington* the donor had neither declared a trust nor made a perfect gift nor had she done everything required of her to make the gift. Accordingly, *Pennington* was an unjustifiable extension of the *Milroy v Lord* principle.[4]

In *Re Ralli* (1964), the High Court decided that a settlor may expressly manifest an intention to transfer the relevant property to third-party trustees (transfer and declaration mode) and, prior to completing the transfer, to declare himself a trustee for the beneficiaries (self-declaration mode). In this event, the trust will be perfect, provided that the third-party trustee acquires the property during the settlor's lifetime. In other words, the self-declaration of trust is regarded as conditional on an effective transfer of the property to the third-party trustee. This condition is required to be satisfied during the lifetime of the settlor in order to perfect the trust, i.e. to render it unconscionable for the settlor to reclaim the property. The court had also decided that it was immaterial how the third-party trustee acquired the relevant property. The mere fact that the property had reached the hands of the intended trustees was sufficient to constitute the trust. The logic of this test extended the *Milroy v Lord* principle. In addition, the court decided on a separate ground that the rule in *Strong v Bird* (1874) (imperfect *inter vivos* gifts where the will appoints the donee as executor) was extended to residuary gifts created in a will.

Moreover, in *Choithram International SA v Pagarani* (2001), the Privy Council decided that where the settlor appoints multiple trustees, including himself, and declares a present, unconditional and irrevocable intention to create a trust for specific persons, a failure to transfer the property to the nominated trustees is not fatal, for his (settlor's) retention of the property will be treated as a trustee. Trusteeship for these purposes is treated as a joint office so that the acquisition of the property by one trustee is equivalent to its

---

4   Express the controversial nature of the **Pennington** rule.

acquisition by all the trustees. There was no distinction between a settlor declaring himself to be the sole trustee and one of a number of trustees.

In *Fletcher v Fletcher* (1844), the court construed the subject matter of a covenant (to transfer property on trust) as creating a chose in action, namely the benefit of the covenant. This intangible property right may be transferred to the trustees on trust for the relevant beneficiaries, thus perfecting the trust. What is needed to assign such a right or chose is a clear intention on the part of the assignor to dispose of the chose to the transferee, but it is questionable whether the settlor had the benefit of the covenant. However, the *Fletcher* principle was subsequently restricted in *Re Cook* (1965) to debts enforceable at law, as distinct from any other choses in action.[5]

Where a trust is perfectly created, the beneficiary is given a right *in rem* in the trust property and may protect his interest against anyone, except a bona fide transferee of the legal estate for value without notice. In short, he has a *locus standi* to enforce the trust, simply by proving that he is an authorised equitable owner of the property. He may bring the claim in his own name and is entitled to join the trustee as a co-defendant. On the other hand, if the intended trust is imperfect, the transaction operates as an agreement to create a trust. This involves the law of contract, as opposed to the law of trust. An agreement to create a trust may only be enforced in equity by non-volunteers. The rule is that 'equity will not assist a volunteer' and 'equity will not perfect an imperfect gift'. To obtain an equitable remedy, the claimant is required to establish that he has furnished consideration. Valuable consideration refers either to common law consideration in money or money's worth or marriage consideration in equity. Common law consideration is the price paid by each party to an agreement. 'Marriage consideration' takes the form of an ante-nuptial settlement made in consideration of marriage, or a post-nuptial settlement made in pursuance of an ante-nuptial agreement. The persons who are treated as providing marriage consideration are the parties to the marriage and the issue of the marriage, including remoter issue.

It follows that if the trust is imperfect and the claimant wishes to obtain equitable assistance, he is required to demonstrate that he has furnished valuable consideration. If this is the case, the imperfect trust will be treated to all intents and purposes as though it was perfect. In other words, the claimant who has furnished valuable consideration will derive from the agreement to create a trust all the benefits accorded to a beneficiary under a perfect trust: see *Pullan v Koe* (1913).

On the other hand, where the claimant is a volunteer and a non-covenantee, the court refused to issue directions in his favour to enforce the covenant at law on the ground

---

5   The **Fletcher** rule is highly controversial and ought to be stated accompanied by its limitations.

that the volunteer ought not to obtain relief indirectly when he could not obtain the same directly: see *Re Pryce* (1917). In *Re Kay* (1939), the court extended the principle further by preventing the volunteer non-covenantee from bringing a claim in damages. The Contracts (Rights of Third Parties) Act 1999 has modified this principle only to the extent that it allows a non-party to a contract to bring a claim in his own right. If he is a volunteer the remedy will be damages.

However, there are well-established exceptions to the general rule that equity will not assist a volunteer, such as the rule in *Strong v Bird* (1874), *donatio mortis causa* (DMC) and proprietary estoppel.

QUESTION 2

In 2008, Alfred, in contemplation of his marriage with Bette, covenanted with Tim to transfer £50,000 to him to be held on trust for Bette for life, remainder to any of the children of the marriage absolutely. The marriage duly took place. A few months later Alfred made a bargain with his father-in-law, Freddie, that in consideration of receiving 10,000 shares in Cashflow Ltd (a private company), Alfred will settle his yacht, *Orca*, on trust for Bette for life, remainder to her brother, Charlie, absolutely. Alfred duly executed another covenant with Tim to settle his yacht, *Orca* on trust for Bette for life with remainder to Charlie.

Alfred failed to make any transfers to Tim in accordance with the covenants although he has been registered as the new owner of 10,000 shares in Cashflow Ltd.

In 2009, Bette died leaving a son, Donald. Alfred still refused to transfer any of the properties to Tim in respect of the covenants.

In 2010 Alfred met Ede and decided to spend his declining years with her. In January 2011, knowing he did not have long to live, he handed Ede the deeds of his house, and said, 'When I die this house and all its furniture is for you.' He also delivered to Ede the share certificates to 10,000 shares in Cashflow Ltd.

In February 2012 Alfred died. Amongst his personal effects was a will, executed in 2010, which declared that all his property was to be distributed to Oxfam, a registered charity. Ede was appointed executrix of Alfred's will.

Advise Donald, Charlie, Freddie, Ede and Tim as to their rights, if any, in the above transactions.

[Ignore any applications under the Inheritance (Provision for Family and Dependants) Act 1975.]

How to Answer this Question

❖ Are the trusts of the covenants perfect and, if not, what are the consequences?
❖ DMC of the house?
❖ The *Strong v Bird* rule regarding the shares?

Answer Structure

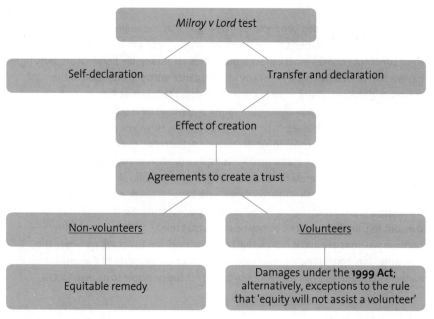

This diagram indicates the requirements for the creation of an express trust, notes its effect and lists the remedies that may be available to a claimant.

ANSWER

Alfred executed two covenants with Tim on separate occasions to transfer £50,000 and the yacht, *Orca*, to him to hold on various trusts, but failed to transfer the properties. Two questions arise in these circumstances: whether the covenants create trusts of the relevant properties in favour of the intended beneficiaries; alternatively, whether the covenants are enforceable as agreements to create trusts.

The test for creating a perfect trust was laid down by Turner LJ in *Milroy v Lord* (1862). This involves the settlor, Alfred, choosing one of two modes of creating the trust:

(a)   a transfer of property to the trustees, subject to a direction to hold upon trust for the beneficiaries; or

(b)   a self-declaration of trust.

Applying this test to the facts of the problem, we have been informed that Alfred failed to transfer the relevant properties (£50,000 and the yacht) to Tim, the intended trustee.[6] Thus, it would appear that the intended trust is imperfect. Further, the court will not automatically imply the second mode for creating an express trust as laid down in *Milroy v Lord*, namely, a self-declaration of trust, in order to constitute Alfred a trustee: see *Richards v Delbridge* (1874). The reason for the rule is that, despite the transferor's intention to benefit another by means of a transfer (whether on trust or not), the transferor ought not to be treated as a trustee if this does not accord with his intention, for otherwise all imperfect trusts will become perfect.

Alternatively, the intended beneficiaries may argue that the subject matter of the covenant involves the 'benefit of the covenant', as distinct from the cash and the yacht, which constitute choses in action. Such properties are intangible personal property rights that are transferred by operation of law in accordance with the intention of the transferor. If this argument were to succeed, it would follow that Tim would have acquired the respective properties from Alfred and would be required to hold the same on trust for the beneficiaries: see *Fletcher v Fletcher* (1844). However, the *Fletcher* rule is restricted to one type of chose in action, namely debts enforceable at law: see *Re Cook* (1965). A debt enforceable at law involves a legal obligation to pay a quantified amount of money. It does not concern a covenanted obligation to transfer shares, paintings or indeed yachts. It follows that in accordance with the *Fletcher* principle only the covenant to transfer £50,000 is capable of constituting a perfect trust. No trust exists of the covenant to transfer the yacht. It may be noted that the *Fletcher* rule is a highly controversial principle and it is arguable that it is restricted to occasions where the covenantor has agreed that his executor will transfer the property to the covenantee trustee. This argument has the tendency to restrict the principle to its own facts.[7]

6   State the principle of law as clearly as possible and apply the same to the facts.

7   The **Fletcher** rule with its limitation ought to be considered when dealing with constitution questions.

If the trust in respect of the covenant to transfer £50,000 to Tim is perfect (in accordance with the *Fletcher v Fletcher* rule) it follows that the beneficiaries, who are given proprietary rights in the trust property, are entitled to enforce the trust: see *Jeffreys v Jeffreys* (1841). Thus, Bette, during her lifetime, and Donald acquire equitable interests in the covenanted sum and are entitled in their own right to bring claims to protect their interests. Similarly, Tim, as trustee, may bring claims on their behalf.[8]

On the other hand, if the trusts of the covenants are imperfect (i.e. the covenant to transfer £50,000 and the yacht) on the ground that the subject matter of the trust has not been transferred to Tim, the intended trustee, the trust is imperfect and the principle is that 'equity will not perfect an imperfect trust' and 'equity will not assist a volunteer'. The unfulfilled covenants will amount to agreements to create trusts and be enforceable, if at all, in contract law.

Subject to the Contracts (Rights of Third Parties) Act 1999, in order to enforce the covenants to create trusts, the claimants are required to establish that they have furnished valuable consideration. Consideration refers either to common law consideration in money or money's worth or marriage consideration. Common law consideration is the price paid by each party to an agreement. 'Marriage consideration' takes the form of an ante-nuptial settlement made in consideration of marriage, or a post-nuptial settlement made in pursuance of an ante-nuptial agreement.[9] The persons who are treated as providing marriage consideration are the parties to the marriage and the issue of the marriage, including remoter issue. Relating this principle to the facts of the problem, it would appear that Bette (and her estate on her behalf) and Donald (if he is an issue of the marriage between Alfred and Bette) are non-volunteers, having provided marriage consideration. Freddie appears to have provided common law consideration and is also treated as a non-volunteer. The other parties connected with the covenants, namely Tim and Charlie, are volunteers and are not entitled to equitable remedies.

The non-volunteers are entitled in their own right to seek equitable assistance and, if necessary, obtain equitable remedies. At the instance of these claimants (Bette's estate, Donald and Freddie) the imperfect trusts will be treated to all intents and purposes as though they were perfect. In other words, the claimants who had furnished valuable consideration will derive from the agreements to create trusts all the benefits accorded to a beneficiary under a perfect trust: see *Pullan v Koe* (1913). In particular, Freddie, as a non-volunteer, is entitled to bring a claim in equity for specific performance to enforce the agreement to transfer the yacht to Tim, subject to a trust: see *Beswick v Beswick* (1968). This is the position even though Charlie is a volunteer and may obtain a benefit from the claim of Freddie; but it must be appreciated that neither Tim nor Charlie, as

---

8   State the effect of the trust being treated as perfect.
9   It is imperative to state clear definitions of relevant concepts.

volunteers, may be able to force Freddie to bring such a claim in equity for specific performance: see *Re Pryce* (1917) and *Re Kay* (1939).

By virtue of s 1 of the Contracts (Rights of Third Parties) Act 1999, a third party to a contract is entitled 'in his own right' to enforce a term of the contract if, *inter alia*, the 'term of the contract purports to confer a benefit on him'. This is clearly covered by the covenant to transfer the yacht to Tim on trust *inter alia* for Charlie. Section 1(5) declares that 'any remedy' will be available to the claimant, on the assumption that he is a party to the contract. The effect is that Charlie, a volunteer, is entitled only to damages against the estate of Alfred for breach of contract. The quantum of damages may be calculated by reference to the value of the yacht on the date of the breach of contract.

The delivery of the deeds to the house to Ede by Alfred in 2011 indicates that no perfect *inter vivos* gift of the house to Ede has taken place. The appropriate formalities involve a conveyance of the legal title. This has not been achieved. In any event the accompanying words indicate that the delivery is conditional on the death of Alfred. It is also evident that Ede is a volunteer as defined above. The issue is whether a valid DMC may be established on the facts. A DMC involves an *inter vivos* transfer of control over property by the donor while contemplating death, but on condition that the gift will become perfect on death. In this event, the donor's personal representative (Ede) is required to hold the legal title to the property on trust for the donee, Ede. If such a claim is successful, the donee stated under the will (Oxfam) will not acquire the property. This is a true case of 'equity perfecting an imperfect gift', or 'equity assisting a volunteer'.

There are a number of conditions that are required to be satisfied in order to establish a valid DMC. These are:

- ❖ the donor is required to contemplate death;
- ❖ the donor is required to transfer the property *inter vivos* and conditional on death;
- ❖ the donor is required to transfer dominion over the property during his lifetime: see *Cain v Moon* (1896).

The first two requirements are questions of fact and may be established by reference to the scenario posed. Alfred is aware that he does not have long to live and he makes the delivery of the deeds expressly conditional on death. The material issue in this problem is whether Alfred had transferred control over the property to Ede during his lifetime. The test is whether Alfred had lost control over the house during his lifetime and, at the same time, whether Ede had acquired control over the asset through the title deeds, the essential indicia of title. Despite the earlier *obiter* pronouncement by Lord Eldon in *Duffield v Elwes* (1827), to the effect that land cannot be the subject matter of a DMC, it was widely believed that this view was too broad and was finally tested in the Court of Appeal decision in *Sen v Headley* (1991). The court took the view that Lord Eldon's opinion could not be supported in respect of unregistered land and decided that the title deeds are the essential indicia of title to such property. As far as the furniture is concerned there is no evidence of the transfer of dominion over such assets and *prima facie* Ede would not be entitled to this.

The delivery of the share certificates to 10,000 shares in Cashflow Ltd, a private company, is insufficient to transfer the legal title to those shares. The formalities to be complied with require Alfred to execute a share transfer form in Ede's favour and send the form, along with the certificates, to the registered office of the company for consideration of registration of the transferee. There is no evidence that Alfred had done this and therefore there is no valid *inter vivos* transfer of the legal title to the shares to Ede; but Ede was appointed executrix of Alfred's estate. Would the rule in *Strong v Bird* (1874) be applicable on these facts to perfect the imperfect gift? The rule in *Strong v Bird* is based on the assumption that where an *inter vivos* gift is imperfect by reason only of the fact that the transfer to the intended donee is incomplete, the incomplete gift will become perfect when the donee acquires the property in the capacity of executor of the donor's estate.

Much depends on evidence of Alfred's intention. The mental element postulated by the rule in *Strong v Bird* is a present, continuous intention on Alfred's part to make an *inter vivos* gift to Ede. Was Alfred's intention concerning the delivery of the share certificates conditional on death (similar to the delivery of the title deeds) or was it unconditional? This is a question of fact. If the intention was unconditional, there is no evidence that its continuity was broken.

QUESTION 3
Is it possible to say with certainty when any potential dealing with trust property will amount to a 'disposition' within s 53(1)(c) of the Law of Property Act 1925? Why is it important to have some measure of certainty in this area?

Aim Higher ★
It is of crucial importance that the policy of enacting **s 53(1)(c)** of the **Law of Property Act 1925** is clearly understood. This is to prevent fraud and to allow trustees to chart the movement of the equitable interest. The judgments in the leading cases, *Grey, Vandervell* and *Oughtred*, ought to be digested by students before attempting examination questions on this subject.

Comman Pitfalls? ✗
Students sometimes fail to grasp that **s 53(1)(c)** of the **LPA 1925** is applicable to subsisting interests only in either land and personalty, and the sub-section may overlap with **s 53(1)(b)** of the **1925 Act**, e.g. a declaration of trust by a beneficiary of his equitable interest in land.

How to Answer this Question

- ❖ The distinction between the creation of a trust and a 'disposition' of a 'subsisting equitable interest' under a trust (s 53(1)(c) of the LPA 1925).
- ❖ Cases where the courts have established that a proposed transaction amounts to a 'disposition' and therefore requires writing (especially *Grey v IRC* (1960), *Oughtred v IRC* (1960) and *Neville v Wilson* (1996)).
- ❖ Cases in which the courts have established that a proposed transaction does not amount to a 'disposition' and therefore does not require writing (especially the *Vandervell* cases).

Answer Structure

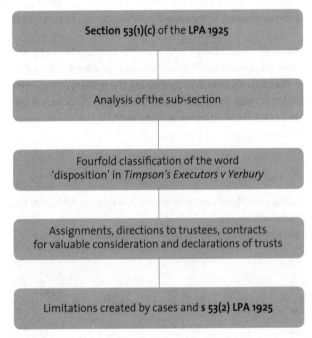

Section 53(1)(c) of the LPA 1925

Analysis of the sub-section

Fourfold classification of the word 'disposition' in *Timpson's Executors v Yerbury*

Assignments, directions to trustees, contracts for valuable consideration and declarations of trusts

Limitations created by cases and s 53(2) LPA 1925

This diagram indicates the broad and restricted meaning of the expression 'disposition' within s 53(1)(c) of the LPA 1925.

ANSWER

Section 53(1)(c) of the Law of Property Act (LPA) 1925 lays down certain requirements of formality which must be satisfied for the effective disposition (that is, transfer) of equitable interests under trusts that already exist, i.e. 'subsisting trusts'.

According to s 53(1)(c) of the LPA 1925, 'a disposition of an equitable interest ... subsisting at the time of the disposition must be in writing'.[10] This means that if a trust already exists, so that there is a beneficiary who has an equitable interest, any attempted 'disposition' (that is, transfer) of that equitable interest must actually be in writing. Such a rule is, of course, designed to ensure that the location of the equitable interest is clear and manifest, not only to provide certainty per se, but also to prevent fraud on the part of the trustee and to ensure that the proper person (that is, the current holder of the equitable interest) may enforce the trust and receive the benefit of the trust property.[11] It ought to be noted that s 53(1)(c) of the LPA 1925 is applicable to both personal and real property. This is the position despite the definition of 'equitable interests' in s 205(1)(x) of the LPA 1925. The statutory definition refers to equitable interests in the context of land. Despite this definition, the effect of the decisions of the courts, including the House of Lords, has been to construe s 53(1)(c) of the LPA 1925 as incorporating both realty and personalty. However, as far as this essay is concerned, there are two important issues to be considered. First, although the creation of trusts of land must be *evidenced* in writing (see s 53(1)(b) of the LPA 1925), any disposition of an equitable interest under an existing trust of land must actually be *in writing*. Second, although the creation of trusts of personalty requires no writing at all, once again the disposition of an equitable interest under an existing trust of personalty must actually be *in writing*. Consequently, it is vital, in the cases of both trusts of land and trusts of personalty, to be able to distinguish between the creation of a new trust and the transfer of an equitable interest under a trust that already exists.

It is clear that 'disposition' is to be given a wide, natural meaning, such as it would enjoy in everyday use (*Grey v IRC* (1960)). The starting point for the meaning of the word 'disposition' can be the judgment of Romer LJ in *Timpson's Executors v Yerbury* (1936), where he identified four different ways by which a beneficiary might dispose of an equitable interest.[12] In addition, there are other circumstances, not covered by Romer LJ, which should also be considered.

First, when the beneficiary wishes to transfer (or 'assign') his equitable interest directly to another person, as where B, the beneficiary, wishes to give her equitable interest to C (*Timpson's Executors v Yerbury* (1936)). Likewise, if a beneficiary is able, under the terms of a trust, to direct her trustee to deal with the trust property in any manner she (the beneficiary) chooses, as is the case in a 'bare' trust, a direction by the beneficiary to the trustee to hold the property on trust for another person is a disposition of that interest within s 53(1)(c) of the LPA 1925 (*Grey v IRC* (1960)). The point is simply that the bare trustee must carry out the original beneficiary's wishes and the net result of the

---

10　Narrate the material elements of the statutory provision before analysing and discussing the provision.
11　The policy governing the provision is an important aspect of the section.
12　This is a key decision that classifies transactions that may amount to 'dispositions'.

beneficiary's direction is that the equitable interest has passed to a third person. Again, if the beneficiary under a trust declares herself trustee of her own equitable interest for another – as where T (trustee and legal owner) holds on trust for B (original beneficiary), and B then declares herself trustee of that equitable interest for C – this may well amount to a disposition if the original beneficiary (B) 'drops out of the picture' thus leaving the trustee effectively holding on trust for C. A beneficiary who declares this 'sub-trust' will drop out of the picture when she has no active duties to perform in relation to the new beneficiary, so effectively disposing of her interest to C (*Grainge v Wilberforce* (1889) and implicit in *Neville v Wilson* (1996)). Although this view of a sub-trust is not necessarily adhered to by all commentators, it is consistent with the policy behind s 53(1)(c) of the LPA 1925, as it prevents hidden (that is, purely oral) dealings with equitable interests. Of course, if the original beneficiary (sub-trustee) does not drop out of the picture, then a new trust has been created and no disposition of a 'subsisting' equitable interest has occurred. A contrary view was expressed by Brian Green to the effect that the sub-section makes no distinction between a declaration of trust of part of, or the entire, equitable interest and in addition, the inelegant distinction between declarations within s 53(1)(c) and declarations outside the sub-section is at odds with the House of Lords' decisions in *Grey v IRC* and *Oughtred v IRC*. In *Nelson v Greening* [2007] EWCA 1358, the Court of Appeal appears to have affirmed the approach adopted by Brian Green. Fourth, it is consistent with the policy of s 53(1)(c) of the LPA 1925 that a surrender of the equitable interest by the equitable owner to the trustee should also count as a disposition. This was not considered by Romer LJ in *Timpson's Executors v Yerbury* (1936) and we might argue that a surrender of the equitable interest merely extinguishes the trust and does not 'dispose' of an interest.

The last example of a transfer of an equitable interest considered by Romer LJ in *Timpson's Executors v Yerbury* (1936) may, or may not, amount to a 'disposition' so as to bring it within s 53(1)(c) of the LPA 1925, although the balance of authority is now that it does not. The case where the issue arose (*Oughtred v IRC* (1960)) was primarily concerned with whether stamp duty was payable on a written document and not whether that written document was actually necessary to transfer the equitable interest under the trust. The facts of the case suggest that, where T holds on trust for B, but B orally agrees by contract to sell his equitable interest to C, if that contract is specifically enforceable, it appears that B holds his equitable interest on constructive trust for C (because, under a specifically enforceable contract, 'equity treats as done what ought to be done'). Furthermore, when B drops out of the picture on payment of the purchase price by C, no writing is necessary to confirm the transfer of the equitable interest because s 53(1)(c) of the LPA 1925 does not apply to the 'operation of . . . constructive trusts' (s 53(2) of the LPA 1925). This was the position argued in *Oughtred v IRC* (1960) although, in the case itself, the majority decided that stamp duty was payable on the later written document. Although this implies that the oral contract did not effectively transfer the equitable interest (that is, that writing was necessary), the judgments are not conclusive. The matter turns on the difficult question of what exactly has been passed to the purchaser by the specifically enforceable contract. So, if the equitable interest of the original beneficiary passes under the constructive trust, then writing is not necessary because of s 53(2) of the LPA 1925; if, however, the purchaser merely obtains a right to that equitable interest which cannot be denied by the original beneficiary, then any later transfer of that interest will need to be in writing because it will be a disposition within s 53(1)(c) of the LPA 1925. Admittedly, this seems complicated, but the essence of the matter is whether the constructive trust which arises from the contract (if the contract is specifically enforceable) actually passes the equitable interest to the purchaser so as to negate the need for writing because s 53(2) of the LPA 1925 is an exception to s 53(1)(c) of the same Act. In *Neville v Wilson* (1996), the Court of Appeal accepted specifically that the equitable interest of the vendor can pass to the purchaser under a constructive trust and this appears now to have confirmed that no writing is needed in such cases: that is, that s 53(1)(c) of the LPA 1925 does not apply.

Finally, we come to those cases where dealings with existing equitable interests under a trust clearly do not amount to a 'disposition' within s 53(1)(c) of the LPA 1925 and, therefore, do not require writing to be carried into effect. This may be so for a variety of reasons. First, as noted above, there are those cases where the beneficiary declares herself trustee of her equitable interest but does not drop out of the picture. This is a new sub-trust and not a disposition of a subsisting equitable interest (*Grainge v Wilberforce* (1889)). But note also the arguments revised by Brian Green (see above).[13] Second, according to *Vandervell v IRC* (1967), the unification of the legal and equitable interests in the hands of a third party does not amount to a disposition within s 53(1)(c). The reason for this is that the third party (C) is now the absolute owner of the property, both at law and in equity. In other words, the mischief which s 53(1)(c) of the LPA 1925 was intended to prevent is not present and the case is different from *Grey v IRC* (1960) because, now, the legal and equitable titles are unified in the recipient. Third, no writing is required for disclaimers of the equitable interest, as where the intended beneficiary orally disavows acceptance of the interest (*Re Paradise Motor Co Ltd* (1968)). This is despite the fact that a disposition is defined as including a disclaimer in s 205(1)(ii) of the LPA 1925 because disclaimers do not represent hidden dealings with equitable interests of the type which s 53(1)(c) of the LPA 1925 is intended to prevent. Fourth, nominations by beneficiaries under staff pension funds do not require writing under s 53(1)(c) of the LPA 1925 (*Re Danish Bacon Co Ltd Staff Pension Fund* (1971)). Fifth, variation of trusts made by virtue of powers under the Variation of Trusts Act 1958 do not require writing even if they involve a reshuffling of the beneficial interests (*Re Holt* (1969)). Sixth, and most controversially, it appears from *Re Vandervell's Trusts (No 2)* (1974) that a declaration of new trusts *by the trustees* with the consent of a beneficial owner who is absolutely entitled to the property does not have to be in writing, even if the result is that the trustees now hold the trust property on the same terms for different beneficiaries. To many, this will look like a

---

13   It is advisable to state the views of academics on controversial issues of law.

transfer of the equitable interest from the original beneficiary to a new equitable owner. Alternatively, the principle in *Re Vandervell (No 2)* (1974) may be vindicated on the grounds of equitable estoppel as laid down in the *High Trees* (1947) case. However, be that as it may, *Re Vandervell (No 2)* is a highly complex case and perhaps the best that can be said for it is that it was decided with reference to its own special facts and should not be regarded as laying down any general principle.

NOTE

For further discussion of *Re Vandervell (No 2),* see Harris (1975) 38 MLR 557 and Green (1984) 47 MLR 385.

QUESTION 4

'In order for a settlor to create a valid *inter vivos* trust of property he owns absolutely, it is necessary both to constitute the trust perfectly and to meet certain statutory requirements.'

▶ Discuss.

Aim Higher

Understanding the distinction between the creation of a trust on the one hand by self-declaration and, on the other, a transfer and declaration is crucial as the methods are mutually exclusive.

Common Pitfalls ✘

This is a fairly broad question that deals with the key elements related to the creation of an express trust. It is imperative to adopt a clear structure in presenting the principles raised in the cases and avoid simply trotting out a catalogue of cases. It is unnecessary to deal with exceptions to the rule that 'equity will not assist a volunteer' in any detail.

How to Answer this Question

- ❖ Summary of the nature of the trust concept.
- ❖ The need for control over the trust property to be effectively conveyed to the trustee, or alternatively retaining the property as trustee (*Milroy v Lord* (1862)).
- ❖ The elements that give rise to the constitution of a trust.
- ❖ The statutory requirements for the validity of trusts of certain kinds of property (s 53 of the Law of Property Act 1925).
- ❖ The consequences of imperfect creation (briefly).

Answer Structure

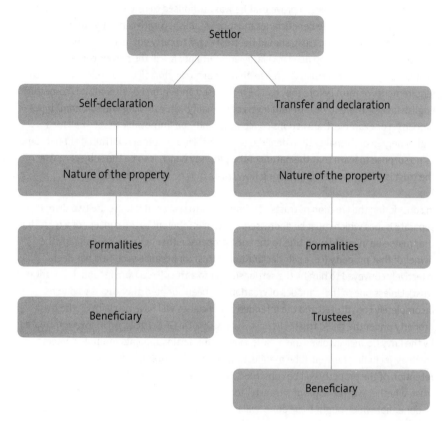

This diagram refers to the various steps that are required to be complied with in order to create a valid express trust.

ANSWER

The trust concept has been heralded as a unique and popular creation of equity over the centuries. When an express trust is created the settlor loses all control over the property and is treated as a stranger to the trust, unless he retains an interest as trustee or beneficiary (*Re Bowden* [1936] Ch 71).[14] The trustee acquires control of the property, subject to a declaration of trust in favour of the beneficiary. Consequently, he will be subject to a bundle of onerous duties created by the trust instrument, or by statute, or by general principles of equity. The effect is that the trustee may be subject to the most stringent standards of behaviour with serious consequences if he neglects his duties or breaches the

---

14 It is sound examination technique to state the rationale for the rule as this assists in understanding the test that has been laid down by the courts.

terms of the trust. Indeed, the trustee is prohibited from deriving any benefit from the trust property except where he can prove that he was authorised to receive or retain the profit. Similarly, the rights of the beneficiaries must be established with certainty so that they may be allowed to enforce the trust, should the trustee fail to carry out its terms. The effect is that there is an underlying need for clarity and certainty for all the parties concerned when establishing an express trust. Of course, that is not to say that all trusts must fulfil the same requirements of form before they can be recognised and enforced. After all, it is common in English law for there to be different levels of formality when dealing with different types of property. For example, transactions concerning land – an immovable asset – call for a higher degree of formality than dealings with other kinds of property. Thus, it should come as no surprise to learn that the nature of the property which is to be the subject matter of the trust is relevant when considering how trusts may be validly created.

In considering the creation of trusts, it is important to realise that there are two distinct and separate issues which must be addressed.[15] First, it is inherent in the concept of a trust that the trustee be invested with title to the trust property, either because he is already the owner of that property (i.e. a self-declaration of trust) or because such title has been effectively conveyed to him by the settlor subject to a trust (i.e. a transfer and declaration of trust). Unless one of these modes of creation has been adopted, the trust is said to be incompletely constituted and the intended beneficiaries will have no claim on the trust property under the failed trust (*Milroy v Lord* (1862) 4 De GF & J 264). An innovation created by the Privy Council involves the occasion where the settlor appoints multiple owners as trustees, including himself. If he manifests an irrevocable intention to create a trust, his retention of the property will be construed as one of the trustees, thereby constituting the trust, whether with or without a transfer to the other trustees. The maxim, 'equity regards as done that which ought to be done' will be applicable: see *Choithram v Pagarani* [2001] 1 WLR 1.[16] In cases where the trust property needs to be conveyed to a trustee, it is necessary to examine the particular type of trust property in order to determine what must be done for an effective transfer of the title. The requirements will be different for each type of property. Second, there are 'external' formality rules, imposed by statute, which regulate the way in which trusts *per se* can be created. These are to be found in the Law of Property Act (LPA) 1925 and they are designed to ensure that the creation of trusts of certain kinds of property is not open to doubt and to minimise the potential for fraud by the trustee. Failure to fulfil these requirements renders the trust unenforceable, even if title to the property is effectively vested in the trustee (s 53 of the LPA 1925).

In the case of a self-declaration of trust, the person who is to be the trustee already has title and, therefore, there is no need to transfer the property. All that is needed is an

---

15   Examiners are impressed by the correct statement of the principle of law presented in legal language.

16   This case (**Pagarani**), or principle, has had an impact on the question whether the trust is perfect. Examinees will find that a reading of the judgment may assist in understanding where this principle fits within the scheme of things.

effective declaration of trust – or rather, a declaration by the current owner of himself as trustee – some clear evidence of a present and irrevocable declaration of trust, as in *Paul v Constance* [1977] 1 All ER 195 and *Re Kayford* [1975] 1 All ER 604, and generally this evidence may take any form except in relation to land; see below. The general rule is summarised in the maxim 'equity looks at the intent rather than the form'.

The second way in which trusts may be created involves the effective transfer of property to the trustee, subject to the trust. As noted at the outset, unless the trustee has title to the property, the trust is incompletely constituted and the beneficiaries have no enforceable claim to the property under the failed 'trust' (*Jones v Lock* (1865) LR 1 Ch App 25). Thus, if S (the owner and 'settlor') decides to create a trust of his book by transferring the book to A on trust for B, legal title to the book must be effectively transferred to A if the trust is to be constituted and B is to have enforceable rights to it. In reality, then, it is essential to know how title to different types of property may be transferred. Indeed, there is nothing special about the rules we are about to consider, as they are the normal rules applicable to the transfer of title to property whenever it is conveyed. It is just that, with trusts, the trustee is receiving the property on behalf of someone else and not for his own use. Typical examples of the formality requirements for the transfer of title in property to a trustee are: a deed or registered disposition for land (unregistered and registered respectively); execution of a share transfer form and registration as owner for stocks and shares; written assignment for choses in action; and delivery of possession or a deed of gift for personal property. It is clear, then, that the particular requirements for the effective transfer of title to a trustee depend upon the nature of the property being transferred and, in this sense, the formality requirements for the creation of a trust are really the formality requirements for the effective transfer of ownership of property generally.

Finally, before considering the 'external' formality requirements for the creation of a trust, it is necessary to consider briefly one or two exceptions to the general principle just considered. First, a trust may be held to have been validly constituted, despite the fact that the trustee has not formally received the legal title, if failure to be invested with that title is because of non-compliance with some condition outside the control of the settlor or trustee. The trust will be constituted with the equitable interest in the property. Thus, in *Re Rose* [1952] Ch 499, a trust of shares in a private company was held to be perfectly constituted despite the fact that the legal title of the trustee had not been formally confirmed at the relevant time by entry in the share register of the company. This was because transfer of legal title was by registration in the company's register but its directors had a discretion to refuse such registration and registration had not yet taken place. Given, then, that complete transfer of the legal title was outside the settlor's (and trustee's) control, lack of compliance was not destructive of the trust.[17] Likewise, in

---

17 The case of **Pennington v Waine** has attracted some criticism in adopting too broad a principle in an effort to perfect the transfer.

Pennington v Waine [2002] All ER (D) 24, the Court of Appeal decided that the execution and delivery of share transfer forms to an intermediary for the purpose of registering the new owner was sufficient to transfer the equitable interest. However, it is unclear whether legal title will be taken to have been effectively transferred if subsequent registration (of the private company's shares or registered land) does not take place and so the exception really allows the trust to be constituted in advance of the time that it technically occurs. Second, according to *Re Ralli* [1964] Ch 288, it may be immaterial that the trustee acquires title to the trust property in a manner different from that which the settlor originally intended. So, even though the settlor has failed to positively transfer title to the trustee during his lifetime, if the intended trustee is also the settlor's executor under his will, when the settlor dies, the executor (and trustee) will obtain legal title by virtue of his position as executor (under the *Strong v Bird* rule (1874)) and the trust will thereby be constituted, albeit in a different manner from that which was intended. Third, there are several other methods by which title to property may be effectively transferred from one person to another without the normal formality rules for that type of property being satisfied. However, these are usually relevant when the transferee obtains the property absolutely and not as trustee – that is, they are used to make gifts, not to perfect trusts. Examples include the principles of *donatio mortis causa* and the law of proprietary estoppel. Fourth, an ineffectual transfer of the relevant property to the nominated trustee will not automatically be treated by the courts as a valid self-declaration of trust, otherwise all imperfect trusts will become perfect. The intention to declare oneself a trustee is very different from the intention to transfer property to another as trustee and they are mutually exclusive: see *Richards v Delbridge* (1874) LR 18 Eq 11.

We shall look now at the other major requirement for the valid creation of a trust: the external formality rules imposed by statute. In essence, these rules are necessary to ensure certainty in dealings with certain kinds of property, especially land. In fact, the position in respect of trusts of property created *inter vivos* is relatively straightforward. First, assuming that title to the property is with, or has been transferred to, the trustee, there are no further formal requirements for the creation of trusts of personalty (that is, not land or interests in land). So, trusts of property other than land may be created orally or in writing and all that is needed is a self-declaration of trust or an effective transfer of title to another as trustee. In the case of land, however, the creation of a trust must be 'manifested and proved' in writing. Although the trust does not have to be *in* writing, there must be written evidence of it, even if that evidence is not contemporaneous with the date of the creation of the trust (s 53(1)(b) of the LPA 1925 and *Rouchefoucauld v Boustead* [1897] 1 Ch 196). Failure to comply with this evidential requirement renders the trust of land unenforceable, although there are exceptions for resulting or constructive trusts of land (s 53(2) of the LPA 1925). Likewise, the court may, in exceptional circumstances, allow oral evidence to prove the existence of a trust of land if this is necessary to prevent fraud by the trustee, as where the trustee dishonestly claims that there is no trust and that he may keep the property *because* of an absence of the necessary writing (*Rouchefoucauld v Boustead*).

These, then, are the necessary formalities which must be met before a settlor can create an *inter vivos* trust of property which he owns absolutely. Of course, if the trust is by will, then different considerations apply (see s 9 of the Wills Act 1837, as amended) and if the subject matter of the trust is itself an equitable interest (so that the trustee holds an equitable title on trust for another), there may be further formality requirements springing from the requirements of writing found in s 53(1)(c) of the LPA 1925. Finally, it is relevant to note that, in some circumstances, it may be difficult to distinguish between, on the one hand, the creation of a trust of pure personalty (no writing) or of land (evidenced in writing) and, on the other, the transfer of an equitable interest in personalty or land under a trust which already exists. The difference is, however, crucial, for the transfer of any equitable interest under an existing trust – be it of personalty or realty – must actually be *in* writing under s 53(1)(c) of the LPA 1925. As the cases of *Grey v IRC* [1960] AC 1 and *Vandervell v IRC* [1967] 2 AC 291 demonstrate, such a distinction is not always easy to draw.

QUESTION 5

Alfred is the sole beneficial owner under a trust that comprises 20,000 shares in Trident Co Ltd (a private company). The trustees are Thomas and Trevor. Discuss the proprietary effect of the following alternative actions:

(i)   Alfred orally declares that he henceforth holds his beneficial interest in the Trident shares on trust for himself for life with remainder to Bernard absolutely;

(ii)   Alfred orally instructs his trustees to hold his beneficial interest in the Trident shares on trust for Bernard;

(iii) Alfred orally instructs his trustees to convey his legal title to the Trident shares to Bernard, at the same time informing Bernard that he is now the outright owner of the shares;

(iv)   Alfred enters into an oral contract with Bernard for the purchase of Alfred's beneficial interest in the Trident shares.

How to Answer this Question

❖   Alfred's interest subsists under an existing trust.

❖   Consider the requirements of s 53(1)(c) of the Law of Property Act 1925 and whether the sub-section is applicable to personal property (i.e. shares).

❖   What constitutes a disposition within s 53(1)(c) of the LPA 1925? See Romer LJ's pronouncement in *Timpson's Executors v Yerbury*.

❖   Whether a declaration of trust of part of an equitable interest is treated as a disposition?

❖   Would an oral instruction to the trustees to hold on trust for another beneficiary constitute an intended disposition?

❖   Would the unification of the legal and equitable interests in the hands of a third party constitute a disposition within s 53(1)(c) of the 1925 Act?

❖   Would a constructive trust that may arise from an oral contract be exempt from the requirements of s 53(1)(c) of the 1925 Act?

Applying the Law

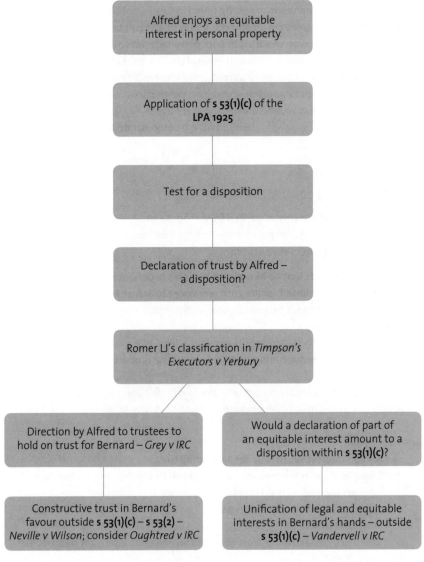

This diagram represents the legal effect of the various transactions entered into by Alfred.

ANSWER

This question concerns alternative oral arrangements entered into by Alfred and requires us to consider the legal effect of each transaction. In particular, the issues relate to the potential disposition of Alfred's equitable interest in the shares.[18] We are told that Alfred enjoys his interest in 20,000 shares in Trident Co Ltd under a trust and Thomas and Trevor are the trustees. It follows that Alfred is an equitable owner of these shares and he is the sole beneficiary. His interest is enjoyed under a 'subsisting' trust for the purposes of s 53(1)(c) of the Law of Property Act 1925 (LPA). A 'subsisting' trust refers to any form of trust that exists irrespective of whether it is express, resulting, constructive or indeed statutory. Section 53(1)(c) requires a 'disposition' of an equitable interest under a subsisting trust to be in writing signed by the disponer or his agent lawfully authorised in writing.[19] This sub-section creates an obligation in writing in order to dispose of the relevant interest. Failure to comply with the requirements of the sub-section will result in the attempted disposition being void. In short, if any of the oral transactions entered into by Alfred is within the confines of s 53(1)(c) the oral transaction will be void and the interest will remain with Alfred.

Before considering the effect of each individual transaction entered into by Alfred there are two preliminary points that underpin the issues. First, s 53(1)(c) of the LPA 1925 is applicable to equitable interests in land and personalty. Despite s 205(1)(x) of the LPA 1925 defining equitable interests by reference to land, the courts have extended the application of the sub-section to personal property in a series of high profile decisions. The justification is that the equivalent to this sub-section was enacted in s 9 of the Statute of Frauds 1677 which was passed to prevent fraud. The mischief or purposive interpretation of the sub-section vindicates the extension of the provision. It is thus unnecessary and too late in the day for the sub-section to be given its literal meaning. Second, as a starting point to the consideration of the width of the expression 'disposition', a partial classification of the term was laid down by Romer LJ in *Timpson's Executors v Yerbury* as including:

- ❖ assignments of interests to donees;
- ❖ directions to the trustees to hold upon trust for another or others;
- ❖ contracts entered into for valuable consideration in order to sell the interest to the other contracting party;
- ❖ self-declarations of trust in favour of other beneficiaries.

(i) Alfred's oral declaration of trust in favour of Bernard

It is clear that Alfred's interest is 'equitable' for it is enjoyed under a trust. It is also clear that Alfred's interest exists in personalty (shares in Trident Co Ltd) and s 53(1)(c) of the LPA 1925 encompasses interests in both realty and personalty. The question in issue here

---

18   It is good examination technique to identify the issues raised in the question.
19   This is a summary of the statutory provision. It is advisable to narrate the provision verbatim.

is whether Alfred's self-declaration of trust of his interest constitutes a disposition within s 53(1)(c) of the LPA 1925. The classification by Romer LJ of a disposition includes a self-declaration of trust and this transaction involves a sub-trust. *Prima facie* the oral declaration by Alfred constitutes an attempt to dispose of his equitable interest and, since it does not comply with the requirement of writing, is therefore void.

On the other hand, academics of the calibre of Professors Pettit and Hayton have advanced arguments to the effect that the expression 'disposition' within s 53(1)(c) does not include the creation of trusts but merely the continuance of trusts. Accordingly, a creation of an interest under a sub-trust by way of a declaration of trust does not constitute a disposition if the declarant has active duties to perform. The reason is that the declarant will not be able to drop out of the picture but is required to perform his duties. Where there are only passive duties on the part of the trustees to perform, the declaration will amount to an intended disposition: see *Grainge v Wilberforce* and *Re Lashmar*. The nature of the transaction seems to vary depending on whether the declarant has active or passive duties to perform. The declaration of trust by Alfred is in respect of part of his equitable interest, namely the remainder interest in favour of Bernard, and therefore imposes active duties on Alfred. The effect is that, according to this view, s 53(1)(c) is not applicable to the creation of this sub-trust. The opposing view was put forward by Brian Green, who, after analysing the main cases, concluded that the sub-section does not draw a distinction between a disposition with or without active duties to perform. In both cases of sub-trusts a disposition is intended and will be effective only when the formal requirements are satisfied. There is some support for this view in *Nelson v Greening & Sykes* [2007] EWCA 1358. On this basis the oral declaration of trust will be ineffective to dispose of Alfred's equitable interest.

(ii) Alfred's oral instruction to the trustees to hold upon trust for Bernard

Since Alfred enjoys an equitable interest under a trust, the question that arises is whether Alfred's oral instruction to the trustees to hold upon trust for Bernard amounts to an intended disposition within s 53(1)(c). If so, then the direction will be void and Alfred will retain his property. This method of disposing of an interest was referred to by Romer LJ in *Yerbury*, see above. Further, the House of Lords in *Grey v IRC* decided that an oral direction by the equitable owner to the trustees to hold on trust for a third party was void. The effect of the decision is where a new equitable owner (Bernard) is intended to be substituted for the previous equitable owner (Alfred), this can only be done by way of a disposition. Since the direction to the trustees is not in writing Bernard does not acquire the equitable interest in the shares.

(iii) Transfer of the legal and equitable interests to Bernard

There are a number of issues to be considered in this aspect of the question: first, the formal requirements to be complied with in order to transfer the legal title to shares in a private company; second, on the assumption that the legal title to the shares has been transferred to Bernard, whether the contemporaneous transfer of the equitable interest in the shares to the same third party (Bernard) requires compliance with s 53(1)(c).

The transfer of the legal title to shares in a private company is complete when the intended new owner of the shares (Bernard) is registered in the company's share register. Alfred as the sole equitable owner of the shares is entitled under the *Saunders v Vautier* principle to direct Thomas and Trevor, the legal owners of the shares, to transfer these shares to Bernard. The procedure to transfer the shares requires a share transfer to be executed by the transferors and this form along with the share certificates is required to be sent to the registered office of the company. A private company usually has the power to register or refuse to register the new owner. We have not been told whether Bernard has been registered. If the proper procedure has been followed and the company refuses to register Bernard a constructive trust will arise in favour of Bernard. The basis for this trust is that the transferors would have done everything in their power to transfer the shares and the decision whether to register Bernard was beyond their control: *Re Rose* and *Pennington v Waine*. This constructive trust would be outside the formal requirements of s 53(1)(c) by virtue of s 53(2) of the LPA 1925: see below.

On the assumption that the transfer of the legal title to the shares has been completed, the next issue is the effect of Alfred's oral statement to Bernard that he is now the outright owner of the shares. Would this constitute an intended disposition within s 53(1)(c) or would it fall outside of s 53(1)(c)? The House of Lords in *Vandervell v IRC* considered the purpose or mischief behind the sub-section and decided that the transfer of the equitable interest, when coupled with the transfer of the legal title to the same individual, was outside the requirements of s 53(1)(c). The reason for this ruling is that the trust will be terminated and there is unlikely to be a fraud, and specifically there will be no need for the trustee to chart the movement of the equitable interest. The effect is that this transaction by Alfred will be effective to dispose of the property to Bernard.

(iv) Alfred contracts to sell his interest in the shares to Bernard

Applying Romer LJ's *dictum* in *Yerbury* it would follow that a contract for valuable consideration to sell Alfred's equitable interest in the Trident shares to Bernard is potentially a disposition within s 53(1)(c) of the LPA 1925. We have not been told of the nature of the consideration, but assuming it is valuable the contract will be valid and binding on the parties. The question in issue is whether Alfred's equitable interest will be transferred to Bernard by virtue of this oral contract. The solution depends on whether a constructive trust arises in favour of Bernard and, if so, whether the trust would fall within s 53(2) of the LPA and exempt the donor from the requirements of s 53(1)(c). In *Oughtred v IRC* the House of Lords decided that when one party executes his part of the bargain, a constructive trust arises in his favour on the basis of the maxim, 'equity regards as done that which ought to be done': see also *Chinn v Collins*. The next question as to whether s 53(2) exempts the disponer from the requirements of s 53(1)(c), was surprisingly only adequately dealt with by one Law Lord, namely Lord Radcliffe. He decided that since a constructive trust (as well as a resulting trust) is created by the courts, it would be regarded as outside the requirements of s 53(1)(c). His view has now been endorsed by the Court of Appeal in *Neville v Wilson*. The effect is that once Bernard has performed in part or as a whole his side of the bargain by paying the purchase monies to Alfred, he, Bernard, will acquire Alfred's equitable interest.

QUESTION 6

To what extent has the Contracts (Rights of Third Parties) Act 1999 ameliorated the position of the volunteer under an imperfect trust?

▶ Discuss, by reference to decided cases.

Aim Higher

Students are best advised that in answering questions of this type they ought to be fully conversant with the law that existed before the introduction of the **Contracts (Rights of Third Parties) Act 1999**, as well as the new rights that have been created under the Act. The reason for this is that the Act can be excluded by an indication of such intention in the contract and, in any event, the contract/covenant is required to confer a benefit on the third party. This question focuses on the implications of the statutory modification of the privity rule and highlights the fact that the maxim that 'equity will not assist a volunteer' remains intact.

Common Pitfalls

Students sometimes do not fully appreciate the remedies that are available to a claimant as a beneficiary under a perfect trust, a non-volunteer and a volunteer under an imperfect trust.

How to Answer this Question

❖ The significance of a perfect trust;

❖ The distinction between volunteers and non-volunteers;

❖ The extent to which a volunteer may enforce an imperfect trust before the introduction of the Contracts (Rights of Third Parties Act) 1999;

❖ The nature and effect of the Contracts (Rights of Third Parties Act) 1999.

Answer Structure

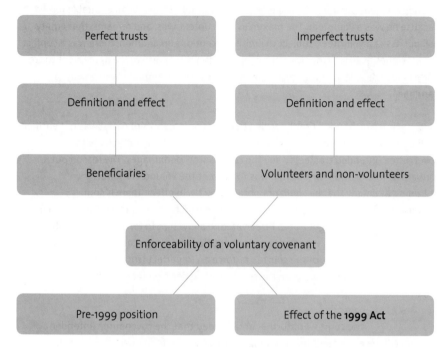

This diagram spells out the remedies that were available to a volunteer before and after the passing of the *1999 Act*.

ANSWER

Under a perfect trust the beneficiary, who may be a volunteer, is entitled to enforce the trust. He acquires an equitable interest *in rem* and is entitled as of right to protect his interest. However, if the trust is imperfect (i.e. the principles in *Milroy v Lord* (1862) have not been complied with) the status of the claimant is of paramount importance. If the claimant is a non-volunteer, he is entitled to assert a right to the property as if the trust is perfect and may be able to obtain specific performance of the promise to transfer the relevant property. Thus, at the instance of a non-volunteer the imperfect trust will be treated as equivalent to a perfect trust. On the other hand, if the trust is imperfect, the claimant is, subject to the Contracts (Rights of Third Parties Act) 1999, required to establish that he had furnished consideration. A volunteer will not be entitled to any equitable remedies.[20]

A volunteer is someone who has not provided valuable consideration. Valuable consideration at common law is money or money's worth or, in equity, marriage consideration.

---

20 Identification of the issues that will be analysed and explored.

The position before the Contracts (Rights of Third Parties) Act 1999 was that an intended beneficiary under an imperfect trust was not entitled to an equitable remedy because he was a volunteer. The maxim in this context was, and remains, that equity will not assist a volunteer, subject to limited exceptions. In addition, there was a conflict of authorities as to whether the volunteer, who is a third party to the agreement to create a trust (such as a deed or a covenant), was entitled to the common law remedy of damages.

In Re Pryce (1917) the High Court decided that the volunteer (third party) was not entitled to directions, the consequences of which would have entitled him to force the covenantee (intended trustee) to sue the covenantor for damages. The reason put forward as justification for this rule was to prevent the volunteer indirectly obtaining a remedy that he could not obtain directly. In effect, there is some justification for the decision, as opposed to the reason for the decision. The volunteer third party's position ought not to be elevated to allow him to force the covenantee to sue for damages. As a volunteer he is not entitled to any equitable assistance and by seeking the directions of the court to enforce an imperfect trust, he was attempting to enhance his position. However, the reason for the decision seems to be excessively broad-based.

In Re Kay (1939) the court went further and decided that the covenantee (intended trustee) will be prevented from bringing an action at law for damages against the covenantor. In this case the court applied the principle laid down in Re Pryce in positively preventing the covenantee from succeeding in such a claim. It was as if the court was attempting to frustrate the covenantee's claim to pursue his common law remedy. The principle in Re Kay, as distinct from Re Pryce, was based on two implied assumptions, namely:

(a) if the covenantee pursued his claim for damages, he would have been entitled to substantial damages, measured by reference to the failure on the part of the covenantor to fulfil his obligations;

(b) the substantial damages received by the covenantee would be held on trust for the volunteer third party.

Accordingly, the covenantee was prevented from pursuing his claim in order to prevent the volunteer becoming a beneficiary under an imperfect trust.

On the other hand, in Re Cavendish-Browne (1916) the High Court decided that the covenantee was entitled to pursue his common law remedy and was awarded substantial damages. The additional issue as to whether the damages were to be held on trust for the volunteer third party was not considered by the court. This case seems to be in direct conflict with Re Kay. Strained efforts have been made to reconcile the decisions on the ground that in Re Cavendish-Browne the property was in existence, namely land in

Canada, whereas in *Re Kay* the subject matter of the covenant was after acquired property. This distinction lies with the facts of the case only and cannot be supported in principle.[21]

In *Cannon v Hartley* (1949) the High Court decided that where the volunteer was a party to the covenant, he was entitled to bring a claim for damages for breach of covenant. The decision is justifiable on the ground that he is a party to the covenant and has suffered loss personally. He does not seek any equitable assistance and pursues his common law remedy for damages only.

In *Beswick v Beswick* (1968) the House of Lords decided that a non-volunteer and party to a covenant was entitled to enforce a covenant in favour of a volunteer. Accordingly, on the death of the non-volunteer, the volunteer (and executor of the deceased) was entitled to enforce the covenant in his favour. In this case the volunteer was able to obtain specific performance.[22]

THE CONTRACTS (RIGHTS OF THIRD PARTIES) ACT 1999

The 1999 Act introduced a long overdue reform of the law. Its purpose was to reform the rule of privity of contract under which a person may only enforce a contract if he is a party to it.

ENTITLEMENT TO SUE

Section 1(1) of the Contracts (Rights of Third Parties) Act 1999 sets out the circumstances when a third party to a contract will have a right to enforce the agreement. These are when the contract was made expressly or impliedly for the benefit of the third party (ss 1(1) and (2)). The third party is required to be identified by name or description, although he need not be in existence at the time the contract was made (s 1(3)).

This provision will be satisfied if A covenants (or makes a simple agreement) with B to transfer property to him upon trust for C. Assuming that A has not transferred the property to B and that C is a 'volunteer', then, as a third party, the requirements above will be satisfied. The effect is that the third party (C) is entitled 'in his own right to enforce' the contract (s 1(1)). This is the typical case with regard to an incompletely constituted trust.

THE REMEDY

Section 1(5) of the Contracts (Rights of Third Parties) Act 1999 declares the remedy which will be available to the third party (C in the above example). Section 1(5) states that for the purpose of exercising his right to enforce a term of the contract, there shall be available

21 It is recommended that you discuss conflicting cases.

22 This question requires a structured discussion of the leading cases.

to the third party any remedy that would have been available to him in an action for breach of contract if he had been a party to the contract (and the rules relating to damages, injunctions, specific performance and other relief shall apply accordingly).[23]

The effect of the provision is to treat C, the volunteer and third party, as if he is a party to the agreement and to grant him such remedies as would be available to him as a party to the agreement. Under the Act, C's position is treated as similar to the claimant in *Cannon v Hartley* (1949). Alternatively, if C has provided valuable consideration for the promise, but is not a party to the agreement (i.e. he has provided marriage consideration), he would be entitled to damages, if this remedy is appropriate (as declared by the Act). But if the remedy of damages is not appropriate, the third party non-volunteer would be entitled to an equitable remedy such as specific performance as in *Pullan v Koe* (1913). This principle has not been changed by the Act, but is simply confirmed by the provision.

IS THE VOLUNTEER ENTITLED TO AN EQUITABLE REMEDY?

The contentious issue is what remedy would C, a volunteer and third party to the contract, be entitled to in an action against A for breach of contract? The remedy that C (the claimant) is entitled to, save for damages, has not been altered by the Act. It is submitted that C, as a volunteer, will only be entitled to damages for four reasons.

First, the policy of the Act was to reform the privity rule and treat the third party in the circumstances laid down in the Act as if he is a party to the contract. On this basis the third party (who is now treated under the Act as though he is a party) is entitled to bring an action against the party in breach *in his own right*, i.e. the claim is not dependent on the means of another. In our example, C may sue A directly without joining B as a co-claimant or a co-defendant.

Second, the reformation of the privity rule does not automatically change the law with regard to equitable remedies. These remain discretionary, but damages are obtainable as of right, subject to the rules regarding the quantification of damages.

Third, s 1(5) confirms that the rules regarding damages and specific performance shall apply. The rules regarding damages are well known, in particular the rules concerning remoteness of damage and the duty to mitigate the loss. These rules remain the same after the Act. In addition, the equitable concept that 'equity will not assist a volunteer' is applicable with equal force after the Act. Since C is a volunteer, he should not expect an equitable remedy, such as specific performance, for he was not entitled to such a remedy prior to the passing of the Act and the Act has not changed this rule. Thus, it follows that since the volunteer non-covenantee (i.e. C) is now treated as though he is a party to the covenant, his status remains a volunteer and as such will not gain any equitable assistance.

23 The statutory provision ought to be defined before entering into a discussion.

Fourth, a volunteer in the eyes of equity is treated as not having lost anything under the contract and, without more, is not entitled in his own right to gain any benefits under the contract. The position is not the same at common law with regard to damages, which is obtainable as of right. Thus, it makes no difference whether the subject matter of the contract to transfer property to B for the benefit of C involves land, shares in a private company or cash. As a contract, as opposed to an imperfect trust, C has lost nothing in the eyes of equity.

In conclusion, the 1999 Act has effected the following changes:

(a)   a reversal of *Re Pryce* (1917) – where a volunteer non-covenantee (C) was not able to force the covenantee (B) to bring an action for damages;

(b)   a reversal of *Re Kay* (1939) – where a covenantee (B) was prevented from bringing an action for damages on behalf of a volunteer non-covenantee (C);

(c)   an endorsement of *Re Cavendish-Browne* (1916) – where a covenantee (B) successfully brought an action for damages on behalf of a non- covenantee (C);

(d)   an approval of the principle in *Cannon v Hartley* (1949) – the volunteer covenantee is entitled to claim substantial damages for breach of covenant, but is not entitled to the equitable remedy of specific performance.

QUESTION 7

A young couple, Wendy and Harold, decided to get married. On the happy occasion, Wendy's father, Frank, who was a pioneer heart surgeon, covenanted with his friends, John and Smith (who were also the executors under his will), to transfer to them £200,000 and a house in Chelsea, to hold on trust for the benefit of Wendy and Harold for their respective lives, thereafter for their children and thereafter for their grandchildren. Failing issue, the trust properties were to be conveyed to Norman, his next of kin, absolutely.

The day after the wedding, Frank, who had made a fortune from his practice at Harley Street, received the shocking news that he had an inoperable brain tumour and that he was unlikely to live longer than 12 months. Frank then decided to sort out his affairs. He called the trustees of the above settlement and told them that he would shortly be transferring the house and cash to them. He also executed a further covenant with the trustees to transfer to them his portfolio of 20,000 shares in Lazerdot.com. At the same time, Frank informed his solicitor that, if he should die within 12 months, he wanted his son, Sam, to have his antique Rolls-Royce motor car. He did this by letter, enclosing a spare ignition key to the car.

Later that night, Frank executed the necessary documents relating to the various properties, except for the cheque for £200,000, which he had filled in but forgotten to sign. He gave the documents to his solicitor to effect the transfers. When he went to the door to see the solicitor off, a bolt of lightning suddenly struck and killed both men instantly.

▶   Consider the issues raised by the events above and advise the executors whether any of the intended beneficiaries and donees are entitled to an interest in any of the properties.

> ### Aim Higher
> In dealing with questions on the constitution of trusts, students are advised to bear in mind that additional issues may include the exceptions to the general rule that equity will not assist a volunteer.

> ### Common Pitfalls
> It is significant to recognise that in *Re Cook*, the settlor's intention was construed as an intention to create a trust as and when the subject matter came into existence and was transferred to the trustees. Thus, *Fletcher v Fletcher* was distinguished on the ground that, in the latter case, the subject matter involved was existing property, whereas in *Re Cook* the subject matter was future property.

How to Answer this Question

- ❖ Whether the requirements for the creation of trusts of the various properties were complied with.
- ❖ Whether the covenant to create trusts is enforceable.
- ❖ The effect of the Contracts (Rights of Third Parties) Act 1999.
- ❖ *Donatio mortis causa.*

Answer Structure

```
                    Milroy v Lord test
```

Effect

- Cheque – Funds not transferred but a chose in action of the benefit of the covenant acquired by trustees
- House – No Legal transfer but possibly transfer of the equitable interest
- Shares – No transfer of the legal title but disposition of the equitable interest
- Car – Transfer of the legal title? Alternatively disposition by way of a DMC

This chart identifies the legal effect of the transactions concerning Frank's properties.

ANSWER

This problem concerns the fundamental principles for the creation of an express trust and the consequences of a perfect and imperfect trust.

A trust is perfectly created when the trust property is 'at home', that is, the trustees have acquired the property subject to the terms of the trust as declared by the settlor. There are two modes of creating an express trust. The first is a transfer of property to the trustees, subject to a declaration of trust by the settlor. This is the transfer and declaration mode. The second mode of creation requires the settlor to declare himself a trustee for the beneficiaries. This is a self-declaration of trust. In order to create a valid express trust one of these modes is required to be complied with. This is the test laid down by Turner LJ in *Milroy v Lord* (1862).

One of the primary issues in this problem is whether a trust attaches to each of the properties specified.

CHEQUE FOR £200,000

Frank had forgotten to sign the cheque that would have transferred the funds to the nominated trustees, John and Smith. Accordingly, there is no transfer of the funds to the trustees. In any event, a cheque is a revocable mandate which is revoked on death, see *Re Beaumont*. The effect is that Frank had manifested an intention to settle funds specified in the cheque, without a transfer of the funds.[24]

At the same time an imperfect transfer will not automatically be construed as a self-declaration of trust with the effect of imposing a trust obligation on Frank, for otherwise all imperfect transfers will be treated as perfect (*Richards v Delbridge* (1874)). In any event Frank did not declare an intention to make himself a trustee. On this basis *Re Ralli* (1964) and *Choithram v Pagarani* (2001) could be distinguished from the facts of this problem.

In accordance with the principle in *Fletcher v Fletcher* (1844), the covenant to transfer £200,000 may be treated as a transfer of a chose in action (i.e. the benefit of the covenant) provided that the cash existed (or its equivalent) at the time of the covenant, and Frank intended the chose to be the subject matter of the trust. Whether Frank intended to create a trust of a chose in action would depend on the circumstances of each case. This involves a question of fact to be construed by the courts. There is very little evidence that Frank intended the subject matter of the trust to be the right created under the covenant, as distinct from the cash sum of £200,000.[25]

---

24 Application of the principles of law to the facts.
25 In constitution questions it is important to consider the **Fletcher v Fletcher** rule.

On the assumption that there is no transfer of property to the trustees (either as funds in a bank account or a chose in action), the intended trust of the covenanted sum will involve an imperfect trust and the maxims that are applicable are 'equity will not assist a volunteer' and 'equity will not perfect an imperfect transfer'. The consequences of such an omission by Frank will be considered later.

THE HOUSE IN CHELSEA

The transfer of the legal title to the house has not been completed by Frank because he died after 'executing the necessary documents' but before the same were sent to the Land Registry. Indeed, Frank delivered the documents to his solicitor for the purpose of securing registration of John and Smith as the legal owners. Unfortunately, the solicitor also died in the same tragedy and presumably before any steps could be taken to transfer the property. The issue here is whether Frank had done everything required of him to transfer the legal title to his trustees John and Smith. This is a question of degree, but, if he had, a constructive trust (involving Frank, or his estate after his death, holding the property as constructive trustee) would arise transferring the equitable interest to the trustees, John and Smith, on trust for the named beneficiaries: see *Re Rose* (1952) and *Mascall v Mascall* (1984). In the recent case of *Pennington v Waine* (2002) the Court of Appeal introduced an alternative basis for resolving the dispute, namely, whether it would be unconscionable for the transferor to deny the transfer. This is a question for the court to decide on the facts of each case. The fact that in *Pennington* the subject matter was shares in a company, as opposed to land (as in the present case), is not material. On the facts of the problem Frank may have been motivated by the marriage of Wendy. He executed a covenant with the intended trustees, John and Smith, and after receiving the tragic news of his medical condition called the intended trustees to inform them that he would shortly transfer *inter alia* the house. He also informed his solicitor of his intentions and executed the transfer document to the house. Drawing the evidence together, it would appear that there is strong evidence to suggest not only that Frank felt that he had done everything required of him to transfer the house, but that it may be unconscionable for Frank's estate to deny the transfer.

In respect of the *Fletcher v Fletcher* (1844) rule, it was decided in *Re Cook* (1965) that that rule is restricted to debts enforceable at law. This limitation restricts *Fletcher* to one type of chose only, namely covenanted obligations to transfer money. Thus the principle would not be applicable to a covenant to transfer the house.

20,000 SHARES IN LAZERDOT.COM

Lazerdot.com appears to be a private company. The significance of this is that the directors of the company have a right to refuse registration of new owners of shares. At the same time the legal title to shares is only transferred if the new owner is registered in the share register of the company. Frank has an obligation to comply with the requirements of the Companies Act 2006 and the Stock Transfer Act 1963 in order to transfer the legal title to shares. The requirements under these Acts impose on Frank the obligation to execute a share transfer form and send the share certificates, along with the form (personally or through his agent), to the company at its registered office in order to secure registration. Frank had 'executed the necessary documents' and delivered these to his solicitor (his agent). Has he done everything required of him? This is a question of fact – see *Re Rose*; *Pennington v Waine* (above) *contra Re Fry* (1946). If he has, the transfer would be effective in equity and he (or his executors) would become a constructive trustee of the shares. In *Pennington v Waine* the court decided that the delivery of the executed transfer documents to an intermediary to secure registration was sufficient compliance with all that was required from the transferor.

THE CAR

Frank has communicated his intention to his solicitor to give the car to Sam, but without delivering the same to the donee unconditionally. Thus, the gift is imperfect *inter vivos* and 'equity will not perfect an imperfect gift', and 'equity will not assist a volunteer'. On the facts, Sam is a volunteer; see later.

Could there be a *donatio mortis causa* of the car? A DMC involves a transfer of dominion over property during the lifetime of the transferor in contemplation of, and conditional on, death: see *Re Craven's Estate* (1937). The requirements of contemplation and conditional on death are subjective questions of fact and on the facts there is some evidence that these requirements are satisfied.[26] However, the controversial question is whether Frank has transferred control of the car to Sam during his (Frank's) lifetime? This is a question of degree. The car is tangible, moveable property and title may only be transferred by delivery accompanied by the relevant intention to transfer. Frank may deliver the car constructively by delivering the symbols of control accompanied by an intention to transfer control. On the facts, Frank has delivered the spare key to his agent (the solicitor), but there is little evidence that the solicitor is an agent for Sam. In any event, delivery of the spare ignition key is not fatal to Sam's claim: see *Woodard v Woodard* (1991).

It is evident that the intended trust of some of the properties may be perfect. Much depends on the view taken by the court. However, if the trust of any of the properties is imperfect, the question that arises is whether the respective claimant is entitled to enforce the covenant to create a trust.

It was stated earlier that the two equitable maxims are applicable with regard to imperfect trusts. A volunteer would not be entitled to equitable assistance if the trust is imperfect. The issue therefore is whether the respective claimants are volunteers and if so, what claims they may pursue.

---

26 An excellent answer would identify questions of fact and distinguish these from questions of law.

A volunteer is one who has not provided valuable consideration, i.e. money or money's worth, or a person who does not come within the marriage consideration. The latter requires a marriage settlement, i.e. an ante-nuptial settlement made in consideration of marriage or a post-nuptial settlement made in pursuance of an ante-nuptial agreement: see *Re Park (No 2)* (1972). The persons within the marriage settlement are the parties to the marriage as well as the issue of the marriage, including grandchildren. Applying this principle to the facts, it would appear that Wendy and Harold, as parties to a marriage settlement, are deemed to provide marriage consideration. The effect is that Wendy and Harold are entitled to enforce the covenant in equity as non-volunteers. Thus, they are entitled to claim specific performance of the agreement as if they were beneficiaries under a perfect trust: see *Pullan v Koe* (1913).

The next of kin is a volunteer and unable to enforce the covenant in equity: *Re Plumtree* (1910). But under the **Contracts (Rights of Third Parties) Act 1999**, the next of kin (third party) is given the capacity to bring an action in his own right. Effectively, this is only in respect of damages, for the rule remains that equity will not assist a volunteer. The volunteer therefore does not have a claim in priority over the non-volunteers.

In any event, John and Smith as the intended trustees are the executors of Frank's will. It is tempting to argue that the rule in *Strong v Bird* (1874) will perfect the imperfect gifts: see *Re Ralli* (1964). But on reflection Frank's intention was to make future transfers to the trustees. This has the effect of excluding the rule in *Strong v Bird*: see *Re Freeland* (1952).[27]

NOTE

The questions raised in this section involve the fundamental principles for the creation of an express trust – formalities and the constitution of a trust. This is a popular collection of topics with examiners.

---

27 Expressly excluding related issues for an implied exclusion may be treated as lack of knowledge.

Secret Trusts

INTRODUCTION

Secret trusts are a peculiar animal. They are special because they allow the creation of valid trusts even though the normal formality rules for the creation of trusts by will not have been met. In this sense, they are an exception to the principles discussed in Chapter 1. However, as we shall see, although 'secret' trusts arise out of testamentary dispositions (that is, wills), there is often little that is secret about either their existence or their terms. Originally, the doctrine of secret trusts was developed to allow testators to make provision for beneficiaries whose identity, or even existence, was best kept quiet, such as illegitimate children or mistresses. Today, however, they are more likely to provide an indecisive testator with a means of avoiding the strict forms required by the Wills Act 1837 (as amended).

Secret trusts are of two types: 'fully secret' trusts and 'half-secret' trusts. In essence, the difference between the two is that nothing of the existence of the trust is revealed in the will of a testator with a fully secret trust, whereas with a half-secret trust, the fact of a trust, but not the identity of the beneficiaries, is revealed in the will. This difference in purpose is reflected in the somewhat different conditions which must be met before the existence of each type of secret trust can be recognised and enforced by the 'secret' beneficiaries. In addition, because both forms of secret trusts do not meet the strict requirements of the Wills Act 1837, there is considerable academic interest in the theory behind the validity of secret trusts, especially how they gel with statutory and common law rules which would otherwise require their invalidity.

There are two general issues which may face a student dealing with secret trusts. First, there are the conditions for the existence of both types of trusts and the manner in which they operate. This requires a knowledge of substantive law and some appreciation of the requirements of the Wills Act 1837 and general equitable principles concerning the validity of trusts. Secondly, there is the largely theoretical argument about the rationale or theory behind secret trusts. While not necessarily of great practical importance, this is fertile ground for examination questions.

QUESTION 8

To what extent is it possible to develop a coherent theory to explain the validity of so-called secret trusts?

Aim Higher

This is a typical 'bookwork' question on the law of secret trusts. It is imperative when answering such a question to avoid a lengthy repetition of the rules concerning the validity of secret trusts – they are straightforward – and to concentrate instead on addressing the precise issues raised by the question.

Common Pitfalls ✘

The theories of enforcement of secret trusts are extremely complex to evaluate within the conventional norms of the law of equity. Students are best advised to analyse the subject carefully as part of their revision plan before attempting this type of question in the examination.

How to Answer this Question

❖ The context of secret trusts: their special status with respect to formalities for the creation of trusts;

❖ Fully secret and half-secret trusts briefly distinguished;

❖ Theories based on fraud: using a statute as an instrument of fraud or disregarding the intention of the testator (old fraud and new fraud);

❖ The declaration and constitution theory;

❖ Views on the different communication requirements.

Answer Structure

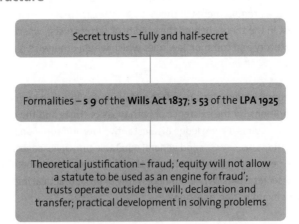

This diagram illustrates the theoretical bases for enforcing fully and half-secret trusts.

ANSWER

The starting point in answering this question is to state the obvious: that is, that both fully secret and half-secret trusts may be valid and enforceable despite lack of compliance with the formalities laid down by s 9 of the Wills Act 1837 and other statutes. Fully secret trusts are not declared in the will at all, with the trustee apparently taking the property absolutely, while in the case of half-secret trusts the existence of the trust is acknowledged in the will, thereby bringing partial compliance with s 9 of the Wills Act 1837, but the identity of the beneficiaries is not.

The lawyer's natural instinct is to search for (and expect) a rational, coherent theory which will explain why the normal rules of statute and common law do not apply. As we shall see, it may be that such a search is fruitless, or that such theories as do exist are not coherent or all-embracing. With that in mind, what can be said about the rationale for secret trusts? There are a number of different views.[1]

Perhaps the most prevalent theory was that secret trusts would be enforced by a court of equity in favour of a secret beneficiary on the ground that 'equity will not permit a statute to be an instrument of fraud' (*McCormick v Grogan* (1869), noted with approval in *Box v Barclays Bank* (1998)). That is, if a fully secret trust was declared unenforceable because it did not comply with the Wills Act 1837, the legatee/trustee would be able to keep the trust property for himself despite the fact that he had accepted the trust obligation during the testator's lifetime. Indeed, the real problem was that he would *try* to keep the property in defiance of the trust by pleading its invalidity for non-compliance with the Wills Act 1837. To accept this could be to accept that the Wills Act 1837 would assist the trustee in his fraud.

Certainly, this rationale has the attraction of simplicity and, indeed, the equitable maxim used here is familiar and well established (see, for example, *Rochefoucauld v Boustead* (1897)). However, a moment's thought will reveal that this rationale cannot explain the validity of half-secret trusts. In half-secret trusts, the testator leaves property to the legatee 'on trust' for unnamed beneficiaries. There is thus no possibility that the half-secret trustee may commit fraud, as he or she is forever barred from the property. At the very least, the half-secret trustee must hold the property on trust for the residuary estate and cannot even claim to be a beneficiary under the trust (*Re Keen* (1937); *Re Rees* (1950)). Simply put, there is no possibility of fraudulent gain by the trustee with a half-secret trust.

The impossibility of explaining both fully secret and half-secret trusts on the basis of *McCormick v Grogan*-type fraud has led to the development of theories that secret trusts are founded on a redefinition of what 'fraud' actually means. Traditionally, 'fraud' would

---

1   This type of essay question needs to have been planned out carefully before the examination.

mean the trustee taking a personal benefit when he or she was meant to hold the property for another and this is what is meant by the *Grogan* rationale. However, some commentators have argued that this is a far too narrow definition of 'fraud' and that a wider view might be taken, which can then be used to justify both fully secret and half-secret trusts. Taking this approach, we might say that secret trusts of both types should be enforced because, otherwise, a 'fraud' would be perpetrated on the testator or the beneficiaries. The testator would be defrauded because he would have parted with his legacy on the understanding that his wishes in respect of it would be carried out (*Re Fleetwood* (1880)). After all, had the secret trustee not agreed to the plan, the testator may have changed his will and made alternative arrangements. This was the view of Lord Westbury in *McCormick v Grogan* (1869). Here, however, lies the flaw in this theory, because it amounts to no more than the bald assertion that a testator's wishes should be respected even if he has put them into effect in a manner that is not acceptable (that is, not in compliance with the Wills Act 1837). Likewise, the argument that the beneficiaries would be defrauded (for example, as put by Lord Buckmaster in *Blackwell v Blackwell* (1929)) if secret trusts were not enforced is equally flawed. Beneficiaries are routinely deprived of property which testators and settlors would desire them to have, for the simple reason that the trust or gift has not been put into effect in the proper manner. In essence, then, both these variants on the 'new fraud' theory are circular and amount only to the argument that the testator's wishes should be respected. There is nothing here to explain why the formalities prescribed by statute for facilitating that intention can be ignored.

A final theory seeks to prise secret trusts away from their link with the Wills Act 1837 altogether and to explain them as ordinary trusts created *inter vivos*. According to this view – sometimes called the declaration and constitution theory of secret trusts – both fully secret and half-secret trusts operate outside the testator's will and should not be regarded as dependent upon it (*Blackwell v Blackwell*). The evidence for this is, apparently, provided by *Re Young* (1951), where a witness to a will was permitted to be a beneficiary under a secret trust, and *Re Gardner (No 2)* (1923), where a beneficiary under a secret trust died before the testator but, nevertheless, his interest passed to his estate. Both of these results would have been impossible if the trust was governed by the Wills Act 1837 because witnesses to wills may not take a legacy and beneficiaries who predecease testators lose their interests.

Assuming, then, that the Wills Act 1837 is not central to the whole matter, how are secret trusts formed under this theory? The rationale is that the communication by the testator to the trustee of the trust and/or its terms amounts to a normal *inter vivos* declaration of trust which is then completed on the testator's death when the property passes into the hands of the trustee. The will is simply the mechanism by which the trustee obtains the property and the trust becomes constituted.

This declaration/constitution theory of secret trusts does have its attractions. It justifies secret trusts on the same basis as other trusts and, in effect, classes them as express *inter vivos* trusts. It means, of course, that the trust does not come into existence until the testator dies, that being when the property passes and the trust becomes constituted. Yet, as ever, there are difficulties. If secret trusts are express trusts, this should mean that such trusts of land must be evidenced in writing as required by s 53(1)(b) of the Law of Property Act (LPA) 1925. However, at least with fully secret trusts, *Ottaway v Norman* (1972) suggests that writing is not required and it would be strange for written evidence to be necessary for compliance with s 53 of the LPA 1925 when none such was required for compliance with the Wills Act 1837. Nevertheless, *Re Baillie* (1886) is unequivocal that writing is needed for half-secret trusts of land. There are other problems, too. If the secret trust does not come into existence until the testator's death, *Re Gardner (No 2)* (1923) must be wrongly decided, as the trust did not exist when the beneficiary died! More importantly, if the relevant date for constitution of the half-secret trust might be the testator's death, why is the date of the will so important for communication purposes? Why is it necessary to declare the trust before the will is made if the will is only a trigger for the constitution of the trust? It is difficult to answer this criticism, save only to say that the communication rule for half-secret trusts is wrong and that post-testamentary communication should be possible.[2] Support for this radical proposition comes from other common law jurisdictions where the distinction between fully secret and half-secret trusts has been abolished (for example, Australia). Nevertheless, there are other explanations of why there is a difference in this respect between the two types of secret trust, although none is altogether convincing. Two of the more cogent theories are, first, that the rule allowing acceptance after the will in fully secret trusts was originally procedural, in that evidence of events occurring after the will (that is, acceptance of the trust obligation) could be admitted by a court to prove a fully secret trust in order to prevent fraud by the legatee/trustee, whereas with half-secret trusts, where the legatee is clearly stated to be a trustee, there is no possibility of fraud and therefore no need to examine events (for example, acceptance) occurring after the will. Second, it may be that the half-secret trust rule is a mistake because of confusion with the law of incorporation of documents. A will may be said to 'incorporate' another document if the will makes reference to that document and if that document was in existence at the time the will was made. It is easy to see how this rule could have been carried over to require acceptance of the half-secret trust at the time the will was made. Of course, it is clear that neither of these theories (nor any other) is wholly satisfactory, and they do not help in finding a rationale for secret trusts generally. What they do illustrate, however, is that any theory concerning any aspect of the law of secret trusts is not watertight.

So, after examining all the relevant theories, we are only a little more aware of a consistent rationale for the validity and enforcement of secret trusts. Indeed, the true answer may well be that there is no coherent theory, no logic and no golden thread that links all the cases. After all, we are dealing with the court's equitable jurisdiction and

2   It is permissible to state that the current law is inaccurate provided that the point is clearly argued.

perhaps the best we can say is that the law of secret trusts has developed organically, with judges solving practical problems in real cases according to the needs of the parties at the time. That they may have had no real theory in mind is not in itself a serious criticism.[3]

QUESTION 9

Thomas executed his will on 1 April, which contained a legacy of £5,000 to Arnold, a legacy of £10,000 to Betty and a legacy of £20,000 to Clive, his brother. In his will, Thomas directed Betty to hold her legacy 'as a matter of trust for such persons as I have communicated to her'. On 1 May, Thomas told Arnold that he wished Arnold to pay his legacy to Thomas's illegitimate son, Zeus. One month later, after a quarrel with Zeus's mother, Thomas told Arnold to keep the money for himself. On 30 March, Thomas telephoned Betty and asked her whether she would be prepared to be a trustee of the money he would leave her in his will. Betty said she would think about it, and received a letter on 2 April enclosing a key to a safe where Thomas said he had deposited instructions as to the destination of the money. Betty immediately telephoned Thomas to assure him she would carry out his wishes. After Thomas's death, a letter was found in the safe directing Betty to pay the money to Lucy. On 1 August, Thomas told Clive that he wished his legacy to be paid to the London Dogs' Home, a registered charity. Clive agreed, but just before Thomas's death, Clive telephoned his brother to withdraw his consent, and indicated his desire to spend 'his legacy' on a world cruise. Thomas died soon afterwards without altering his will in any way.

▶ Advise Arnold, Betty and Clive as to their rights concerning the legacies.

Aim Higher   ★

The peculiarity of secret trusts is that they are regarded as valid and enforceable despite the fact that they do not comply with the strict requirements of formality found in **s 9** of the **Wills Act 1837**. Secret trusts may be valid where either or both the fact of the trust and its details are declared orally or by post-testamentary writing.

Although the matter is not free from doubt, it is arguable that secret trusts operate under the court's equitable jurisdiction, which has always been flexible enough to assist those believed worthy of its protection.

---

3   Explanation of the confused state of the law.

Common Pitfalls

The danger with problems of this type is that students are content to remain with the most obvious answer, namely that the half-secret trust fails. A moment's thought will reveal the danger in this, since it must always be remembered that equity encompasses a flexible set of principles, not rules written in concrete.

How to Answer this Question

❖ Fully secret trusts: communication and acceptance, validity of revocation of trust and substitution of trustee/legatee as sole legatee.
❖ Half-secret trusts: date of communication and acceptance, method of communication and acceptance, possible contradiction of the will.
❖ Fully secret trust: trustee disclaiming trust, whether possible and consequences thereof.

Answer Structure

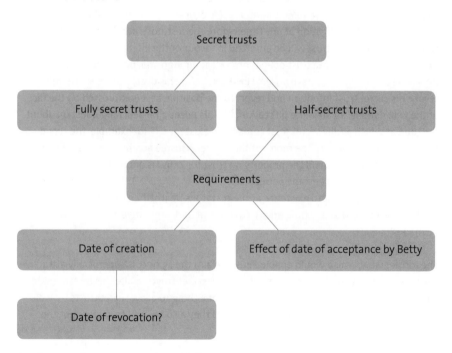

This diagram illustrates a number of fully and half-secret trusts issues raised in the transactions involving Arnold, Betty and Clive.

ANSWER

This question concerns the law of secret trusts. In essence, secret trusts are those trusts which operate in relation to a testamentary disposition but where either the very fact and details of the trust are not declared in the testator's will (fully secret trusts) or where, although the fact of the trust is declared in the will, the identity of the beneficiaries is not (half-secret trusts) (*McCormick v Grogan* (1869); *Re Keen* (1937)). In this question, there appear to be issues concerning the validity of fully secret trusts and half-secret trusts. Each attempted disposition will be discussed in turn.[4]

First, we shall consider the legacy to Arnold, with oral instructions to hold the property for another under a potential secret trust.

In his will, Thomas makes a bequest of £5,000 to Arnold without any limitation on the way in which Arnold may use his gift. On the face of the will, this is an absolute gift to Arnold. Consequently, any claim that Zeus may have to the money may arise only under a fully secret trust.[5] A fully secret trust will arise where, despite an apparently absolute gift, the testator has communicated his intention to the legatee that the property should be held for another and this desire has been accepted by the legatee (*Thynn v Thynn* (1684)). In our case, there is no doubt as to Thomas's intention to create a trust (contrast *Margulies v Margulies* (2000)) and, providing that the legatee/trustee accepts the obligation at any time before the testator's death, there is every chance that the secret trust will be enforced in favour of the intended beneficiary. Arnold's acceptance of the trust obligation is clear enough and, prima facie, a potential fully secret trust seems to have arisen. However, before his death, Thomas attempts to revoke his secret trust intention and revert to the position as it is expressed on the face of the will; namely, an absolute gift to Arnold. This poses a far-reaching question about the time at which a fully secret trust comes into existence. If, for example, the secret trust comes into existence the moment the legatee/trustee accepts the trust obligation, then clearly Arnold will hold the property on trust for Zeus, as once a trust is created, the beneficiaries' rights become perfect (see *Milroy v Lord* (1862)). If, on the other hand, the secret trust comes into existence at the testator's death, then clearly the intended trust can be revoked at any time prior to that event and alternative arrangements can be made.[6]

The former view, which would enable Zeus to claim the £5,000, is superficially attractive because it prevents the testator from using fully secret trusts to alter his testamentary dispositions without making another will. It is one thing to allow secret trusts to avoid the Wills Act 1837 in their formation, but should they also be used to circumvent the

---

4   It is important to define relevant legal concepts.

5   Application of the legal principle to the facts.

6   On controversial issues, examiners require you to raise the issue and evaluate your opinion.

requirements of writing by giving the testator a power of unattested disposition right up to his death? Such a view of secret trusts is implicit in the decisions in *Re Gardner (No 2)* (1923) and *Sonley v Clock Makers Company* (1780), although *Sonley* was a half-secret trust and *Re Gardner (No 2)* has attracted considerable academic criticism.

The alternative and better view sees the secret trust as arising on the testator's death and is therefore revocable until then. The judgments in *Blackwell v Blackwell* (1929) and *Re Maddocks* (1902) support this view. The logic of this approach is that the communication to the trustee during his lifetime, and acceptance thereof, is simply an *inter vivos* intention to create a trust but the trust becomes constituted when the property passes into the hands of the trustee on the testator's death. Thus, the trust may be revoked by the settlor prior to his death. If this is the better view (despite the fact that it allows oral post-testamentary dispositions of property), then clearly Thomas can revoke the trust in favour of Zeus. Further, it seems from the facts that Arnold is to revert to being the beneficiary of an absolute gift as stated on the face of the will and, if the revocation is effective, this will be the final position. Indeed, even if one were to argue that Arnold is to be the new beneficiary under the secret trust (that is, holding on trust for himself), *Irvine v Sullivan* (1869) is clear authority for the proposition that a fully secret trustee can be a beneficiary under his own trust. Arnold may claim his legacy.

Next, there is the gift on trust to Betty, holding for Lucy.

There is a clear intention in respect of the bequest in the will to Betty that she is to be a trustee. Hence, whatever conclusion we come to about the persons ultimately entitled to the £10,000, we know that Betty will not be able to claim the gift. At the very least, she will hold the money on resulting trust for Thomas's estate (*Re Keen* (1937) and *Re Rees* (1950)). However, in order that Lucy may claim the property, she must establish a half-secret trust, wherein the details of the trust were communicated to Betty and accepted by her prior to, or simultaneously with, the execution of the will (*Re Bateman* (1970)). Here is Lucy's first problem as the facts make it clear that, although Thomas asked Betty to be a trustee before the date of the will, acceptance thereof was not made until after the will was executed on 1 April.[7] There are four possibilities. First, the communication rule is applied strictly and the half-secret trust is invalid, with Betty therefore holding on resulting trust for Thomas's estate. Although a perfectly defensible result on the authorities, this seems harsh in the circumstances. Second, it might be argued that Betty had impliedly accepted the trust obligation at the date of the initial telephone call. This seems untenable on the facts as Betty said that 'she would think about it' and the *Moss v Cooper* (1861) principle is not applicable. Third, we could take the robust view that the communication rule for half-secret trusts is wrong and that the

---

7   Identification of the issue as clearly as possible is necessary.

proper approach is that of other common law jurisdictions where the rules for fully secret trusts and half-secret trusts are assimilated. This is attractive, especially because there is no totally convincing explanation for the difference between the two types of trust. However, unfortunately, both *Re Keen* (1937) and *Re Bateman* (1970) are clear enough. Fourth, it can be argued that it is not certain that the communication rule is violated in this case. As *Re Keen* establishes, communication and acceptance must be made before or *simultaneously with* the execution of the will and it is arguable that a process of communication and acceptance that began prior to the execution of the will and which was completed soon after is 'simultaneous' for this purpose.

Assuming, then, that the communication and acceptance of the trust were validly made, Lucy faces other problems. It might be thought that the terms of the trust contradict the terms of the will and this is prohibited by *Re Keen* (for example, as I 'have' communicated). However, this point is met if the above argument about the simultaneous nature of the communication and acceptance of the details is adopted. Likewise, although Betty is not given the precise details of the trust, because they are contained within a locked safe, it is clear from *Re Boyes* (1884) that communication of the means of identifying the beneficiaries is acceptable if it is made at the relevant time (the simultaneous argument again) and if it is out of the power of the testator to change those details. Thus, assuming that Thomas has not kept a key to the safe and cannot change the identity of the beneficiary after his will has been executed, Lucy will be able to claim the £10,000.

The next legacy to consider is that to Clive.

Whether the London Dogs' Home can claim the £20,000 depends on a number of factors. The first and crucial issue is whether there is any attempt at all by Thomas to impose a trust on his brother. Only if the instructions to Clive can be construed as the manifestation of an intention to impose a trust is there any possibility that the charity may claim the gift under a fully secret trust (*Re Snowden* (1979)). The issue is not clear cut, but the fact that 'Clive agrees' to Thomas's suggestion is further evidence, along with the words of the will, of the imposition of a trust obligation, readily accepted. At this point, then, we can say that the Dogs' Home may have a claim to the £20,000 on Thomas's death. Yet, as we have seen when discussing the legacy to Arnold, a fully secret trust does not become constituted – in the sense of giving perfect rights to the beneficiaries – until the testator's death. Here, however, it is not the testator who revokes the trust, but the trustee who attempts to revoke his acceptance of the obligation. Does this destroy the trust and may Clive claim the £20,000? According to *Re Maddocks* (1902), the beneficiaries will have no claim in these circumstances because the trust has not yet arisen but there are *dicta* in the judgment of Lord Buckmaster in *Blackwell v Blackwell* (1929) that indicate that equity will not let such a trust fail for want of a trustee, as is, indeed, the case with half-secret trusts (*Re Smurthwaite* (1871)). Of course, the logic is with the *Re Maddocks* rule, but as a matter of practical justice, perhaps the best view is that, if the testator has had time to amend his will after the trustee's revocation of acceptance but before his own death, the absolute gift on the face of the will takes effect – the property would go to Clive. If, however, the testator had had no time to make alternative arrangements after the trustee's action but before his own death, equity may act to prevent fraud or inequitable conduct on the part of the legatee and either provide a new trustee to carry out the terms of the trust or compel the legatee to hold the property on resulting trust for the testator's estate (the trustee's conscience would be bound: *Westdeutsche Landesbank Girozentrale v Islington LBC* (1996)). The latter of these is more consistent with the idea that the trust had not been formed until the testator's death. In our case, therefore, the issue turns on whether Thomas had time to make alternative arrangements. If he did, we can presume he was happy with Clive keeping the £20,000; if he did not, we should imply a resulting trust for the estate.

QUESTION 10

Joanne, a rich property developer, made her will in 2009. She leaves her personal effects and shares in Build & Co 'to Smith and Jones equally in the knowledge that you will carry out my hopes'. In 2008, she had told Smith that she wanted both Smith and Jones to hold the personal effects in trust for her illegitimate son, Arnie. Smith had readily agreed, although Jones did not know of this arrangement. Moreover, in 2010, Joanne had asked Smith to hold the shares on trust for her lover, Tim, and he had agreed again. In the same will, Joanne leaves her town house 'in the trust of William and Mary for the purpose with which they are familiar'. When Joanne had told William and Mary of her intentions in 2007, they had readily accepted her plan of allowing them to live in the house providing that they left it by their will to the Homeless Charity.

Joanne died in 2012, and Jones has come to claim his share of the personal effects and shares. However, Smith wishes the personal effects to go to Arnie, and although Tim died in 2011, he (Tim) left all his property to Joe – the son of Joanne and Tim – who now claims the shares, despite being a witness to Joanne's will. In addition to this, the Homeless Charity would like to know whether they can expect to receive the town house when William and Mary die, even though both have now denied that they are bound and wish to leave the house to their own son.

▶ Advise the parties.

How to Answer this Question

- ❖ Fully secret or half-secret trusts: a matter of construction.
- ❖ Fully secret trusts and two trustees: whether the agreement of all is required.
- ❖ Half-secret trusts of land.
- ❖ The problem of the predeceased beneficiary under the secret trust.
- ❖ Secret trusts operate outside the Wills Act 1837.
- ❖ The position of witnesses.

Answer Structure

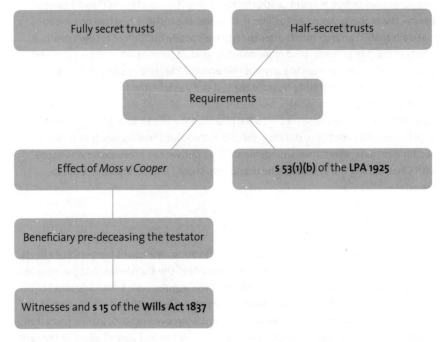

This diagram depicts fully and half-secret trusts and a host of specific issues created by the will of Joanne.

ANSWER

The questions raised by this problem concern the law of fully secret and half-secret trusts. Fully secret trusts arise where property is left to a person absolutely by will but, before her death, the testatrix has asked the legatee to hold the property on trust for a third party and that legatee has agreed (*McCormick v Grogan* (1869)). Half-secret trusts are similar, save that the property is left in the will to the legatee expressly on trust and the objects of the trust (the beneficiaries) are not disclosed, their identity being communicated to the trustee and accepted by him prior to, or simultaneously with, the execution of the testatrix's will (*Re Keen* (1937)).[8] In both cases, the secret trustee will then hold the property on trust for the secret beneficiaries, who may compel the legatee/trustee to hand it over. In our problem, as well as the difficulty of establishing whether any fully secret or half-secret trust exists, there are the added complications of property being left to two or more legatees and the fact that some of the claimants would be disentitled if

8   Full definitions of fully and half secret trusts are crucial in dealing with such questions.

the Wills Act 1837 were applicable, namely, those who predecease the testatrix and those who are witnesses to her will.[9]

Let us consider, first, the shares and personal effects left to Smith and Jones.

The first and most difficult question in respect of the bequest to Smith and Jones is to determine the nature of the trust, if any, that is imposed upon either or both of them. It is only if a trust is established that Arnie and Joe (via Tim) may have a claim to the property. The terms of the legacy to Smith and Jones are equivocal. It is true that Joanne has intimated in her will that the property given to Smith and Jones has been earmarked for some special purpose. Indeed, she comments that she is confident they will carry out her hopes. This might seem to suggest that a half-secret trust can exist, being a trust openly expressed in the will. However, in order to impose a trust on the legatees, the words used must be sufficient to impose a trust obligation as a matter of law: there must be certainty of intention (*Re Snowden* (1979); *Margulies v Margulies* (2000)).[10] In our case, the words used by Joanne are not such as to impose a trust in all circumstances and they are merely precatory (expressions of hope). According to *Re Conolly* (1910), precatory words will not impose a trust if they may also be taken as evidence of an absolute gift. Although the matter is for debate, the better view is that the will of Joanne imposes no trust in respect of the property given to Smith and Jones, especially since Joanne is prepared to be explicit in respect of other property in the same will (for example, the house 'in trust' to William and Mary). Consequently, Smith and Jones are entitled to the property absolutely, at least on the face of the will.

However, the next question is whether the legatees, being absolutely entitled, are subject to a fully secret trust. Certainly, as the facts make clear, at least one of the trustees has been asked to hold the shares and personal effects on trust for third parties and has accepted. As far as the validity of the fully secret trust per se is concerned, it is immaterial that acceptance of the trust of the shares is not given until after the will is executed. Such acceptance may be given at any time up to the testatrix's death (*Re Snowden* (1979)). Note, however, that the property is given absolutely to both Smith and Jones equally and Jones is claiming his portion of both the personal effects and shares. We must determine, therefore, whether Smith's acceptance of the trust obligation (which clearly means he must hold his share for Arnie and Tim) is sufficient to bind Jones as well.

The principles applicable here are set out in *Re Stead* (1900) and, although they are not necessarily logical, they are at least relatively clear.[11] Thus, with a fully secret trust, if the property is given absolutely to the legatees as tenants in common, then only those who

---

9 A brief statement identifying the issues in the problem is advisable.
10 This issue derives from the definition of secret trusts.
11 Considered views on controversial issues are advisable.

accept the trust are bound by it. The reason commonly attributed to this view is that the gift is not tainted with any fraud in procuring the execution of the will: see *Re Stead*. If Smith and Jones are tenants in common of the personal effects and shares, Smith must hold his portion on trust, while Jones may keep his portion absolutely. If, on the other hand, the property is given to Smith and Jones as joint tenants (and this may not be the case, given that the property is transferred 'equally'), then if anyone accepts the trust obligation *before* the will is executed, all are bound, regardless of their own position; but, if acceptance takes place *after* the will, only those who accept are bound. So, assuming Smith and Jones take the property as joint tenants, both will be bound by the fully secret trust in respect of the personal effects, because Smith accepted before the will was executed. Conversely, only Smith will be bound by the trust of the shares as his acceptance came after the will and does not bind Jones. Jones may take the shares absolutely as the will indicates.

The final question in respect of Smith and Jones's legacy is the identity of the beneficiaries of the personal effects and Smith's trust of the shares. Clearly, for the personal effects, Smith and Jones hold the property on trust for Arnie and he may make a successful claim. However, there is a difficulty with Smith's trusteeship of his portion of the shares because Tim, the original beneficiary, has died before the testatrix. The most cogent theory explaining fully secret trusts emphasises that they do not arise (that is, they do not bind the property and give enforceable rights to the beneficiaries) until the testatrix dies (for example, *Blackwell v Blackwell* (1929)) because that is when the trust becomes constituted by the passing of property under the will to the trustee. On this analysis, Tim's estate should not be entitled to the shares, since there is no beneficiary at the time the trust comes into existence. However, there is the direct authority of *Re Gardner (No 2)* (1923) that allows a claim by the successors to a beneficiary who predeceases the testatrix, provided that the trust was communicated and accepted before the beneficiary's death (as here). This may be decisive in favour of Tim's estate and, at least, it makes it clear that Tim is not disentitled by the Wills Act 1837 (which normally voids a gift by will if the legatee dies before the testatrix): this gift is by a trust operating outside the will. Finally, although under the Wills Act 1837 a person may not be entitled to a legacy if he witnesses the will in which the gift is contained, Joe is not disbarred from claiming the shares via Tim because, first, secret trusts operate outside the will and witnesses may claim (*Re Young* (1951)), and, second, Joe can assert that he is not claiming under the secret trust at all, but under the will of Tim, who was the trust's beneficiary.

We must next consider the house left to William and Mary. Although, once again, the terms of the devise to William and Mary is not unequivocal and although use of the word 'trust' does not always impose a trust at law (see, for example, *Tito v Waddell (No 2)* (1977)), it is relatively clear, on the face of the will, that the house has been left to William and Mary expressly as trustees. This is an intended half-secret trust and, at the very least, William and Mary must hold the house eventually for Joanne's estate on resulting trusts

(*Re Keen* (1937)). In such circumstances, William and Mary cannot leave the property to their own son, but can it be claimed by the Homeless Charity? The facts make it clear that Joanne had communicated her intentions to William and Mary, who had agreed to her wishes, before she had executed her will, and this, in principle, raises a trust in favour of the named beneficiary (*Re Bateman* (1970)). Moreover, in *Ottaway v Norman* (1972), it was accepted that an obligation imposed on the trustees under a fully secret trust to leave property in their will to another was perfectly acceptable. Of course, our case involves a half-secret trust, but there is no reason why the same principle should not be applicable. If it is objected that trustees under a half-secret trust are not entitled to be beneficiaries (*Re Rees* (1950)) – as William and Mary appear to be during their lifetimes – we may adopt the judge's reasoning in *Ottaway* that the secret trust comes into existence on the legatee's/trustee's death, and not on that of the testatrix. Hence, William and Mary are not beneficiaries under the half-secret trust and the charity may claim the house.

There is, however, one final problem. The declaration/constitution theory of secret trusts assumes that these trusts are normal, express trusts which operate outside the will. However, the trust property in this case is land and, according to s 53(1)(b) of the Law of Property Act (LPA) 1925, express trusts of land must be evidenced in writing if they are to be enforceable. Indeed, according to *Re Baillie* (1886), a half-secret trust of land must be evidenced in writing if it is to be valid. The half-secret trust of this house is purely oral, and would seem to fail if this reasoning is adopted. Yet the rule in *Re Baillie* (1886) has been subject to much criticism and in *Ottaway*, a fully secret trust of land was upheld on facts similar to these without the need for writing. So, despite the authority of *Baillie*, it might be possible to argue that this half-secret trust should be enforced in favour of the charity, perhaps on the ground that 'equity will not allow a statute (s 53(1)(b) of the LPA 1925) to be an instrument of fraud'. The only problem with this is, of course, that the trustees cannot possibly take the house themselves because they are named as trustees and so fraud in this sense is not possible. We would have to adopt a wider definition of fraud, perhaps a desire to prevent fraud of the beneficiaries. Subject to this last issue being resolved in favour of the charity, they may claim the house on William and Mary's death.

NOTE

Another typical examination problem, this time with the complication of two legatees/trustees. Note, again, that there is more here than first meets the eye, especially in relation to secret trusts of land.

QUESTION 11

Sam has recently died. By his will, he bequeathed his large collection of rare stamps to 'Peter and David absolutely'. In addition, in a separate clause in the will he left his house to William 'on trust for purposes I have communicated to him'.

Before he died, he told Peter that both he and David were to hold the stamps on trust for Becky, his illegitimate daughter. A letter repeating the same instruction to David was found amongst Sam's personal effects after his death. David has informed you that he only became aware of Sam's wishes regarding the stamp collection following his death. Before his death, Sam orally told William that the house was also to be held on trust for Becky.

William was killed in a car crash a week before Sam died.

▶ Advise Becky as to whether she is entitled to any of the properties.

How to Answer this Question

- ❖ Requirements in order to create a fully secret trust.
- ❖ Communication to one of several intended trustees.
- ❖ Standard of proof.
- ❖ Requirements for a half-secret trust.
- ❖ Intended trustee pre-deceasing the testator.
- ❖ Section 53(1)(b) of the Law of Property Act 1925.

Answer Structure

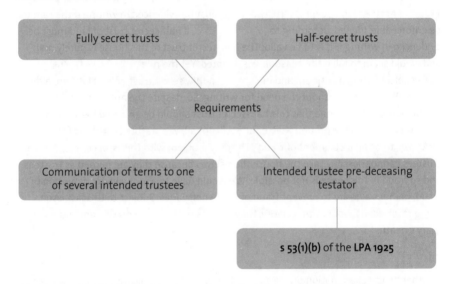

This diagram highlights secret trusts requirements and a number of related issues connected with Sam's will.

ANSWER

Sam's will has effected two transfers – the first concerning a large collection of rare stamps to Peter and David, the second in respect of a house to William. We will deal with the consequences of each of these dispositions in turn.

THE STAMP COLLECTION

The transfer in the will is to Peter and David apparently beneficially on the face of the will. There is no indication that these two individuals take other than for their benefit. However, before Sam died he told Peter that both himself and David were required to hold the collection on trust for Becky, Sam's illegitimate daughter.[12] This arrangement raises the possibility of a fully secret trust being created in favour of Becky. We will now examine how far this is the case.

A fully secret trust is one in which the legatee takes the property beneficially on the face of the will but subject to an understanding between the testator and themselves concerning the property during the lifetime of the testator. The *existence* of the trust, as well as its *terms*, are fully concealed by reference to the will. This appears to be evident in the problem. In this context, the court draws a distinction between a mere legacy on the one hand, and a legacy subject to a secret trust.[13] The essence of the distinction is that in a legacy subject to a secret trust, the testator communicates the terms of the trust during his lifetime to the legatees. In this respect, it is immaterial that the communication of the terms is made before or after the execution of the will, provided that it is made before the testator's death. Applying this principle to the facts of the problem Sam, during his lifetime, has communicated the terms of the trust to Peter, namely that both legatees are required to hold on trust for Becky. Thus far, it is clear that Peter has knowledge of the terms of the trust and is subject to an equitable obligation to carry out the testator's wishes. Has Sam, during the relevant time, communicated the terms of the trust to David? We are told that a letter was found among Sam's personal effects repeating the instruction to David. But the issue is whether this letter was received by David during Sam's lifetime.[14] It would appear that this is not the case. The conclusion here is that David was unaware of Sam's wishes. The implications of this finding will be explored below.

The next requirement for the creation of a fully secret trust is that the intended trustees must accept the terms of the communication made to them. Acceptance for these purposes may be expressly declared by the trustees in the sense that they positively acknowledge the existence of an obligation to act as trustees. There is no evidence that this is the case on the facts of the problem. But acceptance may also be inferred by the silence or acquiescence of the trustee, during the testator's lifetime: see *Moss v Cooper* (1861). Of course this can only be the case where the trustee is aware of the terms of the communication. The rationale is that it would be a fraud on the testator (not to mention the intended beneficiary under the trust) for the trustee to deny the agreement

---

12 It is advisable to extract salient facts from the problem in order to focus on the issue.

13 Application of the legal definition to the facts.

14 The legal issue may be identified in the form of a question. It is important to address that issue by reference to the law.

made with the testator. Accordingly, Peter, by implication, has agreed to become a trustee for Becky.

Would David be obliged to hold on trust or would he take part of the property beneficially? To put the question another way, the issue is when a testator leaves property by will to two persons apparently beneficially, but informs one of the apparent legatees of the terms of the trust, would the person who is unaware of the trust be bound to hold upon trust or not? The solution adopted by the courts, which is far from adequate, depends on the status of the co-owners and the time when the communication was made to those who are aware of the trust. If the informed legatee or devisee was told of the terms of the trust before or at the time of the execution of the will and the multiple owners take as joint tenants, the uninformed legatee is bound by the terms of the trust communicated to the informed legatee. The reason commonly ascribed for this solution is that no one is allowed to claim property under a fraud committed by another. This was stated by Farwell J in *Re Stead* (1900). The assumption that is made is that the informed trustee attempted to defraud the testator, irrespective of the reason for failure to inform the ignorant trustee. On the other hand, if the communication of the terms was made subsequent to the execution of the will, only the person aware of the terms of the trust is bound, for in this case there is no fraud. On the facts of the problem, Peter and David take as joint tenants for they are co-owners without any words of severance, but we are not told when Sam communicated the terms of the trust to Peter. If the communication was made before or at the time of the execution of the will, this would be sufficient to subject David to a trust in favour of Becky. If the communication was made later, David will take part (half) of the property beneficially, and Peter will hold the other portion on trust: see *Re Stead*.

The final point involves the standard of proof to establish the trust. If there is no fraud the standard of proof is a balance of probabilities, but if there is an allegation of fraud the standard exceeds a balance of probabilities but is not as high as beyond a reasonable doubt: see *Re Snowden* (1979). There is no clear definition of fraud, but it has been suggested that where the intended trustee denies the existence of a trust, this involves an allegation of fraud. Since David disputes the existence of an obligation on his part (failure to communicate), it is arguable that this imposes a higher standard of proof on Becky.

THE HOUSE

The terms of the will indicate the existence of a trust but the details of the trust are concealed. This is consistent with an intended half-secret trust. In order to create such a trust, the testator is required to communicate the terms before or at the time of the execution of the will. If the terms of the trust are communicated after the execution of the will, even during the testator's lifetime, the evidence is not admissible: see *Blackwell v Blackwell* (1929). The reason commonly attributed to this rule involves compliance with the formal requirements under s 9 of the Wills Act 1837 in respect of post-will communications. Commentators have suggested that it is a confusion of probate rules with trusts rules. In any event the courts have not demonstrated a willingness to modify the principle. Applying this principle to the facts of the problem, we are told that Sam told William of the terms of the trust before his death. But we are not told specifically at what time the communication was made.[15] If the communication was made before or at the time of the execution of the will, Becky would be entitled to prove the terms of the trust, otherwise the intended trust will fail and the property will be held on resulting trust for Sam's estate.

There are additional problems in that William has pre-deceased the testator; would this have an effect on the potentially valid half-secret trust? Although there are no decided cases, it is arguable that since the trustee takes as trustee on the face of the will, the trust ought not to fail, provided that the terms of the trust could be established. This is in accordance with the maxim, 'equity will not allow a trust to fail for want of a trustee'. The alternative is that the intended half-secret trust fails by virtue of the probate doctrine of lapse. This rule, it may be pointed out, is applicable where a person takes beneficially under a will. In half-secret trusts this is not the case. An additional issue is whether the terms of the trust could be established in the absence of both William and Sam. If this is not the case, a resulting trust will arise in favour of Sam's estate.

Another issue concerns the lack of writing in respect of the terms of the trust. The argument here is that s 53(1)(b) of the Law of Property Act (LPA) 1925 enacts that a 'declaration of trust in respect of land or any interest therein must be manifested and proved by some writing signed by the person able to declare the trust or by his will'. Clearly, the will does not declare the trust and the subject matter is land, but the issue is whether Sam ought to have manifested the terms of the trust in writing. We are told that he orally told William of the terms. Is s 53(1)(b) of the LPA 1925 applicable to the transaction or does s 53(2) of the LPA 1925 exempt the testator from the requirements of s 53(1)(b) of the LPA 1925? Section 53(2) of the LPA 1925 enacts that 'This section shall not affect the creation or operation of implied resulting or constructive trusts.' This involves the classification of half-secret trusts. If they are treated as intended express trusts, s 53(1)(b) of the LPA 1925 may be required to be complied with. In *Re Baillie* (1886) the court decided that half-secret trusts are required to comply with the predecessor to s 53(1)(b) of the LPA 1925. Non-compliance with the sub-section makes the trust unenforceable for lack of evidence in writing. Thus Becky may not be able to enforce the trust of land. If, on the other hand, the trust is treated as constructive, s 53(2) of the LPA 1925 will exempt Sam from the requirements of s 53(1)(b) of the same Act. An argument in support of this view is that the trust is created to prevent fraud. This was the original basis for such trusts and may still be applicable today.

....

15 Where a significant fact is unclear you should assume both ways and apply the appropriate legal principles.

The Inherent Attributes of a Trust
The Three Certainties and the Beneficiary Principle

INTRODUCTION

In the previous two chapters we have looked at the formalities needed to create a trust, the necessity for the trustee to be invested with title to the trust property in order that the trust be properly constituted, and the curious exception to some of these rules found in the law of secret trusts. We have not yet begun to explore the factors which are elemental in the trust concept. In this chapter, two of the inherent characteristics of the trust will be examined: the requirement of the 'three certainties' and the 'beneficiary principle'.

The 'three certainties' is simply a shorthand description for a set of conditions which, when fulfilled, epitomise the trust. These certainties constitute the minimum set of requirements or terms necessary in order to declare the trust. In simple terms, every trust must be established with:

(a) certainty of intention, so as to indicate that the holder of the property is under a trust obligation and must use the property according to the terms of the trust;

(b) certainty of subject matter, so as to ensure that the property which is the subject matter of the trust obligation is clearly defined or definable; and

(c) certainty of objects, so as to ensure that the beneficiaries to whom the trustee owes his onerous duties are clearly ascertainable and in whose favour the court can enforce the trust should the trustee fail in those duties.

As we shall see, the method of determining whether the three certainties exist may vary from trust to trust, especially with certainty of objects. In addition, where charitable trusts are concerned, the certainty of objects rules to be discussed below are not applicable and reference should be made to Chapter 4 for the definition of 'charity'. Finally, there is no statutory guidance as to the nature of the 'three certainties' and there is no substitute for a thorough grounding in case law.

The 'beneficiary principle' is very closely related to the need for certainty of objects for it expresses the idea that every non-charitable trust must have a human beneficiary. In other words, it is generally impossible in English law to establish a trust for a purpose, unless that purpose can be regarded as charitable (see Chapter 4). Thus, nearly every attempt to place a duty on a trustee to achieve non-charitable aims instead of holding the property for ascertainable individuals is doomed to failure. Once again, the beneficiary principle is easy to state, but difficult to apply in concrete cases because of the sometimes confusing precedents which are available.

QUESTION 12

Why is it important to distinguish a trust from a power?

How to Answer this Question

- ❖ Trusts and powers in outline: certainty of beneficiaries.
- ❖ Discretionary trusts.
- ❖ Powers: types of powers.
- ❖ Similarities and opportunities for confusion.
- ❖ Differences in subsidiary certainty rules.
- ❖ Administrative unworkability and capriciousness.

Answer Structure

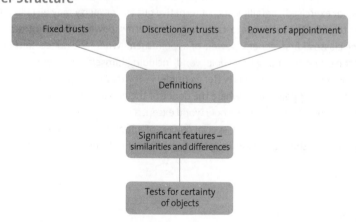

This diagram identifies the main similarities and differences between trusts and powers.

ANSWER

The essential nature of a private trust is that a trustee will hold property on trust for identifiable beneficiaries. Save in the case of charities and a small number of exceptional situations, it is not possible to have a trust for a private purpose as an end in itself. The essential duty imposed upon a trustee is to distribute the trust property according to the wishes of the settlor or testator and in conformity with the terms of the trust, and this is a duty which cannot be delegated to an agent or professional adviser: s 11(2) of the Trustee Act 2000. In this, they will be supervised by the court and be subject to suit by any disaffected beneficiaries: the trust is mandatory and must be carried out. For these reasons, it is of paramount importance that the objects of the trust – the beneficiaries – should be readily identifiable. In the language of Lord Langdale in *Knight v Knight* (1840), 'every trust must have certain objects'.[1] In many cases, of course, the beneficiaries of a trust will be named by the settlor and then there is no doubt that the certainty requirement is fulfilled, as where property is left 'on trust for Mr Smith and Mrs Jones'. However, in other cases, the settlor or testator may have decided to identify the beneficiaries by a class description without naming them individually, as where property is given on trust 'for my relatives' or 'for my friends'. Clearly, gifts on trust for classes of persons who are not named must also have certain objects, for how else will the trustees know how to carry out the trust, and the court be sure that they have done so properly?[2]

In similar fashion, the creation of a 'power of appointment' will only be valid if the objects of the power can be ascertained with certainty (*Re Gulbenkian* (1970)). A power of appointment is literally a power given to a person (who may or may not be a trustee) to decide the destination of property, often the property of a testator or settlor. It is similar to a trust save only that the donee of the power (the person who exercises the power) is not under a duty to distribute the property but has complete freedom whether to do so or not. The power is said to be voluntary, and if it is not exercised the donee of the power may keep the property himself, or the settlor/testator may have provided for a 'gift over in default of appointment' (that is, a direction as to where the property should go if the power is not exercised), or failing such alternative gift the property may be held on resulting trust for the settlor or testator. In general terms, powers of appointment fall into three classes:[3] first, general powers of appointment, where the donee has power to appoint the property among the whole world, including himself. Such powers are akin to absolute ownership of the property (for example, *Re Beatty (deceased)* (1990)); second, hybrid powers of appointment, where the donee of the power has the authority to appoint the property among the whole world except a defined class of individuals (for example, *Re Hay* (1981)); and third, special powers of appointment, where the donee has power to appoint the property among a defined class of individuals (for example,

---

1   Justification for the test of certainty of objects.
2   Nature of the pre-1971 test for certainty of objects.
3   Classification of the types of powers.

Re Gulbenkian (1970)). Obviously, for powers of the second and third type, the excluded or included class of objects of the power must be defined with certainty in order that it is possible to decide whether the power has been validly exercised or not. An example is where the donee has power to appoint 'among his friends' or 'to anyone except his brothers'.

There is, then, a fundamental difference in principle between a trust and a power:[4] the former is mandatory and must be carried out, while the latter is voluntary and may go unexecuted. Unfortunately, in practice, it is very easy to confuse trusts and powers, especially since most powers are given to people who are otherwise trustees and who hold the property itself on trust but have a power (not a trust obligation) over it (being so-called 'fiduciary powers'). In practice, very real problems arise because special powers given to trustees can be virtually indistinguishable from discretionary trusts. A discretionary trust exists where trustees are under a duty to distribute trust property among a class of beneficiaries (which a court will enforce), but have a choice as to which of those beneficiaries shall actually benefit and in what proportions. However, as we have seen, the donee of the power does not have to make any appointment at all and the court will not compel him to do so. In any given case, deciding whether there is a trust or a power – and consequently a duty to distribute or not – depends on the court's construction of the instrument which establishes the arrangement. On this, views can legitimately differ, as in *McPhail v Doulton* (1971), where the question of construction as a trust or power went all the way to the House of Lords.

It is now clear that there are crucial differences between a discretionary trust and a power and, although some case law has tended to blur the distinction somewhat by suggesting that a court might exercise a fiduciary power (one given to a trustee) where the donee is unable or unwilling to do so (*Mettoy Pension Trustees Ltd v Evans* (1990); *Re William Makin & Sons Ltd* (1993)), it is still important to be able to distinguish between the two concepts. For example, the scope of the duties of a trustee under a discretionary trust is wider than those of a donee of a power, even a fiduciary one. Obviously, discretionary trustees must carry out the trust and distribute the property, but their duty to consider when and to whom to distribute the property is much wider than that of a donee of a power. A donee of a fiduciary power has merely to consider from time to time whether to exercise the power, and his survey of the range of objects of the class need not be as extensive as that undertaken by a discretionary trustee (*McPhail v Doulton* (1971)). Indeed, the donee of a personal power (that is, a donee not in a fiduciary position) seems to be under minimal duties, perhaps only to protect those entitled in default of appointment by not exercising the power in favour of anyone outside the class (*Mettoy Pension Trustees Ltd*). A personal (or non-fiduciary) power is a power of appointment granted to a donee of a power in his capacity as an individual, such as the testator's

---

4   Identification of the fundamental differences between a trust and a power.

widow. There is no duty to consider exercising the authority, nor is there a duty to distribute the property in favour of the objects. Indeed, the donee of the power may release the power even if this would mean that he will benefit from the release. Megarry VC in *Re Hay's Settlement Trusts* (1981) declared that the donee of the power is free to exercise the power in any way he chooses unhindered by any fiduciary duties. A fiduciary power is granted to an individual *virtute officio*, such as a trustee. The fiduciary power is similar to a personal power in only one respect in that there is no obligation to distribute the property, but unlike a personal power, the trustees are required to deal with the discretion in a responsible manner. In *Re Hay*, Megarry VC considered the duties imposed on the fiduciary as first, to consider periodically whether or not he should exercise the power, second to consider the range of the objects and thirdly, the appropriateness of individual appointments.

In one respect it has been recognised that discretionary trusts and powers of appointment should be subject to the same principles. The House of Lords, in *McPhail v Doulton* (1971), decided that the test for deciding whether the objects of a discretionary trust were sufficiently certain and the test for deciding whether the objects of a power were sufficiently certain should be the same, not least because the classification of a disposition as a discretionary trust or a fiduciary power usually turns on fine points of construction. It would be inequitable to make their validity (if the tests were different) depend on such subjective issues. Consequently, according to *McPhail*, the test for certainty of objects of a discretionary trust and a power is the *Re Gulbenkian* test, formally applicable only to powers: viz., that it must be possible to say with certainty whether any given individual is, or is not, a member of the class of beneficiaries or objects (the 'given postulant' test). No higher test was needed for discretionary trusts (as was previously the case: *IRC v Broadway Cottages Trust* (1955)) because, even if the court was called on to execute the discretionary trust, it did not have to divide the trust property equally and did not need to know all the members of the class: that, after all, was not what the settlor intended.

The assimilation of the tests for certainty of objects for these two concepts has brought considerable relief to those charged with making the difficult distinction in practice between a discretionary trust and a power. Of course, as we have seen, fundamental differences between the concepts remain and there will always be cases where it is important to make the distinction per se. For example, it seems that 'evidential uncertainty' and 'administrative unworkability' cannot invalidate a power in the same way that it can invalidate a discretionary trust, almost certainly because of the less pressing duties of a donee of a power (*R v District Auditor ex p West Yorkshire MC* (1986)). Likewise, if 'capriciousness' has any application to powers (for example, *Re Manisty* (1974)), it is unlikely that it adds anything to the rules concerning discretionary trusts. However, be that as it may, the decision in *McPhail* should be welcomed because, although there are differences between discretionary trusts and powers, those differences are now related primarily to their operation, not to their validity.

QUESTION 13

Assess the validity of the following dispositions in the will of Thomas, who died in December 2011:

(a)   £10,000 to my Aunt Agatha, knowing that she will use the money in order to secure the future of my daughters;

(b)   my houses in Southwark and Suffolk on trust for my daughters, Amanda and Barbara, for their lifetimes and thence in equal shares between such of my other kinsfolk now living as may be resident in the London borough of Southwark, save only that no person of the Protestant religion shall be entitled to any portion; and

(c)   the residue of my estate to my executors for such of my colleagues at work as they shall in their discretion think fit.

Thomas worked for the National Health Service at various hospitals throughout his life, but spent the last 10 years of his working life in Claremont General Hospital, which was destroyed by fire just after his retirement in 2010.

Aim Higher ★

It is important to appreciate that the three versions of the *Baden* test may cause different results for the validity of the trust or power. All must be considered and *Baden* should *not* be regarded as having a clear *ratio decidendi*.

Common Pitfalls ✗

It is not necessary to decide whether the *Baden* test will be satisfied on the facts of the problem. What is needed are rational arguments demonstrating knowledge of the law, as opposed to conclusions on difficult issues of law.

How to Answer this Question

❖   Brief introduction to the concept of the three certainties;

❖   certainty of intention: precatory words, construction of the gift;

❖   certainty of objects: fixed trusts; conditions precedent; and

❖   certainty of objects: trust or power; test for certainty; construing the gift; evidential difficulties; administrative unworkability.

Answer Structure

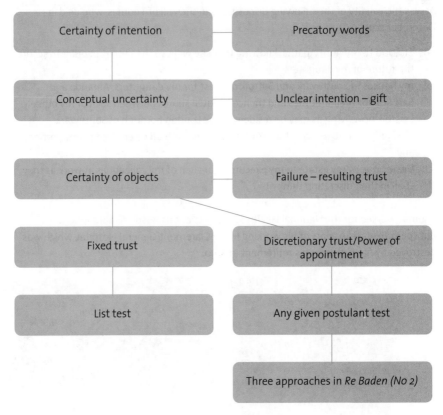

This diagram identifies the 'three certainties' test as an essential feature for the creation of an express trust.

ANSWER

It is a cardinal principle of the law of equity that a trust may only be valid – that is, enforceable by the beneficiaries against the trustee – if it has been created with certainty of intention, certainty of subject matter and certainty of objects (*Knight v Knight* (1840)). This particular problem concerns various aspects of the 'three certainties', and each limb of Thomas's testamentary disposition will be considered in turn.

(a) £10,000 to Aunt Agatha

The issue raised by this disposition is whether the legacy of £10,000 to Aunt Agatha is by way of trust or an absolute gift – in other words, whether there is sufficient certainty of intention to create a trust.[5] If a trust is created, then it becomes necessary to consider

5   This is good examination technique: identifying the issues raised in this part of the question first before launching into a discussion about the issues.

whether there are any valid objects of the trust and whether they are defined with sufficient certainty.

The imposition of a trust over the money requires Thomas to have imposed a mandatory obligation upon Aunt Agatha to carry out his wishes. This is purely a matter of construction of the words used and the surrounding circumstances (*Lambe v Eames* (1871)). It is clear that precatory words (words of expression, hope or desire) will not of themselves impose a trust on the recipient of property in the absence of corroborative evidence (*Re Conolly* (1910)).[6] In our case, the words used by Thomas are stronger than precatory words: Thomas does not 'hope' or 'wish' that Agatha will carry out his wishes, he 'knows' that she will. However, it is still not certain that this is enough to constitute a trust obligation. For example, in *Re Adams and the Kensington Vestry* (1884), a gift 'in full confidence that . . .' was held to be absolute and not mandatory in the way of a trust. On balance, it is likely that the bequest to Aunt Agatha will be construed as an absolute gift, essentially because of the absence of any other indication that this is intended to be a trust.[7] Moreover, even if this disposition was construed to be a trust, there might well be certainty of objects problems. While it is obvious that a trust in favour of 'my daughters' is perfectly certain as to objects, the disposition in this case is 'in order to secure the future of my daughters'. A literal reading of this suggests that this is a trust for *purposes* connected with Thomas's daughters, and trusts for purposes are void (*Re Endacott* (1959)). Of course, it might be possible to construe the disposition (if it were a trust in the first place) in favour of the daughters *per se* (compare *Re Osoba* (1979)) or as a trust saved by the *Re Denley* principle. However, these difficulties in defining the objects of the trust precisely only add to the doubts surrounding the lack of certainty of intention (e.g. *Re Kayford* (1975)). Consequently, in all probability, this is an absolute gift to Aunt Agatha, who may use the property for the benefit of Thomas's daughters if she chooses, but cannot be compelled to do so (*Lassence v Tierney* (1849)).

(b) The houses in Southwark and Suffolk

It is clear from the wording of the second disposition in Thomas's will that a trust is intended. Although use of the word 'trust' does not always impose a trust in law (*Tito v Waddell (No 2)* (1977)), there is nothing here to suggest otherwise. Likewise, the subject matter of the trust is certain, always assuming Thomas did own houses in Southwark and Suffolk. The problem is, then, one of certainty of objects.[8] Clearly, there is no difficulty with the life interests given to Thomas's daughters, who are both named. The disposition will operate under the Trusts of Land and Appointment of Trustees Act 1996, with Amanda and Barbara being given the rights to possession, etc, established by that statute. The problem arises with the class of persons entitled to the

---

6   Clear statement of the approach of the courts to precatory words.

7   Application of the principle to the facts of the problem. Tentative conclusion on a flexible issue is advisable.

8   Clear analysis of the legal issue raised in the question.

reversionary interests, being 'my kinsfolk now living as may be resident in the London borough of Southwark' and then subject to an exclusion against any person of the Protestant religion.

First, it is necessary to determine the nature of the trust affecting the two houses for this will help determine whether there is certainty of objects of the reversionary class. The houses are given in equal shares to the 'kinsfolk', etc, and thus Thomas has fixed in advance the share of each person within the class. The trustees have no discretion to apportion the trust property among the class but must divide it up equally. This is a fixed trust and because the court must be able to execute the trust in default of the trustees and divide the property equally, the test of certainty of the objects is the 'complete list' test laid down in *IRC v Broadway Cottages Trust* (1954). It must be possible to draw up a complete list of all Thomas's 'kinsfolk' who currently reside in the borough of Southwark.[9]

This may prove difficult, not because of the residence restriction, for that should be easy enough to determine, but because 'kinsfolk' is an imprecise concept. It will only be possible to draw up a list of kinsfolk if we know what 'kinsfolk' actually means. Such inherent uncertainty in the concept used by Thomas to define his class may prove fatal unless the court is prepared to redefine the concept for the trustees in the same way that the Court of Appeal redefined 'relatives' in *Re Baden (No 2)* (1973). This should not be ruled out since a court of equity will generally prefer validity to invalidity, especially if the trustees' duties are not otherwise difficult to perform evidentially. Finally, even if the court adopts a benevolent attitude to the fixed trust, there is still the requirement that no person may have a share if he or she is 'of the Protestant religion'. Clearly, the point is that 'not being a Protestant' is to be a condition precedent for entry to the class of beneficiaries. Consequently, the scope of the condition precedent must also be certain because, otherwise, it will be impossible to determine who has been excluded. The test of certainty for conditions precedent is that it must be possible to say with certainty whether one person would or would not fulfil the condition (*Re Allen* (1958) and *Re Barlow* (1979)). As is clear from *Re Tuck* (1978), a condition precedent related to religion can be regarded as certain under this test although, in that case, a third person was given the task of deciding who fell within the religious condition. Subject then to it being possible to define what qualifies a person as 'a Protestant', the condition precedent will be valid. If the fixed trust for the class fails, a resulting trust for the residuary beneficiaries will arise.

(c) The residue of Thomas's estate

The gift of residue for 'such of my colleagues at work' raises, once again, the problem of certainty of objects, those objects being defined by reference to a class description. As regards this disposition, it is clear that the executors are given a discretion as to whom

---

9   Clear identification that the issues raise a combination of points on fixed trusts, conceptual uncertainty and limitations in identifying the beneficiaries.

from among the class they shall select to receive a portion of the residue, and in what proportions. So, this part of Thomas's will discloses either a discretionary trust for the class or a special power of appointment given to the trustees to appoint among the class. Of course, the difference is crucial so far as the executors are concerned because, if this is a discretionary trust, they are under a mandatory obligation to make a selection from among the class and distribute the property whereas, if this is a power, they may decide not to distribute and cannot be compelled to do so. Whether this disposition discloses a trust or a power is a matter of construction and, as *McPhail v Doulton* (1970) shows, the distinction is not always easy to draw. In our case, it is important that there is no gift over in default of appointment, perhaps suggesting that the executors *must* choose from among the class, although the absence of a gift over does not always foretell a trust, since the testator may be content to allow the property to revert to the next of kin if the power is not exercised (*Re Weekes* (1897)). On balance, however, given that the gift to this class is already of the residuary estate and consequently the beneficiaries in default would be difficult to identify, we can legitimately surmise that Thomas intended this to be a discretionary trust.

Since *McPhail v Doulton*, the test for certainty of objects of a discretionary trust and a power have been assimilated and, even if this is a power, the test we must apply is whether it is possible to say with certainty that any given person is, or is not, a member of the class (*McPhail*). Unfortunately, although this test is easy to state, it is difficult to apply because the leading case on its application (*Re Baden (No 2)* (1973)) gives us three alternative approaches.[10] According to Stamp LJ, the traditional, rigid approach is required to be adopted and this requires the class to be defined with precision. This is a strict test and in view of the fire at his last place of work, will there be sufficient employment records to indicate with whom he worked, even if it were possible to say who then qualified as a 'colleague'? Second, even if we take Sachs LJ's approach, it may be difficult to decide whether this discretionary trust is valid. In his view, the test is satisfied if members of the public may prove that they are within the class. The corollary is that evidential difficulties will not invalidate a trust because any person who cannot prove that he or she is a member of the class will be deemed to be outside it. Would the concept of a 'colleague' be clear enough for the courts to determine validity? Finally, we come to Megaw LJ who proposed the least strict version of the 'is or is not' test, believing it to be satisfied if it could be said of a substantial number of persons that they were inside the class, even if it could not be said of every potential person whether he or she was or not. It may be that Thomas's dispositions would satisfy this version of the test. Unfortunately this lax approach has been heavily criticised by commentators.

The conclusion is then that Thomas's third disposition may fail for uncertainty of objects. It may be that a court would be prepared to redefine the concept of 'colleague' so as to

---

10 It is advisable to state and apply each of three approaches to the test.

make it more certain and then apply the 'is or is not' test to the class description so redefined (as in *Re Baden*), but that cannot be guaranteed. Indeed, even then, the executors face one more hurdle, for it may be that the class of the discretionary trust is 'administratively unworkable' and so void for 'secondary uncertainty'. This concept was expounded by Lord Wilberforce in *McPhail* and it is clear from *R v District Auditor ex p West Yorkshire MC* (1986) that if the settlor or testator stipulates a class so large that the trustees cannot effectively fulfil their duties, nor exercise their discretion properly under a discretionary trust, that trust will fail. In our case, Thomas's large number of former places of work may bring the class description within this principle. This will be a matter of judgment. If the gift under the residuary clause is void then the next of kin would be entitled to such surplus funds.

QUESTION 14

Does the 'is or is not' test propounded by the House of Lords in *McPhail v Doulton* (1971) provide clarity in relation to the need for certainty of objects in the creation of a discretionary trust or power?

Aim Higher

This is an extremely complex and fluid area of the law and students are advised to carefully read the judgments in the leading cases. The distinction between certainty of gifts (*Re Allen* certainty of conditions) and certainty of trusts ought to be understood and the various approaches of the Lords Justices of Appeal in *Re Baden (No 2)* carefully considered.

Common Pitfalls

Students attempting this type of question do not always appreciate the rationale and ramifications behind each of the interpretations of the 'is or is not' test. Since there is no consistency in the approach of the courts, students are encouraged to be assertive, provided that they base their arguments on rational grounds.

How to Answer this Question

❖ Explain the 'is or is not' test.
❖ The move to the 'is or is not' test.
❖ Three views of the test: *Re Baden* and redefining concepts.
❖ Other tests of certainty.

Answer Structure

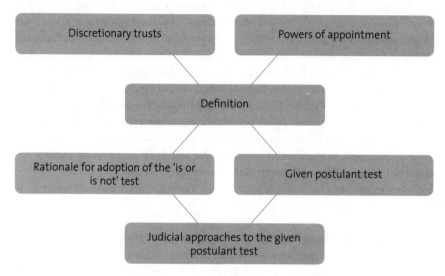

This diagram refers to rationale and judicial approaches underlying the 'any given postulant' test for certainty of objects.

ANSWER

Since the decision of the House of Lords in *McPhail v Doulton* (1971), much ink has been spilt over the meaning of the 'is or is not' test (given postulant test) in relation to the certainty of objects requirements for the creation of discretionary trusts and powers. The central issue arises because both discretionary trusts and powers of appointment give trustees or donees of the power (as the case may be) a discretion to distribute property to specific individuals selected from a class of objects who are themselves defined by reference to a generic term.[11] Thus, property on discretionary trusts 'for my employees' raises the same issue as property to be appointed 'among my friends'. In each case it must be possible to determine who is an 'employee' or who is a 'friend' in order to ensure that the trustees or donees are acting lawfully. Consequently, failure to define the objects of the discretionary trust or power with sufficient certainty will render the trust or power void (*Re Baden (No 2) (sub nom McPhail v Doulton (No 2))* (1973)).

Until the decision in *McPhail v Doulton*, there was a different test for certainty of objects depending on whether the settlor had established a discretionary trust or a power. Prior to 1971, the test for certainty of objects for discretionary trusts was whether it was possible to draw up a complete list of the objects so that, if the trustees made no

11   It is advisable to state the justification for extending the 'any given postulant' test to discretionary trusts.

selection from the class (despite their duty to do so), the court could divide up the property equally between all potential beneficiaries in execution of the trust (*IRC v Broadway Cottages Trust* (1955)). However, in *McPhail*, Lord Wilberforce pointed out that equal distribution among the entire class of potential beneficiaries was probably the last thing the settlor intended (why else give a discretion to the trustees?) and consequently, there was no reason to apply the 'fixed list' test to discretionary trusts. Moreover, given that it was often extremely difficult to distinguish in practice between a discretionary trust and a power, it was not sensible to cause the invalidity of discretionary trusts by insisting on a more stringent test of certainty when the distinction between a trust and a power could turn on the finest point of construction.[12] Consequently, the House of Lords decided that the test for certainty of objects for discretionary trusts should be the same as that for powers: namely, whether it is possible to say with certainty whether any given individual is, or is not, a member of the class of objects specified by the testator or settlor (*Re Gulbenkian* (1970)).

Unfortunately, this test is easy to state but difficult to apply. Following the change in the law in *McPhail v Doulton* the case was remitted to the High Court (*Re Baden (No 2)* (1973)) to determine the validity of the trust. The decision of the High Court was affirmed by the Court of Appeal in favour of the validity of the trust. The three Lords Justices of Appeal in the Court of Appeal took the opportunity to provide a thorough explanation of the 'is or is not' test. What emerged was three individual interpretations of what the test required in practice.

Before examining the judgments in that case in detail, an important distinction needs to be drawn between different kinds of uncertainty of objects, as this may help to explain the issues at the heart of the problem. It will be remembered that the objects of a discretionary trust or power may be defined by reference to a class description: 'employees', 'friends', 'relatives', etc. When deciding if it is possible to say whether any given individual is or is not a member of these classes, it is important to distinguish between 'conceptual' uncertainty and 'evidential' uncertainty. A class description is conceptually uncertain when the words used by the settlor or testator do not have a precise meaning in themselves, irrespective of the factual circumstances surrounding the particular case. For example, if the class of beneficiaries or objects of the power are 'my friends' or 'people with whom I am acquainted', there will be conceptual uncertainty of objects because the concepts used by the settlor are inherently uncertain: the class description is in itself inherently vague and imprecise. Conversely, a class description is evidentially uncertain when it is impossible to determine whether, in fact, a person falls within the class description. The issue is one of evidence, not of the meaning of the words used to define the class. Thus, a trust 'for my employees' may be evidentially uncertain if there is no method of determining who is in fact an employee, even if the concept of an

---

12   Striking similarities between discretionary trusts and powers of appointment.

'employee' is clear enough. As we shall see, it is disputed whether the 'is or is not' test requires conceptual certainty of the class of objects, evidential certainty of the class of objects or both.

Starting first with the judgment of Stamp LJ in *Re Baden (No 2)* (1973), it is clear that he approached the 'is or is not' test literally. In his view, in order for there to be certainty of objects for a discretionary trust or power, it must be possible to say with certainty whether any given individual was or was not a member of the class in fact. In other words, conceptual and evidential certainty of the class was required, for otherwise it would not be possible to say whether anyone *was not* a member of the class. It will be appreciated that this is a rigorous standard as it may mean that a trust or power is declared void even though the settlor has drafted his dispositions very carefully, the fault lying in lack of evidence outside of his or her control. Consequently, there has been much criticism of this view of the *McPhail* test, not least because it requires a degree of certainty barely less than the 'complete list' test so decisively rejected by the House of Lords in that case.[13]

A recognition of these difficulties was at the heart of Sachs LJ's rejection of this literal approach in the second judgment in *Re Baden (No 2)*. In his judgment, the crucial question was whether the class was conceptually certain. If there was conceptual certainty the trust or power would not be invalidated by evidential uncertainty. A person who could not prove evidentially that he or she was within the conceptually certain class would be regarded as outside it. This very practical and workable view has much to commend it because it avoids confusing questions about the inherent validity of the trust or power (conceptual certainty) with difficulties surrounding its execution (evidential certainty). It is, perhaps, the most justifiable of the views to emerge from *Re Baden (No 2)*.

The third judge in the case, Megaw LJ, adopted the least stringent interpretation of the 'is or is not' test and one that nearly every class description will satisfy. In his view, the test was satisfied if it could be said of 'a substantial number' of persons that they were within the class conceptually, even if it were not possible to make a clear decision about every potential beneficiary or object. His reasoning was simply that the trustees/donees of the power could effectively administer the trust or power in such circumstances and, therefore, it should not be invalidated. As indicated, this test will be satisfied by most class gifts because there will be few class descriptions that do not have a central meaning and where it is not possible to say of a 'substantial number' (whatever that means) whether they are in the class or not. Indeed, Megaw LJ's analysis does not sit well with the House of Lords' formulation in *McPhail* that it must be possible to say of *any given person* whether they are or are not within the class. Indeed, it is arguable that Megaw LJ's approach is but a variant from the 'one postulant approach' that was overruled by the House of Lords in *Re Gulbenkian*.

---

13   It is acceptable to present rational criticisms of a judgment.

This is the state of affairs after *Re Baden (No 2)*: we know, in principle, the test for certainty of objects for discretionary trusts and powers, but we have been given different views about how to apply it in practice. Furthermore, it is clear from *Re Baden (No 2)* that it is possible first to construe the settlor's class description and then apply the 'is or is not' test to the class description so construed. So, in *Baden*, Sachs and Megaw LJJ decided that 'relatives' actually meant 'able to trace descent from a common ancestor' and, therefore, on application of the 'is or is not' test, the class so redefined was certain. Stamp LJ, on the other hand, thought 'relatives' meant 'next of kin' and was both conceptually and evidentially certain for that reason. Clearly, this power of construction will allow a court to render most class gifts certain if it so chooses, simply by redefining the testator's class description in a manner that makes the test easier to be satisfied. Another difficulty is that there is no agreement as to whether questions of conceptual certainty can be delegated by the settlor to a third person, as where the settlor directs that his brother may conclusively determine who is a 'friend'. On the one hand, this removes the question of objective validity of the trust or power from the hands of the court (*Re Wynn* (1952)) but, on the other, it has merit in that it clearly reflects the settlor's wishes (*Dundee General Hospital Board v Walker* (1952)). If we then remind ourselves that absolute gifts to individuals subject to a condition precedent (for example, '£100 to any person who is my friend') are subject to a completely different test of certainty (namely, whether it could be said of just one person that he or she satisfies the condition (*Re Barlow* (1979)) and that class gifts and gifts subject to a condition precedent can be easily confused, it is apparent that the certainty rules for discretionary trusts and powers are not defined with as much clarity as we might like. Again, even if the objects of the trust or power are sufficiently certain, there are the further hurdles of 'administrative unworkability' in discretionary trusts (*R v District Auditor ex p West Yorkshire MC* (1986)) and 'capriciousness' with powers (*Re Manisty* (1974)) to surmount. All in all, a person predicting in advance whether a discretionary trust or power has sufficiently certain objects may make a well-informed estimate, but cannot be entirely confident that he or she will be right.[14]

QUESTION 15

George, a wealthy banker, comes to you for advice about a number of financial arrangements he wishes to make for his family and others. He has already drawn up a trust deed which appoints Abbott and Hardy as his executors and trustees and charges them with distributing:

'(a) a reasonable amount of the money from my account at the Bounty Bank, within three years of my death, between such of my employees as my wife shall determine, the remainder to be divided equally between my children; and

(b) £1,000,000 to the inhabitants of my old village of Stanbrooke in such proportions as my trustees shall in their discretion determine.'

---

14 It is acceptable in questions like these to conclude that the law is far from being clear.

During your discussions with George, it transpires that he has several bank accounts at the Bounty Bank and that his employees number over 5,000. Furthermore, your own researches reveal that the village of Stanbrooke now forms part of Greater London and is now officially called the London Borough of Stanbrooke. George also wishes to give his trustees the authority to distribute the residue of his estate among struggling authors and artists resident in the UK, providing that, if the residue is not distributed fully within three years, it should be given absolutely to some charity of his trustees' choosing.

▶ He seeks your advice on all of his proposals.

How to Answer this Question

❖ Trust or power: certainty of subject matter; certainty of objects; conditions precedent.

❖ Administrative unworkability.

❖ Discretionary trust or power: which is preferable when considering the testator's wishes?

Answer structure

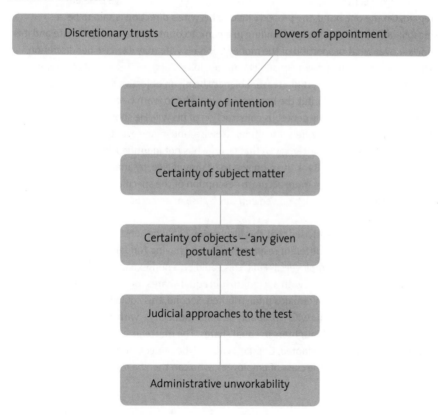

This diagram identifies the essential requirements for the creation of discretionary trusts and powers of appointment.

ANSWER

The various proposals put forward by George need to be considered in the light of the three certainties required to establish a valid trust. In particular, this problem raises preliminary questions about certainty of subject matter and calls for a distinction to be drawn between trusts and powers, as this will define the nature of the trustees' duties. Finally, as George intends to make a number of class gifts – that is, gifts to a group of people who are not named individually but defined by reference to a shared characteristic – it is necessary to consider whether the objects of his trusts or powers satisfy the requirement for certainty of objects.[15]

(a) Reasonable amount of money from George's account at the Bounty Bank, etc

It is clear that George intends to transfer the money in his 'account' to his executors and trustees for them to hold at the direction of his wife. The first point must be to advise George that there is a danger that his disposition will be void for uncertainty of subject matter, irrespective of whether it is a trust or a power. There are two problems in this regard. On the one hand, the property held to his wife's direction is said to be 'a reasonable amount' of money standing in a bank account. This is indeterminate and it is unclear over what proportion of the money George's wife may exercise her discretion. There is apparent uncertainty of subject matter. In *Re Golay* (1965), a trust of 'reasonable income' was held to be certain (reasonableness being an objective limitation that could be decided by the court), but the best advice would be to warn George not to rely on the court adopting a similarly generous construction of his will. He should be specific about the amount given to his wife's discretion. Likewise, and in any event, there is manifest uncertainty of subject matter, given that George has not identified from which of his accounts at the Bounty Bank the money is to be drawn (see, by analogy, *Re Boyes* (1884)). This should be cured by a more accurate description of the specific source of the subject matter of the proposed trust/power, perhaps by use of an account number.

George should also be advised that this disposition could be construed in two ways, each investing his wife with different responsibilities and having fundamentally different consequences for his employees.[16] First, this could be a non-exhaustive discretionary trust in favour of his employees, with a fixed trust in equal shares for his daughters of that amount of money which remains undistributed. Second, this could be a power of appointment given to his wife – probably as a non-fiduciary – with a fixed trust in default of appointment for his daughters in equal shares. The matter is not academic because, if the first construction is adopted, George's wife will be under a duty to distribute at least some money amongst the class of employees, who can then be regarded as beneficiaries

---

15 Identification of the issues in the problem.

16 Where the facts are unclear it is advisable to construe the scenario in a variety of ways. You should then complete the analysis by applying the appropriate principles of law to the various permutations.

under a trust able to compel her to do so. If, on the other hand, the second construction is adopted, George's wife will have a mere power to distribute among the employees, which she may or may not exercise as she chooses. The employees would be merely objects of the power with no enforceable claim to the property, with the daughters being regarded as the beneficiaries in default under the fixed trust.

Clearly, for both George's wife and the employees, resolution of this issue is important. The disposition itself gives little away, although leaving the 'remainder' to his daughters does suggest an intention to benefit at least some of his employees and hence a duty to distribute (a discretionary trust) might be implied. Conversely, it is rare to see the power of discretion under a discretionary trust being given to someone who is not a trustee (the wife), and it might be thought that the reference to George's daughters is intended to be a gift over in default of appointment, thus indicating a power (*Mettoy Pension Trustees Ltd v Evans* (1990)).[17] To avoid this confusion, George should be advised to indicate clearly both the nature of his wife's duties and the rights of his employees. However, in at least one respect, it does not matter whether this is a discretionary trust or power because, since *McPhail v Doulton* (1971), the test for certainty of objects for discretionary trusts and powers has been the same. Moreover, it is likely that it *is* possible to say with certainty whether any given person is, or is not, an 'employee', and thus the class of beneficiaries or objects (as the case may be) is certain.[18] This would be so whether Stamp LJ's, Sachs LJ's or Megaw LJ's analysis of the 'is or is not' test put forward in *Re Baden (No 2)* (1973) is accepted as correct, for there appear to be no evidential problems such as would trouble Stamp LJ. Finally, if this disposition is construed to be a discretionary trust, George should not fear that his disposition will be void for 'administrative unworkability'. There is nothing here to compare with the trust in *R v District Auditor ex p West Yorkshire MC* (1986), as the class of 5,000 does not seem too disparate or large to prevent his wife making a rational selection. Likewise, if this is a power, there is no 'capriciousness' here within the meaning given by Templeman J in *Re Manisty* (1974).

(b) £1,000,000 to the inhabitants of my old village of Stanbrooke, etc

This is clearly an attempt to establish a discretionary trust in favour of a class of beneficiaries defined by reference to a geographical condition. The intention is clear from the words used by George (that is, the trustees *shall* distribute), and the subject matter is certain. Any difficulty that there may be arises from doubts as to the certainty of the objects of the intended discretionary trust. There are three issues here, the first of which may be resolved by construction of George's disposition.

The first potential difficulty arises from the fact that the 'village' of Stanbrooke apparently is no more, having been subsumed by the London Borough of the same name.

---

17 This is a question of intention.
18 Application of the various judicial approaches to the test.

However, although this appears to raise questions concerning the certainty of the objects of the class, it will not be fatal to the validity of George's discretionary trust. For example, it may be possible to identify the old village and, in any event, there is no reason why, on a benevolent construction of the terms of the trust, the London Borough should not be taken to be the relevant geographical limitation. The matter is really one of ascertainability of the class rather than of certainty proper. However, the second difficulty is more pressing: whether, under the *McPhail* test of certainty of objects for discretionary trusts, it is possible to say with certainty whether any given person is, or is not, an 'inhabitant' of Stanbrooke. Much depends on whether the description 'inhabitant' is conceptually certain (compare Sachs LJ in *Re Baden (No 2)* (1973)), for there is unlikely to be any evidential difficulties once the class is geographically defined. In this sense, Stamp LJ's interpretation in *Baden* will not cause difficulties. Thus, if 'inhabitant' can be said to be certain – perhaps construed to mean 'resident' – George's discretionary trust will be valid. This is the most likely result, given the court's preference for validity rather than invalidity. Note, also, that in *R v District Auditor ex p West Yorkshire MC* (1986), a discretionary trust for 'inhabitants' did not fail the 'is or is not' test of certainty. Finally, there is always the danger that a court would decide that a class defined geographically was 'administratively unworkable' in the same way that the court in *West Yorkshire* went on to hold the discretionary trust void even though it had passed the 'is or is not' test. In that case, there were some 2.5 million potential beneficiaries, and it must be a question of degree in each case whether the trustees can exercise their responsibilities under the trust in the light of the size and composition of the class. If there is a danger of this in our case – and to some extent it will depend on the geographical construction given to the trust – George would be best to define his class with greater precision so as not to overburden his trustees.

The final issue raised by George concerns the residue of his estate. George's desire to have his trustees distribute the property among 'struggling' artists and authors, and thence to a charity, might be best achieved by giving his trustees a power of appointment in favour of the artists, subject to an express discretionary trust for charity by way of gift over in default of appointment. There will be no problem with certainty of objects in respect of the discretionary trust for charity because 'charity' is a legal term of art and has, by definition, a certain meaning (see, for example, *Commissioners for Special Purposes of Income Tax v Pemsel* (1891)). A power in favour of 'struggling' artists and authors presents more difficulties, as it may well be that such a description will fail the 'is or is not' test as being conceptually uncertain (*Re Baden (No 2)* (1973)). The likelihood is that 'struggling' will be regarded as too subjective and that the power will fail the test. Indeed, even if George attempts to avoid evidential difficulties by delegating questions of fact to a third party (*Re Coxen* (1948)), it is unclear whether he could also avoid difficulties of conceptual certainty by delegating this issue (*Re Wynn* (1952); *Dundee General Hospital Board v Walker* (1952)). George should rethink this part of his proposed will, perhaps substituting a gift to a charity concerned with authors and artists instead of the power which attempts to benefit them directly.

QUESTION 16

To what extent have the courts withdrawn from the fundamental principle that private purpose trusts are invalid?

How to Answer this Question

❖ The beneficiary principle and its purpose.
❖ Recognised exceptions and the problem of perpetuity.
❖ *Re Denley* principle.
❖ Unincorporated associations: exception to, or application of the beneficiary principle.
❖ *Quistclose* trusts.

Answer structure

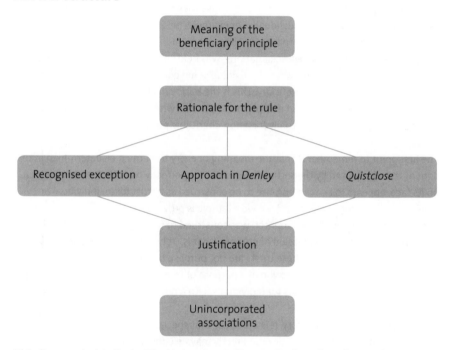

This diagram depicts the justification and exceptions to the 'beneficiary' principle.

ANSWER

When a person accepts the obligation of a trustee, he or she submits both to the jurisdiction of the court of equity and to the onerous duties of trusteeship. It is inherent in the concept of a trust that a court must be able to control and enforce the trusteeship and, if necessary, compel the trustees to carry out their duties.[19] There are several methods by which a court can exercise an effective enforcement jurisdiction, not least by requiring that all trusts have certain objects. Similarly, it is equally important that there must actually be *someone* in whose favour the court can decree performance of the trust and who can apply to the court to enforce its terms. Consequently, with the exception of charitable trusts (which can be enforced by the Attorney General on behalf of the Crown as *parens patriae*), a trust must be made for the benefit of human beneficiaries. There must be a *cestui que* trust in whose favour the court can decree performance (*Morice v Bishop of Durham* (1804); *Re Wood* (1949)). This is the 'beneficiary principle', and it means that, with the exception of charities, nearly all trusts for a purpose are void (*Re Endacott* (1960)).

The beneficiary principle – or the rule against non-charitable purpose trusts as it is sometimes called – is fundamental to the validity of a trust. Many examples abound of trusts for purposes being declared invalid because they are not for the benefit of ascertained or ascertainable individuals. For example, in *Re Astor* (1952), a trust for, *inter alia*, 'the establishment, maintenance and improvement of good understanding, sympathy and co-operation between nations' was held void and in *Re Endacott*, itself a testamentary trust 'for the purpose of providing some good useful memorial to myself', failed for want of a human beneficiary. This is the basic principle. Not surprisingly, therefore, there are a number of exceptional situations where trusts have been held valid despite being apparently or actually for a non-charitable purpose.

The first point to remember is that the meaning of every trust must be determined in the light of the words used by the settlor or testator. It is perfectly possible for a trust which, on its face, appears to be for a purpose to be construed as a trust for an individual or individuals (*Re Sanderson* (1857)).[20] A good example is provided by *Re Osoba* (1979), where a trust 'for the training of my daughter' was construed to be a trust absolutely for the daughter, the testator's expression of purpose (that is, 'for training') having no legal effect. The point here is that these trusts are not purpose trusts at all, and that, as a matter of construction, the indication of a purpose or motive for the absolute gift is of no legal importance. They are trusts for individuals with a non-legal, superadded motive.

In contrast to the above category, it is also clear that special kinds of purpose trusts which actually benefit individuals directly or indirectly may be upheld by the court, providing certain conditions are met. This is known as the *Re Denley* principle, although there may well have been examples of this type of trust before that case (for example, *Re Abbott* (1900)). It is important to realise that these trusts are a true exception to the beneficiary principle. They are trusts for purposes which the court holds valid simply because there are individuals with *locus standi* who can apply to have the purpose carried out.[21] Of

---

19 Justification for the 'beneficiary' principle.
20 This is a question of construction and illustrates the flexibility of the court's jurisdiction.
21 Separate justification for adopting this approach.

course, the individuals directly or indirectly benefited have no equitable interest in the trust property itself: they are not beneficiaries in law. The essence of the matter, as explained in *Re Denley* (1969), is that the beneficiary principle is designed to eliminate purpose trusts of an abstract or impersonal nature, so that any purpose which may be accomplished with certainty and which does thereby confer a benefit directly or indirectly on human beneficiaries should not be declared void. Thus, in *Re Denley*, a trust for the maintenance of a sports ground (a purpose) for use by the employees of a company (the individuals indirectly benefited) was valid on the ground that the employees had *locus standi* to ensure that the trustees put the purpose into effect.

However, because a *Re Denley*-type of trust is a true purpose trust, it must not infringe the rule against perpetuities. Under this principle, those non-charitable purpose trusts which, as an exception to the beneficiary principle, are regarded as valid, must not last longer than the perpetuity period; that is, for no longer than a certain maximum duration (*Morice v Bishop of Durham* (1804)). The reason is that as a matter of public policy, property should not be tied up indefinitely and so be lost to the general economy. The maximum period for which a *Re Denley* purpose trust may last is 125 years as laid down in the Perpetuities and Accumulations Act 2009. More important, however, is the rule that it must be possible to say at the outset of the trust whether its duration will be confined to the perpetuity period. Consequently, in order to avoid perpetuity, the purpose trust must be expressly or impliedly limited to operate within the perpetuity period by the terms of the trust. In *Re Denley* itself, the trust was limited specifically to the perpetuity period and so was upheld by the court.

The *Re Denley* principle is a refinement of the rule against purpose trusts and, in principle, it can operate to validate any purpose trust that meets both the requirements of perpetuity and the need for ascertainable individuals indirectly benefited. In addition, there are some purpose trusts for very specific purposes which are regarded as valid as being anomalous exceptions to the beneficiary principle. These are so-called 'trusts of imperfect obligation'; 'imperfect' because there is no beneficiary as such to enforce the trust. Although the categories may not now be extended (*Re Endacott* (1960)), they have been held valid because the trustees were prepared to undertake the purpose, because the purpose was certain, because there was no perpetuity and because the court had sympathy with the specific motive of the testator on the occasion the validity of the trust was challenged.[22] However, the exceptional nature of these trusts, usually linked to a testator making provision for certain matters after his death, makes it likely that even these exceptional cases will be void if an attempt is made to establish them by *inter vivos* trust. Again, as noted above, because these are purpose trusts, the rule against perpetuities equally applies in such cases.

---

22 Independent justification for these exceptions.

The specific purpose trusts which may be valid under these principles are, first, trusts for the erection or maintenance of tombs or monuments, either to the testator or some other person (*Mussett v Bingle* (1876)), it being assumed in the case of trusts to erect monuments that this task will be completed within the perpetuity period, while trusts to maintain monuments must be limited to perpetuity in the usual way (*Re Hooper* (1932)). Second, there may be trusts for the upkeep of animals after the testator's death, providing, again, that they are limited to the perpetuity period (*Mitford v Reynolds* (1848)). However, the matter is not entirely clear as, in one case (*Re Dean* (1889)), the judge accepted that a purpose trust for the care of an animal could be valid for the life of the animal, and this is not generally taken to be a sufficient perpetuity period in law. Likewise, in other cases, it is not clear whether the gift was for the animal *per se* or to a person provided he looked after the animal (*Pettingall v Pettingall* (1842)). Third, trusts for the saying of masses for the soul of the testator may be upheld (*Re Gibbons* (1917)), although they may occasionally be charitable (*Re Hetherington* (1990)), again if limited to perpetuity. Fourth, and very exceptionally, a trust for the promotion of fox hunting was upheld in *Re Thompson* (1934) on a spurious analogy with the animals cases.

Finally, brief mention should be made of two other matters which relate to the beneficiary principle. First, there are many examples of settlors and testators attempting to give property to *unincorporated* associations – such as the local brass band or gardening club – which appear to fall foul of the beneficiary principle. The problem is simply that unincorporated associations have no legal personality and cannot, therefore, be beneficiaries under a trust. The difficulties this poses have been avoided by construing gifts to unincorporated associations not as gifts on trust for their purposes but as gifts to the individual members of the association who will then use the property to carry out the functions of the association (*Re Recher's Trust* (1972), *Artistic Upholstery Ltd v Art Forma (Ltd)* (1999) and *Re Horley Town Football Club* (2006)). This is so even if the settlor's or testator's gift is expressed to be for a purpose. Once again, what seems to be a purpose trust is not so taken, because of a favourable construction by the court. Likewise, so-called *Quistclose* trusts (from *Barclays Bank v Quistclose Investments* (1970)), whereby a person (A) gives money to another (B) for the single purpose of enabling B to pay his debts to a creditor (C), appear to be purpose trusts – the payment of a debt. However, they have been variously analysed as either a form of the *Re Denley* trust (*Re Northern Developments (Holdings)* (1978)) or as a trust for the creditors with a resulting trust for the provider of the money (A) should the recipient (B) not use the money to pay his debts (*Carreras Rothmans v Freeman Mathews Treasure* (1985) and *Burton v FX Music* (1999)). Whatever their true basis, such trusts are not easily proven – as in *Box v Barclays Bank* (1998).

In conclusion, it remains true that English law refuses to admit the validity of non-charitable purpose trusts as a matter of principle. However, the *Re Denley* principle, the anomalous exceptions, the imaginative constructions placed on gifts to unincorporated associations and, above all, the wide meaning given to charity, means that only the purest examples of purpose trusts which have no element of community benefit are likely to be invalid today.

QUESTION 17 ---

Consider the validity of the following dispositions in the will of Elizabeth, who died in 2012:

'(a) £10,000 for the erection and maintenance of a suitable monument to myself in the village of my birth and for an annual memorial service in the parish church for selected relatives;

(b) £15,000 to the vicar of St Mary's Parish Church to be used as she pleases in the knowledge that nothing will be done which diminishes respect for the church; and

(c) £50,000 to my trustees to be spent on the provision of tennis courts for use by my relatives who are resident in the village.'

Aim Higher

The beneficiary principle is fundamental to the law of trusts and manifests itself in different guises. Problems of perpetuity should not be avoided or ignored as even an otherwise valid purpose trust might thereby fail. The law regarding the perpetuities rule was brought up to date by the **Perpetuities and Accumulations Act 2009**

Common Pitfalls ✗

In dealing with questions on purpose trusts, the prospect of the gift being charitable must be borne in mind.

How to Answer this Question

❖ Anomalous exceptions to the beneficiary principle: severability of gifts and perpetuity.

❖ Trusts, absolute gifts and purposes.

❖ *Re Denley* gifts: the appropriate perpetuity rule.

Answer Structure

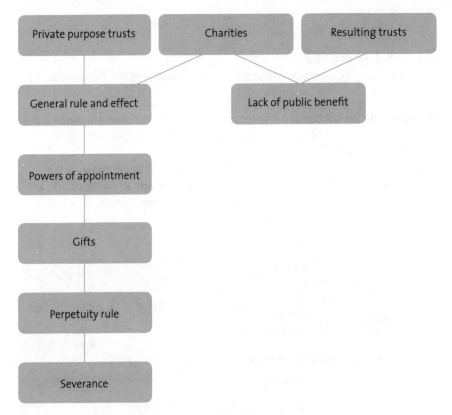

This diagram presents a holistic view of purpose trusts.

ANSWER

In *Re Endacott* (1960), Lord Evershed MR forthrightly stated that 'a trust by English law, not being a charitable trust, in order to be effective, must have ascertained or ascertainable beneficiaries'. This rule against the validity of non-charitable purpose trusts is often seen as a fundamental principle which cannot be violated even if the intended purpose trust is clearly capable of achievement, certain in its objectives, does not tend to a perpetuity and does not offend against public policy. Thus, the lack of a legal person – human or corporate – who can enforce the trust and initiate the court's equitable jurisdiction is regarded as fatal (*Re Shaw* (1952)). Of course, there are qualifications and exceptions to this principle, some dependent on the court giving a benign and purposive construction to the recipients of the property (for example, in the case of an unincorporated association (*Re Recher's Trust* (1972)) and some truly outside the scope of the beneficiary principle. This problem raises several of these issues and calls for both the construction of Elizabeth's will and the application of the *Re Endacott* principle. In addition, because there are circumstances in which special types of purpose trust may be valid, consideration must also be given to the rule against perpetuities. This will be done once the inherent validity of each of Elizabeth's dispositions has been considered.[23]

(a) £10,000 for monuments, etc

This is an attempt to establish a purpose trust or, more accurately, a purpose trust with three different aims: the erection of a monument, the maintenance of that monument and the holding of an annual memorial service. The starting place must be *Re Endacott* itself, for not only does this firmly establish the beneficiary principle in English law, it was a case involving an unsuccessful attempt to establish a trust for the provision 'of some useful memorial to myself'. However, *Endacott* also accepted that there were a limited number of specific purpose trusts whose validity had been accepted by the court, albeit for reasons of sentiment or expediency. One of these, as demonstrated by *Mussett v Bingle* (1876) and *Re Hooper* (1932), is trusts for the erection or maintenance of monuments or graves, at least if the executors of the will are prepared to carry out the trust. *Prima facie*, this would seem to be authority for the validity of Elizabeth's trust for the erection and maintenance of a monument to herself, providing questions of perpetuity can be resolved. Indeed, our case is distinguishable from the failed trust of *Re Endacott*, as that involved a 'memorial', although it seems that even 'monuments' must have a funereal character to fall within the limited exception.

Unfortunately, however, apart from perpetuity problems, there is a further difficulty as the trust is also for an annual memorial service for Elizabeth. While it is possible that a trust for the purpose of saying a mass in private for a testator may be a valid purpose trust (*Re Gibbons* (1917)), it seems that Elizabeth's purpose falls outside that limited exception to the beneficiary principle. There is authority from a former colonial court that a private, non-Christian ceremony to perpetuate the memory of a person may be the subject of a valid purpose trust (*Re Khoo Cheng Teow* (1932)), but it is unlikely that such a trust would be accepted today, especially in the light of the clear direction from *Re Endacott* that the categories of valid purpose trusts are not to be extended. Consequently, questions of perpetuity aside, we seem to have one potentially valid purpose trust and one that is certainly void. It then becomes a matter of construction whether the invalidity of one part of the gift invalidates the whole, for it may be possible to sever the presumptively valid purpose trust, especially if some discrete portion of the £10,000 can be set aside for its completion.[24] The remainder would result to the testator's estate, as would the whole amount if there is no severance or if there were a general perpetuity problem (see below).

---

23   Identification of the issues in the problem.
24   The issue of severance is inherent in the problem.

(b) £15,000 to the vicar of St Mary's, etc

The validity of this gift depends almost entirely on the construction that is placed upon it. There are four possible alternatives.[25] First, this might be an attempt by Elizabeth to give the vicar of St Mary's a power of appointment over the £15,000, where the object of the power is a purpose. There is no rule in English law that makes it impossible to create a power for a purpose, precisely because exercise of the power is entirely voluntary for the donee of the power (the vicar) and thus enforcement (and lack of people to enforce) is irrelevant. However, there must be an intention to establish a power (an intention to establish a void purpose trust is not sufficient: (*IRC v Broadway Cottages* (1955)), the objects of the power must be certain and there must be no perpetuity. In our case, it is not clear that there is an intention to establish a power (for example, there is no gift in default of appointment) and the direction that the vicar may do as she pleases may even indicate an absolute gift. In any event, it is likely that the purpose of the power would be regarded as too uncertain within the test for certainty of objects of powers (the 'is or is not' test) established in *Re Gulbenkian* (1970). The second possibility is that this disposition is regarded as neither a trust nor a power, but as an absolute gift to the vicar of St Mary's *per se*. The point is of some importance as, if this is an absolute gift, the vicar may keep the property for herself and do with it as she pleases. There are several examples of gifts being regarded as absolute despite the fact that the testator has attached some expression of motive or desire to the bequest, including *Re Osoba* (1979) and *Re Andrews* (1905). However, whether we can regard Elizabeth's disposition within this category is unclear, for although it is possible to regard Elizabeth's expressions of hope as without legal effect, imposing no trust at all (that is, the vicar may do 'as she pleases'), it may be important that the vicar of St Mary's is not named, but identified by her office. This does suggest that the money is not intended for that person individually, but in virtue of her official capacity.

A third possibility may be that this is a gift for charitable purposes, being for the advancement of religion (*Re Fowler* (1914)). In some cases, a gift to a clergyman on trust to do as he pleases has been taken to indicate a trust for the advancement of religion (*Re Flinn* (1948)). However, once again, in our case, there is no clear indication that any trust was intended and, even if it were, the general vagueness of the testator's instructions suggests that the gift may be used for other purposes that are not wholly for the advancement of religion: advancement is not the same as non-obstruction. Fourth, this may be a straightforward, non-charitable, purpose trust which is void under *Re Endacott*. So, depending on the construction of the gift, this disposition discloses either no trust or power at all, being an absolute gift; a power for a purpose, which is probably uncertain and therefore void; a charitable purpose; or a void purpose trust.

---

25 This is very good technique to identify the possible solutions.

(c) £50,000 on tennis courts

This appears to be a simple purpose trust: after all, the trustees will be under a mandatory obligation to erect tennis courts. However, instead of being void for want of a human beneficiary, this purpose trust appears to be valid under the *Re Denley* (1969) principle. According to this case, the rule against purpose trusts is intended to invalidate only those trusts which are abstract and impersonal. If a purpose trust directly or indirectly benefits a class of ascertained or ascertainable individuals, it will be valid as the individuals may be given *locus standi* to apply to the court in the event that the trustees do not carry out the trust. The individuals directly or indirectly benefited have no equitable interest in the trust property itself, although they do provide the means of enforcement. Indeed, with the exception of the perpetuity issue, our case is very similar to that in *Re Denley* itself where the purpose was the provision of a sports ground for employees. Applying that case, this disposition is presumptively valid. The executors of Elizabeth's will may have enormous difficulty establishing a charitable purpose on these facts owing to the lack of public benefit.

Finally, we come to problems of perpetuity.[26] According to the rule against perpetual trusts, those non-charitable purpose trusts which, as an exception to the beneficiary principle, equity regards as valid, must not last longer than the perpetuity period, being a period not exceeding 125 years; see the Perpetuities and Accumulations Act 2009. Furthermore, the question of perpetuity must be resolved at the date the disposition comes into effect and, to be valid, there must be no possibility of the purpose lasting longer than the perpetuity period. This usually means that it is necessary for the testatrix to make some express or implied limitation to perpetuity in the trust instrument itself (*Leahy v Attorney General for New South Wales* (1959)). In our cases, although a trust for the erection of a monument will be presumed to be completed within the perpetuity period, a trust for its maintenance must be specifically limited to the period. The same is true for the trust for the annual memorial service, even if it is otherwise valid. Likewise, the *Re Denley*-type trust must be limited to perpetuity. There are no such limitations and all these trusts would seem to fail for perpetuity if nothing else. Similarly, any power given to the vicar of St Mary's would fail were it not exercised within the perpetuity period.

QUESTION 18

Lord Rich wishes to give £10,000 to the Redshire branch of the National Association of Landed Gentry for their general purposes. He discovers that each branch's bank account is in the name of the local officers but that there is a 'Memorandum of Agreement' in which each branch agrees to abide by the rules of the National Association. He comes to you for advice as to how best to achieve his wishes, and he is concerned that the money be effectively prevented from falling into the hands of the local officers personally.

26 Good technique to adopt a holistic approach to the question.

How to Answer this Question

❖ Unincorporated associations: various constructions and respective merits.

❖ Trusts for purposes.

❖ Trusts for individuals as joint tenants or tenants in common (*Neville Estates v Madden* (1962)).

❖ Trusts for individuals and contractual relations (*Re Recher's Trust* (1972), *Artistic Upholstery Ltd v Art Forma (Ltd)* (1999), *Re Horley Town Football Club* (2006)).

❖ Trusts for present and future members of the association (*Bacon v Pianta* (1966)).

❖ Trusts for purposes, with ascertained individuals (*Re Denley* (1969)).

❖ Mandates.

Answer Structure

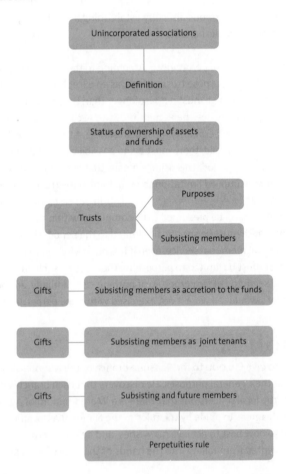

This diagram lists the various judicial constructions of transfers of property to unincorporated associations.

ANSWER

Lord Rich faces something of a problem. As a starting point, it is necessary to consider the nature of the National Association of Landed Gentry in order to discover what action Lord Rich may take to achieve his aims.[27] First, there is no indication here that the National Association of Landed Gentry (or its branches) is a charitable organisation. If it were, the intended donation would cause no difficulties since money given on charitable purpose trusts is perfectly valid and the money would be forever dedicated to the charitable objects (*Commissioners for Special Purposes of Income Tax v Pemsel* (1891)). There is nothing to support this conclusion and it must be discounted. Second, although it is not clear, it is doubtful whether this association has legal personality in its own right. For example, it does not appear to be incorporated as a public or private company, a supposition confirmed by the fact that the bank accounts of the local branches are in the names of the local officers and not the association itself. If the association did have legal personality, it could be the object of a simple trust or absolute gift in its favour and Lord Rich would be able to make his donation safe in the knowledge that the money would be used for the purposes of the association as outlined in its articles of incorporation. Third, the association and its local branches could be regarded as unincorporated associations within the outline definition provided by *Leahy v Attorney General for New South Wales* (1959) and discussed in *Conservative & Unionist Central Office v Burrell* (1982). This does seem most likely and, even if it is true that some contractual relationship must exist between the members of the group before it can be regarded as an unincorporated association in law (*Burrell*), such a relationship will be provided by the 'Memorandum of Agreement' which incorporates the national rules into each local branch, including the Redshire branch. The consequences of adopting this view of the association are considered below. Fourth, it is possible that our association might even lack the necessary formality to be considered an 'unincorporated association'. In that case, its status is *sui generis*, being a collection of individuals combining for a common purpose, and Lord Rich will find it difficult to make a donation for the purposes of the association unless a mandate theory is applied (*Conservative & Unionist Central Office v Burrell* (1982)). This will be discussed below.

The most probable hypothesis is that the Redshire branch can be regarded as an unincorporated association. As noted above, unincorporated associations have no legal personality and cannot be the beneficiaries *per se* of either an absolute gift or a gift on trust. Consequently, it could be that a donation to an unincorporated association for its general purposes should be regarded as a gift on trust for those purposes and, of course, non-charitable purpose trusts are void unless one of the very limited exceptions applies (*Re Endacott* (1960)).[28] This is the heart of the dilemma for persons in Lord Rich's position:

---

27 If the facts of the problem are unclear it is necessary to clarify the issue by assuming relevant facts.

28 State the general rule before dealing with the exceptions.

the unincorporated association cannot itself be the beneficiary of a donation (having no legal personality) and any trust for its purposes *per se* will be void. Fortunately, there are four possible ways to avoid this conclusion, all of which have the effect of making gifts to the association and its members legally possible.[29]

First, a donation to an unincorporated association might be construed as a gift to the present members of the association as joint tenants or tenants in common: see *Cocks v Manners* (1871) (compare *Leahy v Attorney General for New South Wales* (1959)). In other words, there is no purpose trust, but a donation to the members of the association as individuals who, of course, can be the objects of a gift or trust. While this would make the donation perfectly valid – it is like any other trust or gift for an individual – it suffers from the drawback that any of the individual members may use *their* shares of the donation for personal purposes and take their shares with them on leaving the association. The very reason that allows the donation to be valid creates the chance that the donor's motive in making the gift will be ignored. This construction would not, in our case, prevent the officers or anyone else from taking a share of the money and using it as they wish.

Second, a donation to an unincorporated association might be construed, as before, as a gift to the present members of the association individually, but this time on the basis that the subject matter of the donation (the money) is to be dealt with according to the contract which binds the members of the association together. Again, this is a gift or trust for individuals (and therefore perfectly valid), but the rules of the association form a contract between the members which prevent them taking shares for their own use (*Re Recher's Trust* (1972)). The matter is one of contract, not of trust (see *Artistic Upholstery Ltd v Art Forma (Ltd)* (1999)). Likewise, in *Re Horley Town Football Club* (2006) the High Court decided that the donation of a sports ground to a football club to be used as a sports complex by the club was construed as a gift to the members of the club subject to their contractual rights and liabilities towards each other as members of the club. So, if the contract (the rules) provides for the fulfilment of the purposes of the association, the donor can take comfort that his money will be used for the association's purposes, otherwise breach of contract will occur in respect of which a member can sue: *Artistic Upholstery*. Moreover, providing the members' contract (that is, the association's rules) allows the individuals to distribute the property amongst themselves should they so choose, or even allows the present rules to be changed to allow them to do so, there will be no perpetuity problems. Such are the advantages of this 'contract-holding theory' that, if at all possible, all gifts to unincorporated associations will be construed in this manner (*News Group Newspapers Ltd v SOGAT 82* (1986); *Artistic Upholstery*). It allows such gifts to be valid, effectively prevents individuals from gaining a share of the donation unless the association comes to an end, and ensures, so far as the rules (contract) allow, that the donor's money is used for the association's general purposes.

---

29 Identify the possible solutions.

A third solution is really an alternative version of the two constructions just considered: namely, that the donation is construed as a donation on trust or gift for individuals (either as joint tenants, as tenants in common, or as bound by their contract), but this time for the present and future members of the association (*Bacon v Pianta* (1966)).

Unfortunately, this construction suffers from a danger of perpetuity in that the future members of the association may become entitled to the property (that is, they become members of the association) too far in the future, outside the perpetuity period. This would invalidate the gift because 'future interests' (that is, interests of persons not yet members of the class of beneficiaries) must vest within 125 years of the date of the gift. There are ways of remedying the situation (for example, 'wait and see', and class-closing rules under the Perpetuities and Accumulations Act 2009), but this construction should be avoided where possible.

Fourth, there is a possibility that, even if the donation to the unincorporated association is construed as a gift on trust for its purposes, it may be saved from voidness in certain situations by the *Re Denley* (1969) principle. According to this principle, if a purpose trust directly or indirectly confers a benefit on a group of individuals, it may be valid if it is limited to the period of perpetuity (*Re Lipinski* (1976)). The *Denley* principle may apply to any kind of purpose trust in appropriate circumstances, but its application to unincorporated associations is controversial. According to Oliver J in *Re Lipinski*, the *Denley* principle might apply if the association was 'inward looking'; that is, confers a benefit on its members and not on the public at large. That might be the case with our association. However, Vinelott J, in *Re Grant* (1980), doubted whether *Re Denley* could ever save a gift to an unincorporated association, even if *Denley* did validate some other types of purpose trusts. In fact, in our case, even if *Re Denley* was followed, there would be problems of perpetuity.

Finally, if the Redshire branch cannot be regarded as an unincorporated association at all (with a preference for the contract-holding theory), there is the possibility that Lord Rich may make a valid donation via a mandate (*Conservative & Unionist Central Office v Burrell* (1982)). The mandate theory is not fully developed but, essentially, it involves the donor giving a mandate to the treasurer of the group to use the donation in a particular way on behalf of the donor, which mandate becomes irrevocable when the money is so used. However, doubts about who owns the money before it is spent and how the mandate can be enforced mean that this solution should not be adopted unless no other construction of Lord Rich's donation can be adopted.

To conclude, we can give some concrete advice to Lord Rich, encouraging him to ensure that his donation is treated as a gift or trust for the individual members of the association (through clear drafting) and on the understanding that the contract-holding theory applies. This last construction will be presumed by the court if possible and Lord Rich should ensure that there is nothing in the rules of the association which prevents it from being adopted.[30]

QUESTION 19

In 1990, pursuant to a meeting, 20 individuals formed the Benevolent Parachutists Club by each transferring £5,000 to their appointed trustee-treasurer to hold as a fatal accident fund. The minutes of the meeting disclose that the fund was to be invested and moneys paid out on a certain payment scale to the surviving spouse of a member who died as a result of a parachuting accident. Further contributions to the fund have been received by gifts from anonymous donors and by entertainment organised by the members. The payment scale has been updated from time to time but involved one-off capital sums to the recipients. In 2012 the funds of the Club were valued at £20,000.

▸ Advise the treasurer-trustee as to the beneficial ownership of the funds on the assumption that he is the only surviving member of the Club.

Aim Higher

Students are urged to approach problem questions on purpose trusts holistically. First, consider whether the gifts are capable of subsisting as charitable trusts; second, whether the gifts create valid private purpose trusts; and, if not, the consequences of failure – in particular, whether resulting trusts will arise.

Common Pitfalls

Insufficient appreciation of the various approaches adopted by the court to avoid the beneficiary principle in the context of unincorporated associations.

How to Answer this Question

❖ Consideration of whether the Club is charitable.
❖ Status of unincorporated associations.
❖ Status of gifts to unincorporated associations.
❖ Status of gifts on trust for unincorporated associations.
❖ Distribution of surplus funds on dissolution.

---

30 The conclusion on flexible issues of law need not be specific.

Answer Structure

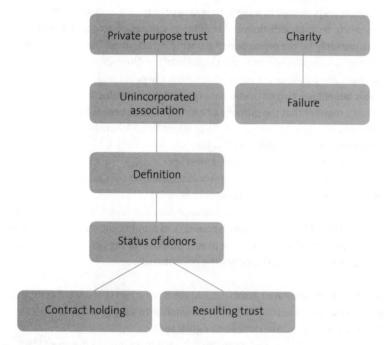

This diagram illustrates the nature of unincorporated associations and the status of holding its assets.

ANSWER -

The Club has never been incorporated. It is therefore an unincorporated association. Thus, unless its assets are held for charitable purposes, they belong in a sense to its members, for the time being. If, on the other hand, the Club's assets are held in charitable trusts, then none of the members can have a claim to its beneficial ownership. The first question is whether the Club is capable of being classified as charitable. Charities with an annual income exceeding £5,000 are required to register with the Charity Commission. It is unclear how much annual income has been received by the Club.[31]

In order to achieve charitable status the Club is required to satisfy two requirements:[32]

(1) The purpose of the association must be of a charitable nature in the sense that it falls within one or more of the charitable purposes stated in s 3 of the Charities Act 2011. Section 3(1)(g) of the Act refers to the advancement of amateur sport which

....

31 Classification of the status of the Club.
32 Discussion of the issue as to whether the Club is a charity.

includes the promotion of health by *inter alia* physical exertion. Even if parachuting by amateurs is treated as a sport, the purpose of the Benevolent Parachutists Club appears to be to provide financial benefits to spouses of deceased members rather than primarily for the promotion of parachuting activities. This would involve a question of construction as to the purposes of the Club.

(2) All charitable purposes are required to satisfy the public benefit test. The test of public benefit has two distinct meanings. First, the enactment in s 4 of the Charities Act 2011 requires that the purpose advocated must be beneficial to the community, and second, the purpose must not be confined to such a small section of society as to deny the element of public participation: see *IRC v Baddeley* (1955); or without a nexus between the donor and the donee: see *Oppenheim v Tobacco Securities Trust Co* (1951) and *Re Compton* (1945). It would appear that the Club comprises 20 members at the most and it exists to benefit the spouses of these members in the event of the latters' death. This would appear to comprise a link with the donors (members) and the beneficiaries (spouses) and may not satisfy the public benefit test. In short, the Club promotes a private purpose for the benefit of spouses of its members which would not satisfy the public benefit test.

The Club is an unincorporated association which is not a legal person but comprises a group of individuals joined together with common aims usually laid down in its constitution, creating mutual duties and rights: see *Conservative and Unionist Central Office v Burrell* (1982).[33] The label, Benevolent Parachutist Club, is a means of identifying the members of the Club and claims may be made or defended by the members collectively or through the officers of the association as representatives of the members. The issue in these types of cases involves the identity of the owners of assets of the association. In this respect Cross J in *Neville Estates Ltd v Madden* (1962), in an *obiter* pronouncement, outlined various constructions concerning gifts or trusts in favour of unincorporated associations. He laid down three propositions:

❖   gifts to the members of the association as joint tenants: see *Cocks v Manners* (1871);
❖   gifts to the existing members as an accretion to the funds of the Club; and
❖   gifts on trust for the purposes of the association: see *Re Lipinski* (1977).

The prima facie rule with regard to gifts to the association concerns the second of these propositions: see *Re Recher's Will Trusts* (1972).[34] In this case Brightman J in an *obiter* pronouncement declared that a gift to the association may be construed as a gift to the members of the association on the date of the gift, not beneficially, but as an accretion to the funds of the society which is regulated by the contract (evidenced by the rules of the association) made by the members *inter se*. Thus, a subsisting member on the date of the

---

33   Definition of an unincorporated association.
34   Where there are several judicial solutions to an issue it would be prudent to express a preference.

gift is not entitled *qua* member to claim an interest in the property but takes the property by reference to the rules of the society. A member who leaves the association by death or resignation will have no claim to the property, in the absence of any rules to the contrary. Accordingly, the transfer in 1990 of £5,000 by each of the members of the Club will be construed as a gift to the members collectively for their benefit, but subject to the contract made with each other as manifested in its constitution. The effect is that no one member is unilaterally entitled to claim any part of the fund except in accordance with the rules of the Club.

The donations to the Club by anonymous persons and entertainment are construed in a similar vein. On the dissolution of the Club these donors are not entitled to a return of the funds donated by these means. A material factor concerns the intentions of the transferors.[35] First, the donors in the same category are treated as having the same intention. Accordingly, all the anonymous donors are deemed to have a like intention. Secondly, since the intention has not been expressed, the court is required to consider whether there is any evidence of an implied intention that the transferor retained an interest in the property. In *Re Gillingham Bus Disaster Fund* (1958), the High Court decided that funds donated anonymously were contributed for a specific purpose which failed and the funds were to be held on resulting trust for the contributors; but the court could easily have come to the opposite conclusion, namely that the donors, being anonymous, manifested an intention not to have the property returned to them. They would then have parted with their funds 'out and out', leaving no room for a resulting trust. In other words, the transfer of the funds anonymously creates an irrebuttable presumption that the donors had parted out and out with the funds. This is the better view and the solution adopted by the High Court in *Re West Sussex Constabulary Trusts* (1971).

With respect to the fund-raising activities for the Club by means of entertainment, it would appear that on authority the donors are not entitled to a return of the funds on a dissolution of the Club. Those who attended these events with the motive of increasing the endowment of the Club created a relationship of contract, not trust. The contributors received the consideration for which they bargained, namely entertainment. Indeed, there were no direct contributions to the Club funds; only the profits of the entertainment were received by the Club. This was the view of Goff J in *Re West Sussex Constabulary* (1971). The effect is that the surplus funds of the Club originating from a variety of sources form an endowment which becomes available for distribution on a dissolution of the association.

Turning to the issue regarding the surplus funds on the date of the dissolution of the Club, it is worth pointing out that, subject to any liquidation clauses in the constitution, the modern rules governing the distribution of funds are based on the law of contract

35 Status of donations to the Club.

rather than the law of trusts. The court will infer a contract between all the members to the effect that ex-members of the Club on the date of dissolution cease to have any interest in the funds: see *Re Bucks Constabulary Fund (No. 2)* (1979). The earlier solution based on a resulting trust has fallen out of favour. The resulting trust solution was based on the notion that the members (or spouses) were all equally entitled to a contingent benefit on the happening of certain events; a resulting trust in their favour was considered to be the fairest way of distributing the fund. The division will be in favour of the subsisting members of the association on the date of dissolution: see *Re Printers and Transferrers Society* (1899) and *Re Houbourn Aero Components Ltd* (1946).

The issue posed in the problem involves the destination of property rights in the event that all the members have passed away save for one. The question is whether the sole surviving member of an unincorporated association is entitled to the surplus funds of the Club or whether the Crown is entitled to it on a *bona vacantia*. It is clear that the association will cease to exist because the contract between the members will come to an end. There can be no association since one cannot associate with oneself: see *Re Bucks Constabulary* (1979). On the death of the last surviving member, prior to the liquidation of the Club, the Crown will be entitled to the surplus as opposed to the estate of the last deceased member: see *Cunnack v Edwards* (1896); but the issue in the problem is distinguishable because the treasurer-trustee (member) is still alive and wishes to establish an interest in the surplus funds of the Club. On this issue Walton J in *Re Bucks Constabulary* (1979) in an *obiter* pronouncement declared that if the society is reduced to a single member, neither he nor his personal representatives will be entitled to the surplus funds and thus the assets become ownerless and may be taken by the Crown.

However, in the recent case, *Hanchett-Stamford v AG* (2008), the High Court refused to follow the *obiter* pronouncement of Walton J and decided that the sole surviving member was entitled to the surplus funds of the association. The court pointed out that the thread that runs through the main cases is that the property rights of an unincorporated association are vested in its members subject to their contractual rights and duties. On the date of the dissolution of the association the subsisting members are entitled to the assets. It would be illogical if a different rule were to be adopted where the membership of the association falls below two. In addition, the deprivation of the property interest in the surviving member would be a breach of Article 1 of Protocol 1 of the European Convention on Human Rights which guarantees the peaceful enjoyment of possessions. No public interest is served by the appropriation by the state of such member's share in the Club's assets.

In conclusion, the treasurer-trustee as the sole surviving member of the Benevolent Parachutist Club will be able to claim the surplus assets of the Club.

The Law of Charities

INTRODUCTION

Charitable trusts are valid public purpose trusts. This means simply that it is perfectly possible to establish a trust for the achievement of a purpose, provided that the purpose in law is regarded as charitable. As far as charities are concerned, it is not important if there is no human beneficiary capable of enforcing the trust, because the Attorney General can take action in respect of all charitable trusts on behalf of the Crown. Moreover, valid charitable trusts are not subject to certain aspects of the perpetuity rule and may be of unlimited duration. Furthermore, when compared to valid private trusts (that is, trusts for human objects), charitable trusts have other advantages; they enjoy considerable fiscal privileges including exemption from many taxes. Hence, many of the decided cases involve the Inland Revenue seeking to deny charitable status. Likewise, there are special rules applicable to the failure of charitable trusts (the principles of *cy-près*) which may oust the normal rules of resulting trusts, and there is a separate body of rules dealing with the administration of charities and the conduct of business by charitable trustees.

Obviously it is of singular importance to be able to distinguish between charitable purposes and non-charitable purposes. The former will be valid and enforceable, as well as having other advantages over private trusts, and the latter will be void unless they fall within one of the exceptions to the beneficiary principle considered in the previous chapter. The Charities Act 2006 enacted for the first time a statutory definition of charities after centuries of reliance mainly on case law to lead the way on the type of activities that would be given charitable status. The 2006 Act introduced a statutory definition by reference to a two-step approach – the listing of a variety of charitable purposes and the public benefit test. The 2006 Act has been repealed and replaced by the Charities Act 2011. This is a consolidating statute that repeals the diverse statutory provisions that are applicable to charities and insert the same in one statute. The Charities Act 2011 came into force on 14th March 2012. The 2011 Act contains a list of 13 charitable purposes – 12 specific charitable objects, and a residual category of charitable purposes designed to maintain the courts' discretion to determine the type of novel activity that ought to be treated as charitable. This is intended to be a comprehensive list of charitable activities. Most of the purposes, in any event, were charitable before the Act was passed. The meaning of 'charity' is to be found principally in case law and the opinions of the Charity Commissioners (now the Charity Commission).

QUESTION 20

Bernard died last year leaving a will providing the following legacies:

'(a) £1,000,000 to be used to train Great Britain's most promising young amateur athletes for the forthcoming Olympic Games;

(b) £2,000,000 to be used to raise awareness of schoolchildren in London of the dangers of possessing a knife in a public place;

(c) £150,000 upon trust to apply the annual income for such charitable or benevolent objects as my trustees shall select.'

▶ Consider the validity of these bequests.

> ## Aim Higher
>
> In *IRC v McMullen* (1981), the majority of the Law Lords adopted a restrictive construction to recreational facilities by deciding that the persons who may benefit from the trust must be deprived of the facilities in the first place.

> ## Common Pitfalls ✗
>
> Students do not always appreciate that the pre-2011 case law on charities is still relevant today. Sections 3(1)(m)(i) to (iii) and 3(3) of the 2011 Act endorse the common law approach to charitable objects and s 4(3) consolidates the case law meaning of public benefit.

How to Answer this Question

❖ Trusts for the advancement of amateur sport within s 3(1)(g) of the Charities Act 2011.

❖ The provision of recreational facilities within s 5 of the Charities Act 2011.

❖ Advancement of education within s 3(1)(b) of the Charities Act 2011.

❖ Perpetuities rule and charities.

❖ Certainty of charitable objects.

❖ Discretionary trusts/powers of appointment.

❖ Resulting trust.

Answer Structure

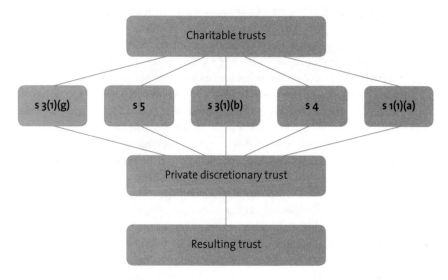

This diagram illustrates the tests to determine the charitable status of gifts in Bernard's will.

ANSWER

A charitable trust is a public purpose trust that may result in individuals or members of the public deriving direct benefits. It is enforceable by the Attorney General on behalf of the Crown. If any of the purposes, as stated in Bernard's will, fail to satisfy the tests for charitable status, consideration is required to be given as to the validity of the purposes as private trusts. If the purposes fail on this score, the relevant property will be held on resulting trust for the residuary beneficiaries under the will.[1]

(a) £1,000,000 to be used to train Great Britain's most promising young amateur athletes for the forthcoming Olympic Games

Prior to the Charities Act 2011 the promotion of sport was not regarded as a charitable activity: see *IRC v City of Glasgow Police Athletic Association* (1953), where the House of Lords held that the provision of facilities for the recreation of police officers was not exclusively for charitable purposes. However, s 3(1)(g) of the Charities Act 2011 has now recognised that the advancement of amateur sport is to be treated as a charitable activity and the training of athletes for the Olympic Games clearly promotes such activity. 'Sport' for these purposes has been broadly defined 'as sports or games which promote health by involving physical or mental skill or exertion': see s 3(2)(d) of the Charities Act 2011. Thus, the charitable status of such activity is dependent on the way the facility is organised. The

---

1   Analysis of the issues that will be considered.

facts of the problem indicate that the sporting activities are restricted to amateur sport and this would appear to satisfy the requirements laid down in s 3(2)(d) of the Act.

The public benefit requirement is now obligatory to prove in respect of all charities without the aid of presumptions: see ss 4(1) and (2) of the 2011 Act.[2] Section 4(3) consolidates the case law meaning of public benefit that existed before the passing of the Act. This involves a two-step test of demonstrating a benefit to society. The change in the law introduced by s 3(1)(g) has this effect by reference to the purpose. In addition, those eligible to receive benefits must comprise a large enough group to be considered as the public and without a personal or private relationship being used to limit those who may benefit. Again this test appears to be satisfied in that there is no connection between the donor, Bernard, and the intended beneficiaries.

Further, s 5 of the Charities Act 2011 confirms the charitable status of recreational activities provided that a number of basic conditions are satisfied. The facilities are required to improve the 'conditions of life' of those who will use them and these persons have need for the facilities because of their youth, disability, and social and economic circumstances. In *Guild v IRC* (1992), the Law Lords adopted a 'benign construction' of the test of 'deprivation' and decided that recreational facilities are provided with the object of improving the conditions of life of the beneficiaries, irrespective of whether or not the participating members are disadvantaged. It would appear that the gift to train promising young athletes for the Games will satisfy this test.

In any event the gift is capable of being charitable under s 3(1)(m) of the 2011 Act, the miscellaneous category.

(b) £2,000,000 to be used to raise awareness of schoolchildren in London of the dangers of possessing a knife in a public place

The issues created by this gift in Bernard's will concern the advancement of education within s 3(1)(b) of the Charities Act 2011 as well as s 3(1)(j) (relief of those in need by reason of their youth) and s 3(1) (m) (the miscellaneous category).

The first issue is to determine what is meant by education and second to consider whether this gift promotes education. Prior to the Charities Act 2011 the advancement of education was treated as a charitable purpose within the preamble to the Statute of Elizabeth 1601. Section 3(1)(b) of the 2011 Act consolidates this purpose. Section 3(3) enacts that terms used in the Act are to be given the same meaning under existing charity law. Thus, the interpretation of the term 'education' under the general law will be consistently applied. Education has been interpreted fairly broadly by the courts. It is not restricted to teaching activities in schools and universities but covers any form of worthwhile instruction, including research or cultural advancement. In *Re Shaw's Will Trust* (1952), the

---

2   Charities questions require discussion of the purposes and public benefit.

court decided that the promotion in Ireland of self-control, elocution and the arts of personal contact was charitable. Likewise in *South Place Ethical Society* (1980), the promotion of ethical principles was treated as a charitable purpose under this head.

It would appear that the gift in Bernard's will may be treated as a form of education of schoolchildren. Nothing has been said in the will concerning the methods of raising such awareness. One such method may involve activities within the school setting. In this event, the narrower meaning of education that was considered in *Re Shaw* (1957), involving an element of teaching, will be satisfied.

The public benefit test will be satisfied if the subject of education is for the public benefit. In other words, the court takes into consideration the usefulness to society or educational value of the subject matter that will be advanced. In *Re Pinion* (1965), the gift of a collection of paintings to the National Trust lacked any artistic merit and failed on this ground. In view of the spate of senseless attacks on young people involving knives, there cannot be any doubt that measures to deter the carrying of weapons in public places have a great deal of public value. An additional consideration is whether the restriction to schoolchildren in London only will fail to satisfy the public benefit test. The satisfaction of the test is a question of law for the judge to decide on the evidence submitted to the court.[3] In essence, this test will be satisfied if the potential beneficiaries of the trust are not numerically negligible and there is no bond or link between the donor and the intended beneficiaries. The number of schoolchildren in London is not negligible and there is no nexus with Bernard.

One minor point ought to be made and that is whether this gift includes a political element masquerading as education.[4] A trust for political purposes will fail as a charity on the ground that the court is incapable of deciding whether a political programme is for the public benefit: see *McGovern v AG* (1982). There is very little evidence that the gift in Bernard's will promotes a political purpose. The gift is not designed to change the law but simply to raise awareness of the dangers in carrying a weapon.

(c) £150,000 upon trust to apply the annual income for such charitable or benevolent objects as my trustees shall select

There are two issues in connection with this gift: first, whether the test for certainty of charitable objects is satisfied and second, the ultimate distribution of the fund.

A charitable trust is subject to a unique test for certainty of objects, namely whether the objects are exclusively charitable. It is unnecessary for the testator to specify the charitable objects which are intended to take the trust property, provided that the trust instrument manifests a clear intention to devote the funds for 'charitable purposes' only.

....

3   Identify questions of law and distinguish these from questions of fact.

4   Address and expressly exclude related issues.

This principle has been affirmed in s 1(1)(a) of the Charities Act 2011. Thus, a gift 'on trust for charitable purposes' will satisfy this test. The Charity Commission and the courts have jurisdiction to establish a scheme for the application of the funds.

The gift in Bernard's will is devoted to charitable 'or' benevolent purposes. The issue is whether this satisfies the test for exclusivity of charitable purposes. This involves a question of construction of the will. If the word 'or' is interpreted disjunctively, the gift will fail as a charity for benevolent purposes other than charitable are capable of benefiting: see *Chichester Diocesan Fund v Simpson* (1944) and *Blair v Duncan* (1902). Alternatively, if the expression is construed conjunctively to the effect that the gift is made for charitable and benevolent purposes, the gift may be valid as a charity. In *AG of the Bahamas v Royal Trust Co* (1986), the court decided that a gift for the 'education and welfare' of Bahamian children failed as a charity on the ground that the word 'and' was to be construed disjunctively. *Prima facie* the word 'or' is construed disjunctively, but much depends on the context in which the expression is used. The will and surrounding circumstances are required to be taken into account.

In addition, consideration ought to be given to the perpetuity rule. Charities are not subject to the rule against excessive duration. The gift in Bernard's will concerns the application of the income that accrues to £150,000 of capital to be applied for the stated purposes. If the gift fails as a charity, the funds may not be held for private purposes that infringe the perpetuity rule, the reason being that Bernard did not specify how long the income is to be so used.

The next issue concerns whether the discretion imposed on Bernard's trustees creates a non-charitable discretionary trust or a mere power of appointment. A discretionary trust imposes an 'obligation' on the trustees to exercise their discretion but allows the trustees the freedom to decide how, and to whom, the funds may be distributed. On the other hand, a mere power of appointment creates an 'authority' on the part of the trustees to distribute the funds but without imposing a duty to distribute: see *Burrough v Philcox* (1840) contrast *Re Weekes* (1897). The distinction between the two concepts involves a question of construction for the courts to decide. In Bernard's will the word 'shall' was used in respect of the selection. *Prima facie* this imposes an obligation to select, but much depends on the will as a whole and the context in which the will was made.

The test for certainty of objects of a private discretionary trust and mere power of appointment is the 'any given postulant' test, i.e. whether the trustees may say with certainty that any given person is or is not within a class of objects. As a trust, this gift may fail for administrative unworkability as laid down in *McPhail v Doulton* (1971) ('residents of Greater London') and applied in *R v District Auditor ex p W. Yorkshire County Council* (1986) ('inhabitants of W. Yorkshire'). In addition, the gift will fail as a private purpose trust since there is no person with the *locus standi* to enforce the intended trust: see *Morice v Bishop of Durham* (1804). Accordingly, a resulting trust for the residuary beneficiaries under the will may arise. As a mere power of appointment the gift may be valid, provided that the test for linguistic or conceptual certainty has been satisfied.

QUESTION 21

Mark, who has recently died, made a will in 2008 in which he made the following gifts:

(i)   £5,000 to Charles and David upon trust for such charitable or philanthropic objects as my trustees shall select.

(ii) £250,000 to the University of London upon trust to establish and maintain in perpetuity a School of Law Reform.

(iii) £3,000 to the trustees of the South Blankshire Methodist Conference for the promotion of physical recreation for Methodists in South Blankshire.

▶ Consider whether these gifts are charitable.

How to Answer this Question

❖ Gifts devoted exclusively for charitable purposes.

❖ Trusts for the advancement of education.

❖ Exemption of charities from the perpetuity rule – excessive duration principle.

❖ Trusts for the promotion of sport.

❖ Section 5 of the Charities Act 2011 – promotion of recreational facilities.

❖ Public benefit test.

Answer Structure

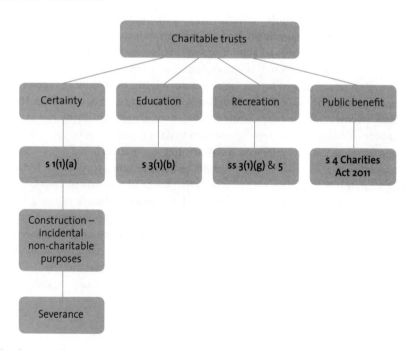

This diagram illustrates the construction and effect of the various purposes stated by Mark in his will.

ANSWER

(i) £5,000 to Charles and David upon trust

Section 1 of the Charities Act 2011 defines a charity as any institution which is established for charitable purposes only and is subject to the jurisdiction of the High Court. Section 3 identifies 13 purposes that are treated as charitable and declares that the institution in question is required to satisfy the public benefit test.

The first question in issue is whether this gift of £5,000 is charitable. In the problem, the will transfers '£5,000 to Charles and David upon trust for such charitable or philanthropic objects'.[5] This raises the question as to whether the test for charitable objects is satisfied.

Charitable trusts, like private trusts, are subject to a test of certainty of objects. A charitable trust is subject to a unique test for certainty of objects, namely, whether the objects are exclusively charitable. This is affirmed in s 1(1)(a) of the Charities Act 2011. In other words, if the trust funds may be used solely for charitable purposes the test will be satisfied. Indeed, it is unnecessary for the settlor or testator to specify the charitable objects which are intended to acquire the trust property: provided that the trust instrument manifests a clear intention to devote the funds for 'charitable purposes', the test will be satisfied.

Referring back to the problem, the question in turn concerns the construction of the expression 'or'.[6] If this conjunction is used disjunctively, as is the norm, it would follow that the test for certainty of charitable objects will not be satisfied as otherwise philanthropic objects that are not charitable would, in theory, be entitled to benefit. In *Chichester Diocesan Fund v Simpson* (1944), a testator directed his executor to apply the residue of his estate 'for such charitable or benevolent objects' as they may select. The executors assumed that the clause created a valid charitable gift and distributed most of the funds to charitable bodies. The court decided that the clause did not create charitable gifts and therefore the gifts were void. A similar result was reached in *Attorney General of the Bahamas v Royal Trust* (1986). The effect will be that a resulting trust for the testator's residuary estate will arise.[7] There is a possibility that the court may, on construction, decide that the non-charitable purposes are merely incidental to the main charitable purposes: see *Verge v Somerville* (1924). However, there is very little evidence on the facts of the problem that may support this contention. Likewise, the doctrine of severance may be too remote a possibility in order to rescue the charitable gift. Severance may be adopted if part of the funds have been devoted for charitable purposes and the remainder (or part) disposable for non-charitable purposes; see *Salisbury v Denton* (1857).

5   It is advisable to extract the salient facts from the problem in order to focus on the legal issue.
6   Application of the principle of law to the facts.
7   Destination of the funds on failure of an express trust.

In this problem there is very little evidence to support the contention that Mark, the testator, intended a division of the £5,000 for the different purposes. Alternatively, the legacy will be valid if the word 'or' is construed conjunctively in the sense that only philanthropic objects that are charitable are entitled to benefit. Again, one would be hard pressed to convince a court of such construction. The court will look at all the circumstances of the case, including the entire will and evidence that exists outside the will, to ascertain the intention of the testator.

(ii) £250,000 to the University of London upon trust

In this problem, the issue is whether the donation of £250,000 to the University for the stated purpose is charitable. Does the gift advance education as declared in s 3(1)(b) of the Charities Act 2011? The donation is to the University of London. This clearly is a charitable body that exists to advance education. If, as is possible, the University is the trustee to promote the stated purpose, the question arises as to whether the stated purpose is charitable. A School of Law Reform within the University exists as a department to undertake the task of examining the extent to which the current law is satisfactory and in appropriate cases to suggest proposals for reform. Section 3(3) of the Charities Act 2011 endorses the common law approach to charitable objects. In the law of charities, education has been interpreted generously and is not restricted to the classroom mode of disseminating knowledge, but requires some element of instruction or supervision. Thus, research is capable of being construed as the provision of education: see *Re Hopkins Will Trust* (1964). In *McGovern v Attorney General* (1981), a definition of advancement of education by way of research was laid down by Slade J. He posited that the requirements are that: (a) the subject matter of the proposed research is a useful object of study; (b) it must be contemplated that the knowledge acquired as a result of the research will be disseminated to others; and (c) the trust is for the benefit of the public, or a sufficiently important section of the public. It would appear that the establishment of a school to study the extent to which the law is in a satisfactory state would clearly satisfy the test laid down by Slade J. An additional issue is whether this purpose is political – for if that is the case the gift will fail as a charity.[8] Political activities include attempts to change the law and gifts to further the objects of political parties. A trust for political purposes is incapable of subsisting as a charity, for the court may not stultify itself by deciding that it is in the public good for the law to be changed: see *National Anti-Vivisection Society v IRC* (1948), concerning the activities of the stated society and *McGovern*, where Amnesty International was declared to be a political organisation. The School exists only to study the extent to which the law is satisfactory; it is not designed to lobby Parliament for changes to be introduced. On this basis it is a charitable activity.

A further point involves the reference to the School being maintained perpetually. Would this infringe the perpetuity rule? Although charitable trusts, like private trusts, are subject

---

8 Related issues ought to be expressly and clearly excluded.

to the rule against remote vesting, charitable trusts, as distinct from private trusts, are not subject to the rule against excessive duration. Indeed, many charities (schools and universities) continue indefinitely and rely heavily on perpetual donations. Accordingly, if the purposes are charitable the gift will not fail for infringing the perpetuity rule.

(iii) £3,000 to the trustees of the South Blankshire Methodist conference

The purpose as stated in this problem raises a number of issues. Is the purpose as declared in the will, namely physical recreation, a charitable activity? In any event, would the public benefit test be satisfied? The donation contemplated appears to promote recreation under the guise of advancing religion, i.e. Methodists in South Blankshire. In other words, the religious element seems to be purely incidental and the real purpose is to promote physical recreation *simpliciter* for such beneficiaries. A similar purpose was considered by the court in *IRC v Baddeley* (1955). Here the House of Lords decided that the gift was void, as recreational activities or sport are not within the preamble to the Statute of Elizabeth or the 'spirit and intendment of the preamble': see *Re Nottage* (1895) and *IRC v City of Glasgow Police Athletic Association* (1953). Section 3(1)(g) of the Charities Act 2011 includes the advancement of amateur sport within the list of charitable purposes. 'Sport' for these purposes has been broadly defined as sports or games which promote health by involving physical or mental skill or exertion: see s 3(2)(d) of the Charities Act 2011. The effect is that the charitable status of such activity is dependent on the way the facility is organised. However, there is little evidence in Mark's will to indicate that the funds are to be used for the promotion of amateur sport.

Section 5 of the Charities Act 2011 consolidates the law regarding the provision of recreational facilities. Section 5 of the Act stipulates that the provision of recreational facilities shall be charitable if two criteria are fulfilled, namely: (1) the public benefit test is satisfied; and (2) the facilities are provided in the interests of social welfare. The 'social welfare' test will be complied with if two 'basic conditions' are satisfied as enacted in s 5(3). The first requirement is continuous as stipulated in s 5(3)(a). The second requirement may be satisfied in alternative ways, either by proving that the facilities are available to a limited class of objects who have a need for such facilities by virtue of one or more of the factors enumerated within s 5(3)(b)(i) (such as a youth club or an organised outing for orphaned children) or s 5(3)(b)(ii) 'the facilities are available to the entire public' (such as a public swimming pool or a public park) or 'female or male members of the public at large' (women's institutes, etc). In *Guild v IRC* (1992), the court decided that the test today is whether the facilities are provided with the purpose of improving the conditions of life of the beneficiaries, irrespective of whether the participating members of society are disadvantaged or not. In short, the material issue concerns the nature of the facilities rather than the status of the participants. On this basis a strong case could be made out that the activities contemplated fall within the requirements of s 5 of the Charities Act 2011.

The definitive issue in this problem is whether the public benefit test will be satisfied. The public benefit test is used to distinguish a public trust from a private trust. A public trust is required to exist for the benefit of the public (the community) or an appreciable section of society. A unique application of this test is reserved for trusts for the relief of poverty. The test of public benefit is laid down in s 4 of the Charities Act 2011. Section 4(3) of the Act endorses the common law approach to the public benefit test that existed prior to the introduction of the 2011 Act. The satisfaction of the test is a question of law for the judge to decide on the evidence submitted to the court. In *IRC v Baddeley* (1955) the court decided that the test will not be satisfied where the intended beneficiaries comprise a class within a class. The facts of the problem refer to Methodists (a class) in South Blankshire (another class) with the effect that the test may not be satisfied. In addition, the beneficiaries must not be numerically negligible and must comprise a sufficient section of the community to be treated as charitable. These are flexible questions for the court to decide.

QUESTION 22

What is the meaning of 'public benefit' in the law of charity, and how do the courts determine whether it exists?

Aim Higher

The justification of the public benefit test is that the law admitted the special status and privileges of charitable trusts and required in return that the benefits thereby granted are not confined to a select few, especially those with some special status or those with an affinity with the person establishing the charitable trust. In addition, not all purposes which were beneficial to the community were treated as charitable; rather, the courts were concerned with purposes which were beneficial in a charitable sense as divined from the spirit and intendment of the **1601 Preamble**.

Common Pitfalls

The two meanings of the 'public element' are often confused by students. In addition, the courts adopted a diverse approach to this principle that varied with the charitable purpose. It is also important to note that lack of either criterion may invalidate the intended charitable gift.

How to Answer this Question

❖ The need for a public element in charitable purposes in order to justify their exceptional status and their advantages.

❖ Two meanings of public benefit: type of benefit and range of benefit.

- ❖ Varying nature of public benefit according to each purpose.
- ❖ Various decisions.

Answer Structure

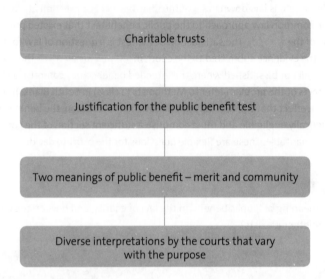

This diagram discloses the rationale and meanings of the public benefit test.

ANSWER

It is a fundamental principle of the law of charities, and affirmed in s 2(1)(b) of the Charities Act 2011, 'that a trust is not charitable unless it is directed to the public benefit'.[9] So spoke Lord Simmonds in *Oppenheim v Tobacco Securities Trust Co Ltd* (1951), confirming a principle that is at the heart of the definition of charity. There is no surprise in this, for not only do charitable trusts have to satisfy less stringent rules for their creation and operation, they also enjoy the protection of the Attorney General and, most importantly, they benefit from extensive fiscal advantages. If the community at large is to subsidise charities financially, it is apparent that the charity itself must be for the benefit of the public.[10] However, while few would argue that charitable trusts must satisfy a requirement of public benefit, there is disagreement as to how this can be both tested and proved. Clearly, as we shall see, 'public benefit' may mean different things in different circumstances and there is no doubt that the degree to which this requirement is applied can vary from charity to charity. Consequently, much turns on the type of charitable purpose being considered and on the precise limitations (if any) which the donor has placed on the gift.

9 Putting the issue posed by the question into context.
10 Justification for the public benefit test.

As a starting point, it must be realised that 'public benefit' has two distinct meanings, although this is not always made clear in the reported cases. First, s 2(1)(b) of the Charities Act 2011 enacts that all charitable purposes must be for the public benefit: that is, it must be inherent in the purpose that it is beneficial to the community. The expression 'public benefit' as used in the Act is given the same meaning as existed at common law: see s 4(3) of the 2011 Act. Nothing that is harmful to the community at large or to the public interest can ever be charitable and perhaps this is why no valid charitable trust can exclude the poor (*Re Macduff* (1896)) and why certain allegedly harmful religious sects can be denied charitable status. In other words, the purpose itself must be beneficial, otherwise the advantages of charitable status will be denied. Second, the purpose which is regarded as beneficial must not normally be confined to such a small section of the population, or be so limited by the stipulations of the testator, as to deny an element of public participation in the purpose.

First, then, what does it mean to say that a charity must be beneficial to the public – that is, of such worth that it requires recognition by the law? Today, charitable trusts are divided into 13 categories as laid down in s 3(1)(a) to (m) of the Charities Act 2011. Prior to the introduction of the Charities Act 2011, if a purpose was shown to be for the relief of poverty, for the advancement of education or for the advancement of religion (currently s 3(1)(a) to (c)), it was presumed to be inherently beneficial (*National Anti-Vivisection Society v IRC* (1948)). The position today is that s 4(2) of the Charities Act 2011 abolishes the presumption of public benefit. Accordingly, all trusts and organisations are required to demonstrate that they satisfy the public benefit test in order to establish their charitable status. Section 4(3) retains the approach of the courts to this question prior to the passing of the Act. In *Independent Schools Council v Charity Commission for England and Wales* [2011] UKUT 421, on a review of the case law the court decided that there was no evidence that a presumption in favour of public benefit was adopted by the courts.

Prior to the introduction of the 2011 Act, proof of public benefit took the form of requiring the courts to consider the Preamble to the Statute of Charitable Uses 1601 and previous cases, and then decide whether there was either a precedent or an analogy for the charitable status of the new purpose (*Williams Trustees v IRC* (1947); *Scottish Burial Reform and Cremation Society Ltd v Glasgow City Corporation* (1968); *Peggs v Lamb* (1994)). It had been suggested in some cases (for example, in *Incorporated Council for Law Reporting for England and Wales v Attorney General* (1971)) that if a purpose was shown to be beneficial to the community *per se*, this should be enough to guarantee charitable status unless some positive harm or unwanted effect can be proven. This approach, which does not appear to have been taken up generally (see the criticism in *Barralet v Attorney General* (1980)), apparently makes it more likely that the meaning of charity will be able to evolve rapidly and in tune with changing patterns of social and economic behaviour as envisaged in s 3 (1)(m) of the Charities Act 2011. However, we must ask whether, in fact, the 'novel' approach really does offer more chance of charitable status than the old 'precedent and analogy' doctrine. In one sense, the new approach merely simplifies the burden of proof when it comes to the beneficial and charitable nature of purposes within s 3(1)(m) of the Charities Act 2011 (the residual category of charitable purposes) and it is highly unlikely that a judge well versed in the law of charities could fail to find a suitable precedent or analogy for a novel purpose that clearly deserved charitable status. In any event, the court is entitled to consider whether the purpose in issue falls within the 'spirit' of a recognised charitable purpose: see s 3(1)(m)(iii) of the 2011 Act. Consequently, despite this rather theoretical argument about how one establishes whether a purpose falls within s 3(1)(m) of the 2011 Act, it is clear that the courts will be more concerned to establish positively the public benefit test in respect of purposes within the residual category as compared to the other more obviously beneficial purposes.

This leads us to consider the second sense in which 'public benefit' is used within charity law: that is, to convey the idea that the public itself, or a sufficient section of it, must benefit from the charitable purpose. Once again, however, this general statement of principle must be qualified for it is clear that charities for the relief of poverty are not subject to as stringent a test of public benefit as other types of charity (*Isaac v Defriez* (1754), *Re Young* (1951), *Re Segelman* (1996)). Likewise, trusts for 'poor relations' are perfectly valid (*Re Scarisbrick* (1951)), and this concession with regard to the public benefit requirement has been confirmed by the House of Lords in *Dingle v Turner* (1972).

With the special status of trusts for the relief of poverty firmly in mind, how is it possible to determine whether a trust is for the public benefit in the sense of casting its benefits sufficiently widely? There are a number of different points to consider. First, it is obvious that the benefits of a charitable trust must not be restricted to a group of people that are numerically negligible (*Oppenheim v Tobacco Securities Trust Co Ltd* (1951)). The point is that the class of persons who may benefit from the charitable purpose must not be narrowly restricted by definition: it matters not that only a small group of people actually enjoy the benefits of the charitable purpose so long as those benefits are available to the public should they come forward (*IRC v Baddeley* (1955)). In *Baddeley*, Lord Simonds drew a distinction between a form of relief accorded to the whole community, yet, by its nature, advantageous only to a few. This type of relief will satisfy the public benefit test. On the other hand, a form of relief accorded to a select few members of the community out of a large number willing to take advantage of it runs a risk of not satisfying the test. Of course, what is 'numerically negligible' depends on the facts of each case and may vary for different types of charity.

Second, and in a similar vein, although the benefits derived from the charity may be limited to a class of persons (not being numerically negligible; for example, the inhabitants of Whiteshire), they may not be confined to 'a class within a class' (*Williams Trustees v IRC* (1947)). Although this can only be a 'rule of thumb', the idea is that one limitation on the class of persons who may derive a benefit from the charity does not destroy the 'public' character of the trust, but a second or third limitation may well make it so difficult for the public at large to qualify for the charitable benefit that there is no real public benefit at all (*IRC v Baddeley* (1955)). However, one must be careful not to rely overmuch on a rigid application of this principle for there are many class limitations (such as age, location or gender) which will not deprive a class of its public character even if combined with another restriction.

Thirdly, and most controversially, it is possible that a trust will not be regarded as charitable, as lacking the essential element of public benefit, if the potential class of persons likely to benefit are united by a common personal bond. This is known as the '*Compton* test' (from *Re Compton* (1945)), and it was confirmed by the House of Lords in *Oppenheim v Tobacco Securities Trust Co Ltd* (1951). Essentially, the point is that if the class intended to benefit from the charity shares a common personal relationship – perhaps they are all employees of one company or relatives of one person – they may not be capable of being regarded as a section of 'the public', even if numerically very great, as in *Oppenheim* itself. However, there are difficulties here and there are doubts whether this 'personal nexus' test is suitable to determine questions of public benefit. The issue was explored in *Dingle v Turner* (1972), although that case was concerned with the relief of poverty which applied a restricted test of public benefit and therefore rendered its criticisms of *Oppenheim* strictly *obiter*. One important criticism is that it is unclear exactly what the personal nexus test is designed to prevent.[11] For example, does the test invalidate trusts where there is a personal connection between the members of the class and the donor of the money or creator of the trust, or does the test invalidate trusts where there is a personal nexus existing between the members of the class *inter se*, irrespective of their relationship to the donor? If the personal nexus test prevents the second type of trust, then it seems rigid and unnecessary and simply replaces judgment with arbitrariness. The objection that not every member of the public has the potential to join this class – because the tie that binds is 'personal' – is not persuasive. Every charity that utilises a class description may exclude certain persons. For example, a trust for 'women in Wales' forever excludes men. Conversely, if it is the former, then at least it can be justified on the ground that it prevents a donor from using the charitable status of a trust to obtain a private benefit for himself (tax relief and employee fringe benefits) and for persons in whom she has a direct interest (relations, employees, etc).

---

11   Questioning the rationale of a principle of law is permissible provided that the arguments are rational.

In short, then, to require a charitable trust to be for the 'public benefit' encompasses a whole range of different policy considerations about the nature of charity. At the very least, being aware of the two distinct meanings of 'public benefit' should enable a more thorough analysis of the essence of 'charity'. Yet, even within these two broad umbrellas there are shades of meaning and different approaches, not least because the range of charitable purposes is diverse, extensive and expanding.[12]

QUESTION 23

Ivor Evans, managing director of Chem Inc, the former state-owned chemical concern, wishes to establish certain trusts with his own money and with that of the company (which he is empowered to do). He desires to take advantage of the generous fiscal arrangements involving charities, both for his own benefit and for the sake of those who will benefit from the charity. He has four objects in view, namely: first, with his own money, to set up a trust to provide scholarships for study in the field of chemistry at a UK university for disadvantaged children living in Cardiff of Welsh-speaking parents; secondly, with his own money, to provide cut-price food and drink for the Cavendish Amateur Rugby Club where his son is a member; thirdly, with the company's money, to establish a conference centre for the fostering of understanding between the UK and the Far East in order to promote trade in agrochemicals; and fourthly, with the company's money, to establish a nursery school for the children of employees.

▶ Advise Ivor Evans of the extent to which these goals can be achieved within the law of charity.

How to Answer this Question

❖ The extent to which a court should consider the motives of a settlor in establishing charitable trusts.

❖ Trusts for education: public benefit, class within a class.

❖ Trusts for a purpose, or for poverty or within s 5 of the Charities Act 2011: also charitable trust for a relative.

❖ Trust for international co-operation or for education: self-interest.

❖ Trust for education: personal nexus test.

---

12 Succinct conclusion that draws together the arguments raised.

Answer Structure

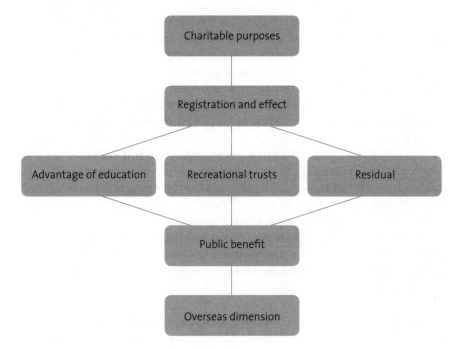

This diagram illustrates the broad nature of charitable purposes.

ANSWER

This question raises difficult issues about the meaning of charitable status, the meaning of public benefit as a test of that status and the extent to which statutory intervention has enabled the achievement of specific kinds of charitable purposes.[13] In general, reference must be made to the new definition of charitable purposes as laid down in s 3 of the Charities Act 2011, the considerable wealth of case law on the meaning of charity prior to 2011, the various ways in which a court will determine whether an apparently charitable purpose has a sufficient element of public benefit as defined in the 2011 Act, the provision of recreational facilities under s 5 of the Charities Act 2011 and the extent to which the fiscal advantages enjoyed by charities should influence a court in deciding whether to declare a trust charitable in the first place.

Clearly, the donor in this case has specific purposes in view, and it is important to advise him at the outset that each purpose should be allocated a specific and certain sum of money, distinct from that set aside for the other purposes. The reason for this is twofold:

13 Summary of legal issues within the question.

first, to ensure that if any one of the four purposes is declared void as a non-charitable purpose trust, it will not then taint any other disposition; secondly, in recognition of the fact that different charitable purposes have different shades of meaning as to whether there is a 'public benefit' and should, therefore, be kept discrete if possible (*IRC v Baddeley* (1955)).[14] In addition, it would be prudent to inform the donor that while his motives in establishing the trusts are usually irrelevant in deciding whether a purpose is charitable – charitable status being a matter of law, not intention (*National Anti-Vivisection Society v IRC* (1948)) – some case law suggests that the donor's desire to achieve fiscal advantages for himself can be relevant in denying charitable status in marginal cases (*Dingle v Turner* (1972); *Scottish Burial Reform and Cremation Society Ltd v Glasgow City Corporation* (1968)). In more recent cases, however, it has been stated that fiscal considerations should not be used to deny the existence of a charity otherwise validly created and that a benign construction of a charitable purpose should be adopted wherever possible (*IRC v McMullen* (1981); *Guild v IRC* (1992)). Consequently, we need only warn Ivor Evans that the trusts should be so constructed as to conform to the conditions required for charitable status, particularly that of public benefit, and that any hint that these were merely tax-reduction schemes should be avoided. What is required is a clear charitable purpose and a clear benefit to the community: if fiscal advantages are thereby given, all well and good.

Turning then to the first alleged charitable purpose, it is immediately apparent that there are two possible ways in which this purpose might be regarded as charitable.[15] First, this could be regarded as an educational charity within s 3(1)(b) of the Charities Act 2011 for, clearly, the primary motive is to establish scholarships for academic study (*McGovern v Attorney General* (1982); *IRC v Educational Grants Association Ltd* (1967)). If this is so, the donor may well have difficulties in establishing that it is for the benefit of the public or a section thereof. The class of persons entitled to such scholarships is quite restricted, needing to fulfil three conditions (being disadvantaged, living in Cardiff, and of Welsh-speaking parents). While the reference to 'disadvantaged' does not negate public benefit (after all, that is the essence of charity), overall this may well be regarded as a 'class within a class' and too narrowly drawn to confer a benefit on the public, as in *Williams Trustees v IRC* (1947), itself a case concerning persons from Wales. In the end, it will be a matter for judgment, although if the donor wishes to avoid these problems he could amend the class-limiting factors.[16] Second, it is possible that this might be regarded as a trust for the relief of poverty, in that it is for 'disadvantaged' persons. It is arguable that this construction would avoid the 'public benefit' difficulties just discussed (*Dingle v Turner* (1972)); the better view is that the purpose of the trust is educational and that the disadvantaged nature of the persons who might benefit is a

---

14   This is good advice on drafting such clauses.

15   Identification of the possible solutions.

16   Having recognised flexible issues of law, it is advisable not to draw a definitive conclusion.

subsidiary factor. In summary, there is a good argument that this will be an educational charity, provided difficulties over the 'public' nature of the benefits thereby conferred can be overcome.

The second intended charity also poses some problems. First, s 3(1)(g) of the Charities Act 2011 has enacted that the advancement of amateur sport is a charitable purpose. This marks a reversal of the law that preceded the introduction of the Act. At common law the promotion of sport *simpliciter* was treated as outside the law of charities because such objective was not within the Preamble to the Statute of Charitable Uses 1601: see *Re Nottage* (1895). 'Amateur sport' has not been defined in the 2011 Act but the court will, no doubt, apply the ordinary dictionary meaning to the phrase and contrast it with professional sport. The expression 'sport' has been defined in s 3(2)(d) of the 2011 Act as 'sports or games which promote health by involving physical or mental skill or exertion'. Clearly the facilities of a rugby club will satisfy this requirement. It is also arguable that the provision of this sport will be charitable under s 5 of the Charities Act 2011 as the facilities are provided in the interests of social welfare, defined in s 5 of the 2011 Act. This provision had been interpreted fairly liberally in *Guild v IRC* (1992). Secondly, the provision of sport within a school or a university has been treated as charitable for the advancement of education: see *Re Mariette* (1915) and *IRC v McMullen* (1981). With regard to the facts of the problem there seems to be no connection between the Cavendish Amateur Rugby Club and the educational environment. Potentially the gift may satisfy the test laid down in s 3(1)(g) of the 2011 Act. Thirdly, a charitable purpose is required to satisfy the test of public benefit. The presumption of public benefit in respect of some charities (if it had been applied by the courts) has now been abolished by virtue of s 4(2) of the Charities Act 2011. Today, all trusts or organisations are required to demonstrate that this test is satisfied. The common law practice of interpreting this test has been expressly retained by s 4(3) of the 2011 Act. In our case, providing that Ivor Evans's donation can be regarded as for the Cavendish Rugby Club *per se* – and not just for the provision of cut-price food and drink to a group who happen to be defined as members of the Cavendish Amateur Rugby Club – we need only ask whether they constitute a sufficient section of the public. Generally, it is clear that members of a club or other institution can qualify as a section of the public, providing that membership is not limited to such a small group as to make it self-selecting, and even this might be overcome if the members then go out into the community as better citizens (*Neville Estates v Madden* (1962)). Likewise, although a personal link or nexus between a donor and the class to benefit from a charity will normally negate any public benefit (*Oppenheim v Tobacco Securities Trust Co Ltd* (1951)), *Re Koettgen* (1954) suggests that there is no objection if merely a proportion of the intended class is linked to the donor. *A fortiori*, the fact that just one person – the donor's son – is a member of the club does not destroy the public nature of its purpose. Whether the test is satisfied on the facts of this problem will depend on the size of membership of the club. If it is negligible, the club may fail to satisfy the public benefit test. The court has a wide discretion in deciding this issue.

Under the third intended trust, Ivor Evans wishes to use the company's money to establish a conference centre. This will be difficult to justify as a charitable trust. In general terms, a trust for the promotion of international harmony and understanding is not charitable (*Re Astor* (1952); *Re Strakosch* (1949)), although it seems that some trusts for the promotion of a trade or occupation may be charitable if they are in some way educational (*Construction Industry Training Board v Attorney General* (1973)). However, following *Re Koeppler* (1984), the establishment of a centre simply as a forum for fostering international relations cannot be charitable unless there is a substantial educational element. There is no evidence of that here, and, indeed, there seems to be a personal motive behind the company's offer to provide these funds.

Finally, there is the aim of establishing a nursery school for the children of employees. The purpose itself seems charitable, being for the advancement of education, at least if the school is non-profit-making (*Abbey, Malvern Wells Ltd v Minister of Local Government and Housing* (1951)). Unfortunately, however, there is a very real possibility that this trust will fail because it violates the 'personal nexus test' and therefore fails to be for the benefit of the public (*Re Compton* (1945); *Oppenheim v Tobacco Securities Trust Co Ltd* (1951)). The test put forward in these cases apparently makes it impossible for the persons intended to benefit from the charitable purpose to share a personal link with each other and with the donor of the charitable funds. In our case, a personal link exists because all the children are of employees of the company and the donor is the employer. The case is on par with *Oppenheim*. Needless to say, the efficacy of this test has been challenged (for example, in *Dingle v Turner* (1972)), but it is designed to ensure that a donor does not derive a private benefit, with fiscal advantages, from what is supposed to be a public purpose. Consequently, even though the motives of Chem Inc may be of the purest kind, the fact that this trust would confer benefits on their own employees, making employment at the company more attractive and the workforce more content, is enough to deprive the intended trust of charitable status.

NOTE

This is a fairly standard question on the law of charity, and it calls for a good knowledge of case law and of the meaning of public benefit. Note, also, that the question does not raise one of the other examinable issues, that of the political nature of charities. Generally, a purpose cannot be charitable if it is political, and this includes those organisations which campaign for a change in the law because it is not appropriate for a court to judge whether a change in the law is of public benefit (see *McGovern v Attorney General* (1982); *Bowman v Secular Society* (1917); *Southwood v Attorney General* (2000)).

QUESTION 24

Consider the validity of the following gifts in the will of Daphne, who died in 2010:

(a) £100,000 to my trustees for the establishment and maintenance of a walled garden within the precincts of St Luke's Church, for the quiet reflection of the parishioners;

(b) £10,000 to my trustees to be distributed to such organisations involved in the protection of the environment and related causes as they shall in their absolute discretion select; and

(c) £50,000 to my trustees for the promotion of tennis in the public schools of Derbyshire.

Aim Higher

Problem questions on charities may involve a variety of issues. It is necessary to present the points in a clear and logical order.

Common Pitfalls

Examinees do not always address the issues raised by reference to the instructions. This question requires analysis of the ultimate validity of the gifts and therefore examinees ought to consider *inter alia* private purpose trusts and resulting trusts in the event of the gifts failing as charitable purposes.

How to Answer this Question

❖ Brief introductory points about the definition of charity;

❖ Possible failure of the stipulated purposes as private purpose trusts;

❖ Trusts for the *promotion* of religion: activities within a religious context *per se* might not be enough;

❖ Trusts for other purposes beneficial to the community and questions of exclusivity of charitable purpose;

❖ Environmental protection – a charitable purpose within s 3(1)(i) of the 2011 Act, but is 'related purposes' too vague?

❖ Trusts for education: issue of public benefit;

❖ Charitable purposes – the advancement of amateur sport, s 3(1)(g) and s 5 (provision of recreational facilities) of the Charities Act 2011.

Applying the Law

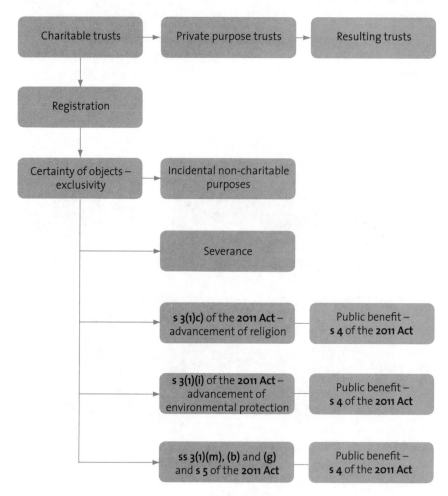

This diagram illustrates the holistic nature of dealing with purpose trusts first as charitable trusts, second as private purpose trusts and finally as resulting trusts.

ANSWER

In this problem, Daphne has attempted to establish trusts for the achievement of certain purposes. It is trite law that a trust cannot exist for a purpose, save in exceptional circumstances or unless that purpose is in law charitable (*Re Endacott* (1960)). As far as Daphne's three distinct dispositions are concerned, it is highly unlikely that any of them falls into the category of valid private purpose trusts. There is nothing here that would fall within the exceptional categories identified in *Re Endacott* and any possibility of the trust for the establishment of a walled garden falling within *Re Denley* (1969) is negated by the fact that this trust (as with the others) is clearly designed to last in perpetuity.[17]

Fortunately, however, charitable trusts do not require human objects and are not void even if of perpetual duration.[18] The crucial question then becomes whether any of these three dispositions falls within the statutory definition of 'charitable purposes' laid down in s 3 of the Charities Act 2011. Before considering this in detail, brief mention should be made of some basic points. First, all charities are required to be registered with the Charity Commission (s 30 of the Charities Act 2011), subject to a number of limited exceptions. Section 37 of the Charities Act 2011 enacts that an institution that has been registered shall be 'conclusively presumed' to be a charity. Thus the first stage in determining the status of these institutions is the application to the Commission for registration. Second, a charitable trust will not exist unless the trust property is devoted exclusively to the charitable purpose: see s 1(1)(a) of the Charities Act 2011 and *Attorney General of the Bahamas v Royal Trust Co* (1986)). Third, all charitable trusts must be for the 'public benefit', see ss 2(1)(b) and 4 of the Charities Act 2011, although this requirement will be satisfied in different ways by different types of charity (*Oppenheim v Tobacco Securities Trust Co Ltd* (1951)). Fourth, the definition of charity is a matter of law as laid down in s 3(1) of the 2011 Act in the form of 13 purposes, independent of the testator's intentions (*National Anti-Vivisection Society v IRC* (1948)). Finally, charitable purposes under the 2011 Act are construed in accordance with the wealth of case law decided over several centuries: see ss 3(3) and 3(1)m) of the 2011 Act.[19]

(a) '£100,000 to my trustees for the establishment and maintenance of a walled garden within the precincts of St Luke's Church, for the quiet reflection of the parishioners'

This particular trust does have the potential to fall within the *Denley* exception to the rule against purpose trusts, although this is unlikely in practice because of the donor's intention to establish a trust in perpetuity. However, it may be that this trust is within the scope of trusts for the advancement of religion within s 3(1)(c) of the 2011 Act and is thereby charitable. There is no doubt here that the proposed trust is connected with a religious establishment and questions concerning the disputed status of some faiths and beliefs are not relevant. The definition of 'religion' within s 3(2)(a) is extremely broad and inclusive: see, for example, *Funnell v Stewart* (1996) 'faith healing'. Yet, it is unclear whether trusts for religious purposes *per se* can be charitable if they are not otherwise for the advancement of religion (*Oxford Group v IRC* (1949)).[20] Furthermore, in our case, the actual purpose seems to be the establishment of a walled garden 'for quiet reflection'

---

17 Outline consideration as to whether the gifts create private purpose trusts.
18 One of the advantages of charitable status.
19 Concise statement of relevant points regarding charitable status.
20 Highlighting the relevant issue in the problem.

and it might be argued that this is not even a religious purpose, as believers are not the only persons able and willing to engage in contemplation (*Re Macaulay's Estate* (1943)). On the other hand, gifts for the maintenance and enhancement of buildings within a church are routinely held to be charitable (*Re Raine* (1956)), as are some matters connected with the church even though they appear far removed from the promotion of the religion itself (*Re Royce* (1940): benefit of church choir).

The matter here is one of construction of the trust instrument in the light of existing case law.[21] The fact that the walled garden must be erected within the fabric of a church is powerful evidence in favour of a charity for the advancement of religion, as is the fact that the anticipated benefit will fall on parishioners (*Re Norton's Will Trusts* (1948)). The only other tenable view is that the reference to 'quiet reflection' may introduce a non-charitable element into the equation and may make the gift void as not being exclusively devoted to charity.[22] Finally, should it be held that this purpose falls within the definition of charity *per se*, it is clear that there is a sufficient element of public benefit. The walled garden would be open to all parishioners and we can legitimately assume that these are neither numerically negligible nor 'a class within a class' (*Williams Trustees v IRC* (1947)). This case is not on a par with *Gilmour v Coats* (1949). In that case, the contemplative nature of the purpose was held to confer no public benefit because the value of prayer could not be proven and because the nuns were cloistered, limited in number and did not participate in community life. Our case, however, may be similar to *Neville Estates v Madden* (1962), where there was a sufficient element of public benefit because the persons enriched by the advancement of religion continued to be members of the community.

(b) '£10,000 to my trustees to be distributed to such organisations involved in the protection of the environment and related causes as they shall in their absolute discretion select'

It is in order for a charitable trust to allow the trustees some discretion in the selection of charitable objects provided, of course, that the trustees are required by the trust to exercise that discretion in favour of objects that are exclusively charitable (*Houston v Burns* (1918)). In this particular case, there are two issues: first, whether the 'protection of the environment' is itself charitable; and second, whether the trustees' ability to use the money for 'related causes' has any bearing on the matter.[23]

As far as the protection of the environment is concerned, this is likely to be a purpose that falls within s (3)(1)(i) of the 2011 Act 'the advancement of environmental protection' and /or

---

21   These are flexible questions of law.

22   This concerns the test of certainty of charitable objects.

23   Concise statement of the issues in this question.

s 3(1)(m) of the 2011 Act, the category of 'other purposes beneficial to the community'. This is despite the fact that there is some doubt as to how we are to determine whether any given purpose is charitable within s 3(1)(m). Section 3(1)(m)(i) to (iii) offers some guidance by reference to the approach adopted by case law. According to Russell LJ in *Incorporated Council for Law Reporting for England and Wales v Attorney General* (1971), a court is entitled to assume that if a purpose is in itself beneficial to the community, it is also charitable in law. On the other hand, the more traditional approach requires that there must be some precedent or analogy with charitable purposes or previous case law before a new purpose which is beneficial in itself can also be regarded as charitable (*Williams Trustees v IRC* (1947); *Peggs v Lamb* (1994)).

Fortunately in our case, a trust for the protection of the environment is undoubtedly regarded as charitable. Certainly, the preservation of historic buildings and gardens is charitable (*Re Verrall* (1916)), as are trusts for natural amenities (*Re Corelli* (1943)). In addition, the Charity Commission explained that a trust to promote conservation must *inter alia* satisfy the criterion of merit or conserve something which deserves protection. This will be dependent on expert evidence in marginal cases. Undoubtedly, the protection of the environment will satisfy the public benefit test. There is no stipulation limiting use of the property to any specific class or type of person and nothing that suggests that the benefits of the charity *per se* are private and intangible. What, then, of the trustees' ability to use the money for 'related causes'? This, again, is a matter of construction. If 'related causes' can be interpreted to mean exclusively environmental purposes, then there should be no problem with the validity of this charitable gift and it is suggested that this is the most sensible view of Daphne's disposition. If, on the other hand, 'related causes' may encompass worthwhile but non-charitable purposes, then the gift may fail as not being exclusively devoted to charity (*Blair v Duncan* (1902)), at least unless the non-charitable purpose is merely subsidiary to the performance of the charitable object (*Re Coxen* (1948)) or can be severed from it (*Lambert v Thwaites* (1866)). Subject, then, to resolving the 'related causes' issue, this is a charitable gift.

(c) '£50,000 to my trustees for the promotion of tennis in the public schools of Derbyshire'

This is the most straightforward of Daphne's dispositions. Section 3(1)(b) of the 2011 Act confirms that the 'advancement of education' is a charitable purpose. The provision of sport within schools is clearly for the advancement of education in that it involves the development of the mind and body. It was recognised by the House of Lords in *IRC v McMullen* (1981) that a trust to provide sporting facilities for schools was itself charitable as furthering the education of pupils. This would seem to cover our case. In addition, the endowment and maintenance of independent (that is, 'public') schools is a charitable purpose, even if some charge is made to parents for tuition fees, providing that the school is not run for profit for the benefit of private individuals: see *Independent Schools Council v Charity Commission* (2011). Moreover, if it should be objected that the scope of Daphne's charitable purpose is limited to a particular area and might fail the test of public benefit (whereas in *McMullen* it was any school within the UK), the trust in *Re Mariette* (1915) was charitable and this concerned the provision of sporting facilities at just one school (and that was an independent one). *A fortiori*, a trust for the promotion of sport in several schools must be charitable.

In addition, the advancement of amateur sport by virtue of s 3(1)g) of the 2011 Act is now treated as a charitable purpose. 'Sport' is defined in s 3(2)(d) as sport or games which promote physical or mental skill or exertion. Clearly tennis satisfies this definition and there is no indication that it is other than the advancement of tennis amongst amateurs and therefore a charitable activity. Finally, the tests of 'public benefit' and 'interests of social welfare' under s 5 of the 2011 Act appear to be satisfied on these facts and will serve as a separate ground to support its charitable status.

QUESTION 25

Consider the validity of the following dispositions in the will of Freddie, who died this year:

(a) £10,000 on trust for the preservation of the habitat of the colony of badgers that is threatened by the work on the Manchester ring road;

(b) £10,000 to the inhabitants of Littleham for the provision of a new swimming pool to be used solely by the residents thereof for such a period as the law allows;

(c) £10,000 to provide scholarships for entry to Cavendish College, my old school, providing that at least 75 per cent of the money be allocated to the sons of old boys; and

(d) £10,000 to my trustees, the income to be used for 30 years by the Lifeboat Association for the provision of rescue crafts, thence on trust for the purposes of the Society for the Promotion of Tiddlywinks.

Aim Higher

This is a difficult problem as it combines the law of charities, non-charitable purpose trusts and perpetuities. It demonstrates the wisdom of a thorough treatment of all purpose trusts and an understanding of the close relationship between the charitable and non-charitable variety.

Common Pitfalls ✘

It is tempting for students to ignore the rule against perpetuities. But the introduction of the **Perpetuities and Accumulations Act 2009** has the effect of simplifying the law and no doubt increases its attraction as a subject for study.

How to Answer this Question

❖ A brief note that this question covers both charitable and non-charitable purpose trusts.
❖ Protection of the countryside, possible political objectives, trusts beneficial to the community.
❖ Recreational charities, restricted classes, *Re Denley* purpose trust.
❖ Educational trust: limited beneficiaries, personal nexus.
❖ Gift to charity, followed by a gift to a purpose trust, perpetuity problems.

Answer Structure

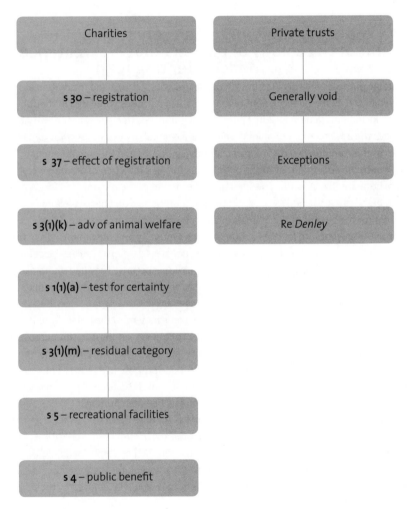

This diagram depicts the multiplicity of charitable purposes and effect of failure of the intended express trust.

ANSWER

Freddie, the testator, has included a number of dispositions in his will, all of which involve consideration of purpose trusts or related concepts. At the outset, it is important to bear in mind two general principles, reliance on which will help determine the validity of Freddie's proposed gifts.[24] First, it is not possible to create a trust for a non-charitable purpose, save in the most exceptional cases (*Re Endacott* (1960) and *Re Denley* (1969)). Such trusts are void and the property will result to the estate of the testator. Second, and in contrast, should a purpose fall within the legal definition of charity, there may be a perfectly valid purpose trust which may last in perpetuity and which will enjoy considerable legal and fiscal advantages. In fact, the dispositions in this problem concern both charitable and non-charitable purpose trusts.

(a) £10,000 on trust for the preservation of the habitat of the colony of badgers that is threatened by the work on the Manchester ring road

Charitable purposes are specified in s 3(1) of the Charities Act 2011 and in addition are required to satisfy the public benefit test. There are 13 purposes stipulated in the sub-section, including a general residual purpose in s 3(1)(m). Section 3(1)(k) of the 2011 Act identifies the advancement of animal welfare as a charitable purpose. Section 3(3) preserves the common law meaning of charitable purposes and the public benefit test. Prior to the enactment of the 2011 Act, trusts for the protection of animals were held to be charitable as within the spirit and intendment of the preamble to the Statute of Charitable Uses 1601. In *Re Wedgwood* (1915) the court upheld an animal welfare trust, not for the benefit of the animals in their own right but on the ground that such trusts may promote feelings of humanity and morality amongst mankind. On this basis a trust has been upheld for a home for lost dogs, in *Re Douglas* (1887). The point is, however, that at common law such trusts are charitable because they benefit mankind – being displays of generosity and human kindness, or as protecting animals useful to man – and not because they benefit the animals *per se* (*Re Grove-Grady* (1929)). Consequently, Freddie's trust must demonstrate some benefit to the public from the protection of these animals, and while the display of human kindness in this purpose is evident, it might not be enough. However, s 3(1)(k) of the 2011 Act specifically enacts that the advancement of animal welfare is a charitable purpose in its own right. Despite these clear words it is reasonable to suppose that the court will imply a limitation, to the effect that in the event of a conflict of interests between humans and animals, the human interest will prevail, as was the case in *National Anti-Vivisection Society v IRC* (1948), where the court decided that the advancement of medical science and research far outweighed the welfare of animals used in such research. In addition, the public benefit test enacted in s 4 of the Charities Act 2011 requires the executors of Freddie's will to demonstrate positively the benefit that would be enjoyed by the

---

24 It is advisable to adopt a holistic approach to the question.

community in preserving the habitat of the colony of badgers as opposed to the work on the Manchester ring road. This could prove to be extremely difficult to justify. Moreover, there is a risk that this purpose will be denied charitable status because of its actual or potential political overtones.[25] It is a clear principle that charities may not engage in political activities and may not attempt to cloak political objectives with more benign purposes (*Bowman v Secular Society* (1917); *McGovern v Attorney General* (1982); *Southwood v Attorney General* (2000)). In our case, this might be seen as an attempt to protect the countryside from transport policies approved by Parliament and this can too easily be regarded as political, especially if it involves a campaigning or propaganda element. So, even if this purpose does manifest a sufficient public benefit, the desire to protect animals may be so bound up with political objectives that its charitable status should be denied.

(b) £10,000 to the inhabitants of Littleham for the provision of a new swimming pool to be used solely by the residents thereof for such a period as the law allows

This is clearly an attempt to establish a trust for a recreational purpose. In general a trust for recreation or sport *per se* is not charitable (*Re Nottage* (1895)), although the matter would be different if the recreation was tied to an educational purpose (*IRC v McMullen* (1981)) or some other charitable object. Conversely, trusts for the provision of land for recreation can be charitable, even if limited to persons from a particular locality (*Re Hadden* (1932)), although this was not extended to an indoor swimming pool in *Valuation Commissioner for Northern Ireland v Lurgan BC* (1968). In the light of this rather clear authority, it seems unlikely that Freddie's trust will be charitable under the general law. Fortunately, that is not the end of the matter. First, it could be that this trust can be charitable under s 5 of the Charities Act 2011 if the recreational facilities are provided in the interests of social welfare, this being where the facilities are provided with the object of improving the conditions of life of the people of Littleham, being persons in need of such facilities by reason of age, infirmity or social and economic considerations (s 5(2) and (3) of the 2011 Act). Moreover, since *Guild v IRC* (1992), it is clear that the persons benefiting from the recreational purpose do not need to be 'deprived' in order to have their conditions of life improved. It is enough if the general conditions of life for members of the public are improved. In our case, provided that the people of Littleham constitute a section of the public (as they are almost bound to do, *Re Hadden* (1932)), this purpose may fall within the Act and be charitable, as was a trust for a similar leisure facility in *Guild*.

Second, even if this purpose is deemed non-charitable, it might still be valid as being within the *Re Denley* (1969) exception to the rule against purpose trusts. Indeed, this does seem to be a trust which indirectly benefits ascertainable individuals and it is limited to the perpetuity period by the reference to 'such a period as the law allows'. In fact, the

---

25 Identification of a non-charitable element.

case is very similar to *Denley* itself and Freddie's estate can be content that, at the very least, he has established a valid non-charitable purpose trust.[26]

(c) £10,000 to provide scholarships for entry to Cavendish College, my old school, providing that at least 75 per cent of the money be allocated to the sons of old boys

In essence, this aspect of Freddie's will encompasses an attempt to establish an educational charitable trust. There is, of course, no doubt that the provision of scholarships is for the advancement of education (*Christ's College Cambridge* (1757)). Unfortunately, there is some doubt as to whether this particular trust is for the 'public benefit', this being an essential requirement of charitable status (*Oppenheim v Tobacco Securities Trust Co Ltd* (1951)), and see s 3(1)(b) of the Charities Act 2011. Public benefit is defined in s 4 of the 2011 Act in accordance with the law that existed before the passing of the Act. Clearly there is a common characteristic shared by most of the persons intended to receive scholarships and this may fall foul of the personal nexus test put forward in *Oppenheim* although, in our case, it is not clear whether being the son of an old boy is 'personal' in this sense. In fact, our doubts about the applicability of the *Oppenheim* test may go further, for there is no common link between the donor of the money and the intended class, merely between most of the class *inter se*. Likewise, there are cases where educational trusts and scholarships for limited classes of persons have been held charitable (*Attorney General v Sidney Sussex College* (1869)). Perhaps the most helpful authority is *Re Koettgen* (1954) where there was a valid educational trust even though the trustees were directed to exercise a preference for employees of a single company in respect of 75 per cent of the total donation. Using that as a reference point, Freddie's trustees may well be successful in establishing the charitable nature of this part of his testamentary dispositions. It ought to be pointed out that *Re Koettgen* was severely criticised by Lord Radcliffe in the Privy Council decision *Caffoor v Commissioners of Income Tax* (1961) as essentially an 'employee trust' and comes close to being inconsistent with the *Oppenheim* case. In *IRC v Educational Grants Association* (1967) the Court of Appeal refused to follow the reasoning in *Re Koettgen*.

(d) £10,000 to my trustees, the income to be used for 30 years by the Lifeboat Association for the provision of rescue crafts, thence on trust for the purposes of the Society for the Promotion of Tiddlywinks

There is clear authority that trusts for rescue services are charitable, being for purposes beneficial to the community (*Re Wokingham Fire Brigade Trusts* (1951)). The Royal National Lifeboat Institution is a charitable organisation and, by analogy, so should be a gift to this Lifeboat Association for the provision of rescue craft. This principle has been affirmed in

---

26 It is good technique to consider the validity of the gift as a private purpose trust after considering the law of charities.

s 3(1)(l) of the Act – the promotion of the efficiency of the rescue services. However, the issue that requires consideration is the legal position with regard to the gift over. After 30 years, the £10,000 capital sum is to be given to the Society for the Promotion of Tiddlywinks, which is most unlikely to be regarded as charitable, being recreational and unlikely to fall within s 5 (*Re Nottage* (1895) and s 3(1)(g) of the 2011 Act). This is, then, a gift to charity, followed by a gift over for a non-charitable purpose. In these circumstances, any potential perpetuities problem will be avoided by the clear, certain and generous perpetuity period of 125 years, introduced by the Perpetuities and Accumulations Act 2009. The effect is that the gift over to the non-charitable society will take effect 30 years after the Lifeboat Association had the use of the income.

Three additional issues may require consideration had the facts been clearer.[27] These are, first, that the position if the Tiddlywinks Society did not exist at the relevant time of vesting. In this event the possibility of a resulting trust of the funds would be a consideration. Second, the validity of a gift to an unincorporated association and the various solutions adopted by the courts would have warranted discussion had the facts been clearer. Finally, the issue arises as to whether the income alone from the trust fund or, alternatively, the entire fund is to be taken by the society. If, on construction, the income is devoted to the society, the gift may fail for infringing the perpetuity period. This issue will be avoided if the entire fund is to be transferred to the society.

QUESTION 26

In what circumstances may a charitable gift be applied *cy-près*?

Aim Higher ★

Cases on the meaning of 'spirit of the gift' (and now included in 'appropriate considerations') in **s 62** of the **Charities Act 2011** are rare and rather inconclusive. The best authority is the Australian case, *Forrest v AG*, referred to below.

Common Pitfalls ✗

Students are strongly advised to appreciate the distinction between the *cy-près* application of funds from cases where one charity succeeds another and takes over its assets. In the second case, there is no failure of the original gift. Of course, if *cy-près* is called for, the property can be distributed to an organisation with similar objects to the original donee – even one which claimed but failed to be a successor in title.

---

27 Additional considerations where the facts are unclear.

How to Answer this Question

❖ Purpose of *cy-près*.
❖ Difference between initial and subsequent impossibility.
❖ Construing the nature of the failure: hence role for *cy-près*.
❖ Statutory modifications to *cy-près*: Charities Act 2011.

Answer Structure

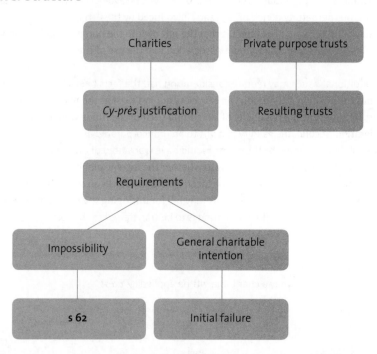

This diagram shows the various steps that need to be overcome before a fund may be applied cy-près.

ANSWER

In the normal course of events, when a trust fails, the trust property will revert to the settlor or to the testator's estate under a resulting trust. This will be so whether the trust fails because of some initial defect, so that all the original trust property is held on resulting trust (*Sprange v Barnard* (1789)), or because the beneficiaries have received all they are entitled to under the trust and some unexpended trust property remains (*Re Abbott* (1900)). However, charitable trusts are different.[28] There is a public interest in ensuring that once money has been effectively dedicated to charity – and all the

---

28 Putting the *cy-près* doctrine in context.

advantages of charitable status have accrued – it should thereafter remain in the public domain and be used so far as is possible in fulfilment of the original charitable purposes. Consequently, when a charitable trust fails, the trust property may be applied by the court or Charity Commission for charitable purposes as near as possible (cy-près) to those originally laid down by the settlor or testator (Re Prison Charities (1873)).

The principles governing cy-près are to be found in the common law as supplemented by what is now s 62 of the Charities Act 2011 (formerly s 13 of the Charities Act 1960 which was repealed and replaced by s 13 of the Charities Act 1993). In essence, property which is subject to a trust for a charitable purpose (and this must be determined before all else) may be applied cy-près when the charitable purpose is either impossible or impractical to achieve, or if one of the events specified in s 62 of the Charities Act 2011 has occurred. Of course, there are conditions to be satisfied before charitable property can be applied cy-près and, if they are not met, the property will then result to the settlor or testator's estate in the normal way: Re Rymer (1895). The basic position is that cy-près will operate when:

(a)   a charitable trust fails; and
(b)   this is a result of either initial impossibility/impracticality or subsequent impossibility/impracticality, itself to be determined under the common law as supplemented by s 62 of the 2011 Act.[29]

In order for the court or Charity Commission to apply a gift cy-près, it is essential that the now failed trust must have been charitable in the first place. This is obvious, but nonetheless crucial, for if the trust was not originally charitable, the property will immediately result to the donor (Re Endacott (1960)). Likewise, it must be clear that the charitable trust has actually failed, and this is not always readily apparent. For example, in those situations where the donor has intended to make a gift on trust to an avowedly charitable organisation, but that organisation does not exist at the time the gift takes effect, it may be that a successor organisation has taken over the original charity and is entitled to receive the donation. The point in cases such as this is that the gift itself has never actually failed, merely that the organisation administering the gift has changed. Indeed, this approach – which is really about successors in title – can be adopted when the 'new' organisation is carrying on the same purposes as the original organisation (Re Roberts (1963)) or when it is not (Re Faraker (1912)). In fact, it matters not that the 'new' charity has a different name or operates in a different geographical area.

Assuming, then, that both the donor's original gift was charitable in law and that there is no legal successor to the now defunct original donee, the property of the charitable trust

---

29 Express acknowledgement that the cy-près doctrine is applicable only to charitable gifts.

may be applied *cy-près* if there is initial impossibility/impracticality or subsequent impossibility/impracticality in the performance of the trust. As noted below, it is very important to be able to distinguish between *initial* failure and *subsequent* failure, because different conditions for *cy-près* apply to each case.

Cases of initial impossibility or impracticality of the donor's original charitable purpose can arise in an infinite number of situations. Typical examples are where property has been given to a specific charity which no longer exists and has no successor in title (*Re Rymer* (1895)); where a named charitable organisation never existed (*Re Harwood* (1936)); where external factors make achievement of the original purpose impossible (*Biscoe v Jackson* (1887): no land available); and where the intended donees cannot use the gift due to the donor's limitations on its use (*Re Dominion Students Hall Trust* (1947); *Re Woodhams* (1981)). Moreover, although the court has always taken a generous view of what was 'impossible' or 'impractical', since the enactment of s 13 of the Charities Act 1960 (now s 62 of the Charities Act 2011) 'the circumstances in which the original purposes of a charitable gift can be altered to allow the property or part of it to be applied *cy-près*' have been considerably extended. In essence, those circumstances now include cases where although possible to carry out the donor's wishes, it is simply absurd, uneconomical, or pointless to do so. Again, typical examples of *cy-près* under the Act are where a charity's income is either too small or too large for the donor's original purposes or where amalgamation with another charity would achieve more effectively those charitable purposes. In short, the court or the Charity Commission now has a *cy-près* jurisdiction where the 'original purposes' (see *Oldham Metropolitan BC v Attorney General* (1993)) are possible but not practical or feasible and if this is apparent at the time the gift takes effect, there is initial 'impracticality'.

Whatever the reason that a charitable trust is deemed initially impossible or impractical (with or without the intervention of s 62), there can be no application of the property *cy-près* unless the terms of the trust disclose a 'paramount intention' to give to charity, otherwise known as a 'general charitable intention'.[30] This was the position before the Act (*Re Wilson* (1913)) and remains so afterwards (s 62(3)). The essence of the matter is that, with initial impossibility or impracticality, the trust property has not yet vested in a charitable purpose. It must be clear that the donor was more concerned with achieving the charitable purpose *per se* than making a gift to the specific charity that is now defunct. Hence the need for a general charitable intention. Not surprisingly, whether such an intention exists is a matter of construction of each charitable gift, although without the existence of such an intention, the property will result to the donor. In one circumstance, however, a general charitable intention will be deemed to exist by force of statute. Under ss 63–66 of the Charities Act 2011 (formerly s 14 of the Charities Act 1960,

----

30 Second requirement for the *cy-près* doctrine.

which was repealed and replaced by s 14 of the Charities Act 1993), property given by anonymous donors shall be deemed to be given for general charitable purposes after suitable advertisements have been made and property raised through collection boxes and raffles etc, and shall be deemed from the start to be made with such an intention. This is an entirely practical solution that will prevent large sums of money from being held indefinitely on resulting trust for donors who might never appear. Section 67 of the Charities Act 2011 empowers the court or the Charity Commission to make a scheme that alters the charitable purposes to such an extent that the court or Commission may consider appropriate. Section 67 also sets out the matters that the court or the Commission may have regard.

Turning now to cases of subsequent impossibility or impracticality,[31] once again the circumstances in which a charitable trust may fail on these grounds are innumerable. The heart of the matter is that the trust property has been given effectively to the original charitable purpose or organisation, but subsequently it has become impossible or impractical to fulfil that purpose, as where there is a surplus of funds after the charitable purpose has been fulfilled (Re Wokingham Fire Brigade Trusts (1951)). Importantly, in cases of subsequent failure, the trust property already has been dedicated to charity and so there is no need to find a general charitable intention before cy-près application can occur. Cy-près may take effect upon the subsequent failure, without more, and this is why it is crucial in practice to be able to distinguish it from cases of initial failure. So, in Re Slevin (1891), there was no need to find a general charitable intention in order to apply the money cy-près: the property became vested in the charity at the testator's death (which did then exist) and so this was a case of subsequent impossibility.

Cases of such obvious subsequent failure are rare for, normally, the achievement of a charitable purpose has simply become outdated or uneconomic, rather than impossible. As such, under the common law, cy-près would not be available and the trust property could not be used effectively. Consequently, in order to allow cy-près application to take place in these circumstances, s 62 of the Charities Act 2011 extends considerably the situations in which the court or the Commission may regard subsequent failure to have occurred. This will now include cases where the charitable purpose has become subsequently impractical or lacks feasibility or is simply uneconomic. Of course, such an extension of the court's powers may well cut across the donor's original intention and for that reason much of the court's jurisdiction under s 62 may be exercised only with regard to 'the appropriate considerations'. The appropriate considerations mean on the one hand the spirit of the gift concerned and, on the other hand, the social and economic circumstances prevailing at the time of the proposed alteration of the original purposes.

---

31 Classification of cases for the purpose of the cy-près doctrine.

While this does not introduce a requirement of a general charitable intention in cases of subsequent failure under the Act, clearly the court cannot proceed immediately to *cy-près* under s 62 without having some regard to the donor's original motives (*Re Lepton's Charity* (1972); *Forrest v Attorney General* (1986), an Australian case construing a similar statutory provision). In fact, s 62 lists five sets of circumstances in which a court may now act in *cy-près* to supplement the position at common law. These include, but are not limited to, cases where the original purposes have been fulfilled (s 62(1)(a)(i)), for example, *Re Lepton's Charity* (1972); where the property may be more effectively used in conjunction with other property (s 62(1)(c)); where the original purposes made reference to an area or class of persons who have ceased to be suitable (s 62(1)(d); see, for example, *Peggs v Lamb* (1994)); and where the original purposes have been provided for by other means (s 62(1)(e)). Obviously, these provisions, along with the other situations listed in s 62, give the court and the Commission considerable power to deal with charitable trust property.

QUESTION 27

Arnold made his will in 2008, in which he left four gifts of £50,000 each to:

(a)   the National Association for the Homeless, an incorporated charity;
(b)   the Whale Protection League, a voluntary association;
(c)   the Cook Home for the Disabled; and
(d)   the Norfolk Bird and Rescue Centre.

When Arnold died this year, it transpired that the National Association for the Homeless had become defunct two years previously and its premises purchased by the UK League Against Homelessness. Likewise, the Whale Protection League had disbanded after disagreements between its members, to be replaced by two organisations, the Whale and Dolphin Sanctuary and the Society for the Humane Harvesting of Whales. It also transpires that there never was a 'Cook Home for the Disabled' and that the Norfolk Bird and Rescue Centre was taken over by the RSPCA and relocated in Cornwall.

▶   Advise as to the proper distribution of Arnold's estate.

How to Answer this Question

❖   *Cy-près*: general purpose.
❖   Initial or subsequent impossibility.
❖   Gifts to institutions, purposes or named funds.
❖   Successor organisations.

Answer Structure

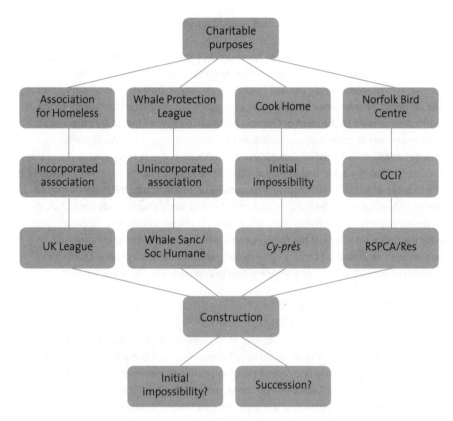

This diagram depicts the various procedures that need to be adopted in order to determine which body will acquire the property under Arnold's will.

ANSWER

Arnold has attempted to distribute his property among several named organisations, none of which exists at the date of his death, at least in their original form. At the outset, it is necessary to determine whether all or any of these gifts are for charitable purposes. If any is not, then the property allocated to that organisation will return to Arnold's estate under a simple resulting trust consequent upon a void purpose trust (*Re Endacott* (1960)).[32] Fortunately, all of the original purposes selected by Arnold appear to be charitable. We are told that the National Association for the Homeless is 'an incorporated charity'; the Cook Home for the Disabled falls squarely within the fourth category of charity identified in *Commissioners for Special Purposes of Income Tax v Pemsel* (1891) or within s 3(1)(d) or (j) of

---

32 Prevalence of the resulting trust where the *cy-près* doctrine is inapplicable.

the Charities Act 2011, being for the relief of the sick; the Norfolk Bird and Rescue Centre will be charitable under s 3(1)(k) of the 2011 Act (Re Wedgwood (1915)), as will the Whale Protection League, providing that it does not engage in political activities.

The importance of deciding that these four purposes are charitable is that it may help determine the distribution of Arnold's estate now that none of the original organisations remain in existence.[33] Simply put, the failure of a charitable trust does not always result in the property being returned to the donor or his estate but may, if certain conditions are fulfilled, be applied by the court or Charity Commission cy-près – that is, for purposes as near as possible to those originally stipulated (Re Wilson (1913)).[34] Broadly speaking, if a charity has failed for 'initial impossibility or impracticality', it may be applied cy-près if there is evidence that the donor had a general intention to benefit charity (Re Wilson). However, if the charity has failed for subsequent impossibility or impracticality, the property may be applied cy-près without the need for such an intention, since it has already been dedicated to charity in perpetuity (Re Peel (1921)). In our cases, it will be necessary to determine, first, whether the charitable trust has failed; second, whether such failure is initial or subsequent; and thirdly, if there is initial failure, whether there is a general charitable intention. Each of the four purposes identified by Arnold will be considered in turn.[35]

(a) £50,000 to the National Association for the Homeless, an incorporated charity

It is clear that Arnold has attempted to give his donation to a charity which, although once in existence, does not exist at the date the gift is to take effect, being on the testator's death. If anything, this may be a case of initial impossibility. However, we are told that the premises of the National Association for the Homeless have been purchased by the UK League Against Homelessness and it is arguable that this institution is in fact the successor in title to the National Association. If that is the case, the correct solution may well be that there has been no failure of Arnold's gift at all but, rather, a continuity between his named charity and its lawful successor, which may then receive the donation.[36]

Whether this is a case of initial failure or a case of a successor charity depends on the construction of Arnold's gift in the circumstances of the case. There are three possibilities. First, it may be construed that Arnold's gift is a gift specifically to the institution named in his will (Re Rymer (1895)). If this is the case, then there is initial impossibility and a general charitable intention needs to be found if the property is to be applied cy-près. Unfortunately, Re Rymer also decides that it is difficult to find a general charitable intention when a specific donee that once existed has been identified with such clarity

---

33 Significance of charitable trusts and the cy-près doctrine.
34 Importance of the donor's intention and the cy-près doctrine.
35 Summary of issues to be considered.
36 Importance of determining whether there has been a failure or alternatively a succession of the charitable purposes.

although, as *Re Finger* (1972) demonstrates, this is not entirely impossible. Second, the original donation can be construed as a gift to the particular purposes undertaken by the original institution, so that if another institution has taken over those purposes, the property will pass to it automatically as the successor in title (*Re Roberts* (1963)). Thirdly, the original donation can be construed as a gift to the charitable fund administered by the original institution, so that if there is another body now administering that fund, the property will pass to it automatically as the successor in title (*Re Faraker* (1912)).[37] In our case, it is unclear which construction to adopt. According to *Re Vernon* (1972) and *Re Finger* (1972), if the charity is incorporated – as here – then the gift should be construed as a gift to the specific institution per se (the first possibility above), while if it is unincorporated the gift should be construed as a gift for the purposes of the original institution. On the other hand, this guidance takes no account of the *Re Faraker* construction. If we follow *Re Vernon*, the donation to the National Association for the Homeless will fail for initial impossibility (being a gift to a specific institution) and will be applicable *cy-près* only if a general charitable intention can be found – something which *Re Rymer*, but not *Re Finger*, says is difficult. Failing such an intention, the property will result back to Arnold's estate. Again, on the basis of *Vernon*, a construction of the gift for purposes does not seem possible. This would mean that the UK League Against Homelessness could not claim the property as of right unless the *Faraker* construction is adopted and the League is now administering the National Association's funds. This we do not know. All in all, a resulting trust seems likely, or *cy-près* if a general charitable intention can be found.

(b) £50,000 to the Whale Protection League, now dissolved and replaced by the Whale & Dolphin Sanctuary and the Society for the Humane Harvesting of Whales

Once again, assuming this gift to be charitable, we must ask first what is the proper construction to be placed on Arnold's original disposition. This is particularly important in this case as there are two organisations who may claim to be the lawful successors in title to the Whale Protection League. We are told that the Whale Protection League was a 'voluntary association' and, therefore, it may be possible (should we wish – see below) to avoid construing this as a gift to a specific institution which has failed (that is, not *Re Rymer*) and so not a case of initial impossibility allowing for *cy-près* only if a general charitable intention can be found. However, it is not easy to choose between the *Re Roberts* construction (a gift for the particular charitable purpose) and the *Re Faraker* construction (a gift to a particular charitable fund). Again, following *Re Vernon* (1972), the unincorporated nature of the original charity might lead us to choose the 'purpose construction', but then we have the dilemma of deciding exactly what the original purpose was. Was it the protection of whales, etc in all circumstances, so that the Whale and Dolphin Sanctuary may claim the gift as carrying on those original purposes? Or was it a gift for the protection

---

37 Identification of the possible methods of construction.

of whales from unnecessary hunting, in which case the Society for the Humane Harvesting of Whales may be the lawful successor to the original purpose? Indeed, precisely the same problem arises if we decide to adopt the *Faraker* construction (gift to a fund) instead of the purpose approach. It is not at all clear which of the rival organisations now administers the funds of the defunct society. Consequently, in the absence of further evidence, we might actually prefer a pragmatic solution and decide that this was, after all, a gift specifically to the Whale Protection League, which failed initially at Arnold's death, but where we can infer a general charitable intention so allowing the property to be applied *cy-près*. If the property is applied *cy-près* (as opposed to going to a successor in title), each rival organisation can receive a share, or none at all, as the court decides.

(c) £50,000 to the Cook Home for the Disabled

The Cook Home for the Disabled has never existed and therefore there is no doubt that this is a case of initial impossibility. Furthermore, there can be no successors in title to an organisation that never was. The property will result to Arnold's estate unless a general charitable intention can be found, in which case it will be applicable *cy-près*. In this regard, *Re Harwood* (1936) decides that, where a gift has been given to an institution which has never existed, a general charitable intention should be presumed unless there is convincing evidence to the contrary. Although somewhat arbitrary, this guidance has been followed in *Re Satterthwaite's Wills Trust* (1966) and in our case affords good authority for a *cy-près* application of the property.

(d) £50,000 to the Norfolk Bird and Rescue Centre

Once again, this donation calls for a decision about the nature of Arnold's gift to the Norfolk Bird Sanctuary. If there is an initial failure of the gift – because it was a gift to that sanctuary and nothing else – the gift may go *cy-près* on the finding of a general charitable intention, or it will result to Arnold's estate. We are told, however, that the Norfolk charity was 'taken over' by the RSPCA and we can infer from this that the RSPCA is to be regarded as the lawful successors in title to the original donees. In other words, there has not been an initial failure of the gift. In view of the fact that the RSPCA operates in protection of all animals – not just birds – it is likely that we can construe the original donation as a gift to the general fund of the Norfolk charity, which fund is now being administered by the RSPCA, as per *Re Faraker*. There is, then, no *cy-près* and no resulting trust, merely a continuation of Arnold's gift in a different form and the £50,000 may be distributed to the RSPCA as successors in title to the Norfolk Bird and Rescue Centre.

There is a crucial difference in law between application of charitable property *cy-près* and distribution of property to a 'new' charity which can be regarded as the successor in title to the original donee. In the second case, there is no failure of the original gift. Of course, if *cy-près* is called for, the property can be distributed to an organisation with similar objects to the original donee – even one which claimed but failed to be a successor in title (as with (b) above).

Resulting Trusts

INTRODUCTION

Resulting trusts are an essential doctrine in the law of trusts. Apart from relatively rare occasions when the subject matter of a trust will pass to the Crown as ownerless property (*bona vacantia*), resulting trusts provide the last practical means of disposing of trust property should the original scheme of a trust fail. In fact, a resulting trust can arise in such a variety of circumstances that there is only marginal merit in considering it on an undergraduate course as a topic in its own right. For example, resulting trusts need to be considered in relation to secret trusts, the three certainties, the beneficiary principle, charities, formalities and constructive trusts. This is not an exhaustive list, and the use of the resulting trust in these and other cases is best considered alongside the substantive law which it services. Moreover, there is now much academic discussion about the proper theoretical basis of resulting trusts: for example, do they arise by reason of the intention of the parties, by operation of law, out of the implied or express acceptance by the resulting trustee of an obligation affecting conscience, or for different reasons in different circumstances. This has practical consequences, as illustrated by the House of Lords' refusal to impose a resulting trust on the defendant in *Westdeutsche Landesbank Girozentrale v Islington LBC* (1996). As indicated above, much of this debate is outside the scope of an undergraduate course, but there are issues here which need consideration. In this chapter, brief attention will be paid to the attributes of the resulting trust *per se* (assuming that 'resulting trusts' share some common attributes), to issues touching on the rationale for the imposition of resulting trusts and to a typical problem-type examination question.

In very general terms, a resulting trust arises when the original arrangement envisaged by the testator or settlor has failed, has not been properly established or has been fully achieved without exhausting the trust's assets. To this extent, it arises out of a disappointed, failed or satisfied purpose of the testator/settlor. In reality the resulting trust arises in order to cure defective drafting of a trust instrument. Although this is a simplistic picture – see, for example, resulting trusts in the context of co-owned property – it explains why, under a resulting trust, the property returns or 'results' to the person originally entitled to it. To put it another way, resulting trusts may be seen as the consequence of the application of the old maxim that 'equity abhors a beneficial vacuum'. How, and in what cases, this is related to the intention of the person originally entitled to the property or to the state of mind (conscience) of the original trustee are difficult and complex issues.

NOTE
Section 199 of the Equality Act 2010 has abolished the presumption of advancement (i.e. the presumption of gifts) with regard to transactions that take effect after the sub-section comes into force.

QUESTION 28
To what extent can it be said that resulting trusts operate to support the equitable maxim that 'equity abhors a beneficial vacuum'?

Aim Higher ★
Given that the categorisation of some resulting trusts as 'automatic' may now be incorrect – as all resulting trusts might spring from intention and a resulting obligation of conscience on the trustee – it could be the case that it may too simplistic to assert that resulting trusts may be seen as primarily filling a beneficial vacuum.

Common Pitfalls ✗
The answers to typical examination questions on resulting trusts are now complicated by the dictum that a resulting trust can exist only where supported by the original donor's intention (*Westdeutsche v Islington LBC*). It remains to be seen whether this goes unchallenged. If it becomes the accepted orthodoxy, the distinction between automatic and presumed resulting trusts will have been exploded.

How to Answer this Question
❖ General nature of resulting trusts and the maxim that equity abhors a beneficial vacuum.
❖ Types of resulting trust.
❖ Differences between resulting trusts arising out of the failure of an express trust and other resulting trusts.
❖ Possible distinction between 'automatic' and 'presumed' resulting trusts.
❖ Rejection of such a distinction in *Westdeutsche Landesbank Girozentrale v Islington LBC* (1996).

Answer Structure

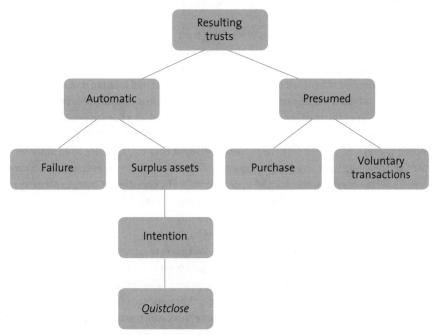

This diagram illustrates the thought processes in deciding which transactions attract the resulting trust.

ANSWER

There are many other situations in trusts law where, for one reason or another, the main purposes of the donor cannot be achieved. The question therefore arises as to who owns the trust property or, more accurately, who is entitled to the beneficial interest under the trust.[1] The solution to this problem (sometimes known as cases involving failure of an express trust) is provided by the principles of resulting trusts. In short, if there are no beneficiaries entitled to the property, the trustee will hold the property on trust for the donor (or his estate): it will 'result back' to the person who provided it in the first place.

It is important to realise, then, that 'resulting trusts' are a very versatile concept. They represent the solution of last resort when determining the ownership of trust property, failing which the property will fall to the Crown as *bona vacantia* (ownerless property), as happened with part of the gift in *Re West Sussex Constabulary Widows Fund* (1971). The circumstances in which a resulting trust may arise are numerous and varied and most

---

1   Contextual nature of resulting trusts.

cases are unique on their own facts, although this does not necessarily mean that the *concept* of resulting trusts cannot be explained by a general theory.[2]

First, one of the most common forms of resulting trust is that which arises when there has been an initial failure of the trust which the donor had intended to establish, either in respect of the whole or part of the trust property. For example, in *Vandervell v IRC* (1967) itself, the donor had attempted to dispose of his interest but had failed to divest himself fully of one portion of his property. Hence, that portion resulted to him. Likewise, if there is complete failure of the trust for uncertainty of objects, or lack of a human beneficiary (a purpose trust: *Re Endacott* (1960)), or where a charitable gift fails initially and cannot be applied *cy-près* (*Re Rymer* (1895)), the property will result back to the settlor. In all of these cases, the resulting trust arises in consequence of the failure of an express trust and, on one view, is said to operate 'automatically' upon that failure by operation of law (*per* Megarry J in *Re Vandervell (No 2)* (1974)). Whether such trusts are correctly described as 'automatic', suggesting, as it does, that they operate independently of the intention of the person originally making the gift, is open to doubt following *Westdeutsche Landesbank Girozentrale v Islington LBC* (1996). In that case, Lord Browne-Wilkinson said that resulting trusts operate because of an intention on the part of the donor to recover the property should the primary purpose fail. Hence, even in cases where there is failure of an express trust in the sense just discussed, a resulting trust will not arise if there is clear evidence of the donor's intention 'to part out and out' with his property. Such an intention, which would negate the existence of a resulting trust, means that the money is ownerless and will pass to the Crown as *bona vacantia* (*Re West Sussex Constabulary*). The equitable maxim raised in the question is supported only to the extent that the parties' intention does not dictate otherwise.

A second example of the use of resulting trusts arises where the primary trust established by the settlor has been completed, yet a surplus of undisposed trust property remains. Again, the traditional view is that the surplus is returned to the donor or his estate under a resulting trust because 'equity abhors a beneficial vacuum'. So, in *Re Abbott* (1900), the initial trust was completed and the surplus was held on resulting trust for the subscribers to the sisters' fund. Again, in *Re Gillingham Bus Disaster Fund* (1958), it was held that surplus funds should result back to the donors. Again, however, intention was an essential element in the use of resulting trusts: evidence of the donor's desire to part forever with his money meant that any surplus will not result (*Westdeutsche*). It is not sufficient that there was an absolute gift to an individual bound up with a non-binding motive to use the money for some specific purpose which then fails. So, in *Re Osoba* (1979), the gift was construed as an absolute gift to the testator's daughter with merely a non-binding direction to use the money for educational purposes. The original gift was absolute, not a gift on trust for educational purposes, and the doctrine of resulting trusts was irrelevant.

....

2   Numerous 'trigger' events that create resulting trusts.

This leads us on to another area where resulting trusts may be important. It often happens that money is given in various ways to an unincorporated association for its members or general purposes, as where a local wildlife group raises money from donors and jumble sales. If this association then comes to an end, the surplus assets must be disposed of: equity abhors a beneficial vacuum. At one time, it was thought that these surplus assets should revert to the donors under a resulting trust (for example, *Re West Sussex Constabulary*). If a resulting trust is adopted, equity is filling the beneficial vacuum created by the failure of the initial gift (subject, as before, to questions concerning the relevance of intention). However, in a majority of recent cases, it is evident that the more favoured solution is to distribute the assets of a defunct unincorporated association among the surviving members of the association (that is, not necessarily among those people who provided the money in the first place). This is because a donation to the association need not be construed as a gift on a trust (which subsequently fails) but as an absolute gift to the members of the association subject to their contractual obligations *inter se*, as created by the rules of the association (*Re Recher's Trust* (1972); *Re Bucks Constabulary Fund Friendly Society (No 2)* (1979)). This construction, which ousts the resulting trust because it denies the existence of a primary trust, is more convenient as it does not require an extensive search for the original donors who may be very numerous and elusive.

Fourth, we come to a type of resulting trust that has come to the fore in recent years, especially in commercial transactions. Thus, if A (the donor) gives money to B (the trustee) solely in order that B may pay his debts to C, if those debts are not paid, the money will result to A under a resulting trust (*Barclays Bank v Quistclose Investments Ltd* (1970)). This may appear quite straightforward, but there are a number of difficulties with this arrangement. For example, if B pays the money to C, A has no claim, so the operation of the resulting trust in favour of A is dependent upon B not carrying out the specific purpose of paying his debts. Does this mean that the trust imposed on B is a purpose trust that is valid under *Re Denley* (1969) (see *Re Northern Developments (Holdings) Ltd* (1978))? Or that the equitable interest in the money is in suspense (*Carreras Rothmans Ltd v Freeman Mathews Treasure* (1985))? Or that A is the beneficiary under an express trust with a power to direct that the money be paid to C, hence excluding resulting trusts altogether? Furthermore, once the trust imposed on B is carried out (that is, he pays his debts), A will have a simple action in debt to recover the money from B: hence A has lost his proprietary right in the property under the resulting trust, to see it replaced by a personal right against B in debt, and all this by B's own actions.[3] In other words, this example of a resulting trust is used in a deliberate way to enable a donor to provide funds for another person (usually a company with which the donor is connected) and to restrict

---

3   Listing of various solutions advisable.

the use of those funds for a specific purpose, failing which the resulting trust comes into operation. The resulting trust is filling the beneficial vacuum, but only for the advantage of the donor, and the solution cannot be adopted where no primary trust existed (*Box v Barclays Bank* (1998)). Furthermore, it is an intended consequence of the parties' actions, in the nature of a deliberate 'failsafe'. It is very different from the 'automatic' resulting trusts considered above which might be thought to arise by operation of law because of an unintentional failure of the original arrangements. This type of resulting trust does seem consistent with the 'intention approach' put forward in *Westdeutsche*.

Finally, brief mention must be made of a different kind of resulting trust.[4] This is the so-called 'presumed' resulting trust. A presumed resulting trust does not arise automatically in order to fill a beneficial vacuum (assuming, post-*Westdeutsche*, that this is an acceptable analysis), but exists because of a presumed intention of the parties to create a trust over property. For example, a person who provides part of the purchase money of a house will be presumed to have intended thereby to acquire part ownership of that house under a presumed resulting trust (*Dyer v Dyer* (1788), subject to the principles laid down in *Stack v Dowden* (2007)), and a person who pays for a lottery ticket may claim the winnings by resulting trust even if, as a matter of form, the ticket is 'owned' by another (*Abrahams v Trustee in Bankruptcy of Abrahams* (1999)). As such, this presumption can be rebutted by evidence that the payment of money was as a gift or loan (*Cowcher v Cowcher* (1972)) or by the circumstances of the payment (*Mumford v Ashe* (2000): money provided in a scheme designed to defraud creditors did not generate a resulting trust for the payer). Of course, in one sense, the resulting trust is filling the beneficial vacuum created by the payer's lack of express intention as to why he is paying the money at all but, in effect, this form of resulting trust is not used to determine ownership of apparently ownerless property, but to give effect to the unexpressed intentions of the parties. It is similar in many respects to the constructive trust approach to acquisition of co-owned property as explained in *Lloyds Bank v Rosset* (1991). As will be obvious, this type of resulting trust is fully consistent with the intention approach to resulting trusts adopted in *Westdeutsche*. There is, however, a problem here. Such 'co-ownership' resulting trusts are now more frequently seen as constructive trusts pure and simple, being examples of a trust imposed to remedy unconscionable conduct on the part of the 'paper owner' of property, as in *Midland Bank v Cooke* (1995), *Stack v Dowden* (2007), *Jones v Kernott* [2011] UKSC 53. Whether such trusts survive as a category of resulting trusts at all is open to question.

QUESTION 29

The Over Village Association, a non-charitable, unincorporated body, existed to safeguard the amenities in the village of Over. It derived its funds from members' subscriptions,

---

4   Status of the presumed resulting trust.

gifts by will and otherwise, the proceeds of local events such as jumble sales and raffles, money in collection boxes and one large anonymous donation. The village has now been granted Protected Status under European Union Regional Funds and its future is secure. The Village Association is about to be disbanded, but there is disagreement as to what to do with the considerable surplus funds that remain. The treasurer comes to you for advice.

How to Answer this Question

- ❖ The link between distribution of funds and validity of gifts.
- ❖ The need to consider each 'source' of finance separately.
- ❖ Resulting trusts, absolute gifts or *bona vacantia*.
- ❖ Rules to be adopted by the association, especially the establishment of a winding-up mechanism.

Answer structure

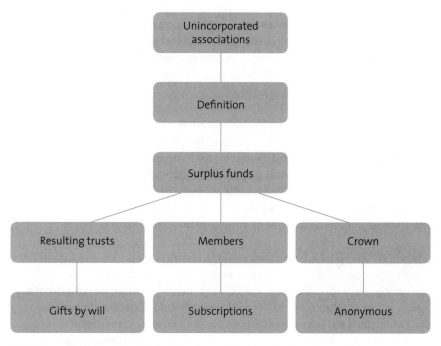

This diagram lists the principles for distributing funds on the liquidation of an unincorporated association.

ANSWER

The dissolution of an unincorporated, non-charitable association presents peculiar difficulties in English law. The absence of incorporation often means that there is no established procedure for winding up the association and its non-charitable status deprives the court of the possibility of *cy-près* application of any property held on trust consequent upon failure (or completion) of the original purposes.[5]

When an unincorporated association ceases to exist there are three possible destinations for any surplus assets.[6] First, the surplus may be returned to the original donors under a resulting trust. This assumes that the money was given to the association on trust in the first place (that trust having been completed or failed: *Re Gillingham Bus Disaster Fund* (1958)) and that the donor had not intended to part forever with his money (*Westdeutsche Landesbank Girozentrale v Islington LBC* (1996)).

Secondly, the surplus assets might be divided up among those members of the association in existence at the date of its demise. This, in turn, depends on recognising that the original donors transferred ownership of their donations absolutely to the members, so that the property could be dealt with according to the members' wishes as expressed and modified by the rules of the association (*Re Recher's Trust* (1972); *Re Bucks Constabulary Fund Friendly Society (No 2)* (1979); *Artistic Upholstery Ltd v Art Forma (Ltd)* (1999)). Thirdly, it is possible both that the original donors of the property have no interest in the surplus assets (no resulting trust) and that the existing members have no claim either (for example, because the rules prevent them taking a share). In such cases, the surplus assets may fall to the Crown as *bona vacantia* (ownerless property) (*Re West Sussex Constabulary's Benevolent Fund* (1971)).

In determining which of these three possibilities is the most appropriate in any given case, it is important to identify precisely the source of the surplus assets and to examine the reason why each original source of funds could be construed as valid in law when it was given.[7] This is particularly important given that an unincorporated association (as here) has no legal personality of its own. The following analysis of each of the ways in which the Over Village Association received money assumes that it is possible to prove that an identifiable part of the surplus assets was derived from each of these methods of donation.

(a) The surplus derived from members' subscriptions

It might be thought that money derived from members' subscriptions is most appropriately returned to those members under a resulting trust, on the basis that the primary purpose of their subscriptions has failed. Indeed, in some cases, this solution has been adopted and each subscriber (whether still a member at the date of dissolution or not) has received a share proportionate to his or her original contributions (*Re Printers and Transferrers Amalgamated Trades Protection Society* (1899), and see *Air Jamaica v Charlton* (1999) in the context of surplus funds of pensions). However, this

---

5   Peculiar nature of unincorporated association.
6   Identification of possible solutions.
7   The possible solutions reflect the sources of surplus assets.

solution presupposes that the members' subscriptions were given 'on trust' in the first place, which trust has now failed or has not exhausted the trust property. If true, this must have been a trust for the purposes of the association even though such trusts for purposes are void under the beneficiary principle (*Re Endacott* (1960)). Alternatively, it is now more likely that income derived from members' subscriptions will be treated as having been given to the association not by way of trust, but as an absolute gift to the members individually, albeit on the basis that the money is to be used in accordance with the rules of the association, this forming a binding contract between them (*Re Recher's Trust* (1972); *Re Bucks Constabulary Fund Friendly Society (No 2)* (1979); *Artistic Upholstery*).[8] This would mean that any surplus derived from subscriptions belongs to the members absolutely (that is, those at the date of dissolution) and may be distributed among them according to their contract (the rules). If the rules prevent the members taking any surplus assets personally when the association dissolves, then either the rules must be changed prior to dissolution (if permitted by the rules themselves) or the property will pass to the Crown as *bona vacantia*. In our case, therefore, the presumption will be that the members at the date of dissolution of the association may share in the surplus assets derived from subscriptions, provided this is permitted by their contract *inter se* under the rules.

(b) The surplus derived from gifts by will and otherwise

This presents a similar problem to members' subscriptions, although now there is a real choice to be made between the resulting trust option and distribution of the surplus assets among the members. With gifts from identifiable persons, there is a distinct possibility that the money will be treated as having been given expressly for the purposes of the association and for nothing else. In other words, a primary trust for the association's purposes was intended which, having failed, the surplus assets attributable to that source result back to the donors unless there is evidence of a clear intention forever to have parted with the money (*Westdeutsche v Islington LBC* (1996)). Of course, there are problems with this interpretation, not least that trusts for purposes are void (*Re Endacott* (1960)) unless they fall within the *Re Denley* (1969) exception. So, unless this is a *Re Denley* trust, in theory the donors should be able to recover the whole of their original gifts – not merely the surplus after the void purpose had been undertaken and failed. However, although the pure logic of this is compelling, the case law suggests that only the *surplus* assets will result to the original donors and this would probably be the case if the resulting trust option was followed with our association (*Re West Sussex Constabulary Widows Fund* (1971)). Similarly, if gifts to the Over Village Association could indeed be construed on a *Re Denley* basis, the donors would be *entitled* only to the surplus funds under the resulting trust (*Re Abbott* (1900)), the primary purpose trust having been valid, but then failed. Finally, we should not discount the possibility that the *Re Bucks Constabulary* construction could be adopted and that specific donations could be

8   Modern view of the destination of surplus assets.

construed as gifts to the individual members of the association under contract, in which case the same considerations are relevant as those considered above when discussing members' subscriptions.[9]

(c) The surplus derived from a large anonymous donation

The surplus attributable to this gift presumptively is to be dealt with in the same way as that arising from specific individual donations (as above). Of course, should the resulting trust option be followed, the anonymity of this donor creates a difficulty, although the court may well direct that the surplus assets be held in court until claimed by the donor on production of satisfactory evidence, as in *Re Gillingham Bus Disaster Fund* (1958). However, the fact that the donor wished for anonymity might lead to the conclusion either: that he or she had intended to disclaim any future interest in the gift and that it should be taken to be an absolute gift to the members of the association to be used according to their contractual rights *inter se* (*Re Bucks Constabulary Fund (No 2)*); or, that a trust for purposes existed but with a resulting trust excluded by intention, with the surplus going to the Crown (*Re West Sussex Constabulary*; *Westdeutsche v Islington LBC*; *Davis v Richards and Wallington Industries* (1990)).

(d) The surplus arising from the proceeds of local events such as jumble sales and raffles

This source of the association's funds presents the least difficulty. In fact, as made clear in *Re Bucks Constabulary Fund (No 2)* (1979), there are two reasons why the resulting trust option should be excluded. First, the people paying for jumble and raffle tickets, etc, are entering into a purchase contract with the association for items of jumble or raffle tickets and they obtain all they are entitled to when that contract is carried out. The 'donors' have no claim on any surplus assets, having received their full contractual entitlement. Second, and in any event, it is not the donor's money which goes to the association but the profit from the jumble sale or raffle after deduction of expenses. Consequently, any surpluses derived from these activities cannot go by way of resulting trust and normally will be treated as an accretion to the general funds of the association to be used by the members individually, subject to their contract *inter se* (*Re Recher's Trust* (1972)). The surplus may be distributed according to the rules of the association as before.

(e) The surplus deriving from money placed in collection boxes

Once again, there is a difficulty here because the identity of the donors may be impossible to establish and, indeed, they are likely to have given in such small amounts that no claim to surplus will be made. Thus, the resulting trust option seems impractical and absurd. However, as Harman J recognised in *Re Gillingham Bus Disaster Fund* (1958), this could be the logical solution, as the donor might well have intended that the money be used for

---

9   Contractual basis of donations by will.

the purposes of the association alone. Why else would he put money in a collection box? However, in *Re West Sussex Constabulary Widows Fund* (1971), Goff J was of the opinion that money derived from street collections was given 'out and out' by the donors, thus depriving them of any future claim to it. In that case, Goff J went further and held that even the members of the Benevolent Fund had no claim to the property because the association was not designed for their benefit, being 'outward looking'. Thus, the surplus fell to the Crown as *bona vacantia*. Further, although this is a rather unattractive solution, and something of a last resort, *Westdeutsche v Islington LBC* confirmed that the existence of a resulting trust depended on the donor having an intention to recover his property. Consequently, where there is no such intention, there can be no possibility of a resulting trust. So, in our case, the Over Village Association may also be described as 'outward looking' and it is possible that both the resulting trust (lack of intention) and gift to members (not consistent with the purpose of the original donation) will be excluded.

This is the picture on the eve of the dissolution of the Over Village Association. Obviously, much depends on the reason why the various donations to the association were valid in the first place and the nature of the contract between the members (that is, the rules of the association). The treasurer should ensure that he or she is acquainted with those rules and the fact that it is possible for the appropriate surplus assets to be distributed to those members in existence at the date of dissolution. Failing that, the property may fall to the Crown as *bona vacantia*. Finally, any surplus derived from property which was subject to a primary trust will result to the donors.

QUESTION 30

Is it possible to identify a unifying underlying theory concerning resulting trusts?

Aim Higher ★

Millett J in *Air Jamaica v Charlton* (1999) advocated the theory that resulting trusts are created as equity's response to the failure of a gift. This view is based on the absence of a positive intention to make a gift of the beneficial interest in favour of the transferee. In short, the resulting trust is based on what the transferor did not intend as distinct from what he intended.

Common Pitfalls ✗

Students tend to shy away from this type of question or are generally unprepared in presenting examination answers, being content to discuss the facts of the cases instead of focusing on the theoretical justifications for resulting trusts.

How to Answer this Question

- ❖ Automatic and presumed resulting trusts.
- ❖ Professor Birks's theory.
- ❖ Swadling's theory.
- ❖ Lord Browne-Wilkinson's theory in *Westdeutsche*.
- ❖ Lord Wilberforce's theory in *Barclays Bank v Quistclose*.
- ❖ Lord Millett's theory in *Twinsectra v Yardley*; *Air Jamaica v Charlton*.
- ❖ Peter Gibson J's theory in *Carreras Rothmans*.
- ❖ Dillon J's theory in *Re EVTR*.

Answer Structure

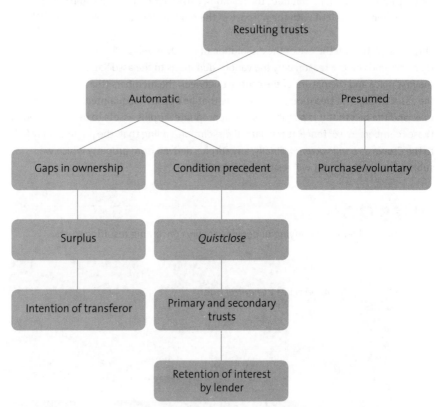

This diagram lists the various theories that have been put forward to justify the creation of the resulting trust.

ANSWER -

In *Re Vandervell (No 2)*, Megarry J classified resulting trusts into two categories, namely 'automatic' and 'presumed' (although his decision was reversed by the Court of Appeal).[10] Automatic resulting trusts arise where the beneficial interest under an express trust remains undisposed of. Such trusts arise in order to fill a gap of ownership. The notion here is that such trusts arise by operation of law irrespective of the intention of the transferor or settlor. The policy which underpins this type of resulting trust involves the destination of the beneficial interest when the instrument creating the intended trust or gift is silent as to the application of the equitable interest. It may be possible to classify the occasions which give rise to an automatic resulting trust into two categories, namely:

(a)   transfers of property subject to conditions precedent that have failed to occur; and
(b)   uncertainty concerning the destination of a surplus of trust funds.

In *Vandervell v IRC* the House of Lords decided that the destination of the equitable interest in the option to repurchase shares was held on a resulting trust for the settlor in order to fill a gap in ownership. Similarly, in *Re Ames* (1884) a trust of a marriage settlement that failed was held on resulting trust for the settlor as a last resort. In *Barclays Bank v Quistclose* (1970) the House of Lords decided that a transfer of funds on a conditional loan arrangement was held on resulting trust for the lender when the relevant condition was not satisfied (or the 'primary' trust failed). Likewise, in *R v Common Professional Examination Board ex p Mealing-McCleod* (2000), the Court of Appeal decided that a *Quistclose* trust was created where a specific loan from Lloyds Bank was made to the borrower for the purpose of security of costs and subject thereto, to be held on trust for the lender.[11]

However, Peter Millett in an article argued that the 'primary' trust idea was fundamentally flawed on the ground that as an intended express trust there was no beneficiary with a *locus standi* capable of enforcing the trust. Such a trust, if there was one, would be inconsistent with the beneficiary principle. In *Twinsectra v Yardley* (2002) Lord Millett described the *Quistclose* trust as a simple commercial arrangement akin to a retention of title clause. This arrangement enables the borrower to have recourse to the lender's money for a particular purpose without entrenching on the lender's property rights more than necessary to enable the purpose to be achieved. The money remains the property of the lender unless and until it is applied in accordance with his directions, and insofar as it is not so applied it must be returned to him (the lender). The significance of this analysis of the *Quistclose* resulting trust is that the lender retains an equitable interest in the sum loaned until the fund is applied to the specified purpose, whereas the view of Lord Wilberforce is that the resulting trust springs back to the lender when the specified purpose is not carried out.[12]

....
10   Classic classification of resulting trusts.
11   Justification of *Quistclose* trusts.
12   Review of the basis of the *Quistclose* trust.

Surplus funds are held on resulting trust for the settlor or transferor on the ground that he had parted with the funds for a specific purpose and by implication had retained an interest in the remainder where the specific purpose remained unfulfilled: see *Re Abbott* (1900). The same principle was adopted in *Re Gillingham Bus Disaster Fund* (1958) with regard to anonymous donors, although this extension was doubted in *Re West Sussex Constabulary Fund* (1971).

On the winding-up of an unincorporated association with surplus assets available for distribution, the resulting trust was the original remedy adopted by the courts. This institution represents, in theory, a solution to the problem, although the more recent cases have considered this basis of distribution with disfavour.[13] This approach was adopted in *Re Printers and Transferrers Society* (1899) and *Re Houbourn Aero Components Air Raid Distress Fund* (1946). The courts have repeatedly stressed that the resulting trust is unsuitable in this context because the members paid their subscriptions on a contractual basis. The distribution of assets ought to be *effected on a contractual basis*. Accordingly, a second solution adopted by the courts is that the members of a society who make their contributions have received, or are receiving, or expect to receive, benefits from the funds of the society during its continuance. On the date of liquidation, such members do not expect the return of their subscriptions or assets of the society, for the members had parted 'out and out' with their subscriptions. Thus the assets of the society may be taken by the Crown as *bona vacantia*. This solution is adopted only as a last resort when the settlor, beneficiary and no one else is entitled to claim the property. The property being ownerless, the Crown will step in to fill the gap: see *Cunnack v Edwards* (1896); *Re West Sussex Constabulary Fund* (1971). But in *Re Bucks Constabulary Fund (No 2)* (1979) the court decided that distribution to the subsisting members on a contractual basis was appropriate.

The 'presumed' resulting trust arises, in the absence of evidence to the contrary, when property is purchased in the name of another, or property is voluntarily transferred to another; for example, A purchases property and has the legal title conveyed in the name of B, or A transfers the legal title to property to B. In both cases the destination of the equitable title has not been specified. In these circumstances, B prima facie holds the property on trust for A: see *Dyer v Dyer* (1788); *Re Vinogradoff* (1935). This type of resulting trust is created in order to fulfil the presumed intentions of the parties. The presumption will, of course, be rebutted by the transferor's contrary intention wherever, on the evidence, that contrary intention is expressed.[14]

Professor Birks's thesis on resulting trusts is that both types of resulting trusts, automatic and presumed, are based on the intention of the settlor/transferor and to prevent unjust

---

13   Liquidation of unincorporated associations.
14   Basis of presumed resulting trusts.

enrichment. If the settlor/transferor does not intend to transfer a beneficial interest to the legal owner, the court will create a resulting trust in order to prevent the unjust enrichment of the transferee. The same principle applies where the transferor disposes of his interest to the transferee by virtue of a mistake or on a total failure of consideration. The transferee does not acquire a proprietary interest in the subject matter of the transfer, but is under an obligation to hold the property on trust for the transferor. The view that the resulting trust is created in order to prevent unjust enrichment appears to be circular. Where the transferee appears to have been 'enriched' by the transfer, it only makes sense to describe the enrichment as 'unjust' if it has already been acknowledged that the transferee holds the benefit under a resulting trust for the transferor. It is the trust which arises as an automatic incident of the transferor's ongoing beneficial interest that renders 'unjust' the apparent beneficial ownership of the transferee. On the other hand, William Swadling has argued that the resulting trust is displaced by evidence of intention which is contrary to the intention to create a trust. If the transferor intended the transferee to have the equitable interest, the existence of a mistake on the part of the transferor does not change things and does not give rise to a resulting trust. The transferor will be able to recover the mistaken payment at common law on a total failure of consideration. Swadling's theory was endorsed by Lord Browne-Wilkinson in the *Westdeutsche* case.

Megarry J's twofold classification of resulting trusts in *Re Vandervell (No 2)* has been the subject of some refinement. Lord Browne-Wilkinson, in *Westdeutsche Landesbank Girozentrale v Islington LBC* (1996), did not fully agree with Megarry VC's classification and declared that resulting trusts arise on two occasions, namely where there is a purchase in the name of another and where there is a surplus of trust funds. He added that both types of trusts are examples of trusts giving rise to the common intentions of the parties. The automatic resulting trust that Megarry J referred to may not arise because the settlor expressly or by implication may abandon any beneficial interest in the equitable interest: see *Re West Sussex Constabulary Fund*. In this case the court decided that the surplus funds were taken by the Crown on a *bona vacantia*.

The comparison of Lord Browne-Wilkinson's classification of resulting trust with Megarry J's categorisation lie with the 'automatic' resulting trust and whether the basis of imposition of the trust is the common intention of the parties (as Lord Browne-Wilkinson suggested). However, Lord Browne-Wilkinson's classification appears to be incomplete because there is no acknowledgment of a resulting trust that arises to fill a gap in ownership (see *Vandervell v IRC*) or an occasion where a transfer to a fiduciary fails *ab initio* (see *Re Ames*). In addition, Lord Browne-Wilkinson opines that both types of resulting trusts arise by reference to the common intention of the parties.

This notion of a common intention resulting trust was also expressed by Peter Gibson J in *Carreras Rothmans Ltd v Freeman Mathews Treasure* (1985). The difficulty with this rationale for the creation of a resulting trust is that the boundaries between resulting and constructive trusts become blurred. It is true that in both cases the courts create the trust. In the case of constructive trusts the courts have deliberately left open the boundaries for the imposition of such trusts. The objective here is to prevent the trustee abusing his position. The court retains the power to monitor the transaction and to impose an order that will redress the imbalance. It is unnecessary for the resulting trust to perform the same task but with the added restriction of restoring the property to the settlor or transferor.

In *Re EVTR* (1987), the court decided that a loan made for a specific purpose imposes a constructive trust on the borrower. But if only part of the sum borrowed was used for the stated purpose, the remaining part of the fund, not so applied, was required to be held on resulting trust for the lender. In other words, both a constructive and resulting trust will arise in respect of the use of part of the funds under a conditional loan arrangement.

In *Air Jamaica v Charlton* (1999), Lord Millett emphasised the relevance of intention in the context of a resulting trust. He also added that the resulting trust will arise whether or not the settlor/transferor intended to retain a beneficial interest. In this case a surplus of pension funds was held on resulting trust for the company and its members.

Essentially, a resulting trust arises as a default mechanism that returns the property to the transferor, in accordance with his presumed (or implied) intention, as determined by the courts. Very often the transferor may not have contemplated the possibility of a return of the property (see *Vandervell v IRC*) but this may be regarded as immaterial if, in the discretion of the court, the circumstances trigger a return of the property to the transferor.

QUESTION 31

Consider the ownership of the equitable interests in the relevant properties, in respect of each of the dispositions made by Alfred of properties which he originally owned absolutely:

(a) A transfer of 10,000 shares in British Telecom plc to his wife, Beryl, subject to an option, exercisable by their son, Charles, at any time within the next five years, to repurchase 5,000 of the shares. The shares have been duly registered in Beryl's name and she pays 50 per cent of the dividends received to Alfred.

(b) A transfer of £50,000 to trustees 'upon trust to distribute all or such part of the income (as they in their absolute discretion shall think fit) for the maintenance and training of my housekeeper's daughter, Mary, until she graduates from university or reaches the age of 25, whichever happens earlier'. Mary, aged 24, has recently graduated from London University.

(c) A transfer of £70,000 to the trustees of his daughter's marriage settlement: 'Upon trust to pay the income to my daughter, Danielle, so long as she does not have an abortion and on her death, to her husband, Ernest, and on his death to pay the capital and income to their children in equal shares.' Five years after the transfer Danielle has an abortion. Ten years after the transfer, Danielle, Ernest and their only child, Frederick, die in a fire.

How to Answer this Question

- ❖ Presumption of a resulting trust (RT) and evidence in rebuttal.
- ❖ Automatic resulting trusts or 'out and out' gifts.
- ❖ Limitation restricted by public policy.
- ❖ Acceleration of postponed interests.
- ❖ Doctrine of *commorientes*.

Answer structure

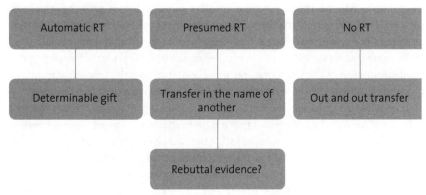

This diagram highlights the principles that are applicable in order to clarify the interests of the various parties.

ANSWER

In each of these transactions the location of the equitable interest is *prima facie* unclear. One solution adopted by the courts over the centuries is the institution of the resulting trust – automatic and presumed. The relevance of such a trust will be considered in respect of each transaction.[15]

(a) A transfer of 10,000 shares in British Telecom plc to his wife, Beryl

We are told that the legal title to the BT shares has been vested in the name of Alfred's wife, Beryl. This involved a voluntary transfer of the legal title to property by a husband to his wife. There has been no indication as to the destination of the equitable interest in

---

15   The last resort nature of identifying interests under resulting trusts.

the shares. The *prima facie* solution adopted by the courts involves a presumption of a resulting trust in favour of Alfred (before the passing of the Equality Act 2010 a presumption of advancement (gift) would have arisen in favour of Beryl as Alfred's wife). Thus, as a starting point Beryl is presumed to be a trustee of the equitable interest in 10,000 shares in favour of the transferor, Alfred. The existence of the resulting trust is a reference to the incidence of the onus of proof, i.e. Beryl bears the burden of rebutting the presumption.

Has the presumption been rebutted? The presumption of resulting trust is an artificial rule for allocating the equitable interest in property when this is unclear. The presumption may be rebutted by evidence that establishes the true intentions of the parties. Such evidence may take the form of oral or written statements as well as the conduct of the parties. However, there are two principles that are applied by the courts in this context – whether the evidence is admissible and, if so, the weight to be attached to such evidence. We are told that Beryl pays 50 per cent of the dividends to Alfred. In the absence of oral or written evidence, this is evidence of conduct that is prejudicial to Beryl in the sense that it may indicate an acknowledgment from Beryl that 50 per cent of the equitable interest belongs to Alfred. Has she consistently paid this amount of the dividends to Alfred? Did she feel obliged to do so? Does Alfred expect to receive this amount when the dividends are paid to Beryl? Are there any mitigating factors that exist in favour of Beryl?[16] These are issues that are connected to the weight of the evidence. Issues of weight are for the tribunal of fact. If the court is convinced that Beryl's conduct acknowledges the interest of Alfred, the presumption of resulting trust will not be rebutted as to 50 per cent of the shares. There does not appear to be any evidence of the conduct of the parties regarding the remaining 50 per cent of the shares. On this basis Alfred will be presumed to retain the equitable interest in these shares as well and the presumption may not be rebutted. The effect would be that Beryl holds 50 per cent of the shares (capital) on resulting trust for Alfred, subject to the terms of the initial transfer. Alternatively, if the presumption is rebutted, Beryl will be entitled to the shares in equity but subject to the terms of the initial transfer.

An additional complication is that the initial transfer of the shares by Alfred to Beryl was subject to an option exercisable by Charles to repurchase 50 per cent of the shares within five years. Thus, the legal right to exercise the option was vested in Charles. This much is clear. The question in issue concerns the location of the equitable interest in the option. This is a voluntary transfer of property rights and accordingly gives rise to a presumption of resulting trust (prior to the Equality Act 2010 a transfer of property by a father to his son would have given rise to a presumption of advancement). The effect is that, *prima facie*, Charles holds the legal right to the option in favour of Alfred. We have not been

---

16   Identification of issues of fact.

given any evidence that could be used in rebuttal of this presumption of resulting trust. Accordingly, Alfred may maintain his equitable interest in the option.

(b) A transfer of £50,000 to trustees

The issue in this problem is whether Mary's beneficial interest terminates when she graduates from London University or, alternatively, whether her interest continues. If Mary's interest terminates, an automatic resulting trust will arise in favour of the transferor as a default mechanism.[17]

The transferor stipulated two alternative events that will trigger a termination of Mary's interest – attaining the age of 25 and graduating from university – and added 'whichever happens earlier'. Mary has recently graduated from London University. This is the earlier event. What effect will this have in respect of the trust? One solution is that a resulting trust arises.[18] The graduation from London University is a determinable condition that signals the end of Mary's interest in the trust. This solution was adopted in *Re Abbott* (1900), where funds were raised for the benefit of two impecunious ladies. On the death of the last surviving beneficiary, creating a surplus of funds, the court decided that a resulting trust for the contributors had arisen.

Alternatively, the court may, on construction, decide that the ultimate intention of the transferor was to benefit Mary 'out and out' with education as the motive for the gift. This was the approach adopted in *Re Andrews* (1905) and *Re Osoba* (1979). There was a similarity in both of these cases in that the transfer on trust was for the education of the beneficiary and they were still capable of enjoying the benefit from the trust. In *Osoba* the court interpreted 'education' liberally and did not restrict it to formal education. In addition, the beneficiaries were still capable of benefiting from the trust. If this approach is adopted to the facts of this problem, it would be possible for Mary to remain a beneficiary and enjoy the income from the property until at least she attains the age of 25. On attaining that age, which is precise and does not create any room for construction, Mary's interest will terminate and a resulting trust will be set up for the transferor.

(c) A transfer of £70,000 to the trustees of his daughter's marriage settlement

There are several issues in this problem. The terms of the trust indicate that the income is payable to Danielle until her death, subject to a restriction that she does not have an abortion. Five years after the transfer Danielle has an abortion. The first issue is whether this clause is void on the ground of public policy. It is not a positive requirement that Danielle must have an abortion (which might be void), but it is a negative prohibition that she does not have an abortion. On this basis it is likely that the clause is valid. The

---

17   Identification of the relevant legal issues.
18   Flexible questions of construction.

next issue concerns the effect of the abortion that Danielle arranged. In particular, would this condition trigger the termination of Danielle's interest? If the court decides that a condition subsequently has taken place and that this brings Danielle's interest to an end, the next issue is the destination of the equitable interest. Ernest, the next in line, is entitled to the income on the death of Danielle, and not merely on the termination of her interest. The issue is whether a resulting trust arises or alternatively, that Ernest's interest is accelerated after Danielle has an abortion. The doctrine of acceleration of a postponed interest is based on the notion that if a prior interest under a trust fails so that the reason for the postponement disappears, a subsequent interest may be brought forward and be enjoyed immediately. The gap in ownership may be filled by an acceleration of a subsequent interest. There is no room for a resulting trust in order to delay the enjoyment of the subsequent interest. Such complications often take place where a draftsman of a trust or will fails to foresee a contingency which has in fact taken place. The court will construe the trust instrument or will in order to ascertain whether there is a gap in ownership and whether the doctrine of acceleration is capable of filling that gap: see *Re Cochrane* (1955). Applying the test to the facts of this case, it appears that no provision is made in the trust for the equitable interest in the events that have taken place. In such an event the court may apply the doctrine of acceleration and bring forward Ernest's life interest after Danielle's interest lapses.

All three parties die in a car crash. For the purposes of inheritance it may be necessary to ascertain the order in which the parties died. If there is no medical evidence to determine the order of death, the doctrine of *commorientes* (endorsed in s 184 of the Law of Property Act 1925) may be adopted to identify when the deaths are deemed to take place. This rule stipulates that the order of deaths is based on the seniority of the individuals. Thus, Frederick is presumed to be the last to die and the property may be distributed to Frederick's heirs.

INTRODUCTION

In the following two chapters we will turn our attention to one of the most versatile of all the forms of the trust concept: the constructive trust. Indeed, so versatile is this concept in the modern law that there really are several types of constructive trusts, all of which bear the same name, but which do not necessarily share the same characteristics or serve the same purposes, save only that they all arise by operation of law consequent upon some defect of conscience on the part of the constructive trustee. In this particular chapter, we will consider two specific kinds of constructive trust. First, there is the constructive trust that is imposed on a trustee or other fiduciary as a consequence of that person using his or her position to make a personal profit or gain. In essence, this constructive trust requires the trustee or fiduciary to hold to account any such profits on trust for the beneficiaries or persons to whom the fiduciary duties are owed: see *Crown Dilmun Ltd v Sutton* (2004). It is in the nature both of a remedy against the trustee/fiduciary for unauthorised activities and a safeguard that ensures that she acts for the benefit of the trust and not for herself. Second, we shall consider the particular principles applicable to the acquisition of interests in land where a person claims a share in a matrimonial or quasi-matrimonial home belonging in law to another. This species of constructive trust is in the nature of a remedy against the legal owner of property, against whom the constructive trust is deployed, in order to achieve equity between the parties.

At the outset, it should be noted that it is notoriously difficult to define with precision the exact circumstances in which a constructive trust may arise. Yet, perhaps that is just as it should be. If there is a common thread that links all types of constructive trust (and that is debatable), it is that they are used to prevent and rectify inequitable conduct. Consequently, some of the material considered in this chapter may well overlap with material considered elsewhere.

QUESTION 32

Discuss the trusts issues raised in each of the situations below and advise the parties concerned:

(a) Sgt Jim Tow was until recently a British member of the UN peacekeeping force in Utopia. He was in charge of the security of food depots. He has accumulated a sum of £50,000 in a London bank account. This money came from bribes he received from some civilian workers of a large aid agency working in Utopia who were illegally selling UN food supplies to private food shops. These facts have now been exposed by a Sunday newspaper.

(b) Peter is the company secretary of two companies, namely X Co Ltd and Y Co plc. Six months ago he passed on to his friend, James, special company information on the two companies. James subsequently sold the information to a third company for £100,000, which he shared with Peter.

Aim Higher

A fiduciary will be required to disgorge any unauthorised profits he makes in breach of his fiduciary duties. This may be achieved by a constructive trust of the profits or he will be personally liable to account in favour of the innocent party. The remedies that are available vary with the circumstances of each case. In particular, relevant issues include whether the contract with the third party has been performed or not and whether the fiduciary still has the property under his control.

Common Pitfalls

Students sometimes fail to appreciate the distinction between breaches of duties by trustees and breaches of fiduciary duties by trustees. Breaches of fiduciary duties only occur when the fiduciary does not act with the beneficiary's best interests in mind.

How to Answer this Question

- ❖ Conflict of duty and interest.
- ❖ Duty to account for bribes received.
- ❖ Whether trust information may be treated as trust property.
- ❖ Knowingly receiving trust property.

Answer structure

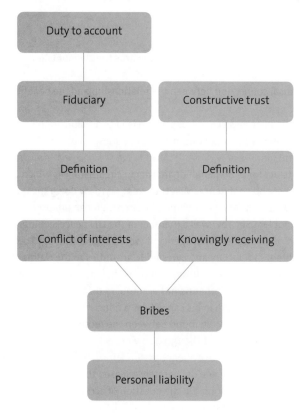

This diagram highlights the personal liability to account for breach of trust and the liability as constructive trustee.

ANSWER

(a) Sgt Tow

Jim Tow has accumulated £50,000 from bribes by illegally selling UN food supplies to private shops. The question is whether he is accountable to the UN agency for these bribes.[1] The general rule is that a person occupying a position of confidence (such as a trustee or fiduciary) is prohibited from deriving any personal benefit by availing himself of his position, in the absence of authority from the beneficiaries, trust instrument or the court. In other words, the trustee or fiduciary should not place himself in the position where his duties may conflict with his personal interest. If such a conflict occurs and the

---

1   Identification of the issues involved in the question.

trustee obtains a benefit or profit, he is accountable to the claimants as if he is a constructive trustee. This is known as the rule in *Keech v Sandford* (1726).

The ingredients of the claim are:[2]

(1)   the defendant holds a fiduciary position towards the claimant; and
(2)   the defendant obtained a benefit; and
(3)   there is a causal connection between the relationship and the benefit.

Failure to establish all of these conditions would lead to a failure in the proceedings. The first issue is whether Sgt Tow is a fiduciary. This is a question of law. The concept was defined by Millett LJ in *Bristol and West Building Society v Mothew* (1996) as someone who has undertaken to act for or on behalf of another in circumstances which give rise to a relationship of trust and confidence. Millett LJ went on to lay down the duties imposed on a fiduciary and added that he is prohibited from making an unauthorised profit. On the facts of the problem Sgt Tow was a member of the UN peacekeeping force in Utopia. He acts on behalf of an international agency. It would appear that Sgt Tow, as a security officer, is undoubtedly a fiduciary and owes fiduciary duties to the claimant; see *Reading v Attorney General* (1951). The next issue is whether he had obtained a profit. This is a question of fact and we are told that he has accumulated £50,000 in a London bank account. Did he receive this sum in his capacity as a fiduciary? This is also a question of fact and requires a causal link to be found between the receipt of the sum and his fiduciary capacity. We are told that the £50,000 was received as bribes for the illegal sales to private shops. This is conclusive evidence that, in effect, he abused his position as a security officer and consciously and deliberately released the food to unauthorised persons in return for remuneration. On the question of accountability for the bribes, the clear rule is that the defendant is required to pay back the bribes that he received: see *Lister & Co v Stubbs* (1890), *Sinclair Investments v Versailles Ltd* [2011] EWCA 347 and contrast *Attorney General for Hong Kong v Reid* (1994). But if the defendant had invested the bribes and received a profit, a more complicated question is involved, namely, whether he is accountable only for the bribes and whether in addition to the bribes he is accountable for the profits derived from the bribes. The solution adopted by the Court of Appeal in *Lister v Stubbs* was that on receipt of the bribe a relationship of debtor and creditor is created. This did not involve the trust notion. However, the Privy Council in *Attorney General for Hong Kong v Reid* refused to follow *Lister* and decided that both the bribe and the additional profit are held upon trust for the persons to whom the duty is owed. On receipt of the bribe, the fiduciary becomes a trustee of the sum for the benefit of the innocent party and is liable to account for this property and any derivative profits. If the bribe is used to purchase other property which decreases in value, the fiduciary is required to account for the difference between the bribe and the undervalue. Alternatively, if the property has increased in value, the innocent party is entitled to claim

---

2   Specification of the elements of the claim.

the surplus, because the fiduciary is not entitled to profit from a breach of his duties. The reason for this rule is that when the bribe is received, it is required to be paid immediately to the claimant; principle – equity considers as done that which ought to be done. Thus, a constructive trust is attached to the bribe. The effect is that the £50,000 in the bank account may be the subject of a constructive trust in favour of the claimant. More recently the Court of Appeal in *Sinclair v Versailles* (2011) refused to follow the Privy Council decision in *Reid* and instead endorsed the *Lister* principle. The effect is that an agent or other fiduciary who receives a bribe has a personal liability to account to the principal for the amount of the bribe as a debtor. The claim is personal and not proprietary and therefore the claimant does not acquire an interest in investments acquired with the proceeds of the bribe.

(b) Peter

Peter, a company secretary, is an officer of the companies X Co Ltd and Y Co plc and is clearly a fiduciary in respect of those companies. He discloses sensitive information concerning the companies to James. On the basis of the analysis in (a) above he is in breach of his duties as a fiduciary in both unlawfully disclosing the information and receiving a profit as a result of the disclosure. He has allowed his duties to conflict with his interest: see *Industrial Developments v Cooley* (1972) and *Regal (Hastings) Ltd v Gulliver* (1942). In *Boardman v Phipps* (1967) an argument was raised as to whether information was capable of being treated as trust property. The House of Lords, by a majority, decided that confidential information was capable of being trust property. On the facts of this problem Peter has used trust property (information) to derive an unauthorised profit and is therefore accountable as a constructive trustee.[3]

Peter's accomplice, James, may also be liable as a constructive trustee and be under a duty to account to the claimants for the profits that he made by selling confidential information (trust property). The test, laid down by Hoffmann LJ in *El Ajou v Dollar Land Holdings plc* (1994), is whether:

* James received trust property,
* in breach of trust; and
* knows that the information is trust property; and
* acts in a way inconsistent with the trust.[4]

On the first issue the court decided in *Boardman v Phipps* that confidential information is capable of being trust property (see above). With regard to the problem there was clearly a breach of trust in that the companies did not authorise the disclosure of the information. Does James have knowledge that the information is trust property?

3   Application of the law to the facts.
4   Identification of the claim.

'Knowledge' for these purposes had been classified by Peter Gibson J in *Re Baden Delvaux* (1983) as including subjective and objective knowledge. This is a question of degree. Since James does not repay the proceeds of sale to the companies, he acts inconsistently with the trust. Accordingly, a court order may be attached to the £100,000 received by James.

Alternatively, in *Re Montagu Settlement Trust* (1987) and more recently in *BCCI v Akindele* (2000) the court decided that the basis of liability when a stranger receives trust property for his own benefit is unconscionability, i.e. whether it would be unconscionable for the defendant to retain the property. The court also decided that the test is subjective knowledge or dishonesty. In *Twinsectra v Yardley* (2002) the House of Lords decided that the test for dishonesty is the combination test that exists in criminal law, i.e. the defendant's conduct is dishonest by reference to the ordinary standards of reasonable and honest people *and* that he himself realised that his conduct was dishonest by those standards. This is both an objective and subjective test.

If James did not receive the trust property but merely assisted Peter dishonestly in a fraudulent design, he (James) will be accountable as if he was a constructive trustee. This was the test laid down in the definitive case of *Royal Brunei Airlines v Tan* (1995). The basis of liability is dishonesty which has been interpreted in *Twinsectra*. Further, in *Barlow Clowes International Ltd v Eurotrust* (2006), the Privy Council decided that an inquiry into the defendant's views about standards of honesty was not required. The standard by which dishonesty is judged is objective. In *Abou-Ramah v Abacha* [2006] EWCA 1492, the Court of Appeal endorsed the approach that was adopted in *Barlow Clowes* (2006) and confirmed that the standard for dishonesty is objective.

QUESTION 33

A trustee must not place herself in a position where her interest and duty conflict.

▶ Discuss, with reference to decided cases.

How to Answer this Question

❖ Constructive trusts imposed on persons already in a fiduciary position in order to ensure that any profit made by virtue of that position is not retained.

❖ There is a duty to the trust but a self-interest to keep the profit: thus, merits of trustee's action are not determinative of their right to keep a profit.

❖ Examples of various circumstances in which this liability can arise.

Answer structure

This diagram illustrates the extent of the fiduciary duty to account.

ANSWER

According to Lord Herschel in *Bray v Ford* (1896), a trustee or other fiduciary must not place herself in a position where her interest and duty conflict.[5] Similarly, a trustee or fiduciary is not permitted to profit from her fiduciary position except when authorised to retain such profit. Consequently, any personal gain attributable to the trusteeship or fiduciary position must be held on constructive trust for the beneficiaries of the trust or the persons to whom the fiduciary relationship is owed (*Aberdeen Town Council v Aberdeen University* (1877)). The essence of the matter is that a trustee (or other fiduciary) owes clear and strict duties to administer the trust property or other assets for the benefit of those entitled in equity to that property or assets. In order to ensure that these

---

5   Clear statement of the principle of law.

duties are honoured in full, there is a virtually absolute bar against the trustee using her position for any personal gain. Such is the strictness of this rule that a constructive trust will be imposed on a trustee or other fiduciary irrespective of any intentional deceit, recklessness or negligence on her part (*Regal (Hastings) Ltd v Gulliver* (1942)).[6] It is enough if the trustee or fiduciary has simply placed herself in a position where her duty to the trust has conflicted with her own interest. In *Crown Dilmun Ltd v Sutton* (2004), the court decided that a fiduciary who concealed information from his employer concerning the opportunity to redevelop property in order to benefit himself, was accountable to the claimant for the profits received.

This overriding principle of equity is of general application, but it is now recognised that there are a number of identifiable situations where the court will intervene to impose a constructive trust on a trustee or fiduciary. These situations represent accepted occasions when a conflict of interest and duty – irrespective of fault – will result in the imposition of a constructive trust and the holding of any gain or profit for the beneficiaries or persons entitled.[7]

First, as a matter of principle, trustees are under a duty to act without remuneration: trusteeship is essentially gratuitous. The trustee's obligation is to ensure the most efficient running of the trust, without the self-interest of creating unwarranted work for which they could be paid (*Robinson v Pett* (1734)). However, even though the rule is strictly applied, it must be emphasised that there is nothing illegal in a trustee receiving remuneration for her work. Rather, any remuneration so received will presumptively be held by way of constructive trust unless there is some applicable rule of law or statute or specific provision in the trust instrument which allows the fiduciary to retain the payment. Consequently, most professionally drafted trusts will contain a remuneration clause authorising the trustees to be paid, and the court retains an inherent jurisdiction to order remuneration if this would be for the better administration of the trust (*Re Duke of Norfolk's Settlement Trusts* (1981)). More importantly, the Trustee Act 2000 contains general provisions authorising the payment of remuneration or stipulating the circumstances in which remuneration can be paid (ss 28–30). They will provide remuneration for nearly all professional trustees, subject to any express terms of the trust instrument. Other means by which the trustee may properly claim to keep any remuneration arise from the existence of a contract to that effect with the beneficiary (although a promise to fulfil existing duties is not good consideration), under certain statutory provisions (for example, s 42 of the Trustee Act 1942; Judicial Trustee Act 1896), under the special rules relating to solicitor trustees (*Cradock v Piper* (1850)) and where the payment is earned during administration of assets abroad (*Re Northcote's Will Trusts* (1949)).

Second, there is a rule that a trustee may not purchase for herself certain types of property, in particular rights in property which should properly be purchased for the

6   Justification of the principle of law.
7   Special application of the general rule.

beneficiaries. So, where a trustee holds a lease for the beneficiaries, if she subsequently obtains a renewal of that lease for herself, the renewed lease will be held on constructive trust for the beneficiaries (*Keech v Sandford* (1726)). This will be so even if it is clear that the landlord would not have renewed the lease in favour of the beneficiaries. The trustee's duty is to act in the best interests of the beneficiaries, not in her own, and there is an irrebuttable presumption of law that a trustee cannot take the benefit of the lease for herself (*Re Biss* (1903)). In similar fashion, it has been held in *Protheroe v Protheroe* (1968) that a constructive trust will be imposed on a trustee who purchases the reversion expectant on a lease which is trust property, once again because the trustee should have been concerned to acquire that reversion for the beneficiary, not for herself. This decision has been subject to considerable criticism, especially as earlier authority (*Griffith v Owen* (1907)) seemed to limit the principle to cases where the lease itself was renewable by custom and hence was already approaching freehold ownership. Nevertheless, the case has been followed without demur and may now represent as firm a rule as that of *Keech* itself (*Re Thompson* (1934) and *Popat v Shonchhatra* (1997)).

Third, as explained in *Tito v Waddell (No 2)* (1977), a trustee is unable to purchase the trust property itself. Simply put, the trustee cannot be both vendor (as trustee) and purchaser of property which she is holding for the benefit of another (*Ex p Lacey* (1802)). This is known as the 'self-dealing' rule, although it should be emphasised that, in some circumstances, a trustee will be permitted to retain her purchase if the reasons for the self-dealing rule are not present.[8] Thus, in *Holder v Holder* (1966) an executor (that is, a fiduciary) who had little to do with the administration of the estate was permitted to retain property which he had purchased openly and at market value, despite the fact that, technically, the self-dealing rule had been violated. However, such cases must be examined closely because the overriding principle is that a trustee or fiduciary must not put herself in a position where her interest and duty conflict: it is usually immaterial once that position is reached whether there was any actual conflict of duty and interest.

Fourth, and in similar vein, the 'fair dealing' rule makes it clear that a trustee may only purchase the interest of the beneficiary if the transaction was at full market value and the trustee disclosed all material facts (*Dougan v Macpherson* (1902)). Again, the trustee must not use her position to gain an advantage when she should be acting for the beneficiaries, and so the sale will be disallowed if the trustee had made use of her position to achieve the purchase. Likewise, a trustee cannot sell her own property to the beneficiary without making full disclosure of all material facts (*Re Cape Breton Co* (1885)).

Fifth, there are a number of cases, involving different factual backgrounds, where the court has imposed a constructive trust on a fiduciary because of a conflict of interest and duty in a business context. For example, it has been held that any fees paid to company directors who

---

8   Exceptional cases where the trustee or fiduciary may purchase trust property.

hold those directorships because of their legal ownership of trust shares must be held on trust for the beneficiaries (*Re Francis* (1905); *Re Macadam* (1946)). As mentioned before, the essence of the matter is that such directors will have received fees only because they were trustees, although if their appointments were not due to their holding trust shares, the fees may be retained (*Re Dover Coalfield Extension* (1908)). Again, in *Williams v Barton* (1927), a trustee who persuaded the trust to employ a firm of stockbrokers from whom he received a commission was held to hold that commission on constructive trust for the beneficiaries, and in *Boardman v Phipps* (1967), a solicitor who made a profit from the purchase of shares, having gained important information while acting as a fiduciary, was required to hold that profit on trust. A further example is provided by *Reading v Attorney General* (1951), where an army sergeant was held to be a constructive trustee of monies received for escorting vehicles unsearched through army checkpoints, although in *Regal (Hastings) Ltd v Gulliver* (1942) it was emphasised that neither fraud nor absence of *bona fides* was necessary to trigger the imposition of the constructive trust in these circumstances (see, also, *LSE v Pearson* (2000)). The presence of a good motive may mean, as in *Boardman*, that a fiduciary is entitled to receive equitable remuneration for her skill in achieving a profit, even though the profit itself must be held on trust for the beneficiaries. Obviously, however, this jurisdiction will not be exercised in favour of a fiduciary who is *mala fides* or whose fiduciary duties positively prohibit personal gain (*Guinness plc v Saunders* (1990)).

Clearly the equitable principle that a trustee must not place herself in a position where her interest and duty conflict has many applications. However, it must not be thought that the types of liability discussed above are exhaustive, or that every case of a conflict of interest and duty can be neatly pigeonholed into one of these categories. By way of example, in *Attorney General for Hong Kong v Reid* (1994), the Privy Council has held that a bribe accepted by a person in a fiduciary position will be held on constructive trust for the person(s) to whom the fiduciary duty is owed, so disapproving of *Lister & Co v Stubbs* (1890), which for many years had decided that no constructive trust could exist in these circumstances. Consequently, following *Reid*, the person to whom the fiduciary duties are owed will be able to call for the bribe, receive any increase in value in the bribe, and trace the bribe as proprietary owner into whatever property is purchased with it. For example, in *LSE v Pearson* (2000), Pearson owed fiduciary duties to the LSE and had accepted secret payments from a supplier. He was to hold such payments on trust for the LSE, irrespective of any corrupt motive. A similar decision was reached in *Daraydan Holdings v Solland Interiors* (2004), where the court affirmed the principle laid down by the Privy Council in *Reid* and refused to follow *Lister*. The cases illustrate that not only is the court's ability to impose a constructive trust always under review, but the principle that a trustee must not place herself in a position where her interest and duty conflict places powerful remedies in the hands of the beneficiaries. However, in *Sinclair Investments v Versailles Ltd* (2011) the Court of Appeal refused to follow *Reid* and decided that the recipient of a bribe owes a personal duty to account to the principal for the amount of the bribe and this principle does not extend to assets purchased with the proceeds of the bribe.

QUESTION 34

The Trustee Act 2000 contains widely drawn statutory authority permitting professional trustees to charge for their services. This is a very desirable reform of the pre-existing law.

▶ Discuss.

How to Answer this Question

❖ Discuss inadequacies in the old law.
❖ Outline Trustee Act 2000 provisions on trustee remuneration.

Answer structure

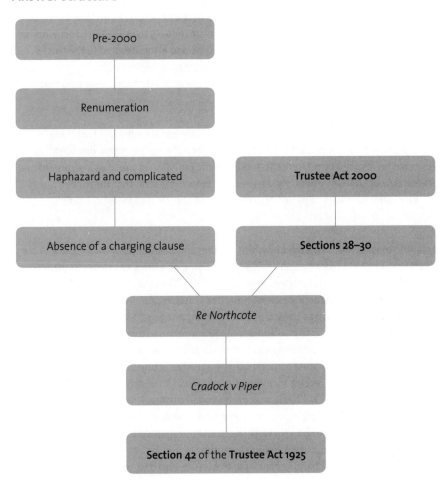

This diagram highlights the changes made by the Trustee Act 2000 authorising trustees to be paid for their services.

ANSWER

The office of trusteeship is inherently gratuitous, springing from the fundamental principle that a trustee must not place himself in a position where his interest and duty conflict (*Bray v Ford* (1896)). Consequently, before the Trustee Act 2000, it was clear both in principle and practice that a trustee should act without remuneration (that is, payment for services rendered), unless there was some specific rule of law or equity under which the trustee could charge.[9] The overriding fear was that the trustee might be tempted to generate income for himself by creating work, thus unnecessarily overloading the trust and acting in his own interest instead of that of the beneficiaries (*Robinson v Pett* (1734)). Of course, it was also true that the gratuitous nature of trusteeship could itself cause problems. For complicated trusts, it is essential that the beneficiaries are able to rely on experienced and professional advisers, but these are unlikely to be willing to act without payment. Even in smaller trusts, the amount of time and effort devoted to the trust's administration may reflect lack of payment and, instead of preventing the overloading of the trust, the absence of payment might result in too little attention being paid to its affairs; a balance needs to be struck.

Prior to the Act, the balance was adopted by acceptance of the principle that there was nothing unlawful in a trustee receiving payment for fulfilling his duties, provided that this could be justified by reference to some specific provision in the trust instrument or a general rule of law. Unfortunately, as discussed below, it is clear that these pre-Trustee Act 2000 principles indicating when a trustee could receive remuneration were haphazard, complicated and altogether unsatisfactory.[10]

By far the most common method by which trustees could have established – and still can establish – a right to receive remuneration is by relying on an express clause in the trust instrument authorising the trustees to be paid (*Willis v Kibble* (1839)). This method will continue to be common for professionally drafted trusts, especially for trusts that employ professional trustees such as banks and investment managers.[11] Such a charging clause can be drafted widely so as to give appropriate recompense to trustees acting in a professional capacity. In addition, under s 28 of the Trustee Act 2000, where such a clause exists and the trustee is a trust corporation or is a trustee acting in a professional capacity, the trustee is entitled to receive such remuneration even if the services rendered could have been provided by a lay (that is, non-professional) trustee. This effectively reverses the old law with respect to 'charging clauses', which were always construed strictly against a trustee and prevented charging for work that could be regarded as not within the professional ambit of the trustee. In this sense, the Trustee Act 2000 supports and enhances the efficacy of charging clauses in trusts (see, also, s 28(4)(a): signature of a

---

9   Outline the pre-2000 principles of law and justification.

10 Criticisms of the pre-2000 rules.

11 Prevalence of express charging clauses.

witness to the will does not invalidate a charging clause in the will in favour of that witness). It is a welcome change to the law and releases trust law from the scope of rules developed at a time when trusts were largely private matters undertaken for private tasks.

In the absence of a charging clause in a trust, the law prior to the Trustee Act 2000 made it difficult for a trustee to claim remuneration. So, although the court had (and probably still has) an inherent jurisdiction to order the payment of remuneration, including authorising payment for the first time or varying an existing charging clause (*Re Duke of Norfolk's Settlement Trusts* (1981); *Foster v Spence* (1996)), the power was limited. The court would not authorise remuneration simply for the benefit of the trustee, but only if the payment of remuneration would be for the better administration of the trust. When deciding whether to exercise its discretion, the court would consider every aspect of the case, including how the administration of the trust would be improved, the need to protect beneficiaries from unscrupulous trustees and the essentially gratuitous nature of trusteeship, and only if there was a demonstrable need for professional trustees or if the trustees could not undertake the proper administration of the trust without devoting more of their own time, would remuneration be awarded.[12]

Second, although it was possible for a trustee to establish a right to remuneration through the conclusion of a contract to that effect with the beneficiaries, the courts looked with scepticism at such arrangements. For example, the trustee might have been forced into an unfavourable contract (or any contract) by a threat from the trustee to abandon his duties under the trust. Consequently, such contracts were rare (*Ayliffe v Murray* (1740)) and, in any event, the trustee must have offered consideration for the beneficiaries' promise to pay, which could not be the promise to carry out the duties under the trust which the trustee is already obliged to perform.

Third, there remain several (relatively limited) statutory provisions that authorise the payment of remuneration to certain types of trustees. It must be emphasised, however, that these provisions do not authorise the payment of trustees generally, but rather are designed to ensure that specific trustees appointed for specific purposes can be paid (for example, under s 42 of the Trustee Act 1925). A trust corporation appointed by the court may be authorised to charge the trust for administering it, and similar provisions exist in respect of the judicial trustee, the public trustee and persons appointed as custodian trustees (s 1(5) of the Judicial Trustee Act 1896; ss 4(3) and 9 of the Public Trustee Act 1906).

Fourth, it remains the case that a trustee may be entitled to retain any remuneration received as a result of administering assets abroad, provided that these are received involuntarily (*Re Northcote's Will Trusts* (1949)). This exception is of limited importance

---

12   Factors relevant in exercising the court's discretion.

and is born more of convenience than of principle. The essence of the matter seems to be that the court regards the payment of remuneration from outside its jurisdiction as presumptively outside its control, unless it is in the nature of a bribe or is otherwise inequitable. Finally, a solicitor trustee has a unique right to receive remuneration for work undertaken on behalf of the trust, provided that these 'profit costs' relate to work undertaken on behalf of the trust generally (and not in respect of his trusteeship alone) and are no greater than those that 'could have been incurred if the solicitor had not been a trustee' (*Cradock v Piper* (1850)). Again, this is a limited exception to the general pre-Trustee Act 2000 principles and is akin to the solicitor trustee being paid for work which is in addition to his normal duties as trustee.

Obviously, apart from the use of the charging clause, which is now made more efficacious by the 2000 Act, there was limited scope for a trustee to claim remuneration. The absence of such a clause meant that a trustee had little hope of claiming remuneration unless one of the limited exceptions applied. It was in order to meet this deficiency that the Trustee Act 2000 now provides, in s 29, methods by which different types of trustees may claim remuneration. First, under s 29(1), a trustee who is a trust corporation (not being a trustee of a charity) 'is entitled to receive reasonable remuneration out of the trust funds for any services that the trust corporation provides', provided that no such remuneration is provided for in the trust instrument or by any other statutory provision. Secondly, under s 29(2) a trustee who acts in a professional capacity (not being a trust corporation, sole trustee or trustee of a charity) is entitled to receive reasonable remuneration if every other trustee has agreed in writing to such payment, again provided that no such remuneration is provided for in the trust instrument or by any other statutory provision. In addition, under s 30 of the Trustee Act 2000, regulations may be made concerning the provision of remuneration to trustees of charities who are trust corporations or who act in a professional capacity.

These are wide powers, with ss 29 and 30 providing, for the first time, a general right for trust corporations, trustees acting in a professional capacity (not being sole trustees) and trustees of charitable trusts to be paid for work done on behalf of the trust. It seems now that it is only sole trustees (not being a trust corporation or charitable trustee) that have no general statutory right to remuneration. This is entirely appropriate in an age where the trust has developed beyond the 'family' trust so common in many of the earlier cases.

NOTE
Questions 33 and 34 addressed the wider issue of when a trustee must avoid a situation where his interest and duty conflict and this raises some issues about remuneration.

QUESTION 35

Barnaby and Alan are trustees of a fund set up in 2009 in favour of Henry and Oliver. The trust property consists of shares in numerous companies, cash on deposit and various property investments. Barnaby is appointed a director of one of the companies in which the trust has a shareholding because the combined total of the trust's shareholding and his own shareholding (which he purchased at the same time the trust invested in the company) makes him a major investor. He is paid £1,000 per annum for this and has received dividends of some £2,000 in respect of his own shares. Getahead plc is a financial services company and attempts to bribe Alan to transfer to them some of the trust's business. Alan is reluctant, but after checking the history of Getahead plc, he persuades Barnaby that they should transfer some £50,000 worth of assets to the company for investment. In return, he receives some shares in Getahead, which doubled in value due to the spectacular success of the company over the next six months. The trust's investment has also doubled. Other trust property includes a leasehold of an office complex in London and, as trustees, Barnaby and Alan are offered the chance to purchase the reversion for £30,000. They refuse, in good faith, on the advice of Getahead, which is predicting a recession. The reversion is, however, placed on the open market, and Alan purchases it for £20,000 at an auction. Alan has arranged a sale in six months' time to a property developer for £35,000.

▶ Discuss.

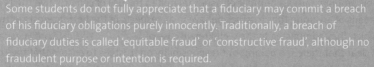

Aim Higher ★

In *Lister v Stubbs* and *Sinclair v Versailles* (2011), in both cases the Court of Appeal decided that ownership of the bribe was the main issue. This was different from a trust obligation and therefore no trust, not even a constructive trust, was created. In short, the bribe involved a personal liability to account but there was no trust. The argument in favour of trust had confused ownership with obligation, whereas in *AG for Hong Kong v Reid*, Lord Templeman reasoned that the receipt of a bribe involved a debt and then proceeded to create a constructive trust of the bribe based on the maxim 'equity regards as done that which ought to be done'.

Common Pitfalls ✘

Some students do not fully appreciate that a fiduciary may commit a breach of his fiduciary obligations purely innocently. Traditionally, a breach of fiduciary duties is called 'equitable fraud' or 'constructive fraud', although no fraudulent purpose or intention is required.

How to Answer this Question

- ❖ Brief introduction to profits by trustees.
- ❖ Directors' fees.
- ❖ Share purchase because of information received while in a fiduciary position.
- ❖ Bribes.
- ❖ Interests in property.

Answer Structure

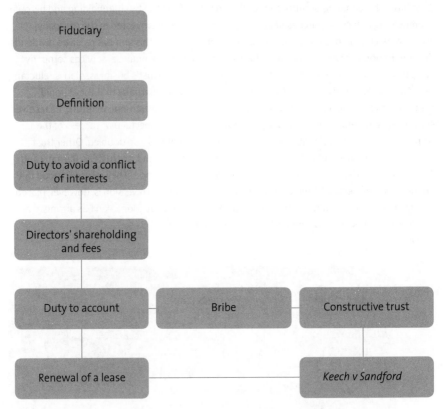

This diagram charts the fiduciary nature of trustees' liability to account and consider the rationale of liability for the receipt of bribes.

ANSWER

This problem raises a number of issues related to the use of constructive trusts as a means of ensuring that trustees behave in all respects in the best interests of the trust which they administer. In the well-known case of *Bray v Ford* (1896), Lord Herschell made it clear that there is a paramount responsibility on trustees to ensure that they do not place themselves in a position where their self-interest conflicts with their duty to the beneficiaries.[13] In order to give effect to this principle, the courts are prepared to impose a duty to account on a person who makes a personal profit or gain by virtue of his fiduciary position. The effect of this is that the profit or gain is then also held for the benefit of the beneficiaries, on the same or similar terms as those governing the subject matter of the

13   Clear statement of the general rule and its effect.

trust or fiduciary relationship proper. Indeed, such is the nature of this jurisdiction that the imposition of a duty to account does not depend on the trustee or fiduciary being *mala fides* but can be imposed if he is entirely honest and acting for what he perceives to be the best of motives (*Regal (Hastings) Ltd v Gulliver* (1942); *LSE v Pearson* (2000)). It is within this framework that the actions of Barnaby and Alan must be judged.

(a) The actions of Barnaby in respect of the company shares

It has been made clear in a line of cases that if a trustee is appointed a director of a company by reason of the fact that he is the legal owner of shares (that is, he holds the shares on trust for others), any fees thereby received by way of remuneration must be held on the same trusts for the beneficiaries (*Re Francis* (1905); *Re Macadam* (1946)).[14] The point is simply that a trustee is under an obligation to account as constructive trustee for any profits received by virtue of the trusteeship (*Aberdeen Town Council v Aberdeen University* (1877)). Our case is not, however, quite straightforward. As was pointed out in *Re Dover Coalfield Extension* (1908), a director trustee is not bound automatically to hold any personal profits on trust for the beneficiaries, but only after proper enquiry as to the facts of the particular case.[15] Thus, if Barnaby became a director without reliance on the trust shares, he may retain his £1,000 per annum, even if the shares thereafter help him maintain his position (*Re Dover Coalfield*). Whether this is so in Barnaby's case is not clear from the facts of the problem. In addition, there is a hint of another difficulty, in that Barnaby acquired his shareholding at the same time as the trust invested in the company. If this private purchase was made possible because of Barnaby's position as trustee, there is every possibility that he will be deemed to be a constructive trustee of the shares themselves, in similar fashion to the result in *Boardman v Phipps* (1967). In that case, a solicitor was held to be a constructive trustee of profits made in certain share transactions because he had acquired the knowledge and opportunity to buy the shares by virtue of his fiduciary position. If this is the case with Barnaby, not only will he hold his director's fees and shares on trust for Henry and Oliver (the trust, of course, having reimbursed Barnaby for the cost of the shares), but the £2,000 of dividends will pass to the beneficiaries as well, being income from trust property. Note, however, that if there is a provision in the trust instrument authorising Barnaby to receive remuneration for the performance of his duties as trustee, he may be able to retain some of the fees (*Re Gee* (1948)), and if Barnaby is acting 'in a professional capacity' he may be able to claim 'reasonable remuneration' under s 29(2) of the Trustee Act 2000, if the other trustee agrees in writing. Likewise, if he has behaved honestly and fairly throughout, the court might exercise its inherent jurisdiction to award him a sum by way of equitable compensation (*Boardman*).

....

14 Extension of the trust property.
15 Recognition that some issues are dependent on their facts.

(b) Alan and Getahead plc

It is a serious matter for a trustee to accept a bribe as an inducement to breach his obligations to the beneficiaries and it may well involve him in criminal liability. Furthermore, it is now clear that the receipt of a bribe will impose a personal obligation on Alan to account to the trust for the proceeds of the bribe: see *Lister v Stubbs* (1890). This principle was affirmed by the Court of Appeal in *Sinclair v Versailles* (2011). The effect is that on receipt of the bribe Alan becomes a debtor to the trust for the amount of the bribe. On the other side of the coin lies the decision of the Privy Council in *AG for Hong Kong v Reid* (1994) which expressed disapproval of the *Lister* decision and decided that the bribe itself will be held on constructive trust for the beneficiaries. The *Reid* principle was applied in *LSE v Pearson* (2000) and *Daraydan Holdings v Solland Interiors* (2004)). Consequently, applying the *Reid* principle, any increase in value of the bribe (or in the property that now represents it) in the hands of the recipient will also accrue to the beneficiaries. On the other hand, applying the Sinclair rule Alan will be accountable for the amount of the bribe. In our case, it is not clear whether any bribe has in fact been given and received.[16] We are told that Alan is 'reluctant' to accept Getahead's offer and the fact that he investigated that company would seem to suggest that he pursues their employment as investment managers for reasons that are entirely proper. Indeed, a bribe is traditionally defined as 'a gift accepted by a fiduciary as an inducement to him to betray his trust' (*Reid*) and, in this case, it is not clear that Alan has been induced by Getahead's gift or that he has actually betrayed his trust; that is, he may not have breached his fiduciary duties. It is not conclusive that no loss was caused to the beneficiaries as a result of these dealings, as a payment may still be a bribe even if every person benefits (*Reading v Attorney General* (1951)).

It is clear from cases such as *Williams v Barton* (1927), *Reading v Attorney General* (1951) and *Regal (Hastings) Ltd v Gulliver* (1942) that any personal gain received by a trustee by virtue of his fiduciary position must be accountable to the beneficiaries, even if there was no dishonesty, again as was emphasised in *LSE v Pearson*. In fact, since *Reid*, it is now clear that the difference between bribes and perfectly honest payments to trustees is that bribes will trigger a greater range of remedies than purely honest payments. Both, however, will involve the imposition of a duty to account on the recipient. It follows that Alan may well find himself to be accountable to the trust for the shares he has received in Getahead plc because, even if they are not a bribe, they have been received as a consequence of his position as trustee. So, also, with their increase in value (*Regal (Hastings) Ltd* and *Crown Dilmun v Sutton* (2004).

Finally, for the sake of completeness, we should note that, if this were a bribe, then any contract between Getahead plc and the trust can be set aside at the option of the beneficiaries (*Bartram v Lloyd* (1904)) and the briber can be sued in fraud or for money

---

16 Objective statement of conflicting principles of law.

had and received. If, on the other hand, this is not a bribe, Getahead plc will not suffer the intervention of equity, and the duty to account/constructive trust will fall on Alan alone because of the unauthorised profit. Again, as in the previous discussion, if Alan has behaved honestly, he may receive equitable compensation for his diligence, although in *Guinness plc v Saunders* (1990) it was emphasised that this jurisdiction should be exercised sparingly.

(c) The leasehold reversion

In *Keech v Sandford* (1726), it was established that, if a trustee holds a lease on trust for beneficiaries, then the trustee is barred as a matter of law from taking a renewal of the lease for himself, even if the landlord would not have granted a renewal to the beneficiaries as such. Any lease which the trustee may acquire in this way would be held on constructive trust for the beneficiaries, even though no breach of trust has been committed. Similarly, it also appears that a trustee may be precluded from purchasing the freehold reversion of a lease, at least where the lease was renewable by custom or the trustee obtained the chance of purchasing the reversion because of his position as trustee (*Griffith v Owen* (1907)). In *Protheroe v Protheroe* (1968), the court went further, holding that a trustee purchasing the reversion of a trust lease would be subject to a constructive trust, irrespective of the type of lease involved or the manner in which the opportunity arose (and see also *Popat v Shonchhatra* (1997)). Consequently, it would appear that Alan will hold the freehold reversion on trust for Henry and Oliver and must account for the profit he has made (or will make) on its resale (*Re Thompson* (1934)).

The strict approach of the *Protheroe* rule has attracted some criticism, not least because it fails to take account of the varied circumstances in which a trustee or fiduciary may become privately entangled with trust property. Perhaps, then, it might be possible to argue that a trustee may not be bound to hold a freehold reversion on constructive trust for the beneficiaries if the circumstances reveal no potential conflict of interest and duty. This may now be the position in respect of the 'self-dealing' rule, which occurs when a trustee or fiduciary seeks to purchase the trust property itself: *Holder v Holder* (1966). There seems little objection to extending it to the *Protheroe*-type situation. Therefore, in our case, the fact that Barnaby and Alan were advised not to purchase the reversion on behalf of the trust, and that Alan secured it on the open market at auction, could be used to discount the possibility that he (Alan) be a constructive trustee of the reversion.

Finally, there is always the possibility that Alan will be caught directly by the original rule in *Griffith v Owen* (1907), irrespective of its extension by *Protheroe*. So, if Alan had acquired either the knowledge or the opportunity to purchase the reversion in his capacity as trustee, he will be called to account for that reason alone (see, also, *Boardman v Phipps* (1967)) and he may find it difficult to defend this claim by pleading the fairness of his transaction. In the end, the court must exercise its discretion, for the imposition of a constructive trust is never automatic. Thus, even if Alan did learn of the opportunity to purchase the reversion when acting as trustee and is thereby fixed with a constructive trust, the circumstances will be relevant in determining whether he is entitled to receive equitable remuneration within the principle of *Boardman v Phipps* (1967). After all, Alan has taken the risk in the open market against the advice of Getahead plc and it appears that the trust will profit from that risk.

QUESTION 36

The principles concerning the imposition of a constructive trust on an owner of real property in circumstances of cohabitation are generous to the claimant. In fact, they are so generous that it would cause little difference to adopt statutory co-ownership of such property.

▶ Discuss with reference to decided cases.

Aim Higher

Some commentators have argued that the type of constructive trust that is applicable in the context of the family home is remedial and criticise the use of such a trust on the grounds that they arise through the exercise of judicial discretion and individual fairness to the parties: see *Stack v Dowden* (2007) and *Jones v Kernott* (2011). An additional point that is worth mentioning is that in *Oxley v Hiscock* (2004) the Court of Appeal commented on the three approaches to the quantification of the interests of the parties in the family home.

Common Pitfalls

Some students tend to be very selective in the principles that they state with respect to this type of question. There are several contrasting principles that are applicable in this area of the law and examiners consider how well candidates appreciate and present their arguments.

How to Answer this Question

❖ Role of constructive trusts: *Pettitt v Pettitt* (1970), *Gissing v Gissing* (1971), *Lloyds Bank v Rosset* (1991).

❖ The elements of a successful claim to co-ownership by means of a constructive trust.

❖ A remedy for inequitable conduct, but widely or narrowly defined: *Burns v Burns* (1984), *Grant v Edwards* (1986), or *Lloyds Bank v Rosset* (1991).

❖ Difficulties in quantifying the beneficial interest: restitutionary or remedial constructive trust: *Midland Bank v Cooke* (1995).

❖ Whether statutory co-ownership would serve the same purposes as the law of constructive trusts.

❖ The approach of the House of Lords in *Stack v Dowden* (2007) and *Jones v Kernott* (2011).

Answer Structure

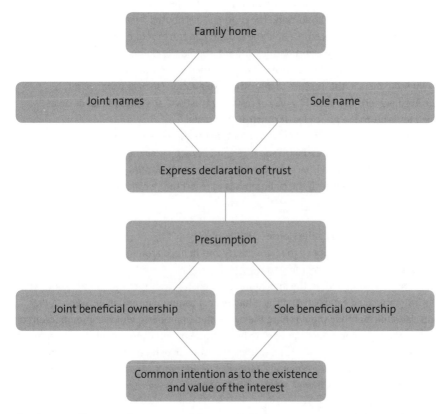

This diagram illustrates the primacy of the remedial constructive trust in declaring the interests of the parties in the family home.

ANSWER

One of the most common uses of the constructive trust in English law is as a device for settling disputes about the ownership of real property. For a variety of reasons, a property shared by a couple as their home may, at law, be owned only by one of them and attract the law of constructive trusts (*Tinsley v Milligan* (1993)). In this context, constructive trusts are not used as an arm of the family court but, apparently, as a remedy for inequitable conduct (*Gissing v Gissing* (1971)).[17]

17 Significance of the constructive trust.

Disputes of this nature arise typically when the legal title to the house is held by one party to the relationship (or, occasionally, jointly with a non-occupier – *Grant v Edwards* (1986)) and the other occupier (the claimant) seeks to rely on words or deeds to prove that he or she should be entitled to a share of ownership. This usually follows a breakdown in the parties' relationship, or some financial catastrophe which requires the property to be sold and the proceeds distributed.[18] If the claim is successful, the legal owner will henceforth hold the property on trust for himself and the claimant, in whatever portions the court decides. Indeed, should the claimant have made direct contributions to the purchase price of the property (by lump sum or mortgage payments), then, in the absence of any other explanation (such as a loan or gift to the legal owner), an interest by way of resulting trust will arise and there will be no need to resort to the principles of constructive trusts: *Drake v Whipp* (1996). The resulting trust route is fairly clear and, although the evidence may be disputed, the parties know in advance and with some certainty exactly how the claimant may establish an interest and how the legal owner may avoid granting one. Unfortunately the same may not be true if the claimant has to resort to the constructive trust as a means of claiming that interest.[19]

As originally conceived by the House of Lords in *Pettitt v Pettitt* (1970), the law of constructive trusts as applied to real property was hedged around with limitations and was quite circumspect. According to *Pettitt* itself and *Gissing v Gissing* (1971) which followed shortly thereafter, the imposition of a constructive trust was possible only when the claimant could establish that there had been a common intention between owner and claimant that they should share the ownership of property, which common intention had been relied upon by the claimant to her detriment. This common intention had to be real (not invented by the court) and would arise from an express oral assurance about ownership relied upon detrimentally. Moreover, even then a constructive trust would not be imposed on the legal owner of the property unless this was necessary to remedy his inequitable conduct (*Gissing v Gissing*).

However, in the 1970s, under the influence of Lord Denning in the Court of Appeal, constructive trusts began to be used widely as a device for granting an interest to claimants (usually deserted female lovers) in the property of their cohabitee. It soon became apparent that the *Pettitt* decision could be 'adjusted' to justify nearly any reordering of property rights that seemed appropriate to the judge. Cases such as *Falconer v Falconer* (1970), *Heseltine v Heseltine* (1971) and *Eves v Eves* (1975) showed that the constructive trust route to a share of ownership could, in fact, be used to satisfy a claimant whenever the court thought it just and equitable to do so.[20]

18   Trigger events that give rise to a need for a solution.

19   The original solution involved the resulting trust in limited circumstances.

20   The flexible nature of the constructive trust.

In reality, at the heart of this expansion of the role of constructive trusts was a dispute over what kind of conduct could give rise to the common intention sufficient to support the claim. Thus, in *Burns v Burns* (1984), the unmarried Ms Burns was denied a share in her partner's property because she had made neither a contribution to the purchase price of the house (that is, there was no resulting trust) nor had she been promised any interest in it. Similarly, in *Lightfoot v Lightfoot-Brown* (2004), the court decided that there was no evidence of a constructive trust by which capital payments were made for the benefit of the family home without any discussion between the parties. In contrast, in *Grant v Edwards* (1986), the judgments suggest that a common intention could be inferred from the conduct of the parties, including the performance of everyday domestic duties, even though, in that case, the legal owner had made an express oral assurance to the claimant.

In itself, the fact that there was a difference between the traditional approach of *Burns* and the expanded jurisdiction of *Grant* is not critical. However, the clear consequence of *Grant* is that a court could, if it wished, 'discover' or 'impute' the common intention and impose a constructive trust simply because the parties shared the occupation of the property and jointly undertook normal obligations of cohabitation – such as house cleaning, child rearing and payment of household expenses. This is very different from the relative objectivity of the *Pettitt* requirements and would have the result that neither party could predict with *any* degree of certainty when a constructive trust would be imposed. Nor can the legal owner so order his affairs so as to *avoid* behaving inequitably. If matters had remained as this, statutory co-ownership would have been a blessing: at least it would have brought certainty.

However, this is not the end of the matter. In 1991, the House of Lords in *Lloyds Bank v Rosset* attempted to return the law to the spirit of *Pettitt* and to establish reasonably clear guidelines for the future use of constructive trusts. According to Lord Bridge in *Rosset*, a constructive trust to achieve co-ownership would be imposed when an express oral promise or assurance as to shared ownership had been made and had been relied on by the claimant in circumstances resulting in detriment. Importantly, Lord Bridge doubted whether anything other than an express oral assurance could raise a constructive trust (except payments to the purchase price of the property: also known as a resulting trust).

However, Lord Bridge in his guidelines omitted to mention the significance of indirect contributions. These involve a link between the mortgage payments and the expenses undertaken by the claimant: see Lord Pearson in *Gissing v Gissing*. Despite Lord Bridge's omission, it is clear that he did not intend to overrule such evidence. A recent illustration of such contributions and their effect is *Le Foe v Le Foe* (2001). In this case the court construed the *Rosset* principles and concluded that the claimant would be entitled to an interest by way of indirect contributions in exceptional circumstances.

In addition, Lord Bridge's statement in *Rosset* equates the interest of the spouse with that of a cohabitee. This ignores the significance of s 37 of the Matrimonial Proceedings and Property Act 1970, as amended by the Civil Partnership Act 2004 (substantial improvement of property by one spouse or civil partner). In addition, on a divorce, judicial separation or nullity decree, the court has a discretion to award a spouse or civil partner an interest in the house under ss 23–25 of the Matrimonial Causes Act 1973. This discretion is not limited by the *Rosset* principles.

This should have settled matters. Constructive trusts remedy assurances unconscionably denied; they do not allow the manipulation of property rights for other (albeit worthy) reasons. This is consistent with later House of Lords authority discussing constructive trusts generally, as in *Westdeutsche Landesbank Girozentrale v Islington LBC* (1996), in which Lord Browne-Wilkinson stated that constructive trusts were imposed where a person's conscience was bound, not because there might be justice in doing so. Nevertheless, difficulties remain. In *Midland Bank v Cooke* (1995), an interest in property was established by means of payments towards the purchase price (a resulting trust), but the claimant's share of ownership was quantified on the basis of the parties' entire conduct and was not proportionate to the amount paid (see the contrary result in *Huntingford v Hobbs* (1993)). This is again the use of a wide discretionary constructive trust.

In *Stack v Dowden* (2007) the House of Lords restated the principles that are applicable when a conveyance is taken in the joint names of a cohabiting couple without an express declaration of trust as to beneficial interests. The constructive trust solution was advocated. The starting point is that equity follows the law and the beneficial interests reflect the legal interests in the property. The same principles apply where there is sole legal ownership – the rebuttable presumption will be sole beneficial ownership. The onus of proof will lie on the party seeking to show that the parties intended their beneficial interests to be different from the legal title. A holistic approach to quantification of the interest is conducted by the courts. Many factors other than financial contributions may be taken into account to ascertain the parties' intentions, including advice or discussions at the time of the transfer, the purpose for which the home was acquired, and the nature of the parties' relationship. Thus, strict mathematical calculations as to who paid what may become less significant. The facts in this case were unusual and the defendant succeeded in establishing a common intention of the parties which was different from an equal share in the property. Lord Neuberger issued a strong dissenting judgment in favour of the traditional resulting and constructive trusts principles. He suggested that, in a sense, it would be wrong in principle to construct an imputed intention on behalf of the parties because in the discretion of the courts this may produce a fair result. This approach would be likely to create manifest uncertainty and unpredictabilty in the law.

In *Jones v Kernott* [2011] UKSC 53, the Supreme Court endorsed the approach of the majority of the Law Lords in *Stack* and decided that orthodox principles of constructive trusts will be adopted in order to quantify the beneficial interests of the parties in the family home. The single regime of the common intention constructive trust will be applicable in cases where the property was taken in joint names as well as cases where the house is in sole ownership. Where the property is in sole ownership, the starting point is whether the other party has a beneficial interest in the property in the first place. If this is the case, the second issue is the value of that interest. There will be no presumption of joint beneficial ownership but the common intention of the parties will have to be deduced objectively from their conduct. Whereas, where the title is in joint names the starting point is that equity follows the law and the parties will be treated as joint tenants in law and equity. If the parties had not given any real thought to their beneficial interests or where the circumstances were fundamentally changed it was imperative to consider what reasonable and fair minded people would have thought about their beneficial interests at the time the circumstances had changed. The courts will attempt to infer the intention of the parties by reference to their conduct and surrounding circumstances. However, in the absence of such evidence the court is entitled to impute a common intention based on an objective standard, but by reference to the facts of the case.

In conclusion, then, it is not true that the imposition of a constructive trust now lies squarely in the discretion of the court, although the broader rules of *Stack v Dowden* and *Jones v Kernott* have the potential for promoting an element of uncertainty in the law. So, in present circumstances, there is no *need* for statutory co-ownership because the law remains reasonably certain. This was the view of the Law Commission in its Report in 2002. However, that does not mean that statutory co-ownership should not be imposed *as a result of a deliberate choice*. But, this is a choice for Parliament to make and should not be rendered otiose by a return to the discretionary, uncertain and unstable use of the constructive trust advocated in some cases. Of course, the constructive trust (like equity itself) retains an inherent flexibility. That is not the same, however, as having completely open-ended rules and uncertain legal concepts.

QUESTION 37

Cassandra is the registered proprietor of a large house in London. In 2008 she met Donald, a young merchant banker, and soon she had invited him to live with her. Donald willingly accepted, not least because he was about to be evicted from his own flat through his inability to pay the rent. At first, Donald insisted that he shared the expenses of running the house, but it soon became clear to him that Cassandra had more money than sense, and he accepted her generosity without complaint. After some time, Cassandra began talking about 'the future', and although he was not entirely committed to the relationship, Donald played along, especially as Cassandra had told him that the house was as good as his own now that they were together. This slice of luck encouraged Donald to abandon even what little financial caution he possessed, and he had soon spent nearly all of his savings on various luxury, but unnecessary, items of furniture for the house and far too many visits to the casino. By this time, Cassandra was becoming a little annoyed at Donald's behaviour, and after one terrible row, in which she had told him to leave, Donald promised to mend his ways. Subsequently, he became altogether more responsible and even began to redecorate the house at his own expense and overhaul the garden. Unfortunately for him, this had come too late for Cassandra, and now she has decided to throw Donald out of the house.

▶ Donald is devastated and comes to you for advice as to whether he can claim a share in the house.

Aim Higher

The answer to this question illustrates the danger of becoming too rigid in the use of constructive trusts. The question requires knowledge of the relevant law but also an understanding of the role and purpose of constructive trusts in these types of cases. As will be apparent, the general theory of trusts put forward in *Westdeutsche Landesbank Girozentrale v Islington LBC* (1996) is very important.

Common Pitfalls X

Questions concerning interests in the family home are regularly asked in land law examinations and occasionally in examinations on trusts law. Students ought to be encouraged to reconcile the principles laid down in the leading judgments in the five House of Lords decisions in *Pettitt v Pettitt, Gissing v Gissing, Lloyds Bank v Rosset, Stack v Dowden* and *Jones v Kernott*. Note that in *Stack*, Lord Neuberger arrived at the same conclusion as Baroness Hale but by a different route.

How to Answer this Question

* ❖ General principles of acquisition of beneficial interests through constructive trusts, *Stack v Dowden* (2007), *Jones v Kernott* (2011).
* ❖ The legal owner as constructive trustee.
* ❖ The need for a promise, reliance and detriment, *Lloyds Bank v Rosset* (1991).
* ❖ Quantifying the share.
* ❖ Whether a remedy can be refused on general equitable principles.

Answer Structure

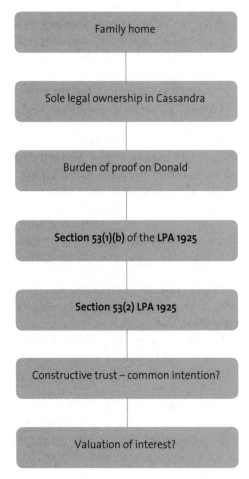

This diagram illustrates the application of the relevant principles in determining the respective interests of the parties in the family home.

ANSWER

This question concerns the acquisition of beneficial interests in property belonging to another through the medium of constructive trusts. In concrete terms, the problem revolves around a contest between the legal owner of the property – Cassandra – and the person who may be able to claim an interest in the property under a constructive trust – Donald. If he is successful, Cassandra will hold the legal title on trust for both of them, in such shares as the court determines.[21]

21 Identification of the issues posed by the question.

By way of introduction, it is important to note that, in our case, there is no express conveyance of the house to Donald as owner, and no express written declaration of trust by Cassandra in his favour. There is no written declaration within s 53(1)(b) of the Law of Property Act (LPA) 1925. So, if Donald is to have any interest in Cassandra's property, it is clear that this must be established under the principles elaborated in *Pettitt v Pettitt* (1970) and codified by the House of Lords in *Lloyds Bank v Rosset* (1991): he must rely on a constructive or resulting trust, as these are exempt from the requirement of writing by s 53(2) of the LPA 1925. Following *Rosset*, a person claiming an equitable interest in property, legal title to which is vested in another, must be able to show either some contribution to the purchase price of the property (that is, a resulting trust) or must prove some oral assurance that he or she was to have an interest in the property, which they have relied upon to their detriment. On the facts as stated, it seems clear that when Donald met Cassandra, Cassandra was sole legal owner of the property and that it was not subject to any mortgage. The property belonged to Cassandra absolutely and had already been paid for.[22] In *Stack v Dowden* (2007) the House of Lords decided that as a starting point the maxim 'equity follows the law' was applicable, i.e. the beneficial interest will *prima facie* be enjoyed by the party with the legal title, namely Cassandra. The burden of proof will therefore lie on Donald to establish an equitable interest by way of a constructive trust. It follows, therefore, that Donald cannot pursue the resulting trust path to an equitable interest – there is no purchase price to which he can make a contribution. It would seem, then, that Donald must rely on the doctrine of constructive trusts: he must plead a promise or oral assurance plus detrimental reliance in order to establish that it would be inequitable for Cassandra to deny him a share in the property. There are a number of factors to consider here.

First, it is clear that Donald readily moved into the house at Cassandra's instigation. However, there is no suggestion at this stage that Cassandra has made any promise or assurance in relation to ownership of the property. As Lord Bridge made clear in *Lloyds Bank v Rosset* (1991), the obligations of common or shared *occupation* of property are not identical with the *obligations* of shared ownership and consequently it is extremely unlikely that a court would be prepared to divine a promise of shared ownership from facts such as ours. Indeed, because in *Rosset* Lord Bridge went so far as to suggest that it was virtually impossible *as a matter of principle* to infer a promise from conduct *per se*, there seems little upon which Donald can base a claim at this stage. Even if by some intellectual gymnastics it is possible to discover a promise made to Donald, there is no evidence of detrimental reliance. Although Donald does vacate his current residence, and even though such action has, in the past, been held to constitute detriment (*Tanner v Tanner* (1975)), it is clear that his actions are prompted by his own circumstances and have little to do with whatever Cassandra may or may not have promised.

---

22 Consideration of the **Rosset** principles before examination of **Stack v Dowden**.

Second, there is little chance that Donald may claim an interest just because he has insisted on paying household expenses. The payment of household expenses is not equivalent to payment of the purchase price of property (*Burns v Burns* (1984)) and (as above) there is no oral assurance to which this expenditure can be linked as detrimental reliance. Indeed, such statements that Cassandra does make (see below) are made *after* Donald spends money. In other words, these monetary payments are not made to the acquisition of the property, nor are they in reliance on a promise. There is no interest to be found on these facts (*Burns v Burns* (1984) and *Lloyds Bank v Rosset* (1991)).

Finally, however, it appears that Cassandra does make a promise of sorts to Donald and it is a matter of construction whether this is sufficient to raise an interest in his favour by way of a constructive trust. First, a problem exists with intention: does Cassandra intend to grant Donald a share in the property by her references to 'the future' and her apparent statement that the house is 'as good as' his? Fortunately for Donald, although *Gissing v Gissing* (1971) suggests that an oral promise (the 'common intention') must be real rather than imagined, it is likely that a court would consider an assurance to have been made if a reasonable person would have believed that the property owner was making a statement about ownership of the property or, indeed, if the actual claimant honestly so believed. In our case, we do not know what Cassandra actually meant, but may a reasonable person in Donald's position conclude that this was an assurance about the ownership of the shared home? This issue is determined by reference to an objective standard. Such a principle is clearly supported by *Midland Bank v Cooke* (1995) which, although distinguishable because in that case there were some payments towards the purchase price, suggests that the court will take a generous view of what the parties 'intended'. The same principle was applied in *Stack v Dowden* (2007) and *Jones v Kernott* (2011). Consequently, Cassandra may find herself in some difficulty having assured Donald that he had a share in the property, even if this was not actually her intention (see, for example, *Eves v Eves* (1975), where the real intention was to deny an interest). Furthermore, it seems clear from the facts that Donald has relied on this assurance in that he has spent his savings on various items of furniture and visits to the casino.

With reference to the alleged detriment, Cassandra might claim that this kind of detrimental reliance is insufficient to found an interest by way of a constructive trust because it was unrelated to the property (money spent at the casino) and part was not necessary for the use and enjoyment of the property (luxury furniture). Indeed, certain cases, such as *Gissing* and *Christian v Christian* (1981), suggest that the detriment suffered as a result of the promise or assurance must be related to the property over which the interest is claimed; for example, spending money on improvements. However, an alternative view is that all that is required is detriment which has been caused by the promise, the nature of such detriment being immaterial. This second approach has much to commend it, especially since it is consistent with the theory that the essence of the constructive trust in these cases is the fact of a promise made and then inequitably denied. The detriment is, on this view, merely the trigger for the trust, not the reason for its existence in the first place. So, following this approach, Donald appears to have a reasonably strong claim to an equitable interest in Cassandra's property. He can show an assurance, reliance and detriment. This means that Cassandra's subsequent attempt to evict him – which may be seen as an attempt to withdraw the promise – comes too late (*Turton v Turton* (1987)). By that time, the equity may have been raised in his favour.[23]

In *Stack v Dowden* and *Jones v Kernott* the court introduced the single regime of the constructive trust as a means of resolving disputes between parties as to the equitable interests in the family home. There are two hurdles for Donald to overcome in order to succeed in his claim to an interest in the house. First, to discharge a burden to prove that Cassandra intended him to have a beneficial interest in the property. This question is determined objectively by the courts. The significant facts have already been identified. It may be doubtful whether Donald may discharge this burden, but if he does, the second issue involves the evaluation of that interest. The courts will consider all the material facts in order to determine what would be fair to the parties: see *Oxley v Hiscock* [2004] EWCA 546

Finally, however, as adviser to Donald, one must issue a word of caution. Although it appears, on a strict application of the *Rosset* principles, that he can claim an interest in Cassandra's property, the court might seek to deny him this by referring to the origins of its equitable jurisdiction in cases such as this. Undoubtedly, the constructive trust is a flexible tool that serves many purposes and can be used in many ways: for example, in *Cooke*, *Stack* and *Kernott*, it was used with maximum flexibility in order to achieve what the courts believed to be equitable results. This was despite the apparent contradiction with *Rosset*. In some cases, constructive trusts appear to treat morally innocent people harshly, but only then in order to do equity to another person who has a greater claim. Yet, what constructive trusts will not be used for is to enable an undeserving litigant to gain a windfall which is not merited: the trust fixes on the conscience of the legal owner of property; it will not be imposed mechanically to assist the undeserving (*Westdeutsche Landesbank Girozentrale v Islington LBC* (1996)). The very essence of the constructive trust is that it is not rigid in application and does not have hard and fast rules. This much was stated by Lord Diplock in *Gissing v Gissing* (1971) and is a feature of the use of constructive trusts in later cases, including those cases difficult to reconcile with each other such as *Lloyds Bank v Rosset* (1990) on the one hand and *Midland Bank v Cooke* (1995), *Stack v Dowden* and *Jones v Kernott* on the other side of the spectrum. Thus, if the constructive trust is rightly to be regarded as a means of remedying inequitable conduct in circumstances where the conscience of the legal owner is affected, a court may well take the view that Donald should not be able to rely on it to claim a benefit which he appears not to deserve.

23 Application of the principles of law to the facts.

QUESTION 38

'When a couple purchase a home in joint names or even in a party's sole name, the resulting trust involving strict mathematical calculations as to who paid what may be less significant in determining ownership of the property.'

▶ Discuss with reference to decided cases.

How to Answer this Question

- ❖ The significance of express declarations of trusts.
- ❖ The status of transactions involving the legal title in joint and sole names.
- ❖ Importance of distinguishing domestic and commercial contexts.
- ❖ Ascertaining the parties' intentions – the holistic approach.
- ❖ Quantifying the parties' shares.

Answer Structure

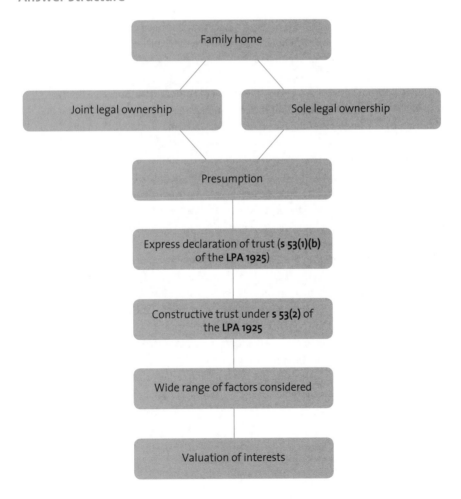

ANSWER

The legal title to property may be conveyed in the joint or sole names of the partners, subject to an express trust of the land for themselves as equitable joint tenants or tenants in common. Such an express declaration of trust will be conclusive of the equitable interests of the parties, in the absence of fraud or mistake or evidence varying the declaration of trust, see *Goodman v Gallant* (1986). In this case, a declaration of trust of joint tenancy was effectively severed by the claimant.[24]

However, the mere fact that the legal title to property is vested in the joint names of the parties does not ultimately entitle the surviving legal owner to an equitable interest in the property, if this does not accord with the intention of the parties: see *Goodman v Charlton* (2002). In this case there was no intention that the transfer of the house into joint names would confer a beneficial interest on the defendant.

Alternatively, the parties may declare the terms of the trust outside the conveyance. Provided that s 53(1)(b) of the **Law of Property Act 1925** has been complied with (evidence in writing), the declaration of trust will be conclusive as to the beneficial interests of the parties, in the absence of fraud or mistake.

In *Stack v Dowden* and *Jones v Kernott*, the House of Lords and the Supreme Court respectively expressed the view that the constructive trust principles are relevant in determining the interests of the parties in the family home. In *Stack v Dowden* (2007), the House of Lords restated the principles concerning the occasion when a conveyance of the legal title to property is taken in the joint names of the parties (or indeed in the sole name of a party), but without an express declaration of trust as to the parties' respective beneficial interests. As a starting point, the maxim 'equity follows the law' will be applicable in order to identify the existence of the equitable interest, subject to evidence to the contrary. Thus, whether we are dealing with joint legal ownership (as in *Stack v Dowden*) or sole legal ownership, the beneficial interest will *prima facie* be enjoyed by the party(ies) with the legal title. Until the contrary is proved, the extent of the beneficial interest will also follow the legal title. Thus, where the transfer of the legal title is in joint names, then *prima facie* the beneficial interest will be enjoyed in joint tenancy until the contrary is proved. The onus of proof is therefore on the party seeking to establish that the beneficial interest is different from the legal title. In *Jones v Kernott* (2011), another case of joint ownership, the Supreme Court decided that the interests of the parties were to be determined in accordance with the principles of fairness and justice and not necessarily to reflect the financial contributions made by the parties.[25]

24 Primacy of the declaration of trust.
25 Significance of recent decisions.

The contrary may be established where the legal owner(s) expressly declare(s) a trust. Such a declaration (as was stated earlier) will be conclusive of the interests of the parties, in the absence of fraud, mistake or variation by subsequent agreement. In *Stack v Dowden* the court decided that a declaration that the survivor of the two legal owners can give a valid receipt for capital monies arising on a disposition of the land did not amount to an express declaration of a beneficial joint tenancy. In this respect the court followed *Huntingford v Hobbs* (1993).

Likewise, on the issue of evidence to the contrary, Baroness Hale in *Stack v Dowden* considered the question whether the starting point ought to be the presumption of a resulting trust, i.e. the beneficial ownership being held in the same proportions as the contributions to the purchase price or by looking at all the relevant circumstances in order to discern the parties' common intention (constructive trust). In Baroness Hale's view the emphasis in the domestic context had moved away from crude factors of money contribution (resulting trust) towards more subtle factors of intentional bargain (constructive trust). Accordingly, strict mathematical calculations as to who paid for what at the time of the acquisition of the property may be less significant today.[26]

In may be noted that in *Stack v Dowden* Lord Neuberger arrived at the same conclusion as the majority, but through a different route. He adopted the same starting point by regarding the equitable interest(s) as following the legal title(s), subject to evidence to the contrary. However, with regard to rebutting evidence he followed the traditional approach by having regard to the resulting and constructive trusts. Where the parties contributed to the purchase price of the property (including mortgage repayments), the beneficial ownership will be held in the same proportions as the contributions to the purchase price. This is the resulting trust solution.

Prior to the decision in *Stack*, The Law Commission (2001, Law Com No 274), in its review of the law relating to the property rights of those who share homes, reported that the law was unduly complex, arbitrary and uncertain in its application. It was ill-suited to determining the property rights of those who, because of the informal nature of their relationship, may not have considered their respective entitlements. In 2002, the Commission published *Sharing Homes, A Discussion Paper* (2002, Law Com No 278) but failed to recommend any proposals for reform.

The presumptions of resulting trust and advancement will not be readily adopted in order to quantify the interests of the parties because such presumptions have outlived their usefulness in this context. It was not until after the Second World War that the courts were required to consider the proprietary rights in family assets of a different

---

26 Flexible approach to the valuation of an interest in the family home.

social class. It was considered to be an abuse of legal principles for ascertaining or imputing intention, to apply to transactions between the post-war generation of married couples, artificial 'presumptions' as to the most likely intentions of a culturally different generation of spouses in the nineteenth century.[27] These sentiments were expressed by the House of Lords in two definitive decisions: *Pettitt v Pettitt* (1970) and *Gissing v Gissing* (1971). In these cases the court decided that settled principles of property law were applicable to determine the interests of the parties in family assets. The resulting trust concerning direct and indirect contributions to the acquisition of the property and the common intention constructive trust will be adopted to ascertain the parties' intentions. The constructive trust will be employed whenever the trustee has so conducted himself that it would be inequitable to allow him to deny to the beneficiary an equitable interest in the land acquired. He will be treated as having conducted himself inequitably if, by his words or conduct, he had induced the beneficiary to act to his own detriment in the reasonable belief that by so acting he will acquire a beneficial interest in the land.

It follows that domestic duties undertaken by a party (such as caring for and bringing up the children), unconnected with a common intention to share the property in reliance on such duties, are insufficient to create an interest in the property, see *Burns v Burns* (1984) and *Grant v Edwards* (1986).

In *Lloyds Bank v Rosset* (1990), the House of Lords reviewed the principles laid down in *Pettitt* and *Gissing* and issued two guidelines concerning the relevant principles. The first guideline involved evidence of agreement between the parties as to the beneficial interests enjoyed by the parties. This is required to be based on express discussion between the parties. The second guideline involved evidence of conduct which concerned contributions (direct and indirect: see *Le Foe v Le Foe* (2001)) to the purchase price.

In *Midland Bank v Cooke* (1995), the Court of Appeal adopted a modified approach to the *Rosset* principles. The approach was that where a party acquired an equitable interest in property by way of direct contributions to the purchase price of the property, the court may take into consideration the conduct of the parties in order to quantify their shares. The court was not bound to deal with the matter on the strict basis of the trust resulting from the cash contribution to the purchase price, and was free to attribute to the parties an intention to share the beneficial interest in some different proportions.

Similarly, in *Drake v Whipp* (1996), the court gave a broad interpretation of the intention of the parties. This intention was not to be measured solely by the direct contributions of

---

27   Fall from grace of the presumptions of resulting trust and advancement in respect of equitable rights in the family home.

the parties, in the absence of evidence to the contrary. The court was entitled to look at all the circumstances of the case to identify the scope of the common intention of the parties, direct contributions being only one factor to be taken into account. The court also classified the types of trust involved in this analysis into constructive and resulting trusts.

In the definitive cases, *Stack v Dowden* and *Jones v Kernott*, the courts decided that the law has moved on in response to changing social and economic conditions. The search with respect to the property is to ascertain the parties' shared intentions, actual, inferred or imputed during the whole course of conduct. In this respect the resulting trust with regard to contributions to the purchase price of the property has fallen out of favour as a decisive principle in deciding the equitable interests of the parties. Instead, the intentions of the parties may be ascertained by a variety of factors (other than financial contributions) including advice or discussion at the time of the transfer, the purpose for which the home was acquired, the nature of the parties' relationship, whether they had children, the parties' personalities, etc. Indeed, the court decided that the *Rosset* guidelines were too narrowly drawn. In quantifying the interests of the parties the court emphasised that the search ought to be identifying the intentions of the parties, as distinct from the view based on fairness laid down by the Court of Appeal in *Oxley v Hiscock* (2004).

In conclusion, the House of Lords' decision in *Stack v Dowden* and the Supreme Court decision in *Jones v Kernott* appear to have broadened the discretion of the courts towards ascertaining the interests of the parties in family assets. Direct financial contributions to the purchase price, involving the resulting trust, may not be given the importance that it occupied during the development of the law.

Constructive Trusts 2
The Liability of Strangers to the Trust

INTRODUCTION

We have seen already in previous chapters that to accept the office of trustee is to open oneself and one's conduct to the closest scrutiny. Not only is the trustee expected to behave at all times with the utmost propriety, but there are also circumstances when even the morally innocent fiduciary may find himself subject to the coercive jurisdiction of the court. Furthermore, it is not only trustees proper who may find themselves in this position, for the reach of a court of equity is both long and powerful. As we shall see in this and the following chapters, third parties may all too easily become embroiled in the trust's affairs and, as far as the various remedies of the beneficiaries are concerned, it is often irrelevant whether these 'strangers to the trust' are innocent, negligent or downright dishonest.

The problems considered in this chapter relate to the liability of a person who is a stranger to the trust – broadly defined as a person who was not originally appointed a trustee or to a fiduciary position. In very general terms, any person who interferes with the operation of the trust or who assists the trustee in a breach of his trust duties may find himself fixed with a constructive trust and answerable to the court and the beneficiaries for any misapplication of the trust property. Of course, it is not in every situation that a stranger to the trust is held liable to the beneficiaries as a constructive trustee. Yet in appropriate cases, when the conditions established by the case law are fulfilled, the constructive trust swings into operation and provides a most powerful remedy.

In simple terms, a stranger to the trust may become accountable to the beneficiaries or be treated as a constructive trustee in four situations:

(a) by dishonestly assisting the trustee in a breach of trust;
(b) by receiving trust property for his own use in the knowledge that it was transferred in breach of trust;
(c) after having received trust property in conformity with the terms of the trust, by knowingly dealing with that property in breach of the terms of the trust; and
(d) by inducing the trustee to commit a breach of trust.

Together, these different examples of accounting as a constructive trustee give the beneficiary some hope of redress in the event of a breach of trust, even if the trustee has escaped the clutches of the court or no longer has the trust property. One note of caution ought to be mentioned. Millett LJ in *Paragon Finance v Thakerar* (1999) opined that the liability of an accessory is strictly not as a constructive trustee because he does not acquire the trust property. His liability is to account to the beneficiaries for any benefits received. This is a 'personal' liability to account rather than an *in rem* liability. Once again, as with so much in the law of trusts, the 'rules' are to be found in case law, although there is some doubt whether the growing volume of case law actually has done anything to clarify the law.

QUESTION 39

Analyse, with reference to decided cases, the circumstances in which a 'stranger' may be liable as a constructive trustee for intermeddling with the management of a trust.

Aim Higher ★

In *Royal Brunei Airlines v Tan* (1995) Lord Nicholls laid down the test for dishonesty as subjective, in that it requires the accessory to know the facts which to a reasonable person would indicate that he was participating in a breach of trust. But the standard of judging dishonesty was objective in the sense that it is determined, not by the defendant, but by the views of honest and reasonable people. This view was clarified by the Privy Council in *Barlow Clowes v Eurotrust* (2006) and endorsed by the Court of Appeal decisions in *Abou-Ramah v Abacha* (2006) and *Starglade v Nash* (2010). In *Twinsectra v Yardley* (2002), it is arguable that Lord Hutton (who gave the leading judgment) confused this test when he adopted the *R v Ghosh* (1982) 'combined' objective and subjective test for dishonesty in criminal law.

Common Pitfalls ✗

Under the heading 'knowingly receiving or dealing', students fail to distinguish whether the liability of the third party is proprietary or personal. Liability is proprietary where the third party unlawfully receives the trust property for his benefit and still has the property, or its traceable proceeds, under his control. On the other hand, liability is personal where the third party knowingly receives the trust property for his own benefit, but no longer retains the property or its traceable proceeds. The courts initially referred to the latter liability as one of constructive trusteeship. Today it is recognised that this is a personal liability to account.

How to Answer this Question

- ❖ The nature of a stranger's liability as constructive trustee and its justification.
- ❖ Trustee *de son tort*.
- ❖ Knowing receipt or dealing.
- ❖ Dishonest assistance.
- ❖ Lack of clarity: position of principle.

Answer Structure

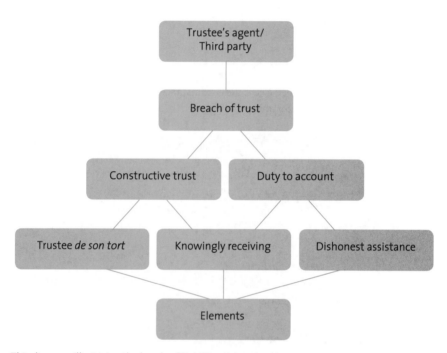

This diagram illustrates the heads of liability of strangers to a trust.

ANSWER

In cases involving strangers to a trust, the court will impose the obligations of a trustee on a person (constructive trust or the duty to account) because that person has so conducted himself in relation to the trust's affairs that in all conscience he should be held accountable to the beneficiaries for any breach of trust that may have occurred. The liability of a stranger may be analysed in the following way.

First, a stranger to the trust may become a constructive trustee because he or she has assumed the duties of a trustee. In other words, if a stranger takes it upon himself to meddle with the trust property as if he were a trustee, equity will treat him as such a trustee (*Mara v Browne* (1896)). This is trusteeship *de son tort* and the essential point is that the person fixed with liability as a constructive trustee has stepped into the shoes of the original trustees or fiduciaries, as in *James v Williams* (1999). It is effectively self-appointed trusteeship. In short, the trustee *de son tort* is a *de facto* trustee. He is a true trustee and is subject to fiduciary duties.[1] His liability is strict and does not depend on dishonesty, and like an express trustee he cannot plead the Limitation Acts as a defence to a claim for breach of trust: see *Dubai Aluminium Co v Salaam* (2002).

Second, equity will impose a constructive trust on a stranger who has received trust property for his own benefit in breach of the terms of the trust. This form of liability is often referred to as 'knowing receipt or dealing' with the trust property (*Baden Delvaux and Lecuit v Société Générale pour Favouriser le Développement du Commerce et de l'Industrie en France SA* (1983); *Houghton v Fayers* (2000)). It is important to realise, however, that the essence of the liability is that the stranger has received property for his own benefit to which he has no right. Consequently, he may be held accountable as constructive trustee for that property or its value to any person having a better claim – that is, the beneficiaries of the trust.

It seems, then, that there are three primary conditions for the imposition of this liability: *Houghton v Fayers*.[2] First, and obviously, there must be disposal of assets in breach of trust or breach of fiduciary duty. Second, the stranger must either have lawfully received property and thereafter applied it for his own purposes in a manner inconsistent with the terms of the trust (inconsistent dealing: *Karak Rubber v Burden* (1972)) or, in the alternative, have received trust property for his own benefit (knowing receipt: *International Sales Ltd v Marcus* (1982)). Thirdly, it seems that the transferee must have some degree of knowledge or notice of the fact that the transfer (or inconsistent dealing) was in breach of trust (*Polly Peck International plc v Nadir (No 2)* (1992); *Westdeutsche Landesbank Girozentrale v Islington LBC* (1996)). This insistence that the stranger be guilty of some degree of 'fault' (in the sense of having some 'knowledge' of the breach) is somewhat at odds with the restitutionary nature of liability – after all, if the root of liability is that X has Y's property, why should X's state of mind be relevant? – but at present it seems securely established in the case law: *BCCI (Overseas) Ltd v Akindele* (2000).

Unfortunately, the precise degree of knowledge required for liability for knowing receipt/inconsistent dealing is uncertain.[3] On the one hand, it has been suggested that, before liability can arise, the recipient must either know or be reckless as to whether the transfer to him or subsequent use of property is in breach of trust. This

1   Justification and nature of trustee's liability as a trustee *de son tort*.
2   Elements of liability for knowingly receiving claim.
3   Uncertain nature of degrees of knowledge.

degree of knowledge equates to the first three of Peter Gibson LJ's infamous categories of knowledge in *Baden Delvaux* (1983) and necessarily has the effect of restricting the circumstances in which a stranger may be liable. It has been applied in cases such as *Carl Zeiss Stiftung v Herbert Smith & Co (No 2)* (1969), *Re Montague* (1987) and, in a commercial context, in *Cowan de Groot Properties v Eagle Trust plc* (1992), *Eagle Trust v SBC Securities (No 2)* (1992). Alternatively, other cases suggest that liability should exist if the stranger is subjectively aware of or is simply negligent with regard to the facts of a breach of trust: in other words, if he should have known that the transfer of trust funds or his own subsequent dealings with them were in breach of trust. This ensures that liability will arise when *any* of the five categories of knowledge in *Baden Delvaux* exists. Cases such as *International Sales Ltd v Marcus* (1982), *Belmont Finance Corporation v Williams Furniture (No 2)* (1980) and the closely argued judgment of Millet J at first instance in *AGIP (Africa) Ltd v Jackson* (1992) support this view. It is implicit in the recent judgment of Ferris J in *Box v Barclays Bank* (1998). Indeed, if it is true that the essence of liability for knowing receipt/inconsistent dealing is that the stranger has received property for his own benefit to which he was not entitled, then (in the absence of a pure 'no fault' restitutionary liability) it is quite appropriate that he should be obliged to return it unless he was innocent of all participation in a breach of trust and it should make no difference whether the alleged transaction in breach arose out of a 'commercial' or 'private' trust.[4] Of course, what a 'reasonable' person should have known or enquired about may vary according to the circumstances – and the nature of the transaction may affect this – with strangers acting commercially being under a lesser duty to enquire and hence a lesser chance of liability (*El Ajou v Dollar Land Holdings plc* (1994) (first instance)). Yet, in principle, negligence should not be a defence to a claim by a person with a better title. In *BCCI v Akindele* (2000), the Court of Appeal tried to overcome these difficulties by noting that the state of knowledge 'must be such as to make it unconscionable' for the recipient to retain the benefit. This reformulation by Nourse LJ clearly is intended to avoid the controversy surrounding the '*Baden* categories' and the uncertainties produced by the 'knowledge/notice' distinction. However, it is not certain that 'unconscionability' is any less opaque than previous attempts to identify the 'core' reason for liability.

Moving now to examine the third general set of circumstances in which a stranger may be made liable as constructive trustee for intermeddling with the trust funds, we come to liability for 'knowing assistance' (as originally stated by Lord Selborne in *Barnes v Addy*). This nomenclature has been changed to 'dishonestly assisting': see *Tan*. A stranger may be accountable as a constructive trustee for dishonestly assisting another to commit a breach of trust (*Barnes v Addy* (1874); *Royal Brunei Airlines v Tan* (1995)). It is important to realise here that, unlike knowing receipt/inconsistent dealing, the stranger may never receive the trust property and, even if he does, it is not for his own benefit.

---

4   Attempting to identify the basis of liability for knowingly receiving claims.

Consequently, this is a form of secondary liability, usually resorted to when for some reason the trustee who has committed the fraudulent breach of trust cannot be found or has insufficient funds to satisfy the claims of the beneficiaries. In addition, the stranger's liability is to account for the profits. Strictly he is not a constructive trustee, for he does not receive the trust property but merely assists in a breach of trust: see Millett LJ in *Paragon Finance v Thakerar* (1999).[5]

However, the liability belongs to the stranger alone, hence it is no longer true that the stranger can be liable only if the trustee himself has behaved fraudulently. This was established by the Privy Council in *Tan*. Of course, it remains true that the stranger must himself be culpable. In *Tan*, however, Lord Nicholls, for the Privy Council, made it clear that what was required was for the assistor to be 'dishonest'.

Necessarily, this leaves some questions unanswered. As the later case of *Brinks v Abu-Saleh (No 3)* (1995) illustrates, the defendant must be proved to have factually assisted in a breach of trust (which was not established in that case). In *Twinsectra v Yardley* (2002), the majority of the House of Lords adopted the criminal law test for dishonesty (as laid down by Lord Lane CJ in *R v Ghosh* (1982)) namely, the defendant's conduct is dishonest by reference to the ordinary standards of reasonable and honest people *and* that he himself realised that his conduct was dishonest by those standards. This involves both objective and subjective questions. In *Barlow Clowes International Ltd (in liquidation) v Eurotrust International Ltd and others* (2006), the Privy Council decided that no inquiry is required to be made as to the defendant's view about standards of dishonesty. Consciousness of dishonesty involved consciousness of those elements of the transaction which made participation transgress ordinary standards of honest behaviour. It did not also require the defendant to have thought about what those standards were. In short, the standard by which the defendant's dishonesty is judged is purely objective. In *Abou-Ramah v Abacha* (2006), the Court of Appeal reaffirmed the notion that the test of dishonesty is objective and requires the court to decide that the defendant knows of the elements of the transaction which makes it dishonest according to the normally accepted standards of behaviour. The objective standard for dishonesty was further clarified by the Court of Appeal in *Starglade Ltd v Nash* [2010] E W C A 1314. The objective test is decided by the court by reference to the defendant's knowledge and experiencee.

Further, there are significant issues concerning the standard of proof required for dishonesty. In *Jyske Bank v Heinl* (1999) it was held that the standard of proof involved a high level of probability greater than a 'balance of probabilities' and the inability of the claimants to meet this meant that the 'assistance' claim in *Akindele* was unsuccessful. However, in *Statek Corp v Alford* (2008), the High Court decided

5   Liability to account but no constructive trust.

that the standard of proof of dishonesty is the traditional civil standard of a balance of probabilities.

Finally, it is clear that the above circumstances in which a constructive trust may be imposed on a stranger cannot be regarded as exhaustive. For example, a stranger will be liable as a constructive trustee if he induces a trustee to commit a breach of trust (*Eaves v Hickson* (1861)). Following the decision in *Lipkin Gorman v Karpnale* (1991), and despite obvious judicial reluctance, it is arguable that the separation of constructive trust liability into these different categories is redundant. Instead, the principle might be that a person can be made liable as constructive trustee for intermeddling with trust property whenever this is necessary to reverse an unjust enrichment, having regard to the defendant's status as a *bona fide* purchaser for value or any defence of change of position.

NOTE

It is a perfectly respectable answer to conclude that the law is in a state of flux and is uncertain as to its practical application (even if the principles are clear). A question such as this cannot really be answered adequately in an examination setting, as there are many more issues which we could consider. Consequently, a general answer is sufficient, provided that there is ample reference to case law.

QUESTION 40

The liability of a stranger for meddling with trust property should be strict. Then, subject only to the defence of change of position, the courts could determine in all the circumstances whether the defendant should return property to the beneficiaries without having to agonise about the defendant's state of mind.

▶ Discuss.

Aim Higher ★

The test of personal liability based on unconscionability as laid down by Nourse LJ in *BCCI v Akindele* (2000) was earlier rejected as meaningless by Lord Nicholls giving judgment in the Privy Council in *Royal Brunei Airlines v Tan* (1994). At the same time Nourse LJ gave little or no guidance as to how this elusive principle would be approached.

Common Pitfalls ✗

The notion of strict liability to be imposed on third parties who intermeddle with trust property was advocated extra-judicially by Lords Nicholls and Millett but rejected by Nourse LJ in *BCCI v Akindele*. The strict liability approach is based on the notion that unless the defendant is forced to disgorge the benefit received he would otherwise be unjustly enriched. Thus, his liability should not be based on knowledge, but merely that he would be enriched at the claimant's expense. The defendant, however, may be able to raise the defence of 'bona fide change of position' in appropriate cases.

How to Answer this Question

❖ Basis of liability for dishonest assistance and knowing receipt.

❖ Confirmation that some degree of fault is required: *Royal Brunei Airlines v Tan* (1995), *Westdeutsche Landesbank Girozentrale v Islington LBC* (1996).

❖ The restitution angle and the change of position defence.

❖ Confusion of language: the problem of semantics.

❖ Confusion of facts: receipt or assistance.

❖ The application of law to facts – a recipe for different interpretations of the law.

Answer Structure

This diagram constructs the essential elements of liability of strangers to a trust and suggested reforms.

ANSWER

The possibility that strangers to a trust – that is, persons not appointed trustees – may be fixed with the obligations and liabilities of constructive trusteeship is settled law. Yet, in many instances, the loss to the trust will be beyond the trustee, or the trustee may have fled the jurisdiction, and this is where the use of constructive trusts becomes vital. In those instances where the loss cannot be recovered from the trustee, constructive trusts enable the beneficiaries to seek redress from someone who has meddled with the trust's affairs or who has been involved in the breach of trust.[6] Such is the power of this remedy that the constructive trustee will be liable not only to return any trust property that he retains (that is, it is held on trust), but also to recompense the beneficiaries personally from his own resources to the full value of their loss.

There is little doubt that, at present, some element of 'fault' on the part of the stranger is required to establish liability (see, for example, *BCCI v Akindele* (2000)). In *Baden Delvaux and Lecuit v Société Générale pour Favouriser le Développement du Commerce et de l'Industrie en France SA* (1983), Peter Gibson J described five degrees or types of knowledge which he thought could be relevant in fixing a stranger with liability to account as a constructive trustee.[7] These may be classified as subjective (first three categories) and objective (latter two categories). However, what Peter Gibson J and, indeed, other judges in other cases, has not made clear is what degree of knowledge is required for which type of liability. Further, it is readily apparent that the distinction between each category of knowledge may be very fine indeed and, what is more, although the 'five degrees of knowledge' are often used as a baseline in other cases, many judges prefer their own formulations or variations of Peter Gibson's categories (see, for example, *AGIP (Africa) Ltd v Jackson* (1992); *Re Montague* (1987); *Eagle Trust plc v SBC Securities (No 2)* (1992); *BCCI v Akindele* (2000)).

Recently, case law has attempted to clarify the position but not, as the question seems to suggest, by removing the 'fault' element from liability. Liability in 'assistance'-type cases is to account to the beneficiaries as though the defendant is a constructive trustee: see *Paragon Finance v Thakerar* (1999).[8] The property has not been received by the stranger for his own benefit (*Barnes v Addy* (1874)). Consequently, it is apparent that such liability should never be triggered by simple factual assistance, but only where such assistance is tainted by personal fault. Further, as is made clear by the Privy Council in *Royal Brunei Airlines v Tan* (1995), the stranger may be liable only where he is 'dishonest': mere negligence, or a deliberate but honest assistance, is not sufficient to found liability (see, for example, *Ferrotex v Banque Français de l'Orient* (2000)). The dishonesty test now replaces the old tests of knowledge based on the *Baden* categories for assistance liability. However, although *apparently* simpler, there were difficulties

---

6   Significance of the constructive trust concept.

7   Rationale of liability for knowingly receiving trust property.

8   Clear basis of liability in dishonest assistance cases.

initially as to what amounts to dishonesty, or how it is proven.[9] *Brinks v Abu-Saleh (No 3)* (1995) suggests that dishonesty implies some knowledge on the part of the stranger, but it was not clear whether this concerns the existence of a trust, or of the fact of breach, or of the fact that the property is another's, or if it has some other meaning. *Armitage v Nurse* (1997) implies that dishonesty arises from intentional or reckless knowledge, but this was held in a different context (see Chapter 9). The test today for dishonesty in this context was laid down by Lord Nicholls in *Royal Brunei Airlines v Tan* (1995). It means that the defendant had acted with a lack of probity or simply not acted as an honest man in the circumstances of the case. This definition was construed by Lord Hutton in *Twinsectra v Yardley* (2002) as involving the criminal law test for dishonesty (as laid down by Lord Lane CJ in *R v Ghosh* (1982)). This test incorporates a combined objective and subjective standard. The defendant's conduct is dishonest by reference to the ordinary standards of reasonable and honest people *and* that he himself realised that his conduct was dishonest by those standards. However, in *Barlow Clowes International Ltd (in liquidation) v Eurotrust International Ltd and others* (2006), the Privy Council decided that no inquiry is required to be made of the defendant's view about standards of dishonesty. Consciousness of dishonesty involved consciousness of those elements of the transaction which made participation transgress ordinary standards of honest behaviour. It did not also require the defendant to have thought about what those standards were. The standard applicable here is objective. In *Abou-Ramah v Abacha* (2006), the Court of Appeal affirmed that the standard is objective and it is unnecessary to show 'subjective dishonesty' in the sense of consciousness on the part of the defendant that the transaction was dishonest. It will be sufficient if the defendant knows of the elements of the transaction which makes it dishonest in accordance with the normally acceptable standards of behaviour. Thus, the standard by which the defendant is judged is objective but with a subjective element. This approach was endorsed by the CA in *Starglade Ltd v Nash* (2010). In reversing the decision of the trial judge, the CA decided that the test is whether the judge is convinced that the defendant's behaviour is or is not within the ordinary standards of honest commercial behaviour.

Turning then to 'knowing receipt', it seems clear that the essence of the liability of the stranger in these cases is that he has received trust property for his own benefit: per Millet J in *AGIP (Africa) Ltd v Jackson* (1992). Liability comprises an obligation to return the property or account for it out of his own resources. Consequently, the liability is primarily restitutionary: to return property which belongs to another. With this in mind, the crucial question is whether the stranger, who has received the property for his own benefit, will be liable only when he was at 'fault' (that is, had some degree of 'knowledge') or whether the liability is strict – so that even an innocent defendant can be liable – subject to a defence of change of position. At present, it seems that liability

---

9   Initial confusion as to the meaning of dishonesty.

is fault-based: see Lord Browne-Wilkinson (*obiter*) in *Westdeutsche Landesbank Girozentrale v Islington LBC* (1996) and, firmly, the Court of Appeal in *BCCI v Akindele*. Yet, as noted below, this has been challenged, although there is little unanimity among the cases for what degree of knowledge is required. It has been suggested in cases such as *Carl Zeiss Stiftung v Herbert Smith & Co (No 2)* (1969), *Re Montague* (1987) and *Cowan de Groot Properties v Eagle Trust plc* (1992) that liability arises only when the stranger had 'want of probity', probably meaning intention or recklessness as to whether the property was transferred in breach of trust, and some case law suggests that mere negligence might be too low a standard in so-called 'commercial' cases where the strangers are professional advisers merely executing the wishes of the trustee (*Cowan de Groot Properties v Eagle Trust plc* (1992); *Polly Peck International plc v Nadir (No 2)* (1992)). Alternatively, other cases suggest that liability should exist if the stranger is simply negligent with regard to the terms of the trust: in other words, if he should have known that the transfer of trust funds or his own subsequent dealings with them were in breach of trust. This ensures that liability will arise when *any* of the five categories of knowledge in *Baden Delvaux* exists. Judgments in cases such as *International Sales Ltd v Marcus* (1982), *Belmont Finance Corporation v Williams Furniture (No 2)* (1980), at first instance in *AGIP (Africa) Ltd v Jackson* (1992) and *Box v Barclays Bank* (1998) support this view. Different again is the approach in *Akindele*, where Nourse LJ seeks to avoid this past confusion by saying that the recipient must act 'unconscionably' before liability can arise. How this differs from 'knowledge' or 'notice' is unclear, although it seems certain that it does presuppose some element of fault.

This doubt about the practical application of the test of 'fault' required to fix a stranger with liability for 'knowing receipt' raises a more fundamental point: namely, whether liability should depend on any fault at all. After all, if liability is triggered by receipt and the obligation is to account for its value (or return it if still held), then should not merely innocent recipients also be liable? Of course, recipients would need a defence, as every circumstance in which X might receive Y's property could not find liability (for example, if X were a *bona fide* purchaser for value). This approach – generally thought to be purely restitutionary – is indicated by the House of Lords in *Lipkin Gorman v Karpnale* (1991) and has been argued forcefully academically by Lord Nicholls writing extra-judicially. Certainly, that was the position with the claim at law and many would argue that there is no reason for any difference merely because the beneficiaries of a trust are pursuing a claim in equity. Lest this is thought to be unfair to the innocent stranger, it is balanced by the recognition of a general defence – 'change of position'. This would be available to any stranger to defeat the imposition of a constructive trust, if the court thought fit, depending on whether the stranger has changed his position in reliance on receipt of the money. As is evident, this introduces an element of discretion into the fixing of receipt liability, but it is not at all clear whether the 'knowledge'-based test really is any more objective.

At present, then, there is no doubt that liability in assistance-type cases (and inducement cases where the inducer never receives the trust property for his own use) is fault-based – that fault being dishonesty. In receipt-based cases (including lawful receipt tainted by subsequent actions in breach of trust), recent case law firmly maintains fault as the basis of liability. However, whether this is logical (see the strict liability position with claims made at law) is open to question, and whether it will survive in the face of powerful restitutionary arguments remains to be seen. However, if questions of 'knowledge' are dispensed with, greater judicial attention will need to be focused on the meaning of the counterbalancing 'change of position' defence.

NOTE

This question reflects the academic debate which is raging over the scope of, and proper conditions for, the granting of equitable remedies consequent on a breach of trust. It is a large issue. It is also relevant in such questions to note the practical constraints under which judges operate and anybody who has read the facts of a commercial 'receipt' or 'assistance' case knows how convoluted the transactions can be.

QUESTION 41

William is the trustee of the Duke of Normandy's Trust Fund and holds various properties on trust for the beneficiaries, Harold and Matilda. The following events occur:

(a)   William decides to employ the services of a stockbroker to help him invest the trust property, and he transfers £50,000 of alpha stock to Richard, a stockbroker, with instructions to invest in Blue Chip plc, an authorised investment. Richard thinks this is a poor choice and persuades William to allow him to invest half the amount in Stockbroker Finance plc, a company that has been tipped to 'boom or bust'.

(b)   William also decides to sell to Jerry half of the freehold property held on trust for a knockdown price in return for 'an introduction fee' of £5,000. Jerry develops the site for an enormous profit, selling luxury houses to wealthy businessmen.

(c)   Harold and Matilda become suspicious of these developments and suggest to William that Catchcon Ltd, a well-known firm of auditors, check the Trust account. William fears that they will find something amiss and immediately asks his accountant (Sharp) to 'use the remaining £100,000 of the Duke of Normandy's Trust Fund to purchase traveller's cheques in my name'. The accountant agrees after speaking to William on the telephone and telling him that such an unusual transaction would require a higher fee than usual.

William has now emigrated to the Bahamas, and it appears that Stockbroker Finance plc has gone into liquidation. Harold and Matilda urgently seek your advice as to whether they have any remedies.

How to Answer this Question

❖   Liability as a constructive trustee for knowing receipt.

❖   Duty to account for dishonest assistance and inconsistent dealing.

❖   Level of knowledge required; meaning of dishonesty.
❖   Appropriate remedy.
❖   Bribes.
❖   Profits.

Answer Structure

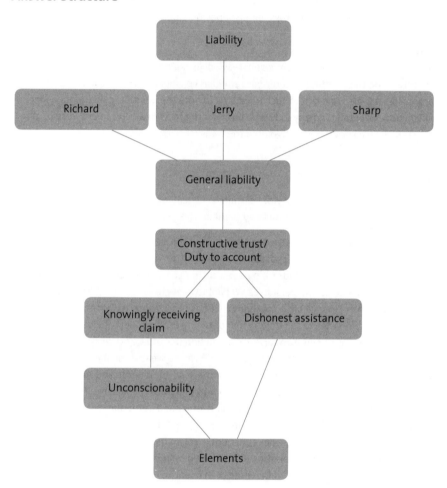

This diagram illustrates the bases of liability of Richard, Jerry and Sharp for intermeddling with the trust property.

ANSWER

It is clear from the facts of this problem that William has committed a series of breaches of trust. Unfortunately for the beneficiaries, he is outside the jurisdiction and the prospects of recovering the lost trust monies from him in a personal action for breach of trust may be remote. Furthermore, it also appears that little of the trust property is in traceable form: Stockbroker plc has gone into liquidation and no mention is made of its assets; Jerry has used the former trust land to build houses which he has sold on to (presumably) innocent purchasers and nothing is said of the money he received on sale. Consequently, with the likely failure of the personal action against the trustee for breach of trust, and with doubts as to the efficacy of the tracing remedy, Harold and Matilda should turn to those persons who have been instrumental in a practical way in these affairs.[10]

In general, a stranger may be liable to account to the beneficiaries as a constructive trustee if he has either knowingly induced a breach of trust (*Eaves v Hickson* (1861)) or dishonestly assisted in a breach of trust (*Royal Brunei Airlines v Tan* (1995)). The stranger may become a constructive trustee if he knowingly received trust property for his own benefit in breach of trust (*Belmont Finance Corporation v Williams Furniture (No 2)* (1980); *BCCI v Akindele* (2000)) or knowingly dealt with trust property in his possession in breach of the terms of the trust (*William-Ashman v Price* (1942)).[11] The consequences of being fixed with a constructive trust are that the stranger is under a duty to return to the beneficiaries any trust property which he still retains and, additionally, to make up any shortfall out of his own assets.

First, let us consider the position of Richard and the investment in Stockbroker Finance plc. It is perfectly acceptable for William to employ the services of a professional adviser or agent when investing the trust property (s 11 of the Trustee Act 2000). Importantly, then, Richard has not received the money in breach of trust, nor has he assisted William in a breach of trust. This eliminates any personal liability to account on these grounds (see, for example, *Brown v Bennett* (1998) and *Box v Barclays Bank* (1998)). However, it is possible that Richard may be liable to account as a constructive trustee in respect of those parts of the trust funds invested in Stockbroker Finance plc for either of two further reasons. First, Richard may be regarded as a constructive trustee because he may have induced William to commit a breach of trust, provided that (a) the investment in Stockbroker Finance plc was indeed a breach of trust; and (b) Richard had a sufficient degree of knowledge of the terms of the trust to trigger liability (*Eaves v Hickson* (1861)).[12]

As to (a), it is not clear from the facts of the problem whether the investment in Stockbroker Finance plc was legitimate or not, although the presumption is that the investment breached William's duty of care under para 1 of Sched 1(1) to the Trustee Act 2000, given the need for Richard to persuade William of this course of action and the volatile nature of Stockbroker's shares. Again, as to (b), it is not clear

....

10 Identification of the issues in the problem.

11 Bringing out the distinction between dishonest assistance and knowingly receiving claims.

12 Application of the principle of law to the facts.

from the facts whether Richard had sufficient knowledge to found liability. In principle, it is reasonably clear that mere negligence on Richard's part as to whether the investment was legitimate (that is, was a breach of trust) is not sufficient to found liability for knowing inducement. What appears to be necessary is either actual knowledge that it was a breach of trust to invest in Stockbroker or a reckless disregard of whether it was a breach. 'Knowledge' within any of the first three of the *Baden* categories is required (or possibly, after *Tan*, even 'dishonesty'). This may or may not exist in our case and liability will depend on a thorough examination of the facts and circumstances of the case. In *Akindele*, the CA introduced the test of unconscionability as a substitute for knowledge.

Second, however, if it is unclear whether Richard actually *induced* William to commit a breach of trust, as opposed to merely facilitating its achievement, it may be possible to fix Richard with a duty to account for dealing inconsistently with trust property in the knowledge that the dealing was in breach of trust. This is a form of secondary liability. However, given that this form of inconsistent dealing is, in essence, another form of assistance liability, it may be correct to assume that liability exists only in conjunction with dishonesty (*Tan*).[13] We must ask whether Richard really was 'dishonest'. The test for dishonesty was originally laid down in Tan as involving an objective standard but with a subjective element. This was interpreted and applied in *Twinsectra v Yardley* (2002), and was believed to involve a two-step approach as declared by Lord Lane CJ in the criminal law case *R v Ghosh* (1982). The first step is whether Richard's conduct was dishonest by reference to the ordinary standards of reasonable and honest people and the second is whether he realised that his conduct was dishonest by those standards. In *Barlow Clowes International Ltd (in liquidation) v Eurotrust International Ltd and others* (2006), the Privy Council decided that no inquiry is required to be made of the defendant's view about standards of dishonesty. Consciousness of dishonesty involved consciousness of those elements of the transaction which made participation transgress ordinary standards of honest behaviour. It did not also require the defendant to have thought about what those standards were. This test was affirmed by the Court of Appeal decisions in *Abou-Ramah v Abacha* (2006), *Starglade Ltd v Nash* (2010). This is a question of fact for the judge to decide by reference to the conduct of the defendant. In our case, perhaps Richard was only negligent and so liable only in tort (*Box v Barclays Bank* (1998)).

The second element of the problem raises similar issues. It seems clear from the facts of the problem that the land was 'sold' to Jerry for his own personal use. This seems to be a case of knowing receipt, being a case where the stranger has received trust property for his own use (*AGIP (Africa) Ltd v Jackson* (1992)). As such, if Jerry is to be liable as a constructive trustee, and thereby be required to satisfy the claims of Harold and Matilda

---

13   Various interpretations of the test for dishonesty.

out of his own resources, it is clear that he must have acted with some degree of knowledge. This requires an understanding that the actions of William were in breach of trust (*Westdeutsche Landesbank Girozentrale v Islington LBC* (1996)), expressed in *Akindele* as to whether it would be 'unconscionable' for Jerry to retain the benefit. Initially, of course, Jerry will claim that he is a *bona fide* purchaser for value of the freehold land and, in consequence, is not liable to the beneficiaries either as a constructive trustee or in tracing (*Re Diplock* (1948)). However, as the facts indicate, Jerry purchases the property for 'a knockdown price' and gives William an introduction fee. Although one must not speculate unduly, the clear inference here is that Jerry is not *bona fides*. Of course, mere suspicion on his part that William is engaged in a breach of trust may not be sufficient to establish Jerry's liability; he must have 'knowledge' (including wilful blindness) of the relevant facts and act 'unconscionably'. To constitute wilful blindness, it must be proved that Jerry suspects the relevant facts exist but makes a deliberate decision to avoid confirming that they exist: see *Manifest Shipping Co v Uni-Polaris Shipping Co* (2001). Unfortunately, what 'unconscionability' means in practice is uncertain. The logic of the situation suggests that simple negligence (that is, any of the five categories of knowledge in *Baden*) should suffice and this is supported by *dicta* in several cases (*International Sales Ltd v Marcus* (1982); *Belmont Finance Corporation v Williams Furniture (No 2)* (1980); *AGIP (Africa) Ltd v Jackson* (1992); *Box v Barclays Bank* (1998)). However, other authority has moved away from such an approach and has placed more emphasis on the 'want of probity' or deliberate fault of the stranger (that is, intention or recklessness). The case for restricting liability in this fashion was strongly argued in *Re Montague* (1987), and a spate of cases involving the alleged liability of professional financial advisers has tended to confirm this view (*Cowan de Groot Properties v Eagle Trust plc* (1992); *Polly Peck International plc v Nadir (No 2)* (1992)). In these so-called 'commercial' cases, the powerful nature of the constructive trust was emphasised and there were fears that commercial transactions would be hampered if mere negligence could trigger the personal liability of the stranger, especially as the stranger might well be liable in any event for breach of contract. As yet, the matter is unclear and the decision in *Akindele*, that it is better to think in terms of unconscionability, may not prove any more helpful. In our case, while there is no doubt that Jerry was negligent, there is also evidence to suggest that he was, at best, reckless and, at worst, that he conspired with William to defeat the rights of the beneficiaries, all for personal gain. In such circumstances, there is a good chance that he would be held liable as constructive trustee for knowing receipt.

The third element of the problem raises similar difficulties. William has clearly embarked on a fraudulent and dishonest course of action which has breached the terms of the trust. The only question is whether Sharp, the accountant, is liable for assisting in this breach of trust. The authorities were fully explored and analysed in *AGIP (Africa) Ltd v Jackson* (1992) and then explained clearly by the Privy Council in *Tan*. It is now relatively clear that the accountant will be accountable for such profits directly connected with knowingly assisting in a breach of trust if he was 'dishonest' and his actions did indeed facilitate the breach. As indicated earlier, there are difficulties over the meaning of dishonesty. In this problem the facts are equivocal. Sharp's higher fee and realisation that the transaction was 'unusual' may be evidence of dishonesty or it may simply be evidence that Sharp appreciated the possibility of fraud – which appears not to amount to dishonesty – *Jyske*. All in all, this stranger may well find himself liable to Harold and Matilda for the balance of the fund that William has taken with him to the Bahamas.

QUESTION 42

Arnold is the agent of Tarquin, the trustee of a settlement in favour of 'the children of Sarah'. Tarquin instructs Arnold to pay £5,000 to Len, who, Tarquin says, is the illegitimate child of Sarah and himself. Tarquin also instructs Arnold to invest £10,000 in the stock exchange in Tarquin Enterprises Ltd, to buy £5,000 worth of tickets in the national lottery (all of which lose) and to transfer £10,000 to Clarence as payment for services rendered to the trust. One year later, Tarquin goes missing with the remaining trust fund monies. Moreover, it transpires that Len is in fact the child of Tarquin and Emily (Arnold's sister) and that the money has all been spent. Tarquin Enterprises have gone bust due to a dramatic withdrawal of cash from their bank account.

▶ Advise the children of Sarah as to their remedies, if any, against Arnold and Clarence.

How to Answer this Question

❖ Liability as a constructive trustee for knowing receipt and dishonest assistance.

❖ Level of knowledge or dishonesty required: whether satisfied.

❖ Profits.

Answer Structure

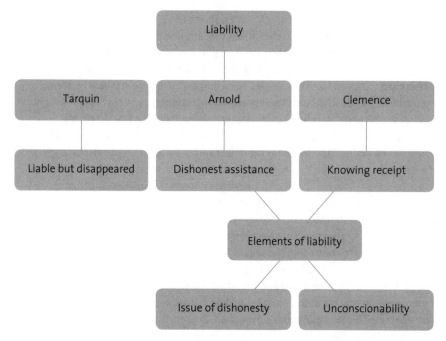

This diagram identifies the nature of the liabilities of Tarquin, Arnold and Clarence for breaches of trust.

ANSWER

In our particular case, it seems that 'the children of Sarah' – the beneficiaries of the trust – would be unable to pursue an action in breach of trust against Tarquin (their trustee) because he has disappeared. Consequently, they must resort to alternative remedies, which, in this case, means attempting to establish that strangers to the trust are fixed with constructive trusteeship because of their interference or involvement with the activities which have caused loss to the trust estate. Importantly, it must be remembered that the liability of the strangers – Arnold and Clarence – can exist only if *inter alia* there has actually been a breach of trust: *Brown v Bennett* (1998). The familiar liability of 'dishonest assistance' and 'knowing receipt' can arise only if the dealings with the trust property disclose a breach of the terms of the trust.[14]

It is a trite principle of trusts law that a distribution of property to non-beneficiaries is a breach of trust. Consequently, a stranger may be personally liable to account as a

---

14   Outline of the issue posed by the question.

constructive trustee if he has assisted in or induced the breach of trust, as *per* the conditions laid down in *Barnes v Addy* (1874) and explained in *Royal Brunei Airlines v Tan* (1995). *Prima facie* then, the distribution of £5,000 to Len is a breach of trust that may generate liability for Arnold. However, this is the only unequivocal breach of trust disclosed by the facts of the problem. For example, it may well be that investing in Tarquin Enterprises Ltd is perfectly within the investment powers of the trust (see, for example, ss 3, 4 and 6 of the Trustee Act 2000) and, if it were, it would be almost impossible to establish Arnold's liability as a stranger. Indeed, whereas Tarquin might be liable for his particular choice of investment – even though it was within his investment powers generally (breach of duty of care: s 1 of the Trustee Act 2000) – Arnold would not be liable as a stranger unless Tarquin's direction to him was part of a design to escape with the trust funds and Arnold dishonestly assisted in this (*Tan*; *Brinks v Abu-Saleh (No 3)* (1995)). Likewise, although it is unlikely, the trust instrument might authorise the purchase of lottery tickets (this would seem to be excluded from the statutory power of investment under the Trustee Act 2000 – see s 4 of that Act as to the standard investment criteria) and Clarence may well have rendered services to the trust in this regard for which he has been paid legitimately. So, without more, it is impossible to determine whether these events disclose a breach of trust. Consequently, the liability of Arnold and Clarence can be discussed only on the assumption that the activities of Tarquin do disclose a breach of trust and would have generated his personal liability. Even then, in itself, this is not enough to establish the liability of the strangers: we must also examine actions of the stranger.

As far as the wrongful distribution of the trust monies is concerned, it has been noted above that this, at least, is a clear breach of the terms of the trust (*Re Hulkes* (1886)). If any liability exists, it will lie in 'dishonest assistance', for clearly Arnold has participated in Tarquin's act which is revealed to be a breach of trust. In order to maintain a successful action against Arnold on this ground, two essential conditions must be fulfilled.[15] First, it must be established that Arnold has assisted Tarquin in a breach of trust. This is a factual matter. Assistance implies positive help although, in this case, it is not difficult to establish. *Tan* makes it clear that the liability is the stranger's and the state of mind of the trustee cannot colour it. A 'simple' breach of trust is enough. Second, *Tan* also makes it clear that the stranger's assistance must be coloured by his own 'dishonesty' before liability can arise. In *Twinsectra v Yardley* (2002), the majority of the House of Lords adopted the criminal law test for dishonesty (as laid down by Lord Lane CJ in *R v Ghosh* (1982)). This involves both objective and subjective questions. Controversy surrounded the *Twinsectra* test. In *Barlow Clowes v Eurotrust* (2006), the Privy Council decided that dishonesty was to be judged by reference to an objective standard. The test was whether the defendant was conscious of those elements of the transaction that made his participation transgress the ordinary

---

15 Specific identification of the elements of the claim.

standards of honest behaviour. In *Abou-Ramah v Abacha* (2006), the Court of Appeal endorsed the decision in *Barlow Clowes* and decided that the test of dishonesty is predominantly objective but with a subjective element and that *Barlow Clowes* does not involve a departure from the *Twinsectra* case. The Court of Appeal decided that the test for dishonesty will be satisfied if the defendant *knows* of the elements of the transaction which make it dishonest in accordance with the normally acceptable standards of honest behaviour. In *Starglade Ltd v Nash* (2010), the CA decided that the test for dishonesty was the principle stated by the Privy Council in *Barlow Clowes* and involved an objective standard. The judge will then consider the conduct, experience and knowledge of the defendant to determine whether his conduct may be characterised as dishonest.

Moreover, there is controversy in respect of the standard of proof of dishonesty. In *Jyske Bank v Heinl* (1999) it was decided by the Court of Appeal that the claimant bears a high standard of proof exceeding the traditional civil standard, but not as high as the criminal standard of proof. However, in the more recent case, *Statek Corp v Alford* (2008), the High Court reverted back to the traditional civil standard of proof of a balance of probabilities. No doubt each case will be unique to its own facts.[16]

In our case, we do not know with certainty Arnold's state of mind or motives, but it might be significant that Len's mother is Arnold's sister. While not conclusive, this does suggest some participation in Tarquin's fraud and, if this is true, Arnold will be accountable as a constructive trustee and will be ordered to repay the £5,000 to the trust fund which Len has now dissipated.

Much the same considerations apply to the two further 'investments' made by Arnold on Tarquin's instructions except that, in both cases, there is no clear evidence of a breach of trust. This makes it impossible to be certain whether the strangers will be accountable for dishonestly assisting Tarquin in his activities. Of course, as above, the possibility that a breach of trust has occurred can be inferred from the nature of the investments ordered by Tarquin, as it is hardly likely that the trust deed authorises investment in one of the trustee's own companies or in a purely speculative lottery and such investments may well be outside ss 3 and 4 of the Trustee Act 2000. Yet this is only a rebuttable presumption. With that in mind, it is again necessary to assess Arnold's state of mind in order to determine whether the beneficiaries have a remedy in a dishonest assistance claim concerning these lost trust funds. Unfortunately, there is nothing in the facts of the problem to help us here and, as we have seen, the fact that no reasonable person would have acted as Arnold did (that is, Arnold was negligent) is not enough to trigger the powerful duty to account in assistance cases (*Tan*). In the absence of further evidence, the matter must rest there.

---

16 Structured discussion of the cases.

The third stage of the beneficiaries' proceedings against the 'strangers' will be an attempt to fix Clarence with constructive trusteeship, this time on the basis of 'knowing receipt'. If this liability is successfully established, Clarence will be required to return the £10,000 to the trust and any profit that it has generated while in his hands (*English v Dedham Vale Properties* (1978)).[17] As a first step, it is apparent that Clarence has received the £10,000 for his own use and benefit, thus establishing clearly that this is a case of 'receipt' (*AGIP (Africa) Ltd v Jackson* (1992); *BCCI v Akindele* (2000)). Yet, before Clarence can be liable, it must be established both that the transfer to Clarence was in breach of trust and that Clarence had sufficient awareness or 'knowledge' of this to make him liable: that is, it is unconscionable for him to retain the benefit (*Akindele*). In fact, although these are separate criteria, it often happens that they are interwoven, as they are in this case. So, if it is true that Clarence has rendered services to the trust, the payment of £10,000 may well be legitimate (that is, there is no breach) – s 14 of the Trustee Act 2000 – and, even if the payment is not legitimate *per se*, Clarence could easily be a *bona fide* purchaser for value (having 'paid' for the money with his services) and thus not be liable. On the other hand, if the transfer to Clarence was in breach of trust – perhaps as part of a scheme to defraud the beneficiaries – Clarence's position must come under much closer scrutiny. If a breach has occurred, Clarence will be liable if he had 'knowledge' of the relevant facts. There is no agreement in the case law as to which level of knowledge is required for 'receipt' liability. Some cases (for example, *Cowan de Groot Properties v Eagle Trust plc* (1992)) suggest that either 'actual knowledge' or 'recklessness' must exist in order to establish liability. In *Re Montague* (1987), Megarry VC also argues powerfully in favour of a minimum standard of 'want of probity'. On the other hand, other cases (*International Sales Ltd v Marcus* (1982); *Belmont Finance Corporation v Williams Furniture (No 2)* (1980); *Box v Barclays Bank* (1998)) indicate plainly that receipt liability can be triggered by mere negligence, and this was also the view of Millet J in his very thorough judgment in *AGIP (Africa) Ltd v Jackson* (1992). Possibly, it is the meaning to be given to the 'unconscionability' test put forward in *Akindele*, but this remains to be seen. In our case, it is not clear whether Clarence has any knowledge of the breach of trust; he may be innocent. An enquiry must be made as to Clarence's understanding of Tarquin's actions and, it is submitted, the better view is that he will be liable as constructive trustee if he was merely negligent or worse: that is, if any of the five categories of knowledge identified in *Baden Delvaux and Lecuit v Société Générale pour Favouriser le Développement du Commerce et de l'Industrie en France SA* (1983) are present.

To conclude, much turns in this case on precise proof of facts which are not apparent from the problem. These are, principally, whether there were breaches of trust and whether the *mens rea* conditions are satisfied. In appropriate cases, the powerful constructive trust will be imposed and the strangers will be held personally responsible

---

17   Statement of liability including the remedy.

for any loss to the trust fund. This will be in addition to the obligation to return any trust property that they do retain, along with any profits that that property has generated in the meantime.

NOTE

These two problem questions are quite general and one should not shy from stating that the precise answer depends on facts which are not made apparent in the question. Of course, this means that the answer requires a discussion of the principles behind the rules.

The Law of Tracing

INTRODUCTION

One of the most effective remedies available to a beneficiary who has been deprived of the trust property as a result of a breach of trust by the trustee is to be found in the law of tracing. 'Tracing' of trust property – either 'at law' or 'in equity' – enables a claimant to identify his ownership of property into whosoever's hands that property falls and to recover it to the extent that the defendant still possesses it. Most importantly, it is clear that a claimant who relies on the tracing process is tracing his or her ownership of the property irrespective of the form the property has taken in the hands of the defendant. In *Foskett v McKeown* (2000), Lord Millett drew a distinction between 'following' and 'tracing'. Both processes involve exercises in locating the assets of the claimant. 'Following' is the process of identifying the *same* asset as it moves from hand to hand. 'Tracing' is the process of identifying a *new* asset as a substitute for the old. For example, if the trustee wrongly distributes trust property – being cash – to X, and X uses that cash to purchase a car, the claimant may 'trace' his ownership through the cash into the car and recover it from X. It should also be noted at this early stage that the remedies attached to the process of tracing and the liability of a stranger as constructive trustee (Chapter 7) are frequently complementary. So, a third party who has received trust property with 'knowledge' that there has been a breach of trust may be a constructive trustee and subject to the tracing process. In the former case (that is, that of constructive trusteeship), he must hold the trust property for the beneficiaries *and* be subject to a personal liability. As we shall see in the case of successful tracing, the defendant may be entirely innocent but must still return the property in its present form to the rightful owners.

In addition, it is reasonably clear that tracing in equity is a 'proprietary' institution in the sense that a successful claimant is asserting his right to the property *per se*: hence, if the defendant is bankrupt, the claimant may recover 'his' property (assuming it exists and is identifiable) and he is not treated as a general creditor and does not have to take only a share of the defendant's assets. It is a matter of 'hard-nosed property rights': *Foskett v McKeown* (2000). Obviously, such a powerful remedy cannot go unchecked and it should come as no surprise that the availability of the remedies attached to tracing in equity are restricted to certain situations. Unfortunately, the precise circumstances in which tracing is available are not universally agreed – either academically or judicially – nor, indeed, is there agreement as to whether tracing 'at law' and tracing 'in equity' are as similar as they first appear. These issues, as well as problem questions testing an awareness of how tracing works in practice, are the staple of examinations.

As inferred already, there are two forms of tracing: tracing 'at law' (common law tracing) and tracing 'in equity'. Tracing at law is available to any person who has legal title to property and its primary purpose is to identify the person whom the legal owner should sue, that being the person into whose hands the property has passed. Once the defendant has been identified, the claimant may then sue on a variety of causes of action as circumstances dictate. These are the action for 'money had and received', being appropriate where the property traced was money, and an action in conversion or for wrongful interference, where the property consists of goods or other kinds of property. We should note, however, that recent case law has tended to 'deconstruct' claims in tracing – especially at law – and to regard the claim as an example of a general restitutionary liability, whereby the defendant should return property to the claimant if the defendant has been unjustly enriched at the claimant's expense, to the extent of the unjust enrichment, in circumstances where there is no defence of change of position (*Trustee of the property of FC Jones v Jones* (1996)). In addition, as we shall see, there is one serious limitation on the effectiveness of tracing at law, for it is impossible to trace at law if the original property has been mixed with any other property (as opposed to having been exchanged for any other), although, again, this may be changing.

Fortunately, tracing into a 'mixed fund' is perfectly possible in equity. Moreover, given that tracing at law requires the claimant to have *legal* title to property, it is clearly not available to a beneficiary under a trust who, after all, has only an equitable title. Consequently, most of the issues examined in this chapter will focus on tracing in equity, that being the remedy available to a beneficiary under a trust and that being the remedy that *does* permit a claim to be made even though the trust property has been mixed with some other, even with that of the trustee himself: *Foskett*. Finally, we shall see that another aspect of the proprietary nature of tracing in equity is that it entitles the claimant both to the property which the defendant has in his possession and to any increase in its value that it may have acquired in the meantime (*Foskett*: entitled to benefits of life insurance because premiums were paid with beneficiaries' money). Until recently, this has not been possible in law, but once again, the move to a generally restitutionary approach may make even this possible (*Trustee of the property of FC Jones v Jones*).

QUESTION 43

What are the essential requirements for a successful tracing claim at law and in equity?

Aim Higher

The courts have drawn a distinction between 'following' and 'tracing'. 'Following' the assets in the hands of the defendant involves the process of identifying the same asset (but not in its substituted form, such as the proceeds of a sale) with the effect that the claimant may attach an order on to the property. 'Tracing' is the process whereby the claimant identifies and protects his interest in the asset, even in a substituted form.

In *Westdeutsche* (1996), Lord Browne-Wilkinson indicated that a thief holds stolen property on constructive trust for the rightful owner as the thief's conscience necessarily is bound. This means that the owner could trace the property through the hands of the thief into the hands of the ultimate recipient. It is an example of the 'act in breach' giving rise to both the claim and the fiduciary relationship necessary to support it. Clearly, this wide view would do much to reduce the practical obstacle placed in the way of tracing by the need to establish the fiduciary relationship. However, in *Shalson v Russo* (2003), Rimer J doubted Lord Browne-Wilkinson's view and stated that a thief has no title to property that he steals and thus cannot become a trustee of it. The true owner retains the legal and beneficial titles to the property. Perhaps the better view is that the thief does acquire title through his act of taking possession, but he does not acquire a better title than his victim.

In *Boscawen v Bajawa* (1995), the Court of Appeal indicated that equitable tracing should be regarded as a route to a defendant for all manner of remedies. So, in that case, once the defendant had been identified as having received the claimant's money (transferred in breach of trust), the claimant was subrogated to (that is, placed in the position of) the mortgagee whom the defendant had paid off with the money. So, it appears that equitable tracing – just like its counterpart at law – is developing a new restitutionary cloak.

Common Pitfalls ✖

Some students attempting this type of question have a tendency to write all they know of the details of cases without a structure and neglecting the policy considerations behind some of the decisions. This essay does not require discussion of the particular rules of equitable tracing (for example, *Re Hallett* (1880), *Re Oatway* (1903), *Clayton's Case* (1816), etc).

How to Answer this Question

❖ The purpose of a tracing claim, both at law and in equity.

❖ Conditions for both claims.

❖ Differences between them: in establishing the remedy and in respect of the defences available to a defendant.

Answer Structure

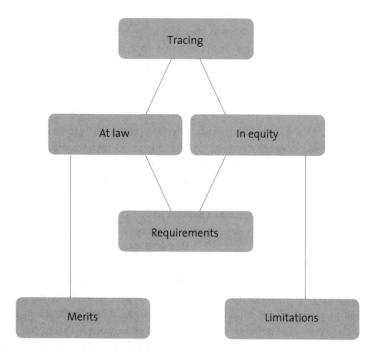

This diagram illustrates the process of tracing at law and in equity.

ANSWER

A tracing claim is a method of asserting ownership to property. Literally, the legal or equitable owner of property may 'trace' his or her ownership through the hands of the different persons who have possessed it and may recover it from the person who currently possesses it. Tracing 'at law' (common law tracing) is a means of following the legal title to property, while tracing 'in equity' signifies a similar right of the equitable owner, such as a beneficiary under a trust. Tracing, both at law and in equity, is not defeated by a change in the external appearance of the claimant's property, but will run against any property which can be identified as encapsulating the claimant's rights of ownership.[1]

---

1   Convergence of tracing at common law and equity.

Common law tracing is a means of following legal title to property through successive persons until the property (or its present equivalent) is identified in the hands of the person against whom the concrete remedy for recovery is pursued. In essence, it is a means to an end, not the end itself (*AGIP (Africa) Ltd v Jackson* (1992); *Trustee of the property of FC Jones v Jones* (1996)). When the present possessor of the property in which the claimant's legal title subsists is identified, the claimant has a choice of remedies against that possessor. If the property is money, then the action will be against the present recipient for 'money had and received' (*Lipkin Gorman v Karpnale* (1991)), whereas if the property is a specific item, then the action will lie in tort for wrongful interference with goods or conversion. In the former case, the amount of the money 'had and received' by the defendant will be returned to the claimant and, in the latter case, the defendant will pay damages representing the value of the item or, in exceptional cases, the item itself may be returned at the discretion of the court.[2]

In the first place, tracing at law (and in equity) requires the property to be in identifiable form. If it has been destroyed, or money has been dissipated, then tracing is of no use: the property and the *legal* title to it are extinct. Second, tracing at law requires the claimant to have had legal title to property. Therefore, as a matter of principle, it is not available to a beneficiary under a trust who is, of course, a person with a pure equitable title. Moreover, it must be clear that the claimant has retained legal title to the property. Given that title to money usually passes with possession, it is often easy to defeat a claim at law, as in *Box v Barclays Bank* (1998) where the legal title had passed from the claimants. On the other hand, some cases – for example, *Lipkin Gorman v Karpnale* (1991) and *Jones v Jones* (1996) – have sidestepped the claimants' *apparent* lack of title (that is, the claimants may have had title to a 'chose in action': a debt now representing the money) and allowed the claim to proceed. Third, the personal nature of tracing at law may cause problems if the defendant has gone bankrupt because, in theory, the personal claim of the tracer will rank equally with other personal claims made on the bankrupt's estate. In practice, the defendant's trustee in bankruptcy may pay the tracer first – in order to avoid a personal claim against *him* as receiver of the claimant's property, although this is an incidental advantage rather than an inherent attribute of tracing at law. Fourth, although there has been much debate, it seems that tracing at law is not available if the claimant's property has been mixed with that of another person and then passed on. The essence of the matter is that mixing at law renders the legal title to the property unidentifiable, in much the same way as if the property had actually been destroyed. This is a serious practical drawback to the efficacy of common law tracing and is a major reason why successful actions are rare. Note, however, that this is an inability to trace against a recipient of the property after it has been mixed. There is nothing to stop the claimant tracing at law against the person who does the

2   Multitude of remedies to complement the tracing process.

mixing because, prior to that person's possession, the property was identifiable. Fifthly, being traditionally regarded as a personal claim, an innocent defendant in an action supported by common law tracing should not normally be required to disgorge profits made by use of the property wrongfully received. The claim is for the value of the property, not *the* property (compare tracing in equity). However, in *Jones v Jones* (1996), the Court of Appeal held, on general restitutionary principles, that if the defendant had no title to the money she had received, then she had no title to the profits she made by using it. In that case, the defendant was compelled to return the value of the initial sum plus the considerably greater profits she made by investing it in the futures market. This may well indicate the way ahead, although we should note that it involves seeing tracing at law as simply a device for reversing unjust enrichment. Finally, it may now be the case that a defendant may be able to plead 'change of position' as a defence to an action triggered by common law tracing (*Lipkin Gorman v Karpnale* (1991)). For example, it may well provide a defence to a claim in money 'had and received' for a person who is a *bona fide* purchaser for value of the claimant's property and to other persons who, in all innocence, have received the claimant's property in circumstances where the court thinks they should not be held personally liable.[3]

Tracing in equity does not suffer from the practical limitations of common tracing and consequently is much more versatile. Importantly, tracing in equity is regarded as proprietary in nature, with the consequence that it attaches directly to the property in the hands of the possessor (no matter what its current form) and gives the claimant paramount rights to recover it, even if the defendant is bankrupt. The defendant has no right to the claimant's property and so it forms no part of the defendant's assets. Furthermore, the proprietary nature of the claim means that the claimant is entitled to any increase in the value of 'his' property while it has been out of his possession, as where shares are purchased with trust money and they rise in value (*Re Tilley* (1967); *Foskett* (2000)). The remedies in equity include a charge over property in the defendant's hands if it represents the claimant's original ownership, or an order for the return of specific assets, or a charge over specific funds, or a charge over a specific portion of the property or funds.[4]

The trigger for a claim of equitable tracing is that the claimant must have an equitable proprietary interest in property and *only* an equitable proprietary interest (*Re Diplock* (1948)). Consequently, a beneficiary under a trust may trace in equity, but a trustee (legal title only) and an absolute owner may not. Secondly, unlike the position at law, it seems that tracing in equity can occur only if there was in existence a fiduciary relationship between the equitable owner and some other person before

---

3   Limitations as to tracing at law.
4   Broader approach to tracing in equity.

the events giving rise to the tracing claim occurred (*Sinclair v Brougham* (1914); *AGIP (Africa) Ltd v Jackson* (1992); and confirmed in *Westdeutsche Landesbank Girozentrale v Islington LBC* (1996)). This will always be the case where the claim arises out of a trust and it is clear that courts may do their utmost to find the required fiduciary relationship in order to facilitate the tracing claim (*Chase Manhattan Bank v Israel-British Bank* (1981)). However, the principle is that there must have been an initial fiduciary relationship.

Thirdly, it is inherent in the equitable tracing claim that the property of the beneficiaries must have been transferred to another person wrongfully. Otherwise, the equitable owner has no right or reason to claim its return. Fourthly, being a claim in equity, equitable tracing is not possible against a person who is a *bona fide* purchaser for value of the property, although it may still be possible to trace against the person who has sold the trust property to the purchaser (*Re Diplock* (1948)). Likewise, it appears that the court has a discretion to disallow tracing against an innocent volunteer (that is, a person who gives no value for the trust property but is innocent of wrongdoing), if to do otherwise would be inequitable in all the circumstances. It is felt that this discretionary limitation in *Re Diplock* is now subsumed in the developing defence of change of position advocated by Lord Goff in *Lipkin Gorman* (1991). Lord Goff formulated the defence on a broad basis. The defence will not be available to a defendant who has changed his position in bad faith; for example, a defendant who spends the claimant's money after knowledge of facts entitling the claimant to restitution. Similarly, the defence will not be available to a wrongdoer, such as a defendant who has acted in breach of his fiduciary duties. In any event, the mere fact that the defendant has spent the money in whole or in part, in the ordinary course of things, does not, of itself, render it inequitable that he should be called upon to repay the claimant. However, if the defendant has spent the claimant's money on a venture which would not have been undertaken but for the gift, such conduct would be capable of being construed as a change of position. In *Niru Battery Manufacturing Co v Milestone Trading Ltd (No 2)* (2004), the Court of Appeal decided that good faith was the touchstone of the defence of change of position and that this concept was incapable of definition. In *Abou-Ramah v Abacha* (2006), the Court of Appeal decided that the requirement of good faith had to be construed not only by reference to the circumstances of the particular transactions in question but by having regard to all the material circumstances of the case.

In conclusion, it is apparent that both tracing in law and tracing in equity can be powerful tools in the hands of persons wrongfully deprived of their property. At present, the conditions for the application of each are different and some would argue that they are fundamentally different in purpose. However, the object of tracing is quite limited: it is to restore to the claimant that of which he has been wrongfully deprived, often in breach of trust. For that reason, a tracing claim in equity may well be accompanied by a personal claim against the trustee for breach of trust. Finally, if it is true that tracing at law and tracing in equity are not logically different – that is, that they are both examples of a restitutionary claim used to restore to the claimant that by which the defendant has been unjustly enriched at the claimant's expense – then, perhaps different considerations should not apply.

NOTE

It is often difficult to describe and analyse the law of tracing in the abstract. The concept of following or tracing the ownership of property is metaphysical, but nevertheless very powerful if one happens to be the defendant in a tracing claim. The 'big' question is whether tracing at law and tracing in equity will survive as distinct classes of action in the face of the new restitutionary approach. Following *Foskett v McKeown*, it seems that they will for some time to come. However, in essays such as this, examples are always useful to illustrate difficult concepts.

QUESTION 44

Charles was the trustee of a large private trust fund. He cashed a cheque for £26,000 drawn on the trust fund and gave the money to James, the trust's financial advisor, with directions to use half to purchase shares for the trust and to use half to invest in antique furniture. James used £7,000 of the money to purchase shares in X Co in the name of the trust, and he delivered the share certificates to Charles as promised. However, he used a further £10,000 to purchase shares in Y Co in his own name, although he has now given these to his daughter as a birthday present, much to her surprise. James puts a further £5,000 in his own bank account, in which he already has some £4,000 of his own money. Out of this account, he purchases shares in Z Co to the value of £3,000, and gives them to his son. He spends the rest of the money from this bank account on a family holiday. The final £4,000 of the trust money was used to purchase antique furniture at a local auction.

The shares in X Co have slumped in value; those in Y Co have remained constant; but those in Z Co have trebled in value. Unfortunately, James has disappeared, and the furniture turns out to be fake and is worthless. Advise Charles of any action he might take to recoup the losses to the trust fund.

Aim Higher ★

In theory, because the question asks one to advise the trustee, it might be possible not to consider equitable tracing at all – because, on one view, the trustee has no equitable title to trace. However, this would not be good *practical* advice given that a partially effective remedy in equitable tracing is available to the beneficiaries.

> ### Common Pitfalls
>
> Students do not always appreciate that tracing at law is simply a means of identifying the defendant, who is then subject to a specific remedy, because the liability of the defendant is personal, not proprietary. In other words, the person identified as the defendant through common law tracing is personally liable to the claimant for either money had and received or wrongful interference with goods, and must, therefore, pay the claimant, whether or not he still retains the property in question.

How to Answer this Question

❖ Tracing at law: existence of legal title and continuance of that title.
❖ Appropriate remedy and defences, if any.
❖ The need to trace in equity: the beneficiaries.
❖ Increase in value of trust property.
❖ New restitutionary approaches.

Answer Structure

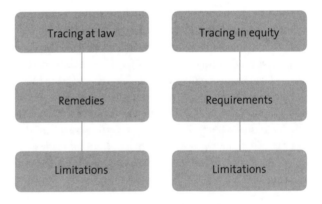

This diagram depicts the nature of tracing both at law and in equity.

ANSWER

This problem raises a number of issues concerning the remedies available to a trustee (Charles) and the beneficiaries for whom he holds the trust property when the trust property is misapplied in breach of trust. However, perhaps the first piece of advice that one may offer to Charles is to warn him of the possibility that he may be sued personally for breach of trust by the beneficiaries. Of course, the acts in breach were committed by James – Charles's agent – but it is clear that Charles might be held personally liable for losses to the trust estate through James's action if Charles did not fulfil his duties in respect of agents under ss 1, 21 and 22 of the Trustee Act 2000, or otherwise delegated a function which he should have exercised personally (see s 11 of the Trustee Act 2000).5 Similarly, there is no doubt that James would have been liable for breaching his contract of agency and probably also as constructive trustee for knowingly dealing inconsistently with trust property (*Karak Rubber v Burden* (1972)).

Despite the availability of these other remedies, it seems that the law of tracing will offer the most hopeful path for recovery of the trust's assets. For example, it is not absolutely certain that Charles's acts or omissions are sufficient to found personal liability for breach of trust and that James has disappeared.6 So, it is only if the trustee, or the beneficiaries on the advice of the trustee, can trace their respective legal and equitable ownership of the trust property that there is hope of substantial redress. In this regard, it is worth noting that the £7,000 worth of shares purchased in X Co in the name of the trust are safe and that the furniture purchased by James, according to his instructions, is also part of the trust estate, even though it is worth very little.

If at all possible, Charles should be advised initially to seek to trace the missing trust funds at law. The advantages of this approach are, first, that there is no need to prove an initial fiduciary relationship (although this would not be a problem for the beneficiaries); second, that an action to recover the property can be made against any persons who have received it, regardless of their state of mind or whether any of them still retains it (*AGIP (Africa) Ltd v Jackson* (1992)); and thirdly, that the defences available to the recipient of the property are fairly limited in scope, even though a change of position defence to a claim at law may now be accepted as valid (*Lipkin Gorman v Karpnale* (1991)).7 If Charles can establish that he – as trustee – retained legal title to the £10,000 which was passed to James, and which James improperly invested in Y Co, he may be able to maintain a tracing action at law against these assets which now lie in the hands of James's daughter. In this connection, Charles will have to establish that he has a legal right of ownership which has survived the transfers to James and subsequently to his daughter. This would not appear to be a problem in this case, especially since James received the money as agent (see *Lipkin Gorman v Karpnale* (1991)). Thereafter, James could not transfer the shares beneficially to his daughter under the equitable maxim *nemo dat quod non habet*. In addition, there is no doubt that a claim to trace at law will survive changes in the nature of the property, providing that it is not mixed with any other property (*Taylor v Plummer* (1815)). Thus, Charles will be able to trace his legal title to the property through James to his daughter. Charles will be able to maintain an action against James's daughter personally for wrongful interference with goods and can expect damages to the value of the property she has received. This liability will persist even if she has disposed of the shares and may be defeated only if she can rely on the defence of 'change of position', recognised in *Lipkin Gorman v Karpnale* (1991) and applied in *Bank Tejaret v HKSB* (1995). This is unlikely in

---

5   Nature of the liability of Charles and James.
6   Lack of clarity as to the personal liability of Charles.
7   Advantages of tracing at law compared with tracing in equity.

the circumstances as there is no evidence that James's daughter has in any way acted to her own detriment in innocent reliance on her receipt of the shares.

The next issue concerns the £5,000 which James places in his own bank account, where there is £4,000 of his own money. James has mixed the trust money with his own money before purchasing the shares and giving them to his son. This is fatal to a claim of tracing at law against James's son because, as far as the common law is concerned, the mixing of property before it is passed to the recipient makes it unidentifiable (*AGIP (Africa) Ltd v Jackson* (1992)).[8] Despite much criticism of this rule and possible contrary authority (*Banque Belge pour l'Etranger v Hambrouk* (1921)), it appears to have been confirmed by the House of Lords in *Lipkin Gorman*. It is possible that Charles might be able to rely on *Trustee of the property of FC Jones v Jones* (1996) to establish a right to the money because, in that case, the Court of Appeal held simply that the claimant could recover on the ground that the defendant never had any right to the money, so had to return it. However, the survival of this claim when mixing had occurred was not addressed in that case, so reliance on it in our case, where mixing has occurred, might be unsafe. For example, the claim to trace at law was rejected in *Box v Barclays Bank* (1998) because the claimant had lost legal title on payment to a bank account. It is possible that Charles could argue that James became a constructive trustee for *him* on the basis that James must have known that he was behaving in breach of trust and so became a trustee on the basis of conscience, following *dicta* in *Westdeutsche Landesbank Girozentrale v Islington LBC* (1996). This would trigger a claim in equity by Charles – the trustee and now beneficiary: *Twinsectra v Yardley* (2002). However, perhaps the best advice is that if the trust fund is to have a good chance of recovering the £5,000, the beneficiaries must be persuaded to pursue a tracing claim in equity against the shares now in the possession of James's son. In fact, there is every chance that an equitable tracing claim would be successful, at least in so far as the trust fund monies remain identifiable. For example, there is an initial fiduciary relationship and the beneficiaries undoubtedly have an equitable proprietary interest (*Re Diplock* (1948)). Moreover, as noted above, so long as the beneficiaries' equitable proprietary interest is identifiable, it is irrelevant that the property is no longer in its original form or that it has been mixed with other property (*Re Hallett* (1880); *Re Oatway* (1903)). The beneficiaries may trace the trust fund money into James's bank account and, following the rule in *Re Oatway* (1903), James will be presumed to have spent £3,000 of the trust money on the shares in Z Co (not following *Re Hallett* (1880) because there are no monies left in the bank account which could satisfy the beneficiaries' claim). Given that James's son is not a *bona fide* purchaser for value, he cannot resist the tracing claim against the shares. But if the circumstances had warranted it, he may have been entitled to the defence of change of position: see Lord Goff in *Lipkin Gorman*. In the present case James's son still retains the shares in Z Co and there is no evidence that he has changed his position. Thus, he may not have a defence to a claim to recover the shares in equity. It should also be noted that the beneficiaries are entitled to the increase in the value of Z Co's shares because tracing in

---

8   Limitations on tracing at law.

equity gives the claimants a proprietary right to property and any increase in its value (*Foskett*). Had the claim been pursued at law – using *Jones v Jones* – this might also have been possible. Finally, as noted above and as *Re Diplock* (1948) makes clear, equitable tracing is unavailable when the property ceases to be identifiable. The money spent by James on a family holiday is lost and, following the traditional approach, the beneficiaries will be forced to rely on personal remedies (if any) against the trustee in order to recover the outstanding £2,000. Again, however, if it is now true that tracing in equity is merely a means to an end (*Boscawen v Bajawa* (1995)), then the fact that some of this property is no longer identifiable may not defeat the claim. Assuming – and it is an assumption that many would challenge – that equitable tracing is merely a means of finding a defendant against whom a claim in restitution can be made, the liability of the recipient will not cease on disposal of the property but he (James) will be held accountable for its value, save only that he might plead change of position.

For the sake of completeness, it should also be noted that both James's daughter and son may incur the additional liabilities of constructive trusteeship if they have knowingly received trust property in breach of trust and, furthermore, the bank which cashed Charles's cheque could, in theory, be liable for assisting Charles in a breach of trust, provided they were dishonest (*Royal Brunei Airlines v Tan* (1995)). Again, both are unlikely on the facts as given (see *Lipkin Gorman v Karpnale* (1991)).

QUESTION 45

Zebedee is the trustee of a trust fund, holding a large amount of money on trust for Dougal and Florence. At the same branch of the bank at which the trust account is held, Zebedee has his own current account which stands in credit at £500. The following events occur:

(a) Zebedee pays £5,000 of the trust fund into his own account;

(b) he then draws out £500 which he invests in the Roundabout Property Co;

(c) he draws a further £3,000 from his account and gives it to his son, Brian, an antique dealer, who uses his skill to make a very successful purchase of a painting at auction;

(d) he draws out a further £1,000, £500 of which he spends on making improvements to his house and the other £500 he gives to his daughter, Ermentrude, so that she can pay off her debt to Loanshark Co;

(e) he pays £500 to the local hospital appeal, which has used the money to purchase some much needed equipment; and

(f) he pays £500 into the current account of the Springboard Trust, of which he is also a trustee and which is in credit at £400. He then buys shares in Magic Co for £700 and entertains his family to dinner with the remainder.

Zebedee has gone bankrupt and the shares in Roundabout Property Co have halved in value. The painting is worth £10,000 and the shares in Magic Co have trebled in value. Advise Dougal, Florence and the Springboard Trust as to their remedies, if any.

How to Answer this Question

- ❖ Breach of trust action is the first resort.
- ❖ In the event of an unsatisfied claim, tracing may be available.
- ❖ Loss of the remedy – change of position.
- ❖ Mixed funds: two trusts.
- ❖ Replacement of trust funds.
- ❖ Innocent volunteers.

Answer Structure

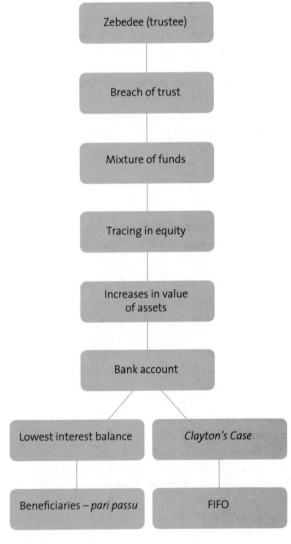

This diagram indicates the nature of the tracing process in respect of the various properties.

ANSWER

Although it is not absolutely clear from the facts of the problem, it is highly likely that Zebedee, the trustee, has committed a series of breaches of trust when disposing of the trust fund monies in the way indicated. Certainly, his mixing of the trust monies with his own may well be a breach of trust and it is highly unlikely that the trust instrument authorises him to make gifts to his children or other causes.[9] However, Zebedee is bankrupt, and personal claims against him will have to be abated in Zebedee's bankruptcy along with the claims of other creditors. In such circumstances, the beneficiaries will wish to pursue such proprietary remedies as they might have, as this will give them a right to their property *per se* in priority to those who are 'merely' creditors. Tracing in equity may well prove to be the route to the most effective remedy.[10]

Fortunately, there is no doubt that Dougal and Florence are entitled to pursue equitable tracing. They will be attempting to pursue their equitable proprietary interest as beneficiaries under a trust as Zebedee stands in a fiduciary relationship to them (*Re Diplock* (1948)). Moreover, as is well known, it is possible in equity to trace ownership into, through, and out of a mixed fund, so the fact that the trustee has mixed the £5,000 of trust money with that of his own will not defeat the tracing claim. Likewise, although some of the final recipients of the trust money may well be innocent (thereby excluding the possibility that they are constructive trustees), none of them are *bona fide* purchasers of the property and so they are not free automatically from equitable tracing, although their status as innocent recipients may have some effect on the precise scope of the remedies granted to Dougal and Florence.[11]

When Zebedee transfers the trust money into his account, it is likely that he is committing a breach of trust and it is immaterial that there has been no loss to the trust estate at this stage. Indeed, as is clear, subsequent events do deprive the beneficiaries of their property and so they will wish to trace their assets into the hands of the persons now possessing them. First, there is the £500 withdrawn from the mixed account and used to purchase shares in Roundabout Co Ltd. The change in nature of the beneficiaries' equitable interest – from money into shares – is not an obstacle to equitable tracing, provided that the shares can be said to have been purchased with the beneficiaries' money in the first place, bearing in mind that Zebedee has £500 of his own money in the mixed bank account.[12] In this regard, *Re Hallett* (1880) decides that a trustee making purchases from a bank account in which funds are mixed must be presumed to have spent his own money first, as there is always a presumption against

9   Consideration of a breach of trust.
10   Primacy of tracing in equity.
11   Limitations on the tracing process in equity.
12   Distinction between following and tracing.

a breach of trust. Yet, in our case, this would mean that the shares in Roundabout belonged to Zebedee, even though, after all the events have taken place, there is no money left in the account to return to the beneficiaries. In these circumstances, when, in effect, there is nothing in the bank account to trace to, *Re Oatway* (1903) makes it clear that the beneficiaries can turn to property purchased out of the mixed fund as being the embodiment of their equitable interest, even if, at the time it was purchased, there was enough money to satisfy their claim.[13] Consequently, the Roundabout shares will belong in equity to Dougal and Florence, although the fact that the shares are now worth only half their original value means that they will have to rely on their personal claim against Zebedee to recover the balance.

In principle, the same considerations apply to the £3,000 which Zebedee then withdraws and pays to his son; this is trust money and capable of being traced. Again, the fact that it was then used to purchase an antique painting will not destroy the tracing claim. Moreover, the added complication that the property (as money, and then a chattel) is in the hands of Brian, a third party, is no bar. Brian is not a *bona fide* purchaser for value, although there is no indication that he knew the money was transferred to him in breach of trust and is unlikely to be a constructive trustee (*Westdeutsche Landesbank Girozentrale v Islington LBC* (1996)). *Re Diplock* (1948) makes it clear that equitable tracing is perfectly possible against an innocent volunteer where the property is identifiable and, in our case, there is no suggestion that Brian has mixed the trust money with his funds before the painting was purchased. Moreover, because tracing in equity is a proprietary remedy, the court will not merely order Brian to repay £3,000 or charge the painting to the value of £3,000. The court is most likely to order the return of the painting itself as this is where the beneficiaries' equitable interest is to be found, especially since the proprietary remedy carries with it any increase in the value of the property (*Re Tilley* (1967); *Foskett v McKeown* (2000)).

The issue of the identifiable nature of the trust property is quite pertinent when considering the next £1,000 which Zebedee withdraws, half of which he gives to his daughter and half of which he spends on his own house. In *Re Diplock*, it was stated that, in some circumstances, the beneficiaries' property could be regarded as unidentifiable and untraceable, or that it may have been used in such a way as to make recovery of it inequitable. In particular, the House of Lords was of the view that it was impossible to trace money that had been used to pay off a debt, both because the creditor could be regarded as a purchaser for value and because the money effectively ceased to exist as independent property. Consequently, at first, unless Zebedee's daughter (or Loanshark Co) has taken the money with knowledge of the breach of trust, and is thereby a constructive trustee, there appears to be no route to a successful recovery of this £500.

....

13   Significance of presumptions in respect of tracing claims in equity.

By way of contrast, however, the Court of Appeal, in *Boscawen v Bajawa* (1995), allowed the claimant a remedy against a defendant who had used monies traced to him to pay off a mortgage. In *Boscawen*, the claimant was subrogated to the creditor who had been paid off.[14] So, in our case, if we follow *Boscawen*, and similar reasoning adopted by the House of Lords in *Banque Financière de la Cité v Parc (Battersea) Ltd* (1998), the claimants will be subrogated to Loanshark Co, and may be able to recover the money by enforcing the debt against Ermentrude as creditors.

Turning to the £500 spent by Zebedee on his house, this might be recovered. It is perfectly possible to levy a charge for a specific amount on property owned by another if this would enable the beneficiaries' interest to be protected. Indeed, although *Re Diplock* suggests that it could be inequitable to levy such a charge on the property of an innocent volunteer where the bulk of its purchase price or improvement costs have been provided by the volunteer, there is no such objection to levying a charge on the property of the trustee who has actually committed the breach of trust. The beneficiaries will be able to take a first charge over Zebedee's house to the value of £500 (or as a proportion of its value) and, being proprietary, this should take precedence over the claims of other creditors. Conversely, however, there are doubts whether the £500 paid to the local hospital can be recovered by the beneficiaries. There is no doubt that the property is traceable *per se*; the facts suggest that the money has been used to purchase identifiable equipment and there is no suggestion that the innocent volunteer (the hospital) had contributed any of its own money to these purchases. Thus, the matter is not entirely within the *Diplock* defences referred to above because the innocent volunteer has not mixed its property with that of the beneficiaries. Yet, it is clear that the court has a general discretion to deny tracing where it would be inequitable to permit it and this may prevent recovery from the hospital. If the court does deny tracing of this £500, it may well take the view that it was, in any event, the £500 of Zebedee's own money which he had in his account prior to the mixing of the trust funds (*Re Hallett* (1880)), as the court may have done with the untraceable £500 given to his daughter but, on these facts, not both. This would ensure, at least, that the final £500 remaining in the account could be regarded as belonging to Dougal and Florence prior to its mixing with the trust money of the Springboard Trust.

If one follows the logic taken above – that is, that one of the untraceable £500 amounts was Zebedee's own money – the mixing of the final £500 with the £400 of the Springboard Trust raises the question of the ability to trace to an asset (the shares in Magic Co) when all claimants to it (Dougal, Florence and the beneficiaries of Springboard Trust) are innocent. In principle, unless the rule in *Clayton's Case* (1816) applies, the two sets of claimants will be able to trace and claim the shares in Magic Co in proportion to their money in the mixed bank account before the purchase took

---

14   Complementary nature of the doctrine of subrogation.

place: that is, in the ratio 5:4 (£500:£400). As before, both parties will be able to retain any increase in the value of their portion of the shares (*Re Tilley* (1967); *Foskett v McKeown* (2000)). The balance in the account would be shared on a similar basis. If, on the other hand, *Clayton's case* does apply, then the beneficiaries of the Springboard Trust will be able to claim that the first £400 worth of Magic Co shares belongs to them, on a 'first in, first out' basis.[15] However, even if it is clear that Zebedee's account is an 'active' bank account within the *Clayton* rule, *Barlow Clowes International Ltd (In Liquidation) v Vaughan* (1992) establishes that *Clayton's* rule is one of convenience only and should not be applied either where the property of the respective claimants is identifiable or where it would achieve an inequitable result. A similar view was echoed in *Commerzbank Aktiengesellschaft v IMB Morgan* (2004). It is suggested, therefore, that the proportionate share rule (*pari passu*, 5:4) should prevail.

In conclusion, it can be seen that Dougal and Florence are able to trace a significant amount of their property through the mixed account into the hands of the (presumably) innocent third parties. That which they cannot claim, and where they still suffer a loss, can be recovered only in a personal action against Zebedee or against any of the third parties who may have had such an awareness of the material facts as to make them liable as constructive trustees.

QUESTION 46

By his will, Terrence appointed Edward and Edwina as his executors and trustees and bequeathed £500,000 to Lucy and £300,000 for the charitable purposes of the War Veterans Association. Edward and Edwina took all proper steps to prove the will and, after making all proper enquiries, paid over the monies to Lucy and the charity. However, Terrence had provided for David and Dee, as his residuary legatees, and they claimed successfully that the will should be set aside on the grounds of Lucy's undue influence over Terrence. Likewise, it appears that the War Veterans Association is not entitled to charitable status, being merely a non-charitable association. It also transpires that Rack, a creditor of Terrence who had been abroad at the time of Terrence's death, is owed a large sum of money, and he now claims £300,000.

Unfortunately, the strain of this was too much for both Edward and Edwina: they turned to gambling and both are now bankrupt. Lucy, however, has spent £100,000 on completely renovating her house, £150,000 on shares in the stock market and £50,000 on a year of high living. The War Veterans Association has spent all the money on providing pensions for disabled servicemen.

▶ Advise David, Dee and Rack as to their rights, if any, in Terrence's estate.

15 Alternative but unpopular solution in **Clayton's Case**.

How to Answer this Question

- ❖ Loss of the remedy.
- ❖ Innocent and culpable defendants.
- ❖ *Re Diplock in personam* remedy – strict liability.
- ❖ Change of position.

Answer Structure

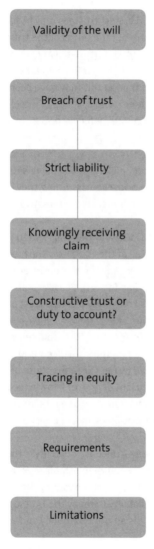

```
Validity of the will
```

```
Breach of trust
```

```
Strict liability
```

```
Knowingly receiving
claim
```

```
Constructive trust or
duty to account?
```

```
Tracing in equity
```

```
Requirements
```

```
Limitations
```

This diagram highlights a claim for breach of trust and the liabilities of strangers as constructive trustees or for accounting.

ANSWER

In the law of trusts, there are many remedies by which a disappointed or defrauded beneficiary may seek to reclaim specific property from third parties, or at least seek damages by way of compensation for the loss they have suffered. The action for damages for breach of trust, the imposition of a constructive trust, the law of equitable tracing and the specialised *Re Diplock in personam* action are perhaps the most widely used. They form the subject matter of this problem.[16]

It is clear that even innocent and honest trustees may be liable in damages for breach of trust if they have failed to carry out the terms of the trust or fulfil their fiduciary duties (*Tito v Waddell (No 2)* (1977)). Unfortunately for Edward and Edwina, it seems that they may have committed breaches of trust in paying the trust money to Lucy and the War Veterans Association, even though this may have been due to an understandable mistake as to law or facts (see, for example, *Re Diplock* itself).[17] It may well be that the two trustees could mount a successful defence to such an action – perhaps under s 61 of the Trustee Act 1925 on the grounds that they have behaved honestly and reasonably and ought fairly to be excused (*Williams v Byron* (1901)). In any event, we are told that they are now bankrupt and so are unlikely to be able to satisfy the large claims of David and Dee for their losses of £800,000, even assuming they had no defence to the action. This means that the two claimants must seek alternative remedies.

As a first choice, it may be that David and Dee will wish to establish that Lucy should be regarded as a constructive trustee of the £500,000 she has received. If this proves to be the case, Lucy will be personally liable for this entire amount, whether or not she retains any of it. Of course, such liability is not easily established, and David and Dee will have to assert that Lucy has knowingly received trust property in breach of trust within the principles discussed in *International Sales Ltd v Marcus* (1982); *AGIP (Africa) Ltd v Jackson* (1992); *BCCI v Akindele* (2000).[18] Undoubtedly, the transfer was in breach of trust – because of the finding of undue influence – and Lucy has received the property for her own benefit, as witnessed by her subsequent use of it. The crucial question then remains whether she has a sufficient degree of knowledge to fix her with liability. Fortunately, whatever doubts there are as to the required degree of knowledge for knowing receipt – intention/recklessness and/or negligence (*Baden Delvaux and Lecuit v Société Générale pour Favouriser le Développement du Commerce et de l'Industrie en France SA* (1983)) or (if different) 'unconscionability' – the finding that Lucy procured the will by her undue influence is enough to establish her knowledge of the relevant facts. She will be a constructive trustee of the money she has received. As noted above, this imposes on her a personal liability to repay the £500,000. Of course, it is quite likely that she will be unable to find this amount of money and we are told that she has spent

---

16 Identification of the issues posed by the problem.
17 The strict nature of liability for breach of trust.
18 Knowingly receiving trust property or unconscionability.

at least £300,000 on specific projects. In such circumstances, while David and Dee may well be able to recover the unspent £200,000 and perhaps even some of the balance out of Lucy's other assets, the beneficiaries would be well advised to resort to the proprietary remedy of tracing.

There is no doubt that David and Dee would be able to satisfy the preconditions for tracing in equity identified in *Re Diplock* (1948): as residuary legatees they have an equitable proprietary interest and there is a clear fiduciary relationship between them and Edward and Edwina. Moreover, *Re Diplock* does indicate that recovery of property through tracing in equity might be refused if the property has been so mixed with that of an innocent volunteer that a successful action would be inequitable (now regarded as a change of position defence: see *Lipkin Gorman v Karpnale* (1991)). Lucy is not 'innocent' and, therefore, there is every chance that David and Dee would be granted a charge over Lucy's house, either to the value of the money spent on it (£100,000) or in the proportion that £100,000 represents of the house's value after improvement (*Re Tilley* (1967); *Foskett v McKeown* (2000)). To some extent, whether the court chooses the fixed charge (£100,000) or the proportionate charge may depend on the value of the house and whether the court feels that the two claimants should benefit from any windfall profit arising from an increase in the house's value. The same considerations apply, *mutatis mutandis*, to Lucy's investment in the stock market. Presumably, the shares she has purchased are registered in her name and the beneficiaries will be entitled to recover them under equitable tracing. Moreover, as there is no suggestion that any of their purchase price was provided from Lucy's own funds, David and Dee will own the shares *per se*, at their current value, although if the shares stand at a loss at the time of their claim, they will have the normal personal action to recover the balance. Finally, it is unfortunately quite likely that the £50,000 spent on 'high living' will be untraceable, having been dissipated on unidentifiable purchases. This amount will have to be the subject of the personal claim against Lucy and/or the trustees.

David and Dee may also be able to maintain a tracing claim against the assets spent by the War Veterans Association. As before, there is no doubt about the nature of David's and Dee's equitable interest or the existence of their proprietary rights. Moreover, it is inherent in a tracing claim that the funds sought to be recovered have been transferred to the recipient in breach of trust; otherwise there is no ground of recovery. In this case, it is clear that the property should never have been distributed to the Association, since it is not a charity. The trust was for a non-charitable purpose, and therefore void, with the money resulting to the residuary legatees under the beneficiary principle (*Re Endacott* (1960)). In fact, these are similar facts to *Re Diplock* itself. Unfortunately, however, like *Re Diplock*, this tracing claim may run into difficulties. As noted above, *Re Diplock* suggests that tracing will not be permitted where it would be inequitable to force the return of the property from an innocent volunteer. It is highly likely that the court would regard it as inequitable to force the disabled war veterans to repay the funds which they have been given as pensions. The court might take the view that David and Dee's claim should fail because of the identity of the defendants and the manner in which the property came to them.[19]

However, that is not the end of the matter. In *Re Diplock*, the House of Lords expressly accepted the existence of a limited *in personam* action, available against the recipients of property, at the suit of unpaid or underpaid creditors or next of kin arising out of a wrongly administered testamentary estate.[20] In our case, given that the estate of Terrence has been wrongly administered, David and Dee and Rack (the creditor) will have a personal action against Lucy and against the officers of the War Veterans Association, all of whom have received funds from the executors and trustees. Importantly, it was made clear in *Re Diplock* that this remedy exists against completely innocent recipients and while this is irrelevant for Lucy, who has personal liability on other grounds, it means that the officers of the Association cannot plead their good faith as a defence. Likewise, because the action is personal (*in personam*), it is irrelevant that the recipients no longer have the property and they must satisfy the claims of the three claimants out of their own funds. As is clear, this is a powerful remedy and this is one reason why currently it exists only in the context of a wrongly administered testamentary estate (and possibly after a wrongful distribution of the assets of a defunct company – *Re Leslie Engineers Co Ltd* (1976)). It is also true that the claimants must exhaust their personal actions against the executors before they can proceed further, although that is not a problem in our case. Finally, however, while at one time it was thought that there was no defence to this *in personam* action – that is, that the innocent recipients had to repay the amount transferred if the preconditions for the remedy were established – it is likely, following *Lipkin Gorman v Karpnale* (1991), that the officers of the War Veterans Association might be able to plead 'change of position' to minimise or deny their liability. This defence does, however, lie in the discretion of the court, and it may well be that, in the light of the bankruptcy of the executors, the court will admit the claim of Rack (who has little chance of a tracing claim being a 'mere' contractual debtor: *Box v Barclays Bank* (1998)), and perhaps David and Dee to the extent that they have not recovered the funds from other sources.

NOTE

These three problem questions show the diverse range of issues that can arise in the law of tracing. Note how useful *Re Diplock* can be: it is authority for nearly every aspect of tracing in equity. Consider also the powerful nature of the *Re Diplock in personam* remedy. This is an invention of equity, limited in nature, but potentially ruinous for the innocent recipients of wrongly distributed funds. It remains to be seen whether *Lipkin Gorman* is authority for the existence of a general, strict liability restitutionary remedy – subject, as always, to the change of position defence.

....

19 Significant limitation to tracing in equity.
20 Significance of the personal action by the unpaid creditors or next of kin.

Breach of Trust

INTRODUCTION

It is perhaps surprising that the last of the beneficiary's remedies to be considered is the personal action for breach of trust. After all, the attempt to fix a stranger with a constructive trust (Chapter 7) and the remedy of tracing (Chapter 8) are triggered by an initial breach of trust by the trustee. Moreover, even in situations where these other remedies are available, if the trustee responsible for the breach is able to satisfy the claims of the beneficiaries in full, a personal action for damages for breach of trust will be the normal course of action and the court may insist that it is pursued before other avenues are followed. As we have seen, the constructive trust and remedy of tracing are used principally against third parties, being persons who have meddled with the trust or who have come into possession of the trust property subsequent to the trustee. In contrast, the action for breach of trust is personal to the trustee in two senses. First, only those trustees who are responsible for the breach of trust may be sued for damages, although the extent of the 'personal responsibility' of a trustee for breach of trust is quite wide. Secondly, the action for breach of trust itself is a personal action and the successful claimant (usually the beneficiary) will become a normal judgment creditor. Consequently, in the event of the trustee's bankruptcy or death, the beneficiary will have to take her chance along with all of the other creditors and claimants and may not receive all of the damages awarded in the breach of trust action. This is why the proprietary remedies discussed in the two previous chapters are so useful when specific trust property is still in existence.

It would be a mistake to believe that the action for breach of trust is not important. It is the first weapon of the wronged beneficiary and one whose net can be cast particularly widely. In general terms, there are four areas of concern to the student although, as ever, this is a somewhat arbitrary classification. First, questions arise as to what actually constitutes a breach of trust and who is responsible for it. This is tied to the standard of care required of trustees and the measure of compensation for a proven breach. Second, there is much case law concerning the circumstances in which a trustee may be liable for breach of trust even though the 'act in breach' was committed by another person, such as an agent or co-trustee. This can be easily confused or interwoven with issues in the first category. Third, the relationship of trustees with each other consequent upon a breach of trust can seem confusing, hence questions concerning the liability of trustees *inter se* and any remedies they may have against each other are often asked in examinations. Fourth, and perhaps less difficult, the student must have an awareness of the trustee's possible defences to an action for breach of trust. Once again, in all of these issues, case law is important although various provisions of the Trustee Act 1925 and the Trustee Act 2000 are relevant and must be examined with some care.

QUESTION 47

In what circumstances may a trustee successfully plead a defence to an established breach of trust?

How to Answer this Question

- ❖ Release/acquiescence by the beneficiary.
- ❖ Participation/consent to a breach of trust by the beneficiary.
- ❖ Sections 61 and 62 of the Trustee Act 1925.
- ❖ Statutory limitation and laches.
- ❖ The joint and several liability of trustees: although a trustee may be liable, an indemnity may be obtained from co-trustees who are more culpable.

Defences to trustees

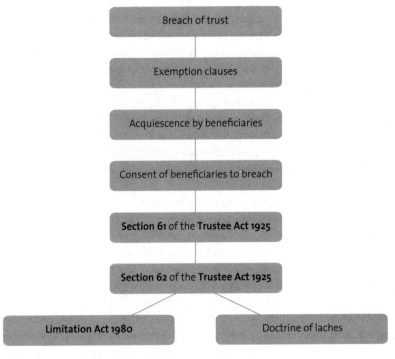

This diagram lists the possible defences that may be raised by a trustee in proceedings for breach of trust.

Aim Higher ★

Students ought to be aware that the nature of the defences and reliefs available to trustees fall into three categories. These are defences available against particular beneficiaries, those available against all beneficiaries and those 'quasi-defences' available to one trustee against another.

Common Pitfalls ✗

This type of question may appear on an examination paper as either an essay or a problem. Students are advised to adopt a structured approach to their answers by first dealing with the possible breaches of trust committed by the trustees and, if appropriate, identifying which trustees have been responsible for these breaches, before considering whether there is a right of contribution or defence available to some of the trustees. Too often, students confuse the various issues, with disappointing consequences.

ANSWER

The personal liability of a trustee for breach of trust extends to all loss which can be causally linked to the breach (*Target Holdings v Redferns* (1996)) and it is generally no defence to the imposition of liability that the trustee was innocent, honest or was acting in the best interests of the trust.[1] Furthermore, as we shall see, although the liable trustees may have rights of contribution against each other, the liability of trustees for breach of trust is joint and several, such that a beneficiary may sue any one or all of the trustees in order to recover the full amount of compensation (*Jackson v Dickinson* (1903)). In order to ensure that liability for breach of trust is not entirely overpowering, and to protect trustees from unscrupulous or culpable beneficiaries, there are a recognised number of defences to a claim of breach of trust. It should be noted, however, that these are 'defences' in a peculiar sense. They do not prevent the liability of the trustee from arising but may, if certain conditions are satisfied, relieve the trustee of the full consequences of that liability. In this way, the strict nature of breach of trust liability is preserved, but some protection is offered to trustees.[2]

We must look now to the general issue of what defences are available to a trustee to relieve him from the consequences of liability for breach of trust. These can be found in both statute and common law. It will be apparent that certain defences are available only against certain claimant beneficiaries. Consequently, a trustee may be relieved

---

1 The strict nature of liability for breach of trust.
2 Nature of defences that may be raised by the trustee.

from liability in an action for breach of trust brought by one beneficiary but may well have to make full restoration to other beneficiaries suing in respect of the same set of circumstances. Many of the defences to an action for breach of trust are relative, not absolute, as befits a relationship springing from the conscience of the parties.

First, a trustee may rely on the principle that a beneficiary who *participates* in, or *consents* to, a breach of trust by the trustee will thereafter be barred from bringing an action for breach of trust (*Life Association of Scotland v Siddal* (1861)). The essence of the matter is that that particular beneficiary has so involved himself with the breach that he should not thereafter be able to deny it and, consequently, it is irrelevant whether the beneficiary actually benefits from the breach or not (*Fletcher v Collis* (1905)).[3] Whether the beneficiary has become so involved will be a question of fact, although it is clear that the beneficiary must be aware of all the relevant facts and understand fully the nature of the transaction which is proposed (*Re Pauling* (1964)). Similarly, the consent must be freely given and it has been said that a beneficiary who consents or participates without independent advice may not be so aware of what is proposed as to bar him from a later action for breach of trust (*Holder v Holder* (1966)). Again, the personal nature of this defence, operating as it does against particular beneficiaries, means that the trustee may still face claims arising from his activities from other beneficiaries not implicated in the breach.

In similar vein, a beneficiary's conduct after the breach may be such as to amount either to a *release* of the trustee or *acquiescence* in the breach sufficient to protect the trustee from later suit by that beneficiary (*Farrant v Blanchford* (1863); *Stafford v Stafford* (1857)). The essential point here is that the beneficiary's conduct after the breach has occurred may be such that it amounts to a personal bar against pursuing an action. As with cases of consent, whether there has been a release or acquiescence is a question of fact and, again, the state of knowledge of the beneficiary is decisive. For cases of release, the classic judgment in *Farrant v Blanchford* emphasises that a release is effective only if the beneficiary was of full age and capacity and had full knowledge of all the circumstances and of his claims against the trustee. This seems to suppose that, unlike cases of consent (and possibly *ex post facto* acquiescence), a release can be effective only if the beneficiary realised he was releasing a trustee from a breach of trust. At first, this seems quite logical yet cases of prior consent require knowledge of the facts and circumstances, but not that they amount to a breach, and this is sometimes said to be the position with *ex post facto* acquiescence as well (*Holder v Holder* (1966)). It would be unfortunate if there was a distinction between consent/acquiescence on the one hand and release on the other and so it is submitted that the general test put forward in *Re Pauling* should be adopted.

---

3   Justification for the defence.

There are circumstances when beneficiaries may be compelled to use their beneficial interests to indemnify the trustees for monies paid out in restoration of a breach of trust. Although the trustee is under a personal obligation to make restoration for loss flowing from the breach of trust, he may recover all or part of that sum from certain beneficiaries. This may be achieved in either of two ways. First, a court of equity has an inherent and discretionary jurisdiction to impound (that is, confiscate) a beneficiary's equitable interest in order to indemnify the trustee when the beneficiary has instigated or requested a trustee to commit a breach of trust (*Chillingworth v Chambers* (1896)) or when the beneficiary had consented to a breach of trust out of which he had received a personal benefit, such confiscation being limited to the benefit received (*Fletcher v Collis* (1905)). Second, this equitable jurisdiction has been extended by s 62 of the Trustee Act 1925 which gives the court a discretionary power to indemnify a trustee out of the beneficiary's interest if the breach of trust was committed 'at the instigation or request or with the consent in writing' of the beneficiary. Once again, the court will not exercise its statutory discretion unless the beneficiary knew and understood all the relevant facts which thereafter amounted to a breach of trust (*Re Somerset* (1894)), although it is only in respect of consent that the trustees' claim to indemnity under s 62 must be supported by writing.

In addition to these defences, all of which rely to one extent or another on the actions of other persons, a 'stand-alone' defence is available to the trustees irrespective of the actions of individual beneficiaries and which can afford a defence to an action by them all. According to s 61 of the Trustee Act 1925, the court has a discretionary power to relieve a trustee of liability for breach of trust, in whole or in part, if it appears that the trustee 'has acted honestly, reasonably, and ought fairly to be excused'. It is clear that, despite the general words of this section, this is not a statutory modification of the strict liability of trustees. The statute does not give the court a general power to exempt all honest trustees but is for those exceptional occasions when there is simply no justification in conscience for the imposition of liability despite the fact that a breach has occurred (*Williams v Byron* (1901)). Moreover, the elements of the defence are to be read conjunctively so that a trustee must establish that he has acted honestly and reasonably and ought fairly to be excused (*Davis v Hutchings* (1907)). In the recent case, *Lloyds Bank plc v Markandan and Uddin* [2012] EWCA 65, the CA refused to grant relief under s 61 of the Trustee Act 1925 to a firm of solicitors on the ground that the defendants did not act reasonably. Consequently, there may be situations, such as the reduced or special circumstances of the beneficiaries, where an entirely honest trustee who has acted reasonably ought *not* to be fairly excused for his breach of trust. Other factors, such as whether the trustee has taken proper advice and whether the trustee had previously undertaken the disputed course of action without any legal difficulties, will be relevant (*Ward-Smith v Jebb* (1964)).

Finally, mention must be made of three further matters. First, the general principles of limitation of actions applies to the action for breach of trust in much the same way as to other personal actions.[4] Thus, except in the case of fraud or where the trustee has possession of trust property or had possession of trust property and converted it to his own use (s 21(1)(a) and (b) of the Limitation Act 1980; and see *Armitage v Nurse* (1997)), no action for breach of trust can be brought after six years have expired from the date the action accrued. There is no period of limitation for cases within s 21(1)(a) and (b), and liability for dishonesty endures without limitation of time (*Armitage*). Second, the liability of trustees *inter se* may be adjusted by a claim for a contribution by those trustees who have been required to make entire restoration against those who have not paid or who are more culpable. This jurisdiction now resides primarily in the Civil Liability (Contribution) Act 1978 (see, for example, *Dubai Aluminium Co v Salaam* (2002)), although there are three situations outside of the Act where one trustee may be made to indemnify completely any others who have actually made restoration to the beneficiaries: where a trustee has received trust money and made use of it (*Bahin v Hughes* (1886)); where the trustee at fault was a solicitor trustee on whose advice the other trustees relied (*Re Linsley* (1904)); and where a trustee is also a beneficiary of the trust (*Chillingworth v Chambers* (1896)). Third, a trustee in breach may escape liability by relying on an exemption clause. These are popular with professional trustees as they mitigate the strict liability of trusteeship. Further, as *Armitage v Nurse* (1997) illustrates, an exemption clause can be effective to exclude liability for negligence and 'equitable fraud' (that is, deliberate but honest breaches believed to be in the interests of beneficiaries), although it cannot exclude liability for dishonesty. Such is the effect of these clauses in relieving liability for a proven breach that the Court of Appeal in *Armitage* made a point of encouraging Parliament to intervene to limit their effect. But the 2006 Law Commission Report recommended that the provision of exclusion clauses in settlements ought to be self-regulated by the trust industry's professional bodies.

QUESTION 48

'A trustee may be liable to pay compensation for his own breach of trust and in some cases for those committed by others.'

Analyse the concept of 'a breach of trust' and assess whether the above is an accurate statement of the law relating to liability for breach of trust.

How to Answer this Question

❖ What constitutes a breach of trust?
❖ Scope of liability for breach of trust.
❖ Prominence of exclusion clauses.
❖ Test of remoteness of damages for breach of trust.
❖ Distinction between primary liability and vicarious liability: the Trustee Act 2000.

---

4   Importance of limitation periods and laches.

❖ Trustees who are liable for breach of trust are jointly and severally liable to the innocent beneficiaries.

❖ Contribution and indemnity as between the trustees (in outline).

Applying the Law

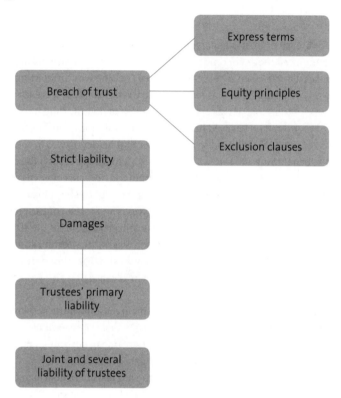

This diagram specifies the sources and extent of liability of the trustees for breach of trust.

ANSWER

It is a fundamental duty of a trustee to manage the trust in accordance with the terms of the trust and rules of equity. Any deviation from this paramount obligation will constitute a breach of trust for which the trustee will be liable personally. This liability may arise in many different situations, but it will be triggered by either a positive act of misfeasance or a failure to act when action was required (an omission). Examples of the former include distribution of the trust property to the wrong people or at the wrong time, investment of trust funds contrary to a restriction in the trust instrument and, of course, the use of the trust property for personal gain. Examples of the latter include failure to distribute the trust property, failure to exercise a discretion, failure to have the trust funds transferred into the trustee's name and failure to review properly the actions of those persons employed to act on behalf of the trust (such as stockbrokers and solicitors). Any act or omission which violates the high standards of stewardship required of trustees (under either the common law or under the duty of care imported for certain powers by s 1 of the Trustee Act 2000) or which is in contravention of the terms of the trust, or which amounts to an inadequate performance of the powers and duties of a trustee, is a breach of trust.[5]

The liability for breach of trust is generally strict in the sense that it is enough that the trustee has committed the act or omission which amounts to a breach of trust.[6] For liability purposes it is irrelevant whether the trustee knew he was committing the breach and did so for his own benefit, or was reckless as to the possibility of a breach occurring or was negligent of the same or was entirely innocent and honest. Thus, it remains a breach of trust for even if he believed he was acting in conformity with the terms of the trust (as in *Re Diplock* (1948)) and did so in the belief that his action was in the best interests of the beneficiaries (*Harrison v Randall* (1852)). Indeed, although the entirely innocent trustee can ask the court to relieve him from the full consequences of liability (s 61 of the Trustee Act 1925), it is clear that the obligations of trusteeship are far reaching and powerful and that even the most judicious and careful of trustees may not escape an action for breach of trust. The only possible exception to the strict nature of the liability for breach of trust is where the breach was entirely technical, and was undertaken for the benefit of the beneficiaries, and was such that the court would have authorised it had the trustee sought its permission in advance (*Lee v Brown* (1798)).

The all encompassing nature of this liability is the main reason why professional trustees insist on the inclusion, in the trust instrument, of a clause excluding liability for certain types of breach of trust. As *Armitage v Nurse* (1997) illustrates, an exemption clause can be effective to exclude liability for negligence and 'equitable fraud' (that is, deliberate and honest breaches believed to be in the interests of beneficiaries), although it cannot exclude liability for dishonesty. Despite some fierce criticism of *Armitage v Nurse*, the Trustee Act 2000 leaves the existing law on exclusion clauses untouched and, further, permits the exclusion of the statutory duty of care imported by s 1 (see Sch 1 and s 7 of the Trustee Act 2000).[7]

Once the liability of a trustee for breach of trust is established, the trustee is under an obligation to make good such loss as flows from the breach of trust, although the loss is not limited to that which is reasonably foreseeable (*Target Holdings Ltd v Redferns* (1996)). In this sense, the essential quality of the trustee's obligation is compensatory, but not being limited by considerations of foreseeability and remoteness of damage (see, for

---

5   Useful technique to state the general rule involving the all embracing duty of the trustee.

6   Good point to make that liability is strict.

7   Important to state the justification for trustees' defences.

example, *Re Dawson (Decd)* (1966)), can be more extensive than damages for breach of contract or those which lie in tort. It is arguable that there is a distinction between breaches of fiduciary duties on the one hand, which involves the test of restitution to the trust, and on the other hand, breaches of non-fiduciary duties which involve the test of compensation to the trust.[8] Of course, that does not mean that the trustee is liable for all loss that flows directly or indirectly from his breach of trust, for there must still be a causal link between the breach of trust and the loss to the claimant (*Swindle v Harrison* (1997)). The essential question is, then, whether it could be shown that the loss would not have occurred but for the breach (*Target Holdings*) and no liability for the total loss will arise if the trustee can show that the loss, or part of it, would have occurred in any event – as where the beneficiaries lose money because of a fall in the value of property rather than because of the admitted misapplication of trust funds (*Target Holdings*), or where the claimant would have acted in the same way had the breach not occurred (*Swindle*). While this seems to be a sensible and obvious conclusion, it does mean that, in some circumstances, a trustee in breach may escape liability because of some fortuitous event that would have caused the loss anyway. Of more concern is whether Lord Browne-Wilkinson is correct to suggest in *Target Holdings* that the rules on causation and breach could be applied differently in 'commercial' and 'traditional' trust cases.[9]

Finally in this survey of the nature of liability for breach of trust, two further supplementary rules may be noted. First, if there is no loss, or no provable loss (*Nestlé v National Westminster Bank* (1992)), the trustee's liability is limited to account for any profits he has received (*Vyse v Foster* (1874)). Second, in general, the losses occasioned by a breach of trust in one transaction cannot be set off against any profits made by them in another (*Dimes v Scott* (1828)), save in the exceptional case where the loss making transaction and the profit making transaction can be regarded as essential ingredients of the same activity (*Bartlett v Barclays Bank Trust Co (No 2)* (1980)).

It is also important to appreciate that it is inherent in the concept of breach of trust, as with other forms of liability, that only those trustees responsible in law for the breach will be liable to the beneficiaries.[10] This is self-evident. However, because it is perfectly possible for a trustee to commit a breach of trust through omission as well as commission, the extent of a trustee's personal responsibility for breach is more extensive than might first be imagined. In simple terms, a trustee will be liable for a breach of trust in the following situations, even though some other person may have committed the acts or omissions that constitute the *actus reus* of the breach.

---

8 The test for remoteness of damages may be difficult to apply.
9 Where a judicial pronouncement is inadequate you should say so.
10 Liability of the trustee is personal. This is an integral part of the question.

First, and most obviously, a trustee will be liable for a breach of trust where he has actually committed the acts in breach, as where a trustee pays money to the wrong persons (*Re Diplock*) or makes off with the trust fund. Second, a trustee may be liable for failing to perform a duty imposed on him by the trust instrument or general law, as where a trustee fails to safeguard the trust's assets. Third, a trustee (A) may be liable for a breach of trust even if the act or omission in breach was committed by a co-trustee (B), but only if A can be said to have failed in his duty to supervise the trust's affairs, which failure facilitated the breach of trust by B: see, for example, *Bahin v Hughes* (1886). This is not liability for B's actions (it is not vicarious), but rather A's primary liability because of his failure to monitor the trust in accordance with his own duty. This duty may spring from the common law, or constitute an aspect of the statutory duty of care imposed on trustees in respect of their powers under the Trustee Act 2000 (s 1 and Sch 1). An example is where a co-trustee pays away money to the wrong beneficiaries and was allowed to do so by the inattention of his colleagues. Fourth, a trustee may be liable even if the act or omission in breach of trust was committed by an agent employed to act on the trust's behalf, but only if it can be shown that the trustee failed in his duty in one of two ways: (a) by falling below the standard of care required by trustees in the appointment of agents, etc. (for example, stockbrokers): s 1 and Pt IV of the Trustee Act 2000; or (b) by failing to review the exercise of the delegable functions of agents as required by s 22 of the Trustee Act 2000. Again, this liability is not vicarious (it is not for the agent's acts), but arises because the trustee has failed in his or her own duty of selection or supervision. Importantly, whatever may have been the position prior to the Trustee Act 2000 with respect to vicarious liability for the acts of agents (see the now defunct ss 23 and 30 of the Trustee Act 1925), s 23 of the Trustee Act 2000 makes it clear that a trustee is not liable for acts amounting to a breach committed by an agent *per se*: that is, liability is triggered only by the trustee's failure in appointment or supervision as indicated above and not because of the agents acts *per se*. This is a welcome and overdue reform and much simplifies this area of the law.

Finally, it should be noted that once the liability of particular trustees for a breach of trust has been established, that liability is, between them, joint and several. In other words, a beneficiary may sue any one of the trustees who has been held liable for the entire amount of the recoverable loss, irrespective of whether any action is taken against any of the others. As against the beneficiaries, those trustees in breach of trust are 'as one' and this is particularly important if some are missing or bankrupt. Of course, in practice, one liable trustee may be more culpable than another and, as a matter of principle, it is unfair that only one of the trustees should be made to bear the entire liability. Consequently, a contribution may be sought from other liable trustees under the Civil Liability (Contribution) Act 1978. Further, in limited circumstances, a liable trustee may be required to pay a complete indemnity to the trustee who has been required to make restitution to the beneficiaries under the principle of joint and several liability. This occurs where the indemnifying trustee was a solicitor on whose advice the other trustees relied (*Re Linsley* (1904)), where the trustee has committed fraud (*Re Smith* (1896)), where the trustee has received the trust property and made use of it for his personal benefit (*Bahin v Hughes* (1886)) and where the trustee is also a beneficiary (*Chillingworth v Chambers* (1896)). Reference may also be made to the potential liability of a trustee who retires: first, for a breach of trust committed while he was a trustee; and second, for breach of trust committed by his successors, if the retirement was designed to facilitate such a breach (*Head v Gould* (1898)). The Trustee Act 2000 has, at last, brought some clarity and certainty to this area of the law.

The above principles illustrate the powerful nature of liability for breach of trust. However, although it may appear that a trustee is being held responsible for an act or omission in breach committed by another person – such as a co-trustee or agent – this is not the case. Although the rules are complicated, the new s 23 of the Trustee Act 2000 has ruled out this pure vicarious liability and has ensured that a trustee is liable only where the breach occurs because of a failure to perform some duty imposed on that particular trustee.

The Office of Trustee and its Powers and Duties

INTRODUCTION

This chapter represents something of a 'sweeping up' of several issues that have not been dealt with so far. Necessarily, in the subjects considered in previous chapters, much has been said about the responsibilities of trustees, their duties towards the beneficiaries and the powers they enjoy in respect of the trust property. Many of these responsibilities are of a general nature – such as the duty to respect the terms of the trust and the power to choose beneficiaries under a discretionary trust – and they should not be forgotten in any general discussion of the nature of trusteeship and the extent of the trustee's powers and duties. In particular, in Chapter 6, we examined the trustee's duty not to make a profit from the trust and this forms an integral part of any discussion of trustee's duties. Thus, it must not be thought that the specific matters considered in this chapter are the only attributes of trusteeship; nor, indeed, should it be assumed that there is any essential thread that ties together the matters dealt with below in a way that excludes consideration of other issues.

The questions considered in this chapter cover several areas: first, the trustee's duty not to delegate any of his essential responsibilities under the trust; second, the appointment and removal of trustees; third, the trustee's power of maintenance and advancement; fourth, the trustee's power of investment; and fifthly, the variation of trusts, being the extent to which the duty to carry out the terms of the trust as originally conceived can be altered by application to the court.

The duty not to delegate is another example of the powerful nature of the trust obligation. It is for the trustee to discharge his specific duties and to exercise any discretionary powers. Any unauthorised delegation of these responsibilities is itself a breach of trust. Indeed, even if a trustee legitimately delegates some administrative function connected with the trust (such as the purchase of shares), that trustee still may be liable for breach of trust even though the act which gives rise to the breach was committed by the person to whom the task was entrusted. Second, although the appointment and removal of trustees may seem a technical matter, it is of considerable practical importance. Trustees die, retire, or simply desire to have nothing more to do with the trust and it is imperative that the good administration of the trust fund does not suffer because of a lack of new or suitably qualified trustees. The relevant principles are to be found primarily in statute, albeit supplemented by case law. Third the power of maintenance and advancement refers to an attribute enjoyed by trustees of certain kinds of trust. In outline, such powers allow the trustee either to use the income from trust property for the benefit of an infant beneficiary before the infant is actually entitled to it (power of maintenance) or to pay a proportion of the trust's capital sum to a potential beneficiary before he or she becomes absolutely entitled to it (power of advancement). These powers may be either expressly included in the trust instrument or implied under ss 31 and 32 of the Trustee Act 1925. Fourth, the investment of trust property is one of the most important of the trustees' responsibilities, for it ensures that the trust fund generates the maximum benefit for all the beneficiaries. Consequently, it is vital that the trustees invest the capital monies lawfully, securely and competently, bearing in mind the need to provide a good income for those immediately entitled and to preserve the capital value of the fund for those entitled in remainder. Most professionally drafted trusts include express powers of investment but a trustee may also take advantage of the provisions of the Trustee Act 2000. Finally, the court's power to sanction a change in the nature or extent of the powers and duties of a trustee (and, indeed, other aspects of the trust) falls within the general law on variation of trusts. As we shall see, this jurisdiction is both inherent and statutory although, because it often involves amending the settlor's or testator's original intentions, the court exercises its power with considerable care and in limited circumstances only. This is particularly so where it is not only the trustees' powers and duties that may be varied but also the nature and extent of the beneficiaries' equitable interests.

QUESTION 49

Explain the circumstances when a court may sanction a variation of the terms of a trust.

Aim Higher ★

It is important to appreciate that in this type of question the student takes a broad view of the various administrative and dispositive provisions that exist to vary the terms of the trust. A detailed examination of the principles under the **Variation of Trusts Act 1958** alone is not advisable.

Common Pitfalls ✗

Case law is important when discussing the **Variation of Trusts Act** as it adds much-needed life to the bare bones of the statute. A similar question could ask the student to discuss the meaning of 'benefit' under the **VTA** when, obviously, considerable case law should be cited.

How to Answer this Question

❖ The need for a power to vary trusts.
❖ Intervention of the court where consents cannot be obtained.

- ❖   Inherent jurisdiction of the court.
- ❖   s 57 of the Trustee Act 1925.
- ❖   s 53 of the Trustee Act 1925.
- ❖   s 64 of the Settled Land Act 1925.
- ❖   Variation of Trusts Act 1958.

Answer Structure

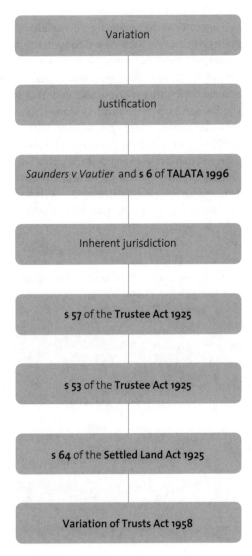

This diagram lists the various tests by the courts and statutes in order to modify the terms of the trust.

ANSWER

It is intrinsic in the nature of a trust that the trustees are under an obligation to carry out the terms of the trust according to the trust instrument, as modified or superseded by the general law. However, there may be many reasons why the details of the trust, the powers and duties of the trustees, or even the nature and extent of the beneficiaries' interests as originally specified, prove impossible to implement in practice. Likewise, the testator or settlor cannot be expected to foresee all possible future contingencies and no amount of expansive or open-ended drafting can hope to cover all possibilities. Therefore there must be some method by which the terms of a trust may be varied, in detail and in substance.[1] Today, the great majority of proposed variations of trust arise because of a desire to minimise the tax liabilities of the trust (see *Re Weston* (1969)), although applications to vary can have other, more altruistic motives, such as a desire to protect the trust property from wayward beneficiaries (*Hambro v Duke of Marlborough* (1994)).

As a matter of principle, it is open to all of the beneficiaries under a trust, providing they are of full age and capacity, to consent to any proposed reordering of the trust (*Saunders v Vautier* (1841) and related powers under s 6 of the Trusts of Land and Appointment of Trustees Act (TOLATA) 1996).[2] However, many of the trusts where a variation would be most beneficial are precisely those where the beneficiaries are either unwilling or unable to consent – for example, because they are infants or members of a hypothetical class, such as future children. In these cases, a variation of the terms of the trust can be achieved only with the aid of the court exercising its inherent or statutory jurisdiction.

The court's inherent jurisdiction to order a variation of trust on the application of either the trustees or interested beneficiaries was examined in detail by the House of Lords in *Chapman v Chapman* (1954). Effectively, this decision limited the court's power to approve a variation to four sets of circumstances only: first, in cases of genuine emergency or necessity where the trustees request the authorisation of the court to enter into a transaction which is not permitted by the trust instrument (*Re New* (1901)). The essence of this jurisdiction is that the court will authorise some otherwise impermissible dealing with the trust property – such as a sale of protected assets – if this is necessary to meet an emergency facing the trust estate. It is not enough that the proposed action would benefit the estate *per se*; there must be real necessity caused by unforeseen events which the requested transaction would remedy (*Re Montague* (1987)). Second, the court will authorise a variation of trust in the sense of consenting on behalf of those who are unable to consent, if this is required to settle a *bona fide* dispute as to the terms of the trust, as discussed, but not permitted, in *Chapman* itself (where there was no genuine dispute). Third, the court will authorise a variation of the beneficial interests of a settlement if this is needed to provide for the maintenance of a tenant for life who is

---

1   The justification in order to modify the terms of the trust.
2   Adjustment of the terms under general principles of law.

otherwise unprovided for (*Re Collins* (1886)). Fourth and finally, the court will act in the now largely redundant situation where a change in the nature of an infant's property (from personalty to realty and *vice versa*) is desired for the purposes of testamentary disposition.[3]

It will be obvious from the preceding discussion that the inherent jurisdiction of the court to authorise a variation of trust is very limited. There is nothing here that allows the variation of a trust because it is expedient or generally beneficial, and such statutory powers as the court possessed at the time of *Chapman v Chapman* (1954) were limited to specific kinds of property or specific circumstances (see below). In fact, such was the concern at the restrictive nature of the inherent jurisdiction revealed in *Chapman* and the limited nature of the existing statutory jurisdiction, that the Law Reform Committee proposed the enactment of a general statute granting the court a greater jurisdiction to authorise variation of trusts. The result was the Variation of Trusts Act 1958.

Before considering the Variation of Trusts Act (VTA) 1958 in detail, brief mention should be made of three other forms of statutory jurisdiction to vary trusts. Under s 57(1) of the Trustee Act 1925, the court is given the jurisdiction to vary the powers of the trustees so as to enable them to achieve transactions connected with the administration of the trust that would otherwise be impermissible. Importantly, this jurisdiction is limited to varying the *administrative* powers of the trustees (such as the power of investment) and does not enable the court to sanction a change in the nature or extent of the beneficiaries' equitable interests (*Re Downshire* (1953); *Mason v Fairbrother* (1983)). Further, the court will only grant an application to vary trustees' administrative powers if it believes this to be 'expedient' for the management of the trust (*Re Craven* (1937)) and the statutory power does not apply to trusts of settled land. Secondly, the court has a limited jurisdiction to authorise certain otherwise impermissible transactions under s 53 of the Trustee Act 1925 in cases where this is necessary to provide for 'the maintenance, education or benefit' of any infant beneficially entitled to trust property (*Re Gower* (1934)), and this can include making the trust more tax efficient (*Re Meux* (1958)). Thirdly, and of real significance, s 64 of the Settled Land Act 1925 gives the court power to authorise the tenant for life to undertake any transaction affecting settled land which 'in the opinion of the court would be for the benefit of the settled land, or any part thereof'. Obviously, this jurisdiction applies only to land within a settlement, and no new settlements may be created after 1 January 1997 (s 7 of TOLATA), but it does permit the court to vary both the administrative provisions of the trust and the beneficial entitlements of the equitable owners (*Re Downshire* (1953)). Indeed, as *Hambro v Duke of Marlborough* (1994) illustrates, s 64 may be used to alter the beneficial entitlements of an equitable owner against his wishes and may even result in the transfer of the land to completely new trusts (see, also, *Raikes v Lygon* (1988)).[4]

....

3   Justification for the **VTA 1958**.

4   Other forms of variation without resort to the **VTA 1958**.

In similar fashion to s 64, the VTA also allows changes to be made to both the administrative powers of trustees and the beneficial interests of the equitable owners, although the court's jurisdiction under this statute is of a general and wide-ranging nature and was entirely novel (*Re Steed* (1960)). However, the Act does not simply empower the court to authorise any variation to the terms of a trust as it thinks fit. Rather, the Act builds upon the *Saunders v Vautier* principle that all of the beneficiaries, if of full age and capacity, can consent to a variation of their trust. Thus, under s 1, the court is empowered to give its consent to a variation or arrangement of the trust on behalf of any of four classes of person who are incapable of consenting for themselves. These are:

(a)   infants with a vested or contingent interest (s 1(1)(a));
(b)   persons who may become entitled to an interest as being a member of a specified class on the happening of a future event, except if that person would be a member of the class if the future event happened on the date of application to the court (s 1(1)(b));
(c)   persons unborn (s 1(1)(c)); and
(d)   persons with an interest under a discretionary trust arising in consequence of a protective trust, where the interest of the principal beneficiary has not failed (s 1(1)(d)).

Although these provisions appear complicated (and s 1(1)(b) has caused difficulties – see *Knocker v Youle* (1986)) – the essential point is that the court will consent for these people (who may be adults or infants respectively) but may only do so if it is satisfied (for classes (a), (b) and (c)) that the variation is for those persons' benefit. Moreover, although the 'benefit' will usually be financial in the form of fiscal advantages (*Re Sainsbury* (1967); *Re Robertson* (1960)), the court can consent to a variation that is of moral or social benefit to the beneficiaries (*Re Weston* (1969); *Re CL* (1969)), and, in exceptional circumstances, this benefit can outweigh any financial disadvantage caused by the variation (*Re Holt* (1969)). In *D (a child) v O* [2004] 3 All ER 780, the court accepted jurisdiction under the VTA 1958 to increase the amount subject to the statutory power of advancement under s 32 of the Trustee Act 1925. Likewise, the court will consider the proposed scheme as a whole and may even consent to a variation that contradicts the settlor's original intentions (*Re Remnant* (1970); but see, *contra, Re Steed* (1960)). There is some doubt, however, whether a completely new scheme which undermines the essential basis of the trust can amount to a 'variation' or 'arrangement' that the court could approve. In *Re T* (1964), it was held that an alleged variation which in fact attacked the very substratum of the trust could not be approved, as it was not a variation but the substitution of completely new trusts. Yet, as *Re Ball* (1968) illustrates, there is a fine line between a substantial variation that leaves the 'substratum' intact and one that does not.

In principle, then, the court now has an extensive jurisdiction to order the variation of trusts and this is in addition to the very specialised jurisdictions under the Matrimonial Causes Act 1973 (see, for example, *Brooks v Brooks* (1996)) and the Mental Health Act 1983.

The court's jurisdiction under the VTA is, however, of a special kind, because in theory, the variation is effected by action of the parties, the court merely consenting on behalf of those beneficiaries who cannot consent for themselves (*Re Holmden* (1968)). This is despite the problems then arising under s 53(1)(c) of the Law of Property Act 1925 when equitable interests are transferred under a variation in the absence of signed writing (see, also, *Re Holt* (1969)). Nevertheless, this theoretical obstacle has not prevented widespread use of the VTA, nor has the passing of this general statute affected the powers of the court under the other statutes discussed above. In particular, provided that the beneficial interests are not in issue, s 57 of the Trustee Act is generally thought preferable for a proposed variation giving wider investment powers (*Anker-Petersen v Anker-Petersen* (1991)).

QUESTION 50

David is a solicitor to a trust. The trustees are Margaret and Norman and the beneficiaries Edward and Francis. The trust instrument contains a clause excluding the trustees from liability for any loss or damage to the income or capital of the fund 'unless such loss or damage shall be caused by their own actual fraud'. The assets of the trust included a painting which David wished to buy. David informed the trustees of his wish and, upon David's suggestion, the trustees approached a valuer, Tony, from whom they sought a valuation of the painting. David was aware that Tony had previously been convicted of an offence involving fraud but did not reveal that fact to the trustees. The trustees themselves made no inquiry as to Tony's character and merely accepted David's nomination of him.

Having been told by David of his wish to buy the painting, Tony puts its value at £100,000, approximately one half of its true market value, and David bought it from the trustees at that price. He has just sold it for £210,000.

▶ Discuss the possible liabilities of Margaret, Norman, David and Tony to the beneficiaries.

How to Answer this Question

- ❖   Trustees' duty of care.
- ❖   Extent of exclusion clause.
- ❖   Fiduciary duties.
- ❖   Knowingly receiving property for one's benefit.
- ❖   Accessory liability.

Answer Structure

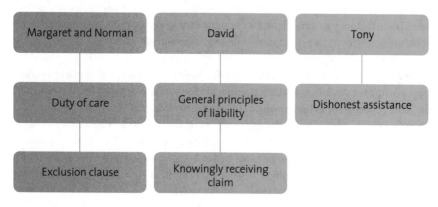

This diagram presents the possible claims that may be brought against the trustees and third parties.

ANSWER

LIABILITY OF MARGARET AND NORMAN

Margaret and Norman are the express trustees under the settlement. They are required to exercise a duty of care. The standard of care as laid down by s1 of the Trustee Act 2000 is such care and skill as are reasonable in the circumstances:

(a) having regard to any special knowledge or experience he has or holds himself out as having; and

(b) if he acts as a trustee in the course of a business or profession, to any special knowledge or experience that it is reasonable to expect of a person acting in the course of that kind of business or profession.[5]

Thus, the section has created an objective/subjective test of the standard of care required from the trustees. The minimum degree of care and skill expected from a trustee is to be determined purely objectively by the court. But this standard of care may be increased by reference to the trustees' special knowledge or experience acquired personally or held out by them. Schedule 1 to the Trustee Act 2000 lists the occasions when the duty of care arises. This includes occasions when trustees enter into arrangements in order to delegate functions to agents, nominees and custodians as well as the review of their actions. On the facts of the problem, the trustees were aware that David, a fiduciary to the trust, wished to purchase the trust property, a sale was made to David, the trustees relied on David's recommendation of a valuer, Tony, and the trustees made no inquiries

---

5   Duties imposed on express trustees.

as to Tony's character; Tony turns out to have had a previous conviction for a crime involving fraud. Did the trustees review the actions of the agent, Tony, with any degree of care? These factors are strong indications that the trustees may not have exercised the appropriate degree of care necessary in the execution of their office.[6]

However, the trustees may be entitled to rely on the exclusion clause that exists in the trust instrument. Assuming that the clause had been validly inserted in the instrument, the issue concerns the extent to which such a clause may protect the trustees from a claim for breach of trust. Such clauses are not, without more, void on public policy grounds. Moreover, provided the clause does not purport to exclude the basic minimum duties of the trustees, it may not be construed as being void for repugnancy to the trust.[7] Some of the minimum duties which may not be excluded are the duties of honesty, good faith and acting for the benefit of the beneficiaries: see *Armitage v Nurse* (1997). In this case the court decided that the expression 'actual fraud' conjures up the notion of dishonesty and is not capable of protecting trustees. In the problem, breach of duties owing to actual fraud is not excluded by virtue of the clause, for such breach is expressly inserted in the proviso. In effect, the settlor intended to protect the trustees from breaches owing to 'constructive fraud' or breaches of fiduciary duties. On this basis the clause may be sufficient to protect the trustees from a claim by the beneficiaries.

DAVID'S LIABILITY

First, David may not be able to claim protection from the exclusion clause, even as a constructive trustee. The clause is intended to protect express trustees and in any event there may be actual fraud involved in David's conduct.

In order to establish the liability of David, the beneficiaries are required to establish the following three cumulative propositions:

(a)   the defendant holds a fiduciary position towards the claimant; and
(b)   the defendant obtained a benefit; and
(c)   a causal connection exists between the relationship and the benefit.[8]

A fiduciary is an individual who is aware that his judgment and confidence are relied on, and have been relied on, by the claimant.

A definition of a fiduciary was offered by Millett LJ in *Bristol and West Building Society v Mothew* (1996) as one who has undertaken to act for or on behalf of another in a particular matter in circumstances which give rise to a relationship of trust and confidence. The distinguishing obligation of a fiduciary is the obligation of loyalty. In

---

6   Duty of care imposed on trustees.
7   Test to determine the validity of the exclusion clause.
8   Elements of liability of a fiduciary.

Boardman v Phipps (1967), a solicitor to a trust was treated as a fiduciary. In like circumstances, David is a solicitor to the trust and would be treated as a fiduciary.

Has David obtained a benefit? This is a question of fact and the issue seems clear that he obtained a benefit, namely a profit of £110,000. Alternatively, he had obtained trust property, namely the painting valued at £200,000 approximately. Did he obtain this benefit as a result of his fiduciary relationship to the trust? Again, this is a question of fact. Did David become aware that the painting was trust property by virtue of being a solicitor to the trust? There is no conclusive evidence on the facts of the problem. However, David informed the trustees of his desire to purchase the painting, he recommended a valuer who was unsuitable to give an independent valuation of the chattel, he failed to disclose material facts to the trustees. The cumulative effect of these facts suggests that David was in breach of his fiduciary duties to the beneficiaries.

There is an additional basis of liability as David purchased the trust property – has he knowingly received trust property for his own use? The basis of liability under this head is that a stranger who knows that a fund is trust property, transferred to him in breach of trust, cannot take control of the property for his own benefit, but is subject to the claims of the trust. He is not a *bona fide* transferee of the legal estate for value without notice. The elements of the cause of action were stated by Hoffmann LJ in *El Ajou v Dollar Land Holdings plc* (1994). These are that the claimant is required to prove first, a disposal of his assets in breach of fiduciary duties; second, the beneficial receipt of the assets or their traceable proceeds by the defendant; and third, knowledge on the part of the defendant that the assets are traceable to a breach of fiduciary duty. The types of knowledge for these purposes were laid down in *Re Baden Delvaux* (1983) as encompassing all types of knowledge, including constructive knowledge.[9]

Alternatively, Megarry V C in *Re Montagu's Settlement* (1987) reviewed the basis of liability under this head and decided that the test is 'want of probity' or 'dishonesty' which requires subjective knowledge of wrongdoing on the part of David. This view was affirmed by the Court of Appeal in *BCCI v Akindele* (2000). In this case, Nourse LJ declared that the categories of knowledge are best forgotten. The test is whether it would be unconscionable for David to retain the property. This is a question of law for the courts to decide. Dishonesty on the part of David may have this effect. In *Twinsectra v Yardley* (2002), the majority of the House of Lords adopted the criminal law test for dishonesty (as laid down by Lord Lane CJ in *R v Ghosh* (1982)), namely the defendant's conduct is dishonest by reference to the ordinary standards of reasonable and honest people *and* that he himself realised that his conduct was dishonest by those standards. In *Barlow Clowes International Ltd v Eurotrust International Ltd* (2006), the Privy Council decided that the defendant's knowledge of the transaction had to be such as to render

---

9   Liability for knowingly receiving trust property.

his participation contrary to the normally acceptable standards of honest conduct. This view was endorsed by the Court of Appeal decisions in *Abou-Ramah v Abacha* (2006) and *Starglade v Nash* (2010). This is an objective standard and the court will consider the conduct of the defendant. On the facts of the problem it is clear that David is aware that the painting is trust property transferred to him in breach of trust. He will therefore become a constructive trustee. As David has sold the painting to a third party, possibly a *bona fide* transferee of the legal estate for value without notice, the remedy available to the beneficiaries is to recover the profit from David.

TONY'S LIABILITY

Tony's liability may be based on the fact that he was an accessory in the breach of trust or dishonestly assisting in a fraudulent breach of trust. The liability here was stated in the classic case of *Royal Brunei Airlines v Tan* (1995) as fault based and involving a duty to account. Assistance involves any act (including an omission when there is a duty to act) effected by another which enables the defendant to commit a dishonest breach of trust.[10] In *Brinks Ltd v Abu-Saleh (No 3)* (1995), it was decided that a defendant is required to lend assistance in the knowledge of, or belief in, the existence of the trust, and the knowledge that his assistance will facilitate the breach of trust. Tony was introduced to the trustees by David in order to value the trust asset and significantly undervalued the painting. It is a question of fact whether this was done dishonestly, negligently or innocently. The test of dishonesty was stated above by reference to the *Twinsectra/Eurotrust/Abacha* decisions. On the facts of the problem it would appear that Tony was aware that he was undervaluing the property with a view to assisting David in acquiring the same at an undervalue. It would seem that the test of dishonesty is satisfied and he will become liable for a breach.

The final point concerns Tony's status. Millett LJ in *Paragon Finance v Thakerar* (1999) opined that the liability of an accessory is strictly not as a constructive trustee because he does not acquire the trust property. His liability is to account to the beneficiaries for any benefits received.

---

10 Tony's liability as an accessory.

Index

abortion: resulting trusts 157–8
acceleration of postponed interest: resulting trusts 158
accessory liability 258
accounting for profits: constructive trusts 174–5, 176, 209–10
actions for breach of trust: defences 234, 238–42; exemption of honest trustees 241, 242; limitation periods 241–2; tracing 229, 234
administrative unworkability: certainties 66, 72, 76, 79; charitable trusts 104; discretionary trusts 76
advancement: power of maintenance and advancement 248, 249; presumption of 140–4, 156
agents: delegation by trustees 64, 248–9; vicarious liability for 246, 247
agreement to create a trust: enforcement 11
amateur sport: charitable trusts 101–2, 117, 124
animals: charitable trusts for animal welfare 126–7; trusts for upkeep of 84
ante-nuptial settlements: marriage consideration 11, 15
appointment of trustees 248
appointment powers: certainties 64, 65, 71, 73; and discretionary trusts 104
assignments: choses in action 11
associations see unincorporated associations
Attorney General: enforcement of charitable trusts 82, 99, 101, 110
automatic resulting trusts 153; and initial failure of trust 142; operation of law 144; or 'out and out' gifts 157; versus presumed resulting trusts 144, 150–2

bankruptcy: and tracing 220, 221, 234
bare trusts: disposition of equitable interests 19
beneficiaries: acquiescence in breach of trust 240; ascertainable 80, 82, 83, 86, 89, 93; beneficiary principle 62–3, 82, 83, 84, 147; certainty of 64; as co-defendants 11; consent/participation in breach of trust 240; definition of role 5; duties of trustees in relation to 167; employees as 78–9; equitable title held by 5; identity unacknowledged in secret trusts 45, 50, 54; indemnification of trustees 241; infant 249; predeceased, under secret trust 55, 56; rights 5, 11, 24, 33; transfer of equitable interests 19–20; trustees as 5, 57, 242; and unincorporated associations 84
bona vacantia (ownerless property): passing to Crown·98, 139, 141, 142, 147, 149, 152
breach of trust: action for 229, 234; beneficiaries' acquiescence in 240; beneficiaries' consent/participation in 240; constructive trusts 237; contravention of terms 244; court powers 241; and delegation of duties 248; dishonestly assisting 194, 198, 202, 211, 212; disposal of assets in 197; distribution of trust property to wrong people 243, 246; elements of 243–4; exclusion clauses 241, 242, 244; failure to act 243, 244, 245, 246; fiduciary versus non-fiduciary duties, breaches of 245; fraud 242; inducement 194, 204–5, 208, 212; joint and several liability 239, 242, 246; limitation periods 241; misfeasance, acts of 243, 244; mixing of trust monies with own funds 229; personal actions for 237–47; remoteness of damage test 244–5; scope of liability for 244; 'stand-alone' defence 241; technical 244; terms of trust 194; tracing 224, 229, 234, 237; by trustees 194, 234, 239, 242, 243, 245–6; undue influence 234; use of property for personal gain 243–4; vicarious liability 246, 247
bribes: constructive trusts 161–3, 168, 176–7; versus honest payments 176

capriciousness: trusts versus powers 66, 79
care, duty of see duty of care

certainties: administrative unworkability
66, 72, 76, 79; beneficiaries 64; colleague,
concept of 71–2; complete list test
(certainty of objects) 70, 73–4; concept of
three certainties 62, 68, 76, 78; conditions
precedent 70, 78; evidential difficulties
66, 69, 71, 75, 79, 80; fixed trusts 70, 78;
intention 9, 55, 57, 62, 68, 69, 79, 88; 'is
or is not' (given postulant) test 66, 72–6;
'kinsfolk' 70; objects see objects, certainty
of; reasonableness test 78; reversionary
interests 69–70; and secondary uncertainty
72; subject matter 9, 62, 68, 69, 78, 79;
subsidiary rules, differences in 66; tests 75;
trusts, distinguished from powers 63–6, 71
cestui que trust 5, 82; see also beneficiaries
change of position defence: strangers to trust,
liability 203, 204, 205; tracing 221, 222, 225,
226, 227, 235
charging clauses: remuneration of trustees
170–1, 172
charitable trusts: administrative unworkability
104; amateur sport 101–2, 117, 124; animal
welfare 126–7; and Attorney General 82,
99, 101, 110; certainty of objects 103–4, 106;
charitable purposes impossible or impractical
to achieve 131, 132, 133, 136, 138; charitable
versus non-charitable purposes 99, 120, 121,
126–7; countryside, protection of 127; *cy-près*
99, 129–34; definitions 101; deprivation test
102, 127; education 102–3, 107, 114, 116, 117, 118,
123–4, 128; enforcement 82; environmental
protection 122–3; ethical principles 103;
exclusivity of charitable purpose 122; gifts
88, 104, 106, 128–9, 136–7; historic buildings,
preservation 123; international harmony
118; limited beneficiaries 128; motives of
settlor 115–16; and perpetuities 99, 104,
107–8, 127, 129; personal nexus test 113, 117,
118, 128; political purposes 103, 107, 127;
poverty relief 111, 112, 116; property 131–2;
public benefit requirement see public benefit
requirement, charitable trusts; purposes
beneficial to community 123, 128; 'related
causes' 123; religion, advancement 111, 121–2;
requirements 95–6; rescue services 128–9,
136, 138; and resulting trusts 104; sport and
recreation 95–6, 101, 108, 124; successor
organisations 137–8; tax avoidance 116; trade
or occupation, trusts for promotion of 118;
and unincorporated associations 137–8;
unlimited duration 99; validity 91, 99; see
also purpose trusts

charities: categories 135; definitions 84, 99–100,
106, 121, 126–7; discretionary trusts for 80;
political nature 118; and secret trusts 52
Charity Commission: requirement to register
with 95, 121
cheques: failure to sign 39
choses in action: tracing 220; trusts of 11, 14, 39
civil partnership: and co-ownership 182
class gifts: certainties 64, 71, 78
cohabitation: constructive trusts 181, 182
common intention trusts: constructive trusts
180, 181, 183, 187; resulting trusts 153–4
common law: breach of trust 244; common law
consideration 11, 15, 33; common law tracing
217–23, 225; *cy-près* trusts 131, 133; rules of 6
commorientes doctrine: resulting trusts 158
communication: fully secret trusts 50;
half-secret trusts 47, 50
conditions precedent: certainties 70, 78
conflicts of interest: business context 167–8;
constructive trusts 161–3, 164–8, 170
conservation: trusts promoting 123
consideration: creation of trusts 11, 15, 31, 33, 42
constructive fraud 164
constructive trusts: and accessory, liability of
195; beneficial interests, acquisition 185,
187, 188, 190; breach of trust 237; bribes
161–3, 168, 176–7; and cohabitation 181,
182; common intention 180, 181, 183, 187;
common uses 179; conflicts of interest
161–3, 164–8, 170; co-ownership trusts 182;
and creation of trusts 10; deceit, recklessness
or negligence 166; directors' fees 167–8,
175; disposition of equitable interests 21,
31; domestic and commercial contexts 191,
192; duty not to make a profit 159–93; and
family home 180, 181, 188, 192; fiduciaries
162–3, 165–8; household expenses, payment
187; indirect contributions 181; inequitable
conduct, remedy for 179, 181; intentions of
parties, 192–3; *Keech v Sandford* rule 162;
knowledge, subjective and objective 164;
leases 167, 177–8; legal owner as constructive
trustee 186; liability 166–8; liability of
strangers to the trust see strangers to
trust, liability; promise, reliance and
detriment requirement 186, 187, 188;
quantifying the share 187, 191, 192–3;
refusal of remedy on general equitable
principles 188; restitutionary or remedial 182;
role 179, 180, 181, 182; self-interest 166, 174;
shares, sale of interests in 31, 32; tracing
207, 225, 227; whether trust information

can be treated as trust property 163–4; types 159; unconscionability 164, 182, 208, 209, 214

contract: agreement to create a trust 11; breach of contract 225, 245; privity of 35, 36; resulting trusts 152; third parties and enforcement of contracts 15, 16, 20, 21, 35–6, 42; and unincorporated associations 91, 97–8

Contracts (Rights of Third Parties Act) 1999: changes made by 37; enforcement of imperfect trust by volunteer prior to 34–5; entitlement to sue 35; nature and effect 35–7, 42; and position of volunteer under an imperfect trust 32–7; remedy available 35–6

co-ownership trusts: civil partnership 182; constructive trusts 178; resulting trusts 139, 144, 180; statutory co-ownership 181, 182–3

covenants: enforcement 11–12, 14, 40; imperfect, consequences 14–15; subject matte, 11, 14; and subject matter of trust 39

creation of trusts 5–42; agreement to create a trust 11; cheques, failure to sign 39; consideration 11, 15, 31, 33, 42; declaration of trust 6, 9; versus disposition of a subsisting equitable interest 18, 19, 20; express trusts 8–9; failure to constitute trus, 6, 24; *Fletcher* rule 11, 14, 15, 39, 40; formality requirement, 6, 9, 16, 17–22, 24, 25–6, 39–40, 45; fully secret trusts 59; gifts, equity not striving to defeat 6–12; joint trusteeship 10–11; *Milroy v Lord* principles 8–9, 10, 14, 33; modes of creation 8–9, 10, 14; oral 26, 29–30; secret trusts 45, 46; self-declaration *see* self-declaration; transfer of property to trustees 6, 9, 17; unconscionability 7, 10, 40; writing requirements 19

Crown: *bona vacantia* 98, 139, 141, 142, 147, 149, 152; and charitable trusts 82

cy-près trusts 99, 129–34; common law 131, 133; examples 132; impossibility or impracticality 131, 132, 133, 136, 138; nature of failure 131, 132, 133; purpose of *cy-près* 130–1, 136; and resulting trusts 142; statutory modifications to *cy-près* 132–4; unincorporated associations 146

damages: breach of trust 237; creation of trusts 12, 16, 34, 35, 36

death: revocation of cheques on 39

debts: constructive trusts 162, 163, 176; enforceable at law 11, 14, 40; purpose trusts 84; resulting trusts 143; tracing 227, 230, 231, 236

declaration and constitution theory: secret trusts 46–7, 57

declaration of trust: absence of, in constructive or resulting trust 186; creation of trusts 6, 9; express 190, 191; form 9; oral 29–30; of part of equitable interest 30; secret trusts 46, 61; self-declaration *see* self-declaration; validity 9

defences: actions for breach of trust 238–42; change of position defence *see* change of position defence; tracing 221–2

delegation by trustees: and duties of trusties 64, 248–9

detrimental reliance: constructive trusts 186, 187

directors' fees: constructive trusts 167–8, 175

discretionary trusts: administrative unworkability 76; and appointment powers 104; certainty of objects requirement 66, 71, 73–4, 79; for charities 80; class description 74; duty to distribute 78, 79; geographical limitations 79–80; incapacity to give consent 253; versus powers 65, 79

dishonesty: consciousness of 199, 203, 208; criminal law test 203, 208, 212, 213, 257; definitions 208, 210; dishonestly assisting breach of trust 194, 198, 202, 211, 212; motives 213; standard of proof 199–200, 213; standards of 199, 203, 208; subjective 203; versus subjective knowledge 164; *see also* strangers to trust, liability

disposition of equitable interests 17–22; active or passive duties of declarant 30; continuance of trusts 30; definitions 19, 21, 29, 30; oral instructions to trustees to hold upon trust 30; where proposed transactions amount to dispositions 19–21; where proposed transactions do not amount to dispositions 21–2; shares, sale of interests in 31–2; sub-trusts 30; transfer of legal and equitable interests 30–1; where void 29, 30

donatio mortis causa (DMC): creation of trust, 12, 16–17, 26, 41

duty of care: arising when 255–6; breach of trust 244; conflict of duty and interest 161–2, 164–8, 170; liability of trustees 244, 255–6; property of trust 166–7; strangers to trust, liability 207

education: charitable trusts 102–3, 107, 114, 116, 117, 118, 123–4, 128; definitions 102; resulting trusts 157

enforcement jurisdiction: certainty of objects
   requirement 82
equitable estoppel: dispositions 22
equitable fraud 242, 244
equitable interests: disposition 17–22, 30; and
   land transactions 29; realty and personalty
   29–30; statutory definition 19; surrender
   20; transfer of 27, 30–1
equitable title: held by beneficiaries 5; transfer
   of 9–10
equitable tracing 216–23, 226–7, 229
equity: beneficial vacuum, abhorring 139,
   140–4; constructive trusts 166; following
   the law, and constructive trusts 182, 183,
   186, 190; fundamental principles 8; gifts,
   not striving to defeat 6–12; looking at intent
   rather than form 9, 25; not perfecting
   imperfect gift 8, 11, 16; regarding as done
   that which ought to be done 24, 31; transfer
   of property effective in 9; volunteers, not
   assisting 8, 11, 12, 15, 16, 34, 36, 42
estoppel: equitable 22; proprietary 12, 26
evidential difficulties: certainties 66, 69, 71, 75,
   79, 80
examination technique 2–3
exceptions: beneficiary principle 83, 84, 86–7,
   87; equity not assisting volunteers 12, 34;
   formality requirements for creation of
   trusts 25–6, 186; purpose trusts 127
exclusion clauses: breach of trust 241, 242, 244;
   duty of care 256
express trusts: clarity requirement 24; modes
   of creation 8–9, 10, 14, 39; and secret
   trusts 47; settlors, consequences for 23;
   significance of express declarations 190, 191

failure to constitute trust: effects 6, 24
family home: and constructive trusts 180, 181,
   188, 192
fiduciary relationships: conflicts of interest
   162–3, 165–8; defined 5; definitions
   256–7; fiduciary versus non-fiduciary duties,
   breaches of 245; loyalty obligation of
   fiduciary 256; share purchases 175; tracing
   229, 235; trusts versus powers 65, 66
fixed trusts: certainties 70, 78
following: and tracing 216
foreseeability: breach of trust 244–5
formality requirements: for creation of
   trusts 6, 9, 16, 17–22, 24, 25–6, 39–40; for
   disposition of equitable interests 17–22;
   exceptions 25–6; property type 24; secret
   trusts 45; statutory 26

fraud: breach of trust 242; definitions 45–6, 57;
   and dishonesty 210; equitable 242, 244; new
   fraud theory 46; prevention of 6, 19, 29, 53,
   57; and secret trusts 45–6, 47, 53, 57, 59–60
future interests: donations 93

gifts: absolute 53, 55, 68, 69, 88, 142, 147; animal
   welfare 84; anonymous donors 97, 148, 152;
   charitable purposes 88, 104, 106, 128–9,
   136–7; class gifts 64, 71, 78; in default of
   appointment 64, 65, 71; donatio mortis causa
   (DMC) 12, 16–17, 26, 41; educational 103;
   equity not striving to defeat 6–12; and future
   interests 93; imperfect 8, 10, 11, 16, 17, 41;
   intentions of donors 97; inter vivos see inter
   vivos gifts or trusts; motives in making 92;
   multiple trustees 10–11; no self-declaration
   following imperfect transfer 10; original
   donors, returned to 147–8; 'out and out'
   157; political purposes 103; presumption of
   advancement 140–4, 156; Re Ralli principle
   10; of residue 70–1; secret trusts 52, 53,
   56; severability 86–7, 106; surplus assets
   derived from 147–8; transferor completing
   everything required 9, 10, 40; on trust
   for unincorporated associations 97; to
   unincorporated associations 84, 91–2, 93, 96,
   129, 143; validity, and distribution of funds
   146; void 106
given postulant ('is or is not') test 66, 72–6,
   79; certainty of objects requirement 73;
   conceptual uncertainty versus evidential
   uncertainty 74; definitions 73, 74; move to
   73–4; three views 74–5

hybrid powers of appointment: trusts versus
   powers 64

imperfect obligation trusts: beneficiary
   principle 83
imperfect trusts 14, 15; enforcement by
   volunteer prior to Contracts (Rights of
   Third Parties Act) 1999 34–5; Milroy v Lord
   principles not complied with 33; nature and
   effect of Contracts (Rights of Third Parties
   Act) 35–7; volunteer, statutory position
   32–7; see also under gifts
inconsistent dealing: constructive trusts 208
inducement of breach of trust: liability of
   strangers to trust 194, 204–5, 208, 212
intangible property rights: transfer of 11, 14
intention: certainty of 9, 55, 57, 62, 68, 69, 79,
   88; charitable 132; cohabitation 182

inter vivos gifts or trusts: beneficiary principle 83; creation of trusts 5, 10, 16, 17, 26, 41; secret trusts 46–7

investment: contrary to restriction in trust instrument 243; powers 248, 249

'is or is not' (given postulant) test 66, 72–6, 79; certainty of objects requirement 73, 104; conceptual uncertainty versus evidential uncertainty 74; definitions 73, 74; move to 73–4; three views 74–5

joint and several liability: breach of trust 239, 242, 246

joint ownership *see* co-ownership trusts

joint tenants: secret trusts 55–6, 60; unincorporated associations 92, 96

joint trusteeship: creation of trusts 10–11

knowing receipt of trust property: constructive trusts 163–4, 197, 203–4, 206–7, 208, 211, 214; knowledge/notice distinction 198; personal benefit 257–8; tracing 234

knowledge: actual 214; categories 198, 202, 208; degree required for liability as constructive trustee 197–8; subjective and objective 164, 202, 257

land, trusts of: equitable interests 29; formality requirements 19, 24, 25, 26; half-secret 47, 56–7

leases: constructive trust of 167, 177–8

legal title: constructive trusts 168; failure to be formally confirmed 25; held by trustees 5, 24; incomplete transfer of 40; joint and sole names 190; sole ownership 182; transfer of 9, 30–1

limitation periods: personal actions for breach of trust 241–2

liquidation: unincorporated associations 144–9

locus standi 11; purpose trusts 82, 89, 104

maintenance: power of 249

mandate theory 39, 91, 93

marriage consideration: creation of trust 11, 15, 33, 42

mixed funds: tracing into 217, 226, 231, 232

monuments and memorials: purpose trusts 84, 87, 89

negligence: breach of trust 244; constructive trusts 166, 208, 209; liability in 208

nemo dat quod non habet 225

objects, certainty of 9, 62, 64, 65, 68, 69, 77, 78, 80, 88; charitable objects 103–4, 106; complete list test 70, 73–4; discretionary trusts 66, 71, 73–4, 79; enforcement jurisdiction 82; failure of trust for uncertainty 142; 'is or is not' (given postulant) test 73, 104; philanthropic 106

omissions: breach of trust 243, 244, 245, 246

pension trusts 146

perfect trusts: creation 8, 10, 15, 33, 39

perpetuities 84, 88; and charitable trusts 99, 104, 107–8, 127, 129; rule against 83, 87, 89

personal nexus test: charitable trusts 113, 117, 118, 128

personal powers: trusts versus powers 65–6

political purposes: and charitable trusts 103, 107, 127

post-nuptial settlements: marriage consideration 11, 15

poverty: charitable trusts 116; charitable trusts for relief of 111, 112

powers: creation for a purpose 88; distinguished from trusts 63–6, 71, 78; fiduciary 65, 66; personal 65–6; void 73; voluntary nature 64, 65

precatory words: certainties 69; secret trusts 55

presumed resulting trusts: versus automatic resulting trusts 144; and evidence in rebuttal 156

presumption of advancement: resulting trusts 140–4, 156

privity of contract 35, 36

professional trustees 172, 175

profits: accounting for 174–5, 176, 209–10

property of trust: absolute ownership 64; *bona vacantia see bona vacantia* (ownerless property); and breach of trust 194, 243–4; certainty of subject matter 9; charitable trusts 131–2; disposition of equitable interests 17–22; distribution to wrong people 243, 246; failure to transfer 14; given absolutely to tenants in common 55–6; inconsistent dealing 208; increase in value 227; interests in 177–8; knowing receipt 163–4, 197, 203–4, 206–7, 208, 211, 214, 234, 257–8; land *see* land, trusts of; liability of strangers to the trust 194–215; nature of, formality requirements 24; obligations of common or shared occupation not identical with obligations of shared ownership 186; self-dealing rule 167, 177; tracing

207, 220, 227; transfer to trustee 6, 9, 25; whether trust information can be treated as 163–4; and trustees' duty of care 166–7; validity of trusts of certain kinds, statutory requirements 24, 25, 26

proportionate share (*pari passu*) rule: tracing 232

proprietary estoppel: creation of trusts 12, 26

public benefit requirement, charitable trusts 96, 99, 102, 103, 106, 107, 115, 116, 121, 124; class limitations 113, 116; *Compton* test 113; decisions 112–13; definitions 128; disadvantaged persons 116–17; meaning of 'public benefit' in charity law 109–14; need for public element in charitable purposes 110; personal nexus test 113, 117, 118, 128; 'precedent and analogy doctrine' 112; type of benefit and range of benefit 111, 114; varying nature of public benefit according to purpose 111–12

purpose trusts: animal upkeep 84; ascertainable beneficiaries 80, 82, 83, 86, 89, 93; charitable *see* charitable trusts; failure 121, 142; individuals with *locus standi* 82, 89, 104; invalidity 81–5, 86; maximum duration 83, 89; *Re Denley* principle 69, 82, 83, 84, 89, 93, 121, 127, 128; rule against non-charitable (beneficiary principle) 62–3, 82, 83, 84; tombs and monuments, erection or maintenance of 84, 87; void, 69, 87, 88, 91, 147, 235

Quistclose trusts: and private purpose trusts 84; resulting trusts 151

recreation *see* sport and recreation

religion: advancement of 88; charitable trusts 111, 121–2; conditions precedent related to 70; contemplation/quiet reflection 121, 122; definitions 121

remoteness of damage test: breach of trust 244–5

remuneration of trustees: charging clauses 170–1, 172; constructive trusts 166, 168, 170–2

rescue services: charitable trusts 128–9, 136, 138

restitutionary approach: strangers to trust, liability 203–4, 205; tracing 217, 221, 223, 224, 236

resulting trusts: abortion 157–8; arising when 139–40, 141–2; automatic 142, 144, 150–2, 153; and charitable trusts 104; classification 153; commercial transactions 143–4; common intention 153–4; *commorientes* doctrine 158; co-ownership trusts 139, 144,

180; and *cy-près* principles 99, 142; 'equity abhors beneficial vacuum' 139, 140–4; initial failure of trust 142–3, 151; members' subscriptions, surplus assets derived from 146–7; postponed interests, acceleration 158; presumed 144, 155–7; public policy 157–8; *Quistclose* trusts 151; and secret trusts 51, 56; surplus assets 98, 146–9; types 140; underlying theory 139, 149–54; unjust enrichment, preventing 153

revision strategy 2

secret trusts 43–61; communication and acceptance 47, 50, 51, 52, 55, 58, 59; creation requirements (fully secret) 59; declaration and constitution theory 46–7, 57; definitions 45, 50, 54, 59; distinction between fully-secret and half-secret 45, 47, 52; enforcement 46; and fraud 45–6, 47, 53, 59–60; fully or half-secret as matter of construction 54–5; fully secret 43, 45, 45–6, 47, 50, 51, 52, 53, 54, 54–6, 59; gifts 52, 53, 56; half-secret 45–6, 47, 50, 51, 52, 54–5, 56–7, 60–1; intended trustee pre-deceasing testator 61; of land (half-secret, 56–7; legacies subject to, distinguished from mere legacies 59; more than one legatee 54, 55–6; one of several intended trustees, communication to 59–60; oral 57; personal effects 56; predeceased beneficiary problem 55, 56; requirements for half-secret 60–1; and resulting trusts 56; revocation, validity 51, 52, 53; shares 56; simultaneous execution of will and communication/ acceptance 52, 54; standard of proof 60; statutory provisions 61; substitution of trustee/legatee as sole legatee 51; trustee disclaiming 52; validity 43, 44–8, 55; and wills 43, 45, 47, 51, 52, 53, 59; Wills Act 1837, operating outside 56; and witnesses 55, 56; writing requirements 47, 61

self-dealing rule 167, 177

self-declaration of trust: creation of trusts 9, 10, 14, 24–5, 26, 39; disposition of equitable interests 30

settled land 252

settlors: as beneficiaries 5; declaration of trust *see* declaration of trust; motives of settlor in creating charitable trusts 115–16; non-compliance by outside control of settlor 25–6; as trustees 5, 9, 10

shares: disposition of equitable interests in 29; dividends 154, 156, 173, 175; LPA 1925, whether applicable to 29; private company, effect of being 9, 12, 17, 25, 26, 30–1, 40; purchase when in fiduciary position 175; registration of transfer 6, 17, 31, 41; sale of interests in 31–2; secret trusts 56; *Strong v Bird* rule 17; and tracing 229–30; transfer of 6, 9, 17

special powers of appointment: certainties 64–5, 71

specific performance: creation of trusts 36

sport and recreation: amateur sport 101–2, 117, 124; charitable trusts 95–6, 101–2, 108, 124; definitions 101, 108; recreational facilities, provision 102, 108, 127–8

spouses: versus cohabitees 182; and co-ownership 180, 181, 188; presumption of advancement 140–4

stamp duty: disposition of equitable interests 20

standard of proof: constructive trusts 186; dishonesty 199–200; secret trusts 60

statutory co-ownership: constructive trusts 181, 182–3

strangers to trust, liability 194–215; application of law to facts 204–5; change of position defence 203, 204, 205; circumstances 195–200; as constructive trustees 196–7; degree of knowledge required 197–8; extent of liability 202; fault requirement 201, 202, 204, 205; investments 213; knowing receipt of trust property 197, 203–4, 206–7, 208, 211, 214; language confusion 202–3; in negligence 208, 209; principle 199–200; proceedings against strangers 214; reasonableness test 198, 208; receipt or assistance 204–5, 211, 212; restitution 203–4, 205; secondary liability 199, 208; significance of 202; strict liability 203; in tort 208; wilful blindness 209; *see also* constructive trusts

strict liability: third parties 203

subject matter of trust: certainty of 9, 62, 68, 69, 78, 79; and covenants 39; creation of trusts 6; formality requirements 27; role of settlor 5

subrogation doctrine: tracing 231

subsisting trusts: definitions 29; formality requirements 18, 19, 20

sub-trusts: defined 5; disposition of equitable interests 20, 21, 30

successor organisations: charitable trusts 137–8

surplus assets, resulting trusts 97–8, 146–9; derived from a large anonymous donation 97, 148, 152; derived from collection boxes 148–9; derived from gifts 147–8; derived from members' subscriptions 146–7; derived from proceeds of local events 148; unincorporated associations 97–8, 146, 152

tax avoidance 116, 253

tenants in common 92; secret trusts 55–6

testamentary trusts: and beneficiary principle 82

testators: definition of role 5

third parties: constructive trusts 237; dishonestly assisting breach of trust 194, 198, 202, 211, 212; dispositions 30–1; and enforcement of contracts 15, 16, 20, 21, 35–6, 42; knowing receipt of trust property 163–4, 197, 203–4, 208, 211, 214; liability of strangers to the trust 194–215; role in creation of trusts 10; and strict liability 203; and tracing remedy 237; *see also* strangers to trust, liability; volunteers

tombs and monuments: purpose trusts 84, 87

tort: degree of liability 245; liability of strangers in 208

tracing 216–36; and bankruptcy 220, 221, 234; beneficiaries, rights of 5; breach of trust 224, 229, 234, 237; change of position defence 221, 222, 225, 226, 227, 235; choses in action 220; *Clayton's Case*, rule in 231–2; common law 217–23, 225; conditions for claims 220–1; constructive trusts 207, 225, 227; defences available 221–2; equitable 216–23, 226–7, 229; in event of unsatisfied claim 229; and following 216; increase in value of trust property 227; innocent volunteer 222, 230, 231, 231–2, 235; mixed funds, into 217, 226, 231, 232; 'money had and received,' action for 217, 220, 221; *in personam* action (*Re Diplock*) 233, 234, 236; property in identifiable form 220; proportionate share (*pari passu*) rule 232; purpose of tracing claim 219, 222–3; remedy, establishing 221, 224–5; replacement of trust funds 231; restitutionary approach 217, 221, 223, 224, 227, 236; subrogation doctrine 231; unjust enrichment 217

transfer and declaration mode: creation of trusts 9, 10, 14, 39

trustees: appointment 248; as beneficiaries 5, 57, 242; breach of trust by 194, 234, 239, 242, 243, 245–6; conflicts of interest 161–3, 164–8, 170; control over trust property conveyed to 24; death of 248; definition of role 5; delegation by 64, 248–9; duties and powers 23–4, 64, 78, 81, 167; duty of care 244, 255–6;

indemnification of 241; investment powers 248, 249; joint and several liability, breach of trust 239, 242, 246; legal title held by 5, 24; liability of 23–4; multiple 10–11, 24; non-compliance by outside control of trustee 25–6; office of 248–58; passive 30; professional 172, 175; and property of trust 166–7; removal 248; remuneration 166, 170–2; retention of property 24; retirement 248; self-dealing rule 167, 177; settlors as 5, 9, 10; solicitor 166; stewardship standards 244; transfer of property to 6, 9, 25; trustee *de son tort* 196–7; and variation of terms of trusts 248, 249–54

trusts: breach of *see* breach of trust; charitable *see* charitable trusts; choses in action 11, 14, 39; constitution, elements giving rise to 24–6; continuance 30; contravention of terms 244; creation *see* creation of trusts; definition problems 5; distinguished from powers 63–6, 71, 77, 78; imperfect 14, 15, 32–7; nature of concept 23–4, 64; perfect 8, 10, 15, 33, 39; public versus private 109; purpose *see* purpose trusts; resulting *see* resulting trusts; secret *see* secret trusts; self-declaration *see* self-declaration; subsisting 18, 19, 20, 29; testamentary 82; validity 68; variation of terms 248, 249–54; void 73

unconscionability: constructive trusts 164, 182, 208, 209, 214; creation of trusts 7, 10, 40; resulting trusts 144; tracing 234
undue influence: breach of trust 234
unincorporated associations: and charitable trusts 137–8; final surviving member 98;

gifts to 84, 91–2, 93, 96–7, 129, 143; liquidation 144–9; status 96; status of gifts to 96–7; surplus assets 97–8, 146, 152; trusts for present and future members of 93
unjust enrichment: resulting trusts 153; tracing 217

valuable consideration: creation of trusts 11, 15, 31, 33, 42
variation of terms of trusts 248, 249–54; court intervention where consents not obtained 251–4; incapacity to give consent 253; inherent jurisdiction of court 251–2, 253–4; statutory provisions 252, 253, 254
vicarious liability: breach of trust 246, 247
void trusts: discretionary trusts 72; 'is or is not' (given postulant) test 73, 75; purpose trusts 69, 87, 88, 91, 147, 235; uncertainty of subject matter 78
volunteers: consideration not provided by 42; damages awards 34, 35; defined 33; equity not assisting 8, 11, 12, 15, 16, 34, 36, 42; imperfect trusts, statutory position under 32–7; innocent 222, 230, 231, 231–2, 235; next of kin as 42; and non-volunteers 11, 15, 33–5, 42

wills: charitable trusts 104; date, importance 47; formality requirements 27; residuary gifts created in 10; and secret trusts 43, 45, 47, 51, 53, 59; surplus assets derived from 147–8; witnesses to 46
witnesses: and secret trusts 55, 56; to wills 46
writing requirements: creation of trusts 6; dispositions 19–21; evidence of in land transactions 26; where not required 21–2; secret trusts 47, 61